by the same author

ASK

NOTHING

PAUL MORLEY

faber and faber

First published in 2000
by Faber and Faber Limited
3 Queen Square London WC1N 3AU

Photoset by RefineCatch Limited, Bungay, Suffolk
Printed in England by Clays Ltd, St Ives plc

A CIP record for this book
is available from the British Library

ISBN 0-571-17799-9

2 4 6 8 10 9 7 5 3 1

e.s.p.

PART ONE

The Conclusion

*Why the beginning is also the end
and then there's the middle.*

He who understands everything about his subject cannot write it. I
write as much to discover as to explain.

ARTHUR MILLER

I never feel mature enough for a strong work. Apparently, I am
waiting to fall into ruin.

JULES RENARD, 1887

ONE

I have only seen one dead body in my life.

It didn't look dead and it didn't look alive and it didn't look anything in between. Significantly, it was positioned inside an open coffin, dressed for an occasion, and cushioned against reality by white satin-covered padding. The coffin was resting on a wooden table or a slab of concrete covered with neatly pleated drapes. It looked as if it was floating, suspended in the air as it seemed suspended in time.

The body looked very quiet, as if it had made enough noise for now, as if it was just thinking, not of something to say, but of how thinking was a thing of the past, and in the future there would be no thinking, and no past. It was very thoughtful-looking. It was perhaps thinking that it would have to do an awful lot of not thinking. Or I was thinking that on its behalf. Or perhaps it wasn't thinking at all. For all that the body had this thoughtful bearing there was also something very thoughtless about its general demeanour.

I have only ever seen one dead body in my life. I could tell just by looking at it that not only had this once been a human being but in some ways, for all its stillness, it still was. The body, the dead thing I was there to see for some living reason, had all the features and angles and curves of a living thing, and it even had an expression you might want to associate with a living thing. It was quite a composed expression for someone who was only putting decomposition on hold. For someone who had been transformed brutally quickly sometime during the past few days from a somebody into a nobody, the expression was acceptably dignified. At the time, I was doing the accepting. Perhaps somebody else doing the accepting might have interpreted the expression in another way. Someone else might have seen a hint of terror. Or a dark suggestion of desperate resignation. Or a chilled sparkle of odd joy. From where I was standing, a couple of vast intimate yards away from the body, I would stick to my conclusion that, under the circumstances, you could say that the expression on the faint face of the solidly dead body was approaching the serene, even the blissful, for all its understandable seriousness. A smile would have been very inappropriate. A smile fixed for anywhere between ten seconds and eternity always looks a little sinister, and the last thing you want on a dead body laid out for friends and loved ones to pay their final respects is anything transparently sinister. The body kept a classically straight face to match the general level of its immediate ambition.

The body was very still indeed, but it was presented in such a way that you felt any split second there might be a flicker, a twitch, a breath, some movement that would actually stop your breath and bring your own flickering and twitching to an instant halt. It was a shocking sight, this thing that was a dead body checking my sense of reality, and I was directly connected to a liquid state of shock. But through it all the body was lifelike enough to make you think that at any moment it might blink. Or burp. Or break into song. What would it sing? 'This is the end, my friend.' Or a love song with a sad ending. 'It's good to touch the green, green grass of home'? Or something about dead souls. 'Heaven Knows I'm Miserable Now'? What about 'Fly Me to the Moon'?

Perhaps it would mime – badly – to the words 'this is the way to step inside'. Drums would be pummelled with detached precision, bass guitar would rumble up from deep out of the ground and a guitar would cut through the atmosphere as if it were an electronically charged knife. Because this was atmosphere you could cut with a knife: cut into shreds.

The voice the body was miming to would croon with a kind of objectless longing, an urgent aimlessness. It would sound like a voice that demanded to be heard. A voice that was young and old at the same time, weak and strong. It would be inviting the listener into a void, or emptiness, or infinity, to watch the basic adventure of man's metaphysical self as it tears itself from life to death. Either that or moaning melodically that it was too cold where it was, or too hot, and there didn't seem to be any natural distance between itself and its surroundings.

A host of angels would ritualistically dance like disordered demons and the body, drained of all spirit, a kind of spent arrow, would continue to mime. Terribly. Its lips wouldn't move at all. It would mime the words 'this is the way to step inside' as if it might continue to do so for ever, and a guitar would slice everything in sight into metallic tatters while some drum's dream rolled over the present like frightened wings and a triumphant bass broke up the past.

But the rigid body had had enough of singing. It couldn't even be bothered to mime. It had had enough of everything. It was covered up to the neck, for somebody's convenience, and it had been delicately made up, no doubt to tactfully hide the last marks and traces made on its mortal body before it stopped thinking. There was not a hair out of place. Then again, all of its hair was out of place – hair on a dead body is pretty much a definition of being out of place. The body was close to being handsome, in a desolate sort of way. Perhaps it was just that it seemed so settled, so confident, so committed to its final position of complete rest and epic listlessness that gave it this appearance of senseless attractiveness. Or perhaps it was just the way the dead body had been disguised, as if it was an actor, to appear alive. The actor seemed to be sleeping. And breathing . . . very slowly. Perhaps one breath an eternity.

Sleeping is a very appropriate way of presenting death, perfect for occasions when the body is lacking its life but for certain social reasons requires the appearance of life. Sleeping is, on the long stretched-out surface of things, a quite close approximation to the look of death. When a dead body needs to be looked at, for someone's convenience, for reasons of comfort and assurance, it is an advantage that there is this apparently coincidental link between the dead body and the sleeping body. It is better for the dead body to look as if it is sleeping rather than for it to look as if it is writing a cheque.

I have only ever seen one dead body in my life. I wondered what I was doing in this room of goodbyes and awakenings looking at something that was fairly dead but which retained the shape and size of life. I'm not sure who had more on their plate as we contemplated each other in this small grey room, a little larger than a coffin, that someone had taken the trouble to decorate. For something that was dead the body had presence. For all its intense muteness, it clearly communicated that death was larger than life. As a young man in his early twenties giving this stiff and vivid dead body a stunned once-over I couldn't help but begin to think that the experience didn't make death any more or less real but it definitely made life a little bit more strange.

The body didn't smell of anything. It smelt of nothing. I wondered when the last time the body as a moving person had cleaned its teeth. I wondered whether when the teeth were cleaned the person doing the brushing had had an epiphany about the absurdity of

5

cleaning their teeth at such a momentous time. If you are going to die any moment and you have a vague notion that you are going to die, or a very specific idea, an idea so specific it puts you in absolute control of your own immediate fate, do you prepare for death by carrying on some of the well-established hygienic routines of modern living? Or are other thoughts a priority? What would those thoughts be? I looked at the body but it didn't want to say even by using sign language what it was thinking in the hours before its death. Unless it was thinking absolutely nothing. Unless its mind was dreadfully blank as it – he – went through the slow irresistible motions of turning with such will and might and exhaustion from life to death.

I wondered if anyone had cleaned the body's teeth after it was dead in the way that they had applied powder to the body's face, in the way that someone had certainly straightened its hair. Actually that's not quite true. I didn't wonder that at the time. But I wonder it now. At the time I didn't consider at all the process that had creatively held the body in this limbo state of deathly lifelikeness. I took for granted that the dead body bore a striking resemblance to the body when it had been alive. I didn't think to think what the body would look like without the crude yet subtle rot-stalling cosmetic support. Now I can't help wondering if there was a notice attached to the door of this waiting-room – and what a wait you can have in such a room – explaining the face-saving particulars of embalming.

NOTICE

Embalming disinfects and temporarily preserves and restores, to an acceptable physical appearance, a dead human body. As human remains begin to decompose almost immediately after death, thereby offering an ideal environment for microbial growth, untreated remains pose a public health concern. While embalming sanitises the body, it also retards decomposition, thus temporarily preserving the body. Embalming restores the body to an acceptable physical appearance following a traumatic death or devastating illness.

Many bereavement experts agree that viewing the deceased confirms the reality of death and helps survivors take an important step towards recovering from their loss.

The embalming process begins with thorough washing and disinfection of the body. The mouth, nose and other openings are closed to prevent excretions which could be a source of disease or infection. Embalming chemicals are then injected into the body through the more accessible arteries while body fluids are drained through corresponding veins.

Embalming fluids kill bacteria and temporarily preserve the body by altering the physical structure of the body's proteins. A latticework of inert firm proteins is created that can no longer serve as a host for bacteria or be acted upon by enzymes. Thus the decomposition process is retarded and the body is sanitised and temporarily preserved.

Thank you for your attention.

Such a note on the door would have given the game away, shattered the illusion of the perfectly presented dead body, undermined the magic trick, the minor miracle. The fact that I cannot recall whether there was such a notice pinned to the door isn't because of faulty remembering but because there wasn't such a notice. It didn't say 'exit' on the door, either.

I have only ever seen one dead body in my life. The dead body I saw might have thought that it was dreaming. As far as I knew, it was dreaming. Or it wasn't dreaming. Or it wouldn't remember its dreams. Maybe I would remember them on its behalf. It was dreaming that it had been alive, once. It was dreaming its life. Or it was dreaming its death. Or both. The dead body gives little away, when it's been dressed, made up and elegantly posed, about its dreams, forgotten or remembered. I looked hard at the well-mannered body for what seemed like less than a second and more than for ever. Sometimes the body appears in my dreams, floating from some engagement to another, as handsome as ever, and as inscrutable. I wonder if I ever appear in its dreams, looking for clues, thinking of something to say. Mostly, I think, I never find a clue, and I never think of anything to say. I couldn't think of anything to say as I looked at the body, which had died so recently it still looked as if it could wake up at any moment. It would wake up and wonder what the intensely black little marks criss-crossing its neck were. It would wake up and it wouldn't be an it any more. It would be a he. A he that would be at a loss to explain what on earth was going on.

7

I think of the body as an it rather than a he. Whatever made it a he had dissolved somewhere between the moment of his death and the moment when he became a memory, a feeling, to those he knew, stronger than the presence of the body that remained. The memory becomes the he, the life that is remembered was lived by a he. The body is an it, separated from the he that it was. It lies in front of me like something that belongs in a dream. A dead body in front of you, all dressed up with nowhere to go, will heavily remind you that, if you are looking for *it*, then a good place to search is a dead body, which is and has been and was and will be nothing but it. A dead body is it incarnate. It is it no more, no less. It is it dead stop. It is where all things end. It is it.

It really is.

As I looked at it, this big bag of it, laid out in front of me dead to the world, reeking of it, stiffened to an ultimate point of absurdity, it beyond it, I realised, in a second that had been split into infinity, that the truth was, I had only seen one dead body *in the flesh*. In the flesh, so to speak. The breathless bloodless it-hammered colossal body bracing flesh. This dead body that I saw in front of me, decadently showing off its magnificent deadness, an unlined glowing deadness no living body could ever hope to duplicate, was and is the only dead body that I have ever seen. The only dead body that I have seen for real, as dreamlike as the occasion seemed. It was real, very real, in the way only it can be. And, as far as the eye could see, it was in the flesh. It was three-dimensional, with in some senses a fourth even a fifth ominously hovering nearby.

I could see the skin on its face and it looked very fleshy to me, if slightly clownish, owing to the make-up applied to bring a little natural colour into its unnatural cheeks. The make-up failed to be perfectly natural, to be perfectly honest. There is a big mysterious difference between flesh colour and flesh itself. The body was a long lonely way from being in the pink.

The flesh colour was a curdled blend of pink and yellow, a yellow-ish pink, a pinkish yellow, a strained sagging colour only the dead could look relatively good in. It was a broken colour that had not yet made its mind up whether to be a colour, as such, or just a shadow, a shadow of death, in hopeless disguise. It was the kind of colour you couldn't believe was going to be still for very long. It was what happens to living colour when there is lack of oxygen and lack

8

of blood. It was generally speaking a lack of colour. A colour that would be at its best on the move, melting, dissolving, changing its tone, changing its appearance. A colour that was never an absolute colour, but a colour in transit, a colour on the way to something else, to somewhere else. It was a colour at a loss in this world that would come into its own in another world. It was a rotten colour that didn't belong to the living, a colour giving lost last cover to flesh that was close to life but closer, much closer, to death. It was an off colour for an off body. You could call this colour 'forlorn yink', although I think the technical term is 'zombie yuk'.

The body was an abandoned blend of doomed flesh and gloomy flesh colour. For something that didn't exist it was very much in the here and now, sharing space with some objects and fabrics that did exist, and the quiet wary me, nervously representing the pale colours of existence. I was not so in the pink myself, but I was I'm sure the colour of something in the room that was lively enough to be breathing. There was warm fluid me, living on the edge of my nerves, and there was cold cadaverous it, having fantastically and permanently charged over the edge of its nerves into implosive abruptness. It was as if it always had been nerveless, careless, doubt-less, less than less, and now it was well on the way to being fleshless, having died in the hairless arms of an absent abyss. The body stretched out in front of me, the exact frozen shape of the past. It represented then. It represented the moment that had passed. It staked a claim for all moments that had passed. Moments that reached so far back into the forever past they met up with a return-ing future. No wonder the face of the body was a peculiar colour.

For now, a now that was having trouble becoming a then, its flesh was not so much human flesh as something beyond flesh. Something that, in this dream-edged reality biased towards the living, was drowsily approaching the spirit of flesh. It conspired to have the distant look of flesh, the smooth ways of flesh if not quite the rough means. I can't say what was hidden away from the face, if there was any flesh elsewhere, some remote body parts, apart from the discreetly messed up neck. And I could see the hands, the hands of it, the hands with nothing left to hold, the hands with nothing left to do. The hands were arranged in such a manner that if this was a person actually asleep you might think that it was a very unlikely, but very peaceful, way of being asleep. You would think they could be faking that they were asleep. They were posing. The flesh of the hands was set into such a position you might consider for a fleet moment that death is such a pose. The ultimate pose. The hands looked very beautiful. All in all, it was a good pose. A pose poised right on the cusp between mortal possibility and impossible immortality. A very glamorous pose, drawn up with such sullen assurance by a mischievous power that was using this body to play around with the endlessness of the end. I'm sure that the he that once livened up this body would have been pleased with the pose and the arch shadow of death that grazed it. Film stars and pop stars and models work hard to create such a cold and splendid pose. Working too hard to achieve such poses can often lead what with one thing and another to an early controversial death. The earlier the death, the better, the more tragic, this final pose. The neat black marks crossing the neck of the body of the man who had died early and was truly in front of me only succeeded in increasing the depressed glory of the final pose. The black marks that danced on the body's neck like some Gothically extravagant beauty spot drew attention to the damned flawlessness of everything else emphasising with sick magnificent force that this was indeed, as he would have wanted, if he had had to choose, a good-looking corpse.

This was a dead body in the flesh, it was no photograph, it was no processed image, but the flesh had stopped, or was stopping being flesh. The body was in a state of having been flesh. I was looking, towards and then away, at the flesh of the dead. I was looking, out of politeness, out of courtesy, out of time, at the skin of a dead body that had been made up with due care and attention to be lifelike. It seemed to me – not at the time, but later, when I had left the room with a view of the dead, the room of colours dead that was part of a church that feebly stretched to the sky – it seemed to me – later, when I was remembering the dead body rather than looking at it as if I should say something – it seemed to me, eventually, that its skin was bad skin. It was wrong flesh. I didn't think this at the time, as I shared this cold room with a dead body and acted as if I too was wearing thick make-up and had no feelings in my fingers, because I didn't think anything other than wonder what I was doing there and what it was doing there and what should I say. What should I do? I didn't think this like there were words in my head. The room compelled me to be profoundly wordless.

There were no words in my mind. There was just a wash of slowed sensation and a sense that my mind was somehow holding its breath. Or a sense that my mind was being held by distorting outside forces and the overall feeling struck me as being something that might make me sob, or giggle.

But I felt that once I had left the room and words – the words that make up thought, the thought that is talking to oneself – had returned, the kind of words that would emerge, they would be to do with awkwardness and dull confusion, and with skewered details of life and death, of the still stillness of the body as an it. And they were. They formed, words and thoughts, found by my mind, little by little, over the years that have passed over my life since I looked in a state of suspended animation at the body locked in a dead weight of cancelled animation. For instance, I didn't think about it at the time, but I remember now – my mind has just deciphered another fragment of the code – that neither of us, me playing Life and it easing through the early stages of Death, was worried about the time. And both of us felt in our own equally dramatic ways that there was nothing much to say. I think, also, that I was in this life-soaked hurry to leave the room of death, but it, the body, the dead one, was in no hurry at all. Its grand lack of hurry gave the body a fine sense of bludgeoned elegance, but then most of what had made the it a he had already hurried away. To wherever. Whenever.

For ever and ever.

I felt faintly funny looking at what flesh was on show and experienced confusion about just what this flesh actually was. It used to be flesh, not that long ago, so you could still call it flesh and get away with it. Everyone would know what you meant. But now it is flesh at some stopped dead place between being and non-being. It's ex-flesh but at the same time it is existing flesh. After death, using this body hanging around in front of me as my research, the body's flesh remains for a little while. It doesn't disappear as instantly as say the soul. The body's had it wrapped around its little finger for long enough, and meanwhile there are still a few steady moments to go before the flesh is finally forced to accept, perhaps through burning, that it is, ultimately, nothing. It has no right to even pretend that it was something. It's nothing without a soul, the word used here to describe whatever it is that makes you a he she or whatever above and beyond being a basic hollow bone-stretched vessel leaking eerie essence. Without life and soul, flesh has a bleak future.*

The it before me was fleshless flesh, or lifeless flesh, or flesh kept flesh for a final few days thanks to science, superstition and compassion, flesh that had been flesh and was now hanging on for dear life, or should that be dear death? It was flesh of sorts, anyway. So even though I have seen many dead bodies in fact and fiction through film and television, seen people shot and stabbed in fake ways and real ways, this was the only dead body that I have seen in my life in real life. The only dead body I have seen that wasn't on the other side of a screen, dreamt up, glassed off, made of light, as removed as yesterday, as faint as thought. The only dead body that, if I was so disposed, I could touch.

I suppose I saw my first dead body on television when I was five or six. I have a feeling that the first one I saw was probably the body of a cat. A cartoon cat. Tom. I saw him smashed and mangled by a plump little cartoon mouse pumped up with frivolous malice. Jerry. Frankly, I saw him destroyed to death. Tom fluttered up towards the sky, and heaven, as an angel, a transparent cat with angel wings and an expression of benign acceptance. Seconds later, he was alive again. Tom and Jerry didn't make death seem so fatal, in the same way that they didn't make violence seem so violent. They made death as funny as violence. I watched Tom and Jerry flirt famously with death and torture, and I laughed at it all. I laughed in the face of death.

I estimate that by the time I was eight I had seen a couple of hundred dead bodies on television, a few on film, of which only about ten were cartoons. It wasn't just the cartoon characters who died only to live again. The numbers of screened-off dead bodies piled up in my life, but the way I saw it death was just part of a game. Part of a war game or a space game or a cartoon game. The dead bodies looked like they were sleeping, dreaming, waiting. They looked like they'd lost the game. Then another game would begin. Sometimes, the dead bodies would go to heaven, which was like earth but fluffier and whiter. Then they would come back to earth, as if nothing had happened. Death was just another part of life, it was

---

* Without flesh, on the other hand, the soul is left out on its own to be as strange as it likes, which, all things considered, is very strange indeed.

enclosed by life, you could die and still be alive. There was a sense that something stopped, but it certainly wasn't life that stopped. At eight, even as I watched cowboys killed in front of my eyes and heard the screams of soldiers as they were halted in their tracks, even as I watched coyotes flattened to the width of paper, even as I vaguely registered that people died and death was dark, darker than night, I hadn't yet begun to believe that death stopped everything. I had no reason yet to suspect that death was anything other than a funny thing that happened on the way to another adventure. The biggest realest deaths I remember were the ones of J. F. Kennedy and the Scottish racing car driver Jim Clarke. TV told me very clearly about both deaths. I was sad about Kennedy when I was six because everyone else seemed upset. I was angry about Jim Clarke when I was eight or nine because he was my favourite and I realised that he would never race again and never win again. It was the end of the game, the end of the race, and there wouldn't be any others. His death made me feel a bit sick in the stomach, and was perhaps the first, above the world-changing Kennedy's, that prompted me to consider death as a rather unsettling disappearing act.

As the body-count mounted, and after Clarke's crash, I got a little suspicious. I don't know if there was necessarily a connection between the dead bodies I was vaguely watching on television and my own growing feeling that death wasn't actually the end of a game but I was soon asking my mother what happened to you when you died. At first, my mother didn't have much of an answer. I think she also had difficulty imagining one. Her initial answer suggested that the route Tom the cat took to heaven and the wings that materialised on his back were, for a cartoon, incredibly realistic. I imagined in a rough, rushed way Jim Clarke racing about a fuzzy heaven with little wings on his back. I desperately hoped that somehow somewhere, really, there was still a Jim Clarke being a Jim Clarke even if he wasn't racing cars and winning races and being exotic and if I only but knew it, damned near erotic, in a manly sort of way.

In my heart of hearts I didn't much trust this image of Clarke cavorting in heaven, and I left behind the confusing death of Jim Clarke, the way it interfered with my wishes and dreams, and found other sports to obsess about, other sportsmen to adore. After the initial shock faded away, I didn't want to think about it too much. Or think about it at all. Deep down in my mind I knew for bumpy sure that there was no such thing as Jim Clarke any more, as ridiculously far-fetched as this seemed. And there was little chance of my new manly hero, John Edrich, the opening batsman for the Surrey cricket team, disappearing as suddenly and unfathomably as Jim Clarke. There would always be John Edrich playing his game and scoring centuries and so everything was all right with the world. Or it was when the sun shone.

Dead bodies continued to be screened and stocked up for me as I grew up. By the time I was thirteen, I must have seen thousands of dead bodies. In the film *Zulu* alone I must have seen 2,356 dead bodies. They littered my life. One or two seen on the news might even have been the dead bodies of people who had actually lived. Chasing dumb entertainment so as to help further numb my growing appreciation that death led not nowhere in particular but nowhere at all, and I do mean all, meant that I was coming across dead bodies by the day by the handful. I might have looked stupid, and pretty vacant, by the time I was thirteen, but I was sensitive enough to know that all those dead bodies being paraded in front of me weren't actually dead. They were as dead as a cartoon cat.

The dead bodies taking their rehearsed position in various screen dramas and thrillers were about as dead as me. They were as dead as me with my eyes shut. As dead as me lying down and dreaming of something else. As dead as me pretending to be dead. Any war victim that I might have seen in the news who was actually as dead as a pre-existing cartoon cat, really dead, as lifeless as a drawing that's never been drawn, seemed as unreal and unimpressive as any actor playing dead by being as still as possible for a few seconds. The screened dead bodies tended to show that death was everywhere, it was all around, it was on top of us and right round the corner, but fiction and make-believe could keep it in its place. Fantasy's job was to control death. To place it right in front of our faces but to wrap it up in cotton wool. To draw constant attention to it and yet at the same time deflect attention by pretending it was no big deal and no one gets hurt, as such. It's nothing, really, and quite easy to get over.

I went to no funerals. All through my teens, none of my family died. None of my friends died. I had a friend whose father died. He was told about it one day at school. When he arrived back in class after being told by the headmaster about his father, he didn't seem that bothered. He shrugged his shoulders and sort of smiled and got on with the day. I was vaguely puzzled but just assumed that's how death was. A bit of news. A change in routine for a while. Me and my friend never talked about his father's death. I never asked if he ever saw his father's body.

I remember when I was twelve or thirteen our next-door neighbour's wife died. He must have seen his wife's body because he discovered it. I remember him being a bit shattered for a few days, chatting aimlessly, or maybe with perfect aim, to my mother about this and that and death. But I didn't really think about it. I didn't want to think about it. I made a decision not to pay too much attention to what I distantly felt was an immensely difficult situation. The neighbour helplessly drifting in and out of my vision swapping small talk and then abruptly not so small talk with my mother made me feel very awkward. I felt awkward enough as it was, as an unkissed and unscintillating thirteen-year-old feeling far too hemmed in by his skin.* The neighbour, who had been married to his wife for about twice the length of my young and flimsy life, made me and my bones feel uncomfortable just looking at him and the way that grief hugged his shoulders. He didn't seem to have the faintest idea what to do next, which way to turn, how to smile in a way that wasn't thin and forced. How can you smile brightly when your lips are trapped by unhappiness? I have no idea, and I didn't even contemplate such a thing at the time.

Then, overnight, as far as I could tell from where I was, lodged within my blank carelessness, he got on with the rest of his life, a life changed into a very different shape because he had seen his wife as a dead body. I wonder how long it was before he too was a dead body someone was looking at with the result that their life was a little more shaded than it had been. I didn't wonder that at the time. I was wondering if and when and how I would ever be kissed.

I wasn't well versed in the art and craft of death. None of my sporting heroes died any more. I became a fan of Jim Morrisson and Jimi Hendrix after they had died. My teen years were mostly a deathless motion, while on the screens all around me images of dead bodies multiplied in the scenic abstract. Death did make a cameo appearance in my life when I was fourteen. I wanted to kill myself.

* As for his bones.

15

After some dark thought, as I adolescently lowered myself into a great dark pit of worked-up helplessness and scorching self-pity, I realised that I couldn't think how to do it. This only increased my misery, and confirmed my sore and sunken sense of failure. I also ended up focusing hard and clear on an interesting understanding – if I did kill myself I wouldn't be around any more. This understanding, which has increased in interest as I've grown older, didn't particularly help me on the suicidal planning front. I wonder now, if I had already seen the dead body that eventually I would get to see it might have offered up some neat black criss-crossed clues about how to go about killing yourself. But I wasn't to see this dead body for a good bad and indifferent few years yet. The dead bodies planted onto the television, the dead bodies strewn over the imaginative wasteland of films, they offered absolutely no clues about how to kill yourself. They supplied a load of fairly unwanted advice about how to play dead.

After I had failed to kill myself and resigned myself to an immediate future full of life and other things equally tentative and uncertain, during my teenage years there wasn't much death to write home about. Mine wasn't so much a suicide attempt as a suicide fumble. I frightened myself before I could kill myself. I think I reached the very last stage you can before you actually get down to business, and although this was life-changing enough for death to make a big move in on my life and eat away some of its alleged charm, death and the dead still remained active and alive only in fiction and fables and films. I was aware that death was following me around, and a lonely melodramatic part of me was repelled and attracted by its creeping absent presence. But death was apart from me. It had not entered me. It had not twisted my brain or chilled the very heart of me, except abstractly. The woodwork teacher at my school died, but, largely owing to the chisels he liked to hurl at boys who were behind in their woodwork exercises, that was a cause for unsuppressed and quite open celebration. Death could be OK.

In the end, the first funeral I ever went to was that of my father. Which made death very much a part of me. But his wasn't the dead body that I saw. I have only ever seen one dead body in my life and I saw it a few years after my father died. I saw the dead body of someone who had hanged himself. The dead body of a young man who had succeeded at suicide even as he felt useless and hopeless and pointless. I saw the dead body of someone who was about my age. The dead body of someone whom I was not related to and only barely knew. It was the dead body of Ian Curtis, the lead singer of the rock group Joy Division.

I don't really know what I was doing there, staring at him when he was at his most exposed and most crestfallen. He certainly didn't know what I was doing there. But one thing I did know for sure. He was dead. The best way to know for sure, to really believe, that someone is dead and gone is to see their body with all the life and character and personality and essence scooped right out of it. You see the patched-up shell of a whole lifetime. You see cancelled existence. You see terrible peace. You reach a hard but inevitable conclusion. That's that, then. That's it. Life – and death – goes on.

I have only seen one dead body in my life and it wasn't the body of my father.

TWO

A book requires all the thoughts you think you've ever had. For example, once upon a time I began a book this way: Here goes nothing.

And I continued: It is worth pointing out that nothing is nothing and yet not precisely nothing.

This book was called *Fragments of Darkness in the Shape of a Man* and it was about the death of my father.

Then I began a book in another way, more or less like this: It was a special day, though it didn't look like it, but it was the day that he was going to die. He knew it.

He just knew it.

It was a special day for a special person, although he didn't particularly look special. He sat in his underpants staring at a space he knew well squeezed between nothing and everything. He was waiting for his wife to iron his trousers. He ate a bowl of cornflakes lathered with sugar and he felt special. Surely soon he would look as special as he felt.

He crunched with feeling on a mouthful of cornflakes and let the intense sweetness cascade through his body with a chill that was thrilling and ultimate. The sensation of being alive melted through him on a fierce course to nothing. Everything was under control. A special control. This level of control pressed deep into him affording him a feeling of almost pleasure. He had forgotten what that felt like just as he had forgotten what he felt like. But today he was recovering both those feelings. Today he was on top of the world. Or, he was at the bottom of the world. But who can tell the difference! Anyway, today he had found something he could concentrate on. He had a plan that would help him sleep and help him find hope.

Today was the day that he was going to kill himself.

That was from a book finally called *Fighting Shy* and it was about the relationship between shyness, melancholia and depression. It was also, I suppose, about my father. There were going to be a couple of chapters on laziness but I couldn't be bothered writing them.

One chapter included a conversation I had with my father over a pint of bitter in a pub. (The conversation was imaginary, and so was the pint of bitter. We never had a drink in a pub.) At one point I pretended that he'd said to me: 'I agree that it is very important to leave an incomplete image of oneself.'

I snorted politely and asked if he wanted another. Another drink, not another image. He declined and rather surprisingly remarked: 'When the habit of seeing things as they are turns into a mania, we lament the madman we have been and are no longer.' I asked him if he wanted some crisps. He soberly replied: 'There is an ancient tradition that says that philosophy is essentially concerned with death – whether with understanding it, reconciling oneself to it or preparing oneself for its inevitable arrival.'

I took that as a yes, and got him a packet of cheese and onion.

Then there was a book that began: 'Life is without meaning,' but I didn't really mean it and I didn't go any further. That book was going to be called *You Think We Have Eternity to Waltz through Your Piddle?*

Another book started: 'I have only ever seen one dead body in my life.' Still another started with a quote from Jules Renard in 1889: 'You aren't mature enough, you say, to write a strong book; are you waiting until you rot?' And then I began a book with a stolen line: 'In the beginning, a short sentence.' Or was it: 'In the beginning, a stolen line'? Whatever, in my dreams, I finished that book. I finished it with a stolen line: 'In the end, we do not rush toward death, we flee the catastrophe of birth, survivors struggling to forget it.' Or was it: 'In the end, a stolen line'?

I wrote a book called *What Is This Thing You Hold in Your Hands If You'll Pardon the Expression?* and this discussed something that Jorge Luis Borges had once said about books: 'What tiresome and laborious folly is it to write lengthy tomes, to expound in five hundred pages on an idea that one could easily propound orally in a few minutes. Better is pretending that the books exist already and offering a summary or commentary.'

Unfortunately, or fortunately, depending on your point of view, my summary or commentary only stretched to 235 words, and so it never became in the real sense a book. I could orally propound the idea in less than thirty seconds. I thought it was quite a poetic 235 words – I had indeed grasped the absolute and expressed it in a few words – but someone who read it said that it was a bit repetitive and could do with some editing.

Then there were books that began in all these ways:

1) One day I might just up and walk away.

2) The days started to feel too long, but they passed by quickly.

3) He was born with a different face.

4) When I was evacuated I remember getting off the train and being handed over to Mrs Morrissey.

5) Time watched him as a cat watches a mouse.

6) 'I give up,' he said.

7) He had never heard of John Cage. He never knew that John Cage once said, 'I have nothing to say and I am saying it and that is poetry.' He never knew that there was John Cage. For him there was no John Cage. I wonder if it would have made a difference to his life if he had been aware of John Cage, even a fan. But he had nothing to say about John Cage and he was saying it and that was that.

8) Dennis Hopper had been married to Michelle Phillips for eight days. She went on the road with Leonard Cohen and she called Hopper and told him that she had decided that music was her future. He was distraught. He screamed, But I need you, I need you, what am I going to do without you? And she said, Have you ever considered suicide?

9) I cannot for the life of me remember what happened.

10) Do I have to say something?

All these opening lines were to different versions of a book called *A Little Something for a Rainy Day*.

And then there was a book called *Death in the Family*, which began somewhere later than the beginning with the words:

THREE

Call me Paul. My father did. Just.

FOUR

Sometime during the year 1956, which was after the war and just before rock and roll, somewhere in some space, and most of all somehow, two young people found themselves together. They fancied each other and they found it in themselves to have sex. It might have been the first time they'd had sex and it might have been the sixth. With each other or with anyone. Perhaps they weren't particularly good at sex. Perhaps one was and the other wasn't. Perhaps they both knew exactly what they were doing. The sex went smoothly and it was rough around the edges. It was dark. It was light. It was hot it was cold. It was messy. It was beautiful. Things happened, fast and slow, and it all rushed in one direction faster than life. Then it was all over. The boy came. He had an orgasm. The girl didn't, although she felt a kind of shock that might have been an orgasm, but what did she know?

The man's orgasm was, for the sake of argument, the thousandth he'd had in his life. As he came there was ringing in his ears that could have been cheering and celebration. He felt dizzy with all the collaborative appreciation that was going on.

The two youngsters didn't know each other well but they knew each other better and better for each second they were fighting each other in this battle of sex. They fought against their parents they fought against their past they fought against their future they fought for their bodies for their soul for their feelings; they thought of nothing they thought of themselves they thought of each other; they fought for space they forced the present through itself and they fought for survival. They fought for life. They fought for breath.

They fought for seconds. In the end, it was a fight that would go on for years. Eventually, one of them would get knocked out.

They were making love and they were making life. They knew it and they didn't know it. They were so alive as they wrestled with bodies and consciousness as they collided in space and time so full of themselves and the moment so motivated and emotional so ordinary and supernatural that they created life out of nothing. Because these two stricken strangers fought the good fight and everything worked as it should there was something about me that made the journey that they say everyone makes. I was produced, I came out of nowhere from somewhere, a rush of sperm fighting towards egg, fighting for position, fighting for life. It was a world so small, so large within itself, the near me must have been at the very centre of the universe, if only for that bursting moment that one spunky sperm out of creamy teeming millions speared a solitary egg and blasted me into the near far. I was my dad's sperm and my mum's egg. I in the storm of creation soared and divided and soaked into the beginning of beginning. The me to be fell apart dividing and sub-dividing and doubling up. The me of sorts was in orbit, float-ing, the me was under sea, the me was bouncing into bits that would make a whole, touching surfaces, drifting, slipping. Then I, if I it was, became embedded into the lining of the womb. The womb of the mother of a me that was being rapidly shaped into existence. My cells divided and divided and they go on dividing even now. I multi-ply, dividing myself into life.

I was a millimetre long. My features started to form. My head was bent down towards the life-saving placenta. And then I was two and a half centimetres long. My hands and feet formed. I was a collection of cells resembling a tiny human being. At six weeks I might have been a human embryo but there wasn't much difference in me from a pig embryo. I might even have been a chicken. In the end, I was human. My mum and dad were human beings. This was my fate. Eons of slow-changing variations had led to me being a human being. There had been such effort over millions of years so that human beings would be reproduced this way and my mother and father couldn't help but continue the whole thing. The survival instincts were just too great. The certainty of evolution was just too overpowering. The arbitrariness of well-established cosmic prin-ciples were simply too compelling. And so there I was, with a life of my own, drying out in the sun, bound by the consequences of gravity, the son that made my mother a mother and my father a father.

What a fight it had been to get us all this far. What an astounding, timely series of accidents, coincidences and fiascos. It was as though we all knew what we were doing. You'd be easily tempted to wonder what was going to happen next.

FIVE

Next, I started to think. And then I started to remember things, and forget things.

SIX

They had six weeks to register my name. There was only a day left, and they still hadn't visited the Births and Registrations officer at the hospital. They were meant to announce that they'd had a son, and have a birth certificate filled out. The trouble was, they weren't really sure what to call me. If I had been a girl, they would have been ready. I would have been Kim Elizabeth. But something in my past-less past made my mind up to be a boy. That confused them, and it meant that there would never be a Kim Elizabeth.

There was a writer, Christopher Morley, who died the day after I was born. If he had died the same day as I was born, then I would have been called Christopher. But he didn't die on the day of my birth, so they didn't name me after him. They didn't feel it was a nice enough name to give their new son if there wasn't any kind of coincidence of dates. I missed being a Christopher by a day. I had no real feelings one way or another about this, as long as people didn't start calling me Chris. As a Chris Morley I would have been very different from the Paul Morley I am. Somehow, Christopher Morley doesn't seem as far removed from Paul Morley as Chris Morley. As Christopher Morley I would have been closer as a personality to Paul Morley than Chris Morley. I think I would have been closer to Paul Morley if I had been called Kim Elizabeth rather than Chris. Apparently, I didn't look like a Chris, or a Christopher, anyway, whatever that entails.

I'm not sure what would have happened if they hadn't registered me in time. Would I not have existed? Would I have been handed a name off the shelf? Reginald. What kind of life would I have led as a Reginald Morley? Would I have been assigned a number? 34526 Morley. I would have preferred that to Reginald, as long as nobody called me 34 for short.

My mother started to panic. 'Come on,' she said to her husband,' we've got to call him something.' For the first six weeks of my life I didn't really have a name. I slept in a drawer that they'd removed from an old chest of drawers, and was just known as 'the baby', 'the boy', 'him', 'it', 'cuddlywups'. I'm not sure about that last one, but it remains a better name for me than Chris.

Yes, thought my father, annoyed to be under pressure, we have to call him something. He was a little angry that he couldn't just think of a name in his own good time. It was no one's business but their own how long they waited before they came up with a name. Except that it was, officially speaking. My father had some vague feeling that he wanted his baby to grow into a name. Soon enough, the baby would look like a name. Perhaps they could let the baby grow enough so that he was able to think up his own name. Funnily enough, if they'd let me grow to the age of about twelve I would have chosen the name Zack. But none of us could wait. I had to have a name by tomorrow. Zack Morley ceased to exist before he even came to exist, which is probably a good thing.

It went right to the wire. There must have been something about me at six weeks old that was connected to who I grew to be, a glint they could see in my eyes, a hint they could see in the slope of my nose, because they plumped for Paul, which is what I am, which is who I am, even though I wasn't then. It's quite a coincidence. Somehow, running out of time, without much of an idea, with no sense of how I would turn out, they managed to get my name right.

I wonder if I would feel the same now if I was Chris Morley.

SEVEN

I arrived, wet and foolhardy and hardly sure of my footing, slap bang into the 1950s. I was dumped there and/or I was meant to be there. It was fate, mistake or fantasy. For all I knew and cared it

23

might well have been 1067 or 674 BC or 1734. It could have been 2233. But my time was to be the end of the twentieth century, and I had no choice but to get used to it. We are coaxed and coerced into being the children of our time whether we like it or not. As soon as we emerge slapped and shocked into this clear and present world we are swiftly encouraged to forget the details of our previous experience of oblivion. We are as close to the chaos of death as we are going to be for quite a while, and instantly we are wrapped up in the chaos of life. No one ever knows for sure whether it is the chaos of life that is controlled, and the chaos of death uncontrolled, or vice versa. A newborn baby will know more than most, having just crossed over in one almighty leap, but nature ensures that the baby cannot spill the beans. The baby is not in a position to be able to give away any big secrets.

Nature makes damned sure that the baby cannot speak during the months it might be able to pass on information about any push-and-pull stillness on any other side. A baby can pull a few faces, produce intriguing moisture and scream out a few noises that might offer hints about the details of nothing and nowhere that are behind and ahead of us, but they are all produced in such a babyish manner we don't really pay any attention. Nature has it well worked out. By the time a baby is beginning to speak, all memories of a previous existence and/or non-existence have been wiped away by the baby-wipe of this existence. The rules and by-rules of this life, this dream of stuff, have blotted out all memories of the past that was a non-past perfectly shaped by its standby nothingness. The baby is persuaded to concentrate on adapting to this world and the life that goes with it, and consequently it loses its grip on where it came from and what it was. Only the vaguest of deep unsettling strangely lit memories remain, squeezed out by the new banality and bravery of growing up in this life, drained of meaning by all the new meaning we have to get used to overnight over years and years.

During the first few months and years of my existence I was firmly and comprehensively turned into the very image of a human being born into the late 1950s. It always happens, with alien exceptions. Whenever we are born, at whatever time of the century, we are conveniently accommodated by that time, by those moments. When we are born matters to the person we become as much as if not more than where we are born. We are moulded quickly and without much second thought to be right for the time. Whatever about us that was right for our past – the pre-past, the past that pretends nothing other than its own pastness, the past that cannot be explained by anyone but a hungry two-month-old baby – it is all discharged by the faint fury of this life and the languages and emotions that help us describe, define, tame and time this faint fury.

We are convinced by everything around us as filtered to us through our parents and their appreciation of everything that it is in our best interests to believe in something rather than nothing. The fact that there might have been something before we were born, as the cry of a newborn baby oddly suggests, does not help us grow accustomed to the slippy, sloppy something that we have been propelled into. And so helped by our parents we forget for good, or for the good of this life, the staggering details of oblivion and learn to hold a fork and piss in a pot. I have been conditioned to accept that this is a fair swap.

I became a human being born into the 1950s in the way that my father became a human being born into the 1930s. I was taught the language, behaviour and gesture suitable for the time in much the same way as my father was for his. We learnt to love, and hate, the local customs of local people stuck in a very local corner of a local galaxy penetrated by local time. We were both turned from nothing into something. We both never got used to it. We were both overwhelmed by the style and fashion of the times immediately around us. We both had a combination of something to look forward to and nothing. We were both infected by the urgency of the date we were expected to write on our cheques and accept was an objective way to fix us in time and space. We were both Morleys. We both had first names given to us by our fathers. And second names.

It's no wonder we were so much the same and yet so different, separated as we were by no time and all the time in the world.

EIGHT

And then what happened was, for a few years, as a young boy forgetting nothing and getting used to something, I lived on the Isle of Wight in a place near a town called Newport. It is the first place I remember living. I was a few months old, or one, or two, or all three. And then I was three or four and we moved.

My father worked as a prison guard at Parkhurst Prison and we lived on a modern estate near the jail. There were a number of quiet roads made up of bland post-war semi-detached houses that were occupied by prison staff and their families.

I remember that there were empty fields at the bottom of our road, and I really do remember the occasional siren whining to announce an escape, and the two-year-old feeling that something dark from the prison was creeping towards me across the open field, and then perhaps settling down and living in these fields for ever. I don't remember anything outside of about half a dozen houses on our road, and a dense dark nowhere between our house and the prison nearby. Sometimes me and my mother would meet my father outside the big brick prison and I remember the massive wooden door at the entrance that looked like the gate of a castle.

I remember coming to on the Isle of Wight. I remember looking at the wrinkled top of the curtains in my bedroom and seeing the faces that I imagined might be the faces of the mysterious beings that lived inside the prison where my father seemed to be most of the time. They had mean nasty faces that seemed to change shape depending on the time of night or the mood I was in. I didn't like sharing my room with these faces. These monsters from the castle where my dad went to and then came back from.

I remember Mum and Dad walking me back from the prison to our house. I was between them and they were swinging me by the arms. They let me go too low and I scraped my knees on the pavement.

I remember seeing a snake wriggling nastily in our back garden. This slimy giant worm was as green as the grass and it was as if the grass just came to life.

I remember a wonderful wooden model of an old sailing ship, gorgeously detailed with miniature sails, and it inspired complete awe inside my young head and heart. It appeared for a couple of days and then just as magically it disappeared for ever for no reason. My dad never did tell me what it was or what it was doing in our house or where it went. I missed it very much.

I remember driving in a big old bottle-green Rover car that wasn't as nice as a Mini or a Morris Minor. I was in the front seat, we were slowly crawling down a big road full of shops, and the car got hit from behind. The jolt and the crack made me sick. I remember driving to the beach in this big old car and it getting stuck in the sand as it tried to park.

I remember these things as part of my conditioning. I don't precisely remember my mother and father being around. I just remember that my mother and father must have been around, and I can just make out their faces, like they are Rock Hudson and Doris Day or something. They were around because they were my mum and dad and I felt that quite deeply and quite indifferently. I don't remember anything they ever said to me. I remember them talking but I don't remember that they actually used words. I don't remember their voices.

I don't remember, but I was told sometime in my life, that in this house near Parkhurst Prison, my mother and father got into a terrible row. My mother was so furious that she tore up their marriage certificate. She ripped it into tiny pieces and flung them around the room. Later, when a kind of peace reigned between them, she tried to put the certificate back together. She sellotaped all the pieces she could find back together. The only bit that she couldn't find was the piece that contained the name of my father.

The first colour I remember separating itself from other colours was red.

I remember my best friend Peter O'Shaughnessy, whose name was just right for him. He lived right across the road from me, and I remember him being run over by a big car that for some reason I have always supposed was a Jaguar. I remember that there was red all over his legs, and I thought that was because the car was red and the red had rubbed off on his legs. Peter lived to tell the tale, and for all I know still lives on the Isle of Wight, and hates the colour red.

I don't remember any of the furniture in the house, or the colour of the carpets. I remember my bedroom like it's a dream but I've lost all of the details. I remember receiving a train set for Christmas that seemed the biggest thing in the world because it completely filled out a pillowslip. I remember some stairs. I don't remember the first time I went to the toilet. I don't remember getting my hair cut. I don't remember having my photograph taken, except I have the photographic evidence in front of me that

I had my photograph taken. I'm three years old and I'm wearing a tie. I look very happy.

I remember our big old car running out of petrol down some Isle of Wight country lane. I remember my dad hitching a lift, and he ran down the road and climbed into the back of this army truck that had stopped for him. The truck drove off with my dad sitting precariously in the back, and he waved at me and I suppose my mum. I don't remember how long it took for him to get back to us with some petrol. I suppose he eventually did, unless I'm still waiting and what I think has been my life has just been the bored agitated fantasy of a two-year-old stuck in a country lane somewhere on the Isle of Wight. There's a chance it might have been, give or take this and that thing.

I do remember, as I watched him run the couple of hundred yards to where the truck had pulled up, feeling a tingling mixture of happiness and sadness. And the first stirrings of some kind of pride. He was my dad. He was all mine. I was all his.

I wonder what made me remember that and not remember other things. There were plenty of things I don't remember. If you consider that I lived on the Isle of Wight for a couple of years or so, and I was awake for say a half of that time, and for a quarter of that time I was doing something that involved activity that could be memorable, then there's about three solid months of stuff to recall. I only seem to remember about thirty-five minutes. The rest of the time is about as blank as the pre-birth past my early life was extinguishing.

I don't remember, for instance, my father losing all the feelings in one side of his face. Apparently he suffered from a temporary paralysis of the facial muscles down one side so that when he smiled at me only half his faced moved. The rest stayed frozen stiff. I'm told by my mother, my one source of proof about this incident, that when he smiled at me like this, half as moving as life, half dead still, I was pretty scared. I don't remember this at all, although it seems such a strong and powerful thing to forget. Maybe I remembered it for a while, and I remembered enough about it to want to forget all about it. Maybe his half and half, on and off face was even scarier than the faces that lurked at the top of my curtains.

Sometimes I think I'll remember all about these things that I've consciously or unconsciously forgotten when I'm older. I'll realise that I've had the image of my father as human gargoyle locked away in my consciousness all ready to be released when the time is right. Or wrong. Perhaps I'll dream about it one day. Sometimes I dream about my father, and these dreams seem as far as I can ever know to be scattered would-be memories mixed with conditioned emotions and unconditioned fantasy. Perhaps I've already had a dream about my father and his paralysed face and I forgot it when I woke up. Just like I forgot that it ever even happened in real life. Some dreams are remembered. Some dreams are forgotten. It's never clear why. I wonder if it's anything to do with what happened to us before we were born, and what will happen to us after we die.

NINE

Time passes. Things happen. Perceptions shift. The past hardens. Something always happens next. Life goes on. It's amazing.
    Meanwhile.

TEN

In the middle of one book I was considering writing, entitled with relish *Extermination*, there was a section that in its own middle said as such: But I often think about death, as I presume Heidegger did, which is not the same thing as facing it. Confronting death must be a very emotional experience, to say the least. Thinking about death, by contrast, seems curiously detached, abstracted, out of touch with the phenomenon it ponders. As Descartes so clearly noted, one never knows better that one is alive – or finds it more inconceivable that one should not be – than when one is thinking.
    Meanwhile, in another book, *Pub Conversations with My Father, Volume 3*, my dad was on his second packet of crisps, and still talking.
    'Why don't I commit suicide? Because I am as sick of death as I am of life. I should be cast into a flaming cauldron! Why am I on this earth? I feel the need to cry out, to utter a scream that will set the world atremble with dread. I am like a lightning bolt ready to set the world ablaze and swallow it in all the flames of my nothingness.

I am the most monstrous being in history, the Beast of the Apocalypse full of fire and darkness, of aspirations and despair. I am the beast with a contorted grin, contracting down to illusion and dilating towards infinity, both growing and dying, delightfully suspended between hope for nothing and despair of everything, brought up among perfumes and poisons, consumed with love and hatred, killed by lights and shadows.'

At which point the pub landlord rang a bell and called out, 'Last orders, puhlease . . .'

And then in the middle of a book called with reluctance *The Very Idea of the Self Brought into Question*, I thought up another series of opening sentences to a number of books that I had or hadn't written. These opening sentences included:

1) What was his name again?

2) He felt hunted – hunted by himself.

3) The fantastic is generally that which leads a person out into the infinite in such a way that it only leads him away from himself and thereby prevents him from coming back to himself.

4) His entire self completely got in the way of him just being someone who was simply capable of getting on with his life.

5) It was as though nothing had happened.

6) The suicide rate in many advanced industrialised countries, not all of them with Scandinavian winters, attests to the popularity if not the rationality of preferring death to any number of social, economic, family, professional, or psychological humiliations.

7) It took me some time to find the party.

8) I never met the comedian Ken Dodd, and I don't think about him every day, and to be honest I haven't thought about him this year at all. Until, funnily enough, now.

9) He agreed with whoever it was, Heidegger or Ken Dodd, Kierkegaard or Dennis Hopper, that said old age is just death without the nothingness.

10) He agreed with whoever it was, Smokey Robinson or E. M. Cioran, Benedict de Spinoza or Ian Curtis, that said tears always have deeper roots than smiles.

It was in the middle of a book to be called *Snapping the Braces of My Confusion*, a book about the death of my father, that I spent nearly forty pages wondering what on earth Kierkegaard was on about when he wrote in *The Sickness unto Death*:

> *To the extent that a person has the truer conception of despair, if he still remains in despair, and to the extent that he is more clearly conscious of being in despair – to that extent, the despair is more intensive. The person who, with a realisation that suicide is despair and to that extent with a true conception of the nature of despair, commits suicide is more intensively in despair than one who commits suicide without a clear idea that suicide is despair; conversely the less true his conception of despair, the less intensive his despair. On the other hand, a person who with a clearer consciousness of himself (self-consciousness) commits suicide is more intensively in despair than one whose soul, by comparison, is in confusion and darkness.*

I was driven to despair trying to work this out. I'm pretty sure that I was clearly conscious of being in despair, but don't push me on that. Ironically enough, my father once told me more or less the same thing in an imaginary pub conversation. I didn't really understand what he was saying either, but that may have been because he had a mouthful of crisps.

As you can imagine, I never finished *Snapping the Braces of My Confusion*. I didn't actually get to start it either. I did get to start *The Memoir of a Man Who Cannot Remember Much* and somewhere in the middle of this book, I was writing the following: If I remember rightly, some Heideggerians see finitude as an essential dimension to the human condition; the narrative structure of a life must have closure, and this is argued for as a matter of conceptual necessity. Perhaps the original version of such positions is Hegel's idea that adult or serious fully free self-consciousness, in the only form that we can really understand it, must know and live with the fact of annihilation.

And then, near the middle if not in the actual middle of a book called *The Sisters of Suicide* there were the words: When I was three, my mother and father had a daughter, and so I had a sister. She was called Jayne Elizabeth, and this name was entirely right for her. This was another amazing coincidence and/or act of shrewdness on the part of my parents. She was definitely a Jayne. Not a Jane. The 'y' has made all the difference. Somehow my parents anticipated that she would be so emphatically full of 'y' and knew that she was a Jayne not a Jane. All of her life she has been a Jayne, as my parents knew, because they were her parents, because they had no choice, because they could see the 'y' in her eyes as soon as she was born.

When I was nine, my parents had another daughter. They named her Carol Ann, and yet again they were right. And yet again my father had a minor run-in with the official at the office of Births and Registrations. The official refused to accept the name, saying that it was a boy's name. He must have been a fan of Carol Reed, the director of *The Third Man*. My father was incredulous, stunned that anyone would think that Carol was a boy's name. He was adamant that he would not add an extra 'e' to make it Carole. She was not a Carole. She was a Carol. He knew what he was talking about. The official eventually relented, muttering darkly about the idiocy and indeed danger of giving a girl a boy's name. My father won the day, and my sister was Carol without an 'e', because the 'e' would have been enough to change her entire personality and turn her into something and somebody that she wasn't at the moment of birth and that she wasn't going to become. The 'y' in Jayne shifted the emphasis the right way towards the personality and nature of my first sister. The non-appearance of an 'e' in Carol created just the correct weight of my second sister's character and being. Just about the first thing I think of when I think of my sisters is that Jayne has a 'y' in her name, and Carol doesn't have an 'e'. After that, I lose track a little. In relation to Jayne, the girl with the 'y' in her life, I am always three years old, and I always seem to be a nine-year-old in my relative dealings with Carol, the girl who was never burdened with an unwanted silent 'e'.

My father was not a flamboyant chooser of names. In no way did he stretch any envelope of names. He was plain but fair, and in his own way he consistently hit the nail of the name firmly on its head. He named his children Paul, Jayne and Carol, and that's exactly what and who they were. I often wonder how he could have been so sure.

In the middle of a book called *Fun versus Futility* there was a chapter about cleaning cookers. This was a twenty-chapter book and the chapter 'On Cleaning Cookers' was chapter ten, so I'm quite correct when I say that it was in the middle of the book. It was dead in the middle of the book. The cooker was used as a symbol of something or other to do with the constant battle in life between futility and fun.

I could count the number of times I have cleaned an oven on the fingers of one hand, in fact on the fingers of one finger. I have an excuse, though, for why I am reluctant to clean a cooker. Cleaning a cooker makes me think of death. Cleaning a cooker catapults me right back to the lucid desperate few hours just after I had officially heard that my father had died.

How old was I when my father died? That's a very good question, and it's something I intend to find out. At some point, I must ask my mother: Just how old was I when my father died? (There are other questions I must ask her as well, on the way to finding out about what the hell happened since, say, my father was born. Perhaps in some book I am writing, even this one, I will get to ask her.) For the moment, I will take a guess. I was nineteen, or twenty, or twenty-one. I might have been eighteen.

My mother's eldest sister, Jill, who I thought looked like Princess Margaret and who I called Auntie Jill, had arrived during the morning we had found out that my dad was dead. Finding a flattened family of sons and daughters and sisters and brothers and wife and mother shocked out of their shells, she tried to protect us from our sodden suffering by issuing tasks for us to perform. My job was to clean the cooker. I was in such a state I was prepared to do anything if asked, even clean a cooker, which was something I had never done. And the cooker I was cleaning didn't seem to have been cleaned for months if not years. It was covered with grease marks and burnt-in grime and blackened food. It was encrusted with dirt and scarred with fat that had merged into the very material of the cooker itself. Auntie Jill made me clean the cooker and I set to work with the feeling that I would be cleaning this lump of metal and muck for the rest of my life and it didn't matter because nothing, really, mattered. Life was coated with filth and shit that could never be budged. I started to clean the old crappy cooker to prove to myself and the rest of the world that the ingrained dirt of life could never be lifted. Life could never be cleaned. Dirt marked it through and through inside and out. Life was black with murk and mould that no amount of cleaning fluid, scrubbing or optimism could remove.

I rubbed and scoured the cooker for over an hour. I cleaned all parts of the cooker for so long I soon forgot how long I'd been cleaning the oven. I was cleaning the oven to forget, to forget some trouble, and I scrubbed and rubbed and washed to forget my worries, forget my shock, forget the time, even, if possible, to forget myself. I scoured myself into such a state in order to reduce life to the simple act of cleaning an uncleanable old cooker. There was nothing to life and beyond life other than the fact of cleaning a cooker that had been disabled by scorched fat and maimed by baked-bean sauce. Sauce that had harmed the metal of the cooker as if it was acid. My whole life became about me cleaning a cooker. I rubbed and scrubbed myself into such a state I was aware only of what I was doing. I lifted as much charred filth off the neglected surfaces of the cooker as I possibly could, using as much physical and mental strength as I could muster given my brand new father-less status. I shifted the grotty filth like it was my memory. I stripped away memories as I stripped away concrete-hard cooking spills. I scratched at the cooker as if I was scratching away parts of my past. I concentrated on the cooker like I'd never concentrated on any-thing before and as I bleached away shrivelled up patches of grot and grit I felt similarly shrivelled-up memories being washed away.

I rubbed and rubbed so hard the cooker seemed to shrink in size. I kept going until the cooker seemed to melt down to the size of a boiled sweet. I slipped it into my mouth and sucked on the smooth surface of the shock-flavoured sweet. I sucked and sucked so that the sweet shrank in size. I sucked until the sweet was just a sliver of cracked shock biting into my tongue. I sucked until I was sucking nothing but a slimy fragment of shock with holes in. I sucked until the cooker was the size of next to nothing and then I spat this saturated little particle of shock out into the air and the cooker leapt back at me becoming the size of a cooker and as dirty as hell. I couldn't get rid of it that easily.

It was just me and the cooker. My hands were cold and wet, smeared with soap suds and flakes of black dirt. I was on my knees reaching inside the oven pulling out lumps of ancient burnt food. The smell of wretched rancid lard and fresh detergent, a mix of the stale past and the vivid present, pierced my skull and added bent intoxication to the weird way the news of my father's death had left me slightly stoned. Brain cells were surely dissolving as completely as some of the cooker crap was under this unexpected and urgent

34

assault of elbow grease, water and detergent. Memories were being squeezed out as definitively as dirty water was from the scrappy bit of cloth I was using to clean up this animal of a cooker.

I have no idea what tasks my sisters and my mother had been given as they went through their motions elsewhere in the house. It was just me and the cooker. The cooker got cleaner in a half-hearted sort of way. Bits of clean surface appeared amidst the immortal filth. At some point, somehow, I stopped cleaning the cooker, as if I had done the job. My task seemed completed, because it wasn't really about turning an old cooker into a new one. My task was to use up an hour that, because it was not long after I had heard my father was dead, was a long and deadening hour. My task was to move a little further away from the jolting moment I had heard that my father was dead. My task was to find something to do as I got used to the news that I had no father. My task was to find ways to get on with life at the moment that life caved in on me.

I vaguely noticed that little patches of the cooker shone in a blank perfunctory sort of way. I resigned myself to the fact that most of the dirt was never going to be removed. It was stuck for life. It had grown to become part of the cooker. I left the cooker to its own devices and got on with a life that was very different from how it had been before the cleaning of the cooker. I don't like to clean cookers, as the cleaning of the cooker is so intertwined with the freshly minted misery I experienced as I cleaned the cooker in the minutes after I found that my father had been killed. Cleaning a cooker takes on an added dimension of shitty melancholy over and above the merely everyday misery of having to clean up such an awkward and large object. Cleaning a cooker is something I associate with dreary escape, something you have to do when you have memories to dislodge, something to do when your life has fallen away from under you. Cleaning a cooker seems to me to be one of the most momentous things to do in your life. I can't shake away that feeling in the same way I couldn't clean away most of the dirt that was welded to the cooker I was told to clean the morning I found out that my father had disappeared for good. The cooker I cleaned that morning was so dirty it looked as though it had been in an explosion. I cleaned it in such a slow daze as if I too had been in an explosion.

And then there was the fall-out, a lot of which ended up in the middle of a number of books I could and couldn't write.

ELEVEN

In the middle of a book to be called *Sing a Song of Suicide* I wrote a chapter about Joy Division that I called 'Listen to the Silence'. It could equally have been called 'Some Fall-Out after Cleaning A Cooker'. The chapter might have become part of the book I never wrote about Joy Division that was never called *The Nothing Special*. This would have been a book about how for a time I seemed more troubled by the death of Ian Curtis than by the death of my father.

I wrote this chapter something like twenty years after I had cleaned a cooker in some drastic morning confusion. I first met Ian Curtis, the Joy Division singer, a couple of years after I had cleaned this cooker in an intense burst of present-tense mind-rubbing scrubbing. He was a quiet young man and I was a quiet young man and we used to swap talk so small you would need a microscope to see it. The truth of how we really felt about things splashed in isolated pools of black water no bigger than puddles littered throughout the gaps in our small hesitant talk. After we had shyly talked smallness into the ground, dead unaware of any concealed splashing going on as performed by our deeper, hidden thoughts, Ian would go on stage and sing loud sad songs that, it turned out, were shortening his life-expectancy. And I would go away and write about his songs and singing still vaguely bothered by the death of my father, and write with dreadful seriousness about the dreadful seriousness of Joy Division's music. Because of the way my father had been killed, I imagined, or really believed, or just knew for sure, that their songs conjured up splashy truths about the way death, and its associated effects, can warp life. Ian and I never once talked about this, we never talked about the death of my father, or the fact that I had never seen his body. But once we shared a packet of cheese and onion crisps and talked about nothing, although we didn't really think of it as nothing. We thought of it as something. Something about the weather, or Patti Smith, or the bus route from Stockport to Manchester. It was nothing really, nothing hiding something that was splashing around in a black depthless pool of water.

Ian's death didn't make me want to attack a cooker with shock-dragged vim and vigour. But it did remind me of why one day I was so willing to spend an hour doing nothing but wiping and tugging away at an old electric cooker that looked like the grotty shape of death in scummy metal form. And it meant that eighteen years after his death, I would write, for the sake of argument, the following:

1) I suppose Joy Division are like my Elvis Presley. In the ways that pop music opens you up and helps explain things, how it cleans you out and clears a way forward, let me say for the sake of the promise I might have made about how pop opens you up and explains things that when I was fourteen Marc Bolan with a wave of his magic wand and a rhythm that rhymed with sex space and time showed me the light. And Joy Division with a dizzying swoop into the unknown and a rhythm that rhymed with thought showed me the dark.

For me they were both the absolute peak of pop. Bolan stuck stars onto his skin, and that was pretty exciting. Joy Division pierced their skin – put a hole in their being – with their cracked and cracking obsessiveness. That was oddly exciting. I think because Bolan slickly skated over the surface of life with a mischievous smile and made a pop that went with life all the way, and because Joy Division dived under the surface and made a pop that sometimes turned back on life, then Bolan seems to belong to my past. Listening to him now I'm reminded of the faint young teenager who was cracking open the world, and using Bolan as a kind of cosmic key. He is, alas, behind me, a fabulous fling, the star I lost my virginity to, the pop prince of innuendo. Joy Division still point me towards the future. They wrote songs on a journey towards a place and a world of imagination that is like a journey that I'm still on. It wasn't music that meant something to me only as a teenager. Their music is a soundtrack to an adventure that I'm still following. Their music is the soundtrack to the end of this adventure, it is a soundtrack to how you see and sense this end, how you deny it, how you deal with it. It's a soundtrack to how life goes in different directions, and around odd corners, and under itself, towards its end. It's a soundtrack to how the end is as near as anything and as far away as a dream. It's a soundtrack to the question: Where *will* it end? It's a soundtrack to the following paragraph: '. . . and if it is the living, existential experience of the individual that matters and has precedence over any abstract concepts it may elicit, then the very act of confronting the void or continuing to confront it is an act of affirmation. The blacker the situation and the deeper the background of despair against which this act of affirmation is made, the more complete and the more triumphant must be the victory that it constitutes. The uglier the reality that is confronted, the more exhilarating will be its sublimation into symmetry, rhythm, movement and noise.'

2) With Joy Division, you hear a group with a brilliant record collection, who have great discrimination, and whose intention was to absorb and dominate these influences, to equal and surpass. When they started to get good, they started to rub all these noises together, to blend temperatures, to mix blatant antic rock directness with shy nervy avant-garde indirectness. They took their influences and fumbled and twisted them into something original. They took the gaunt tick-tock motion and frosty deadpan adroitness of Kraftwerk. They inherited the hyperactive and gormless artistry of Iggy and the Stooges. They gingerly stalked space and intimately scratched time because they had heard the gelled indulgence of Can. They gnashed and flashed with their guitars and drums as abrasively as MC5.

There was this sarcastic, alternative thing about them that they nicked in their bedrooms from the likes of the Stooges, The Doors and The Velvet Underground. The way they used guitars as bursting abuse, melodies as a ripe sign of bitter-sweet intelligence, beat to beat up time, the way hate was as great a subject as love, the secrecy and hardcore drama of thought as sexy a subject as sex, the way fear and loathing was as great a pop subject as love. These surly, self-sacrificial Americans revealed to them the edgy, and many potential edges to hurl themselves over.

They wanted to be as fishy and theatrical as the green-skinned Bowie and as randomly precise as The Velvet Underground. They were touched up by the sleek and bleak Roxy Music of *For Your Pleasure*. They loved how Bowie lost himself to himself in the tall and tense songs on *Station to Station* and they loved the becalmed insanity of Brian Eno on *Another Green World*. They loved it when Eno and Bowie worked together on *Low* and *Heroes* and worked up a tender, fractured sound that was all at once angelic and diabolical.

They fancied being as unsentimentally epic as Pink Floyd and as

38

sentimentally violent as Led Zeppelin. They would be as male and as pale as Nick Drake and as blunt and infernal as The Sex Pistols. In the wet dead north-west with its low-slung dirty blue sky such delectably subversive stuff was the surreal thing; it showed there was a way out over the grey walls and through the sharp and hostile everydayness of things. And so all these distant and not so distant decadent musicians banking up in the lives of the four impressionable young men shared this thing about 'not belonging' and not wanting to belong and they had this flamboyant and tenacious urge to tell the truth about the world through great, sly and liberating lies.

It was as if the world could be a better place because of the imagination, and why not? Just at the right time in this history of things along came punk rock (turning private emergencies into public urgency) and that fitted right in with all this other stuff, not least because a lot of what punk was had slipped and slithered out of all this other stuff. It was The Sex Pistols tonguing out of the mouths of Stooges that harassed the group that became Joy Division into galactic north-west technological rock and roll action, and they adapted to and pretty quickly transcended this frenzied coincidence of The Sex Pistols, Kraftwerk, The Doors, Brian Eno and Television (and you never know Peter Hammill and Black Sabbath, or J. G. Ballard and Albert Camus, or Franz Kafka and Chic, or Neu and Isaac Asimov, or Mott the Hoople and Dostoevsky . . .).

3) And there was much more that helped the group be mysteriously more than the sum of their influences. There was the Manchester damp, and the phantoms and omens called into empty being by the hills and moors that lurked at the edges of their vision. It wasn't soft, where they lived. It was stained green and unpleasant. There were times when it seemed to be at the edge of the edge of the world, buried under a grievous history. You really had to dream your way out of such a tranquillised, inert land/mindscape. You really had to use your imagination to make believe that there was anything else but nothing else. In this slowed and woeful land your mind would ache for release. And so would your body.

4) What about their record company, Factory? Not so much a record company as a state of mind, an organisation in constant graceful disarray, and a company of free-thinking sub-maniacs who were responsible for pushing and pulling Joy Division through their

short, frantic career. Factory encouraged them and guided them and held them tight to their chest. They helped them and hindered them. They indulged them and spoilt them and disciplined them. In some ways, Factory drove Joy Division. In other ways, the group drove the record company. They certainly drove each other up the walls of their mutual adventure. Together they erratically defied the boring rock gravity of following certain rules of presentation and promotion. Factory helped wrap the darkness of Joy Division in darkness – they wrapped a shroud of provocative anti-glamour around the group, either for protection or to expose even more dramatically the enriched drama of the music.

Factory Records were unusual. Since when has a record company been a combination of villain, pantomime dame, benefactor, wicked stepmother, clown, love, butler, coach, pervert and performance artist? Joy Division could only have been the Joy Division they became because they were a big part of the Factory family.

Factory was a mad, maddening male communion of north-west television presenter Tony Wilson, a sort of cross between Jerry Springer and Malcolm McLaren, actor and will-o'-the-wisp Alan Erasmus, record producer Martin Hannett and Joy Division's manager Rob Gretton. Joy Division couldn't have become the Joy Division they became without Gretton, the quiet fanatic who managed them like he was on a quest for some rock and roll Holy Grail. He loved the group like a child, like a brother, like a father, like a friend, like a fan, and he watched over them with such belief and commitment. He followed them to the ends of the earth and then, oddly enough, beyond. He died a relatively young man: perhaps he lived as long a life as the myth of the group demanded from its manager.

It was Wilson who had a zealous need to create rock history using Joy Division as his tool. He was a seedy idealist, a vulnerable creep, a lovable rogue. He loved the rock myths of Hendrix, The Doors, the Pistols, myths made up of death and danger and cultural derring-do. He loved the idea of his beloved Manchester being the home of a fantastic new rock and roll cult, a massive new youth myth based around the life, and then the death, of Joy Division. He had the lead-lined conceit and the whipped-up energy of a fan who wanted to make rock and roll history. It's always the fans of rock and roll history, the fans who believe in it religiously, who make rock and roll history. He was greedy for the thrill of being associated with a bona fide cultural event.

When Ian Curtis was alive, and so therefore were Joy Division, Wilson hustled hard and shamelessly to ensure the group were destined to fulfil a rock and roll fate that would see them as notorious, as known, as classic as The Doors, or The Velvet Underground. He wanted to be part of something that sold the noise of dreams to the whole world, something that changed the very nature of pop culture.

While Ian was living, and Joy Division were more and more communicating the details of Ian's careering life, Wilson was convinced that they could be a British group as massive and as iconic as the Stones, The Who, Led Zeppelin. A group that could create the images and moods of a decade, a generation, even a century. A group that could change the mind of the entire world. Curtis's death didn't stop Wilson in his tracks. It whetted his appetite even more. The violent suicide of the lead singer gave Wilson strong raw material to play with. He wasn't the type to play down such an episode, and as far as he was concerned it didn't mean that any myth that was growing around the music of Joy Division died with the singer. Such a death was a massive shot in the arm to the myth, and he was determined to use the black energy of the suicide to maintain his belief that Joy Division had cultural and iconic importance. What this importance was could be made up along the way. Rock and roll history is always made up of spontaneous and unpredicted moments that are then rationalised in comparatively comfortable hindsight.

Curtis had made earlier attempts to commit suicide, and these failures perhaps encouraged Wilson to consider the possibilities of what could happen to the reputation of the group if their singer destroyed himself. After all, the group made a music that seemed to point towards suicide. The later songs that Joy Division were writing were the increasingly sensitive Curtis's autobiographical way of dealing with his depressive struggles to live, his struggle with love, they were songs about the burden of the future, and the death of sensation, and death itself. They were the songs of someone losing touch with the conditions of everyday reality, songs about someone slipping into something else, someone discovering new levels to reality. The songs of somebody drugged by his own predicament.

41

A suicide would certainly suggest that this doom-laden, energetically exhausted and gracefully self-obsessed music wasn't any kind of fake. The intensity of the music would be sealed into permanent myth by the suicide of the singer – the utter reality of such an action could only succeed in lighting up the darkness of the songs and confirm that the songs were made up of dense and packed truth.

Wilson felt before Curtis died that he had a modern post-punk Pink Floyd on his hands. He saw Joy Division as a potential supergroup taking out their uncompromising view of madness and desperation into the commercial world and developing into rock greats who were serious and artistic about what they did. He felt that the group were good enough and powerful enough to dominate the 90s and beyond with their sonic drama and imageless image. Eventually, he would claim that Joy Division set up the territory and cleared the way for the success of U2. He considered that U2 became what Joy Division would have become without the suicide of their singer. Legends in their own rock and roll life time.

At the time, once Curtis had died, Wilson, fascinated by the cosmetically cosmic shape of rock and roll history, was convinced that the suicide could help Joy Division become a modern post-punk Doors, and Curtis as mythically malleable, as posthumously iconic, as Jim Morrisson. Curtis killed himself on the eve of a tour Joy Division were about to make of America, a tour Wilson and comrades were hoping would be an integral part of the plan to establish Joy Division as the first real post-punk supergroup. The abrupt disintegration of the group, the shocked and melodramatic response of a small but influential number of fans and critics, meant that instead of an American tour propelling the group towards anti-superstar status, it was a suicide. Wilson, with amoral glee, playing a slippy game of manipulation and fantasising endlessly about creating some hard-edged north-west equivalent of The Sex Pistols, set to work. Rumours, lies, facts, fictions, hypes, all started to shimmer around the ex-group and their ex-singer. Within a matter of weeks after Curtis's death, the group had their first hit single. 'Love Will Tear Us Apart' contained in its lyric and melody and weary dynamic all the information you might require about why Ian Curtis killed himself in the way that a seed contains everything that eventually becomes a tree. The song was his agony and desperation compressed into the irresistible shape of a great, moving pop song. It probably would have been a hit even if Curtis hadn't killed himself. Already the rumours about his suicide attempts and his horribly random epileptic fits were adding to the fever that was spreading in pop circles regarding the nature and commitment of the group.

As it was, Joy Division began their first few weeks of unintentional non-existence with a hit single, and the strange facts of the strange fate of Ian Curtis ensured that Joy Division were destined to find a place in any list of rock and roll weirdness and rock and roll greats. Just how high their position would be in such arbitrary lists would be down to the to-ing and fro-ing, the egging and fretting, of Wilson and his cohorts. And down to how writers would respond to the suicide and Factory's creative and commercial exploitation of it . . .

5) I responded, and continue to respond . . . surrounded by fallout . . . from one thing and another.

6) All of this, all of this before and after, all of this make-up and varnish, all of these coincidences, and transmissions, and transitions, and (r)apt moments, and exotic settings, and wild distortions, it all added up, and multiplied, and put the group, what with one thing and a bloody other, into this unique position where they were both the last ever great rock and roll group (after The Velvet Underground, the Stooges, MC5, The Doors, Television, The Sex Pistols) and the first ever great rock and roll band (before Sonic Youth, The Pixies, My Bloody Valentine, Nine Inch Nails, Nirvana, Smashing Pumpkins, Radiohead . . .) and so somehow they were some twisting turning point some tunnel of light and dark and love and heart that you must journey through from one era to the next from one noise to another if you are to make any sense of the urgency and desire of great rock music . . . Joy Division summoned up in their time and place, summed up in their local way, with such certainty and uncertainty, with such chilling heat, all the great rock and roll that there ever was and ever will be.

7) Joy Division are, in my order of things, which is pretty correct all things considered, the dead centre of the rock universe. They sounded like the greatest rock group of all time, and they ended up all mangled and martyred like a great rock and roll group. They just kept going faster and faster until they suddenly stopped, slammed into themselves by the force of love and the temptation of some other life.

43

8) Or death. Because there was this death in the family. And rock and roll, the greedy bastard, loves early death and gaudy sacrifice. The myth of rock and roll loves death as the lions loved the Christians. Death in rock and roll, and there just isn't enough of it, chronically cosmically represents the ideal levels in rock of madness, danger, self-belief and self-deception. At the extremes of desire, death proves rock and roll, certifies its acts of rebellion. It's not all play-acting. And death proved Joy Division weren't playing with all those extreme surreal eerie themes. Death – general, individual – rams home into amplified eternity the essential black-hearted glamour that rock and roll aspires to, instantly, brutally creates the kind of immortality that all entertainers – even the frail, unformed and boyishly, conscientiously alienated Ian Curtis – desperately crave. Immortality without death might be preferable, and mid-song, mid-ecstatic moment, soul-deep in modern fame, caught in the glare of awed attention, an entertainer might glimpse a sort of immortality. But it needs a messy, publicised mixture of show-business and death to achieve an authentic immortality, a rock and roll immortality. In Ian's case, there was the show business, there was the death, and there was the fact that the dreams written into his songs, the life-suffering death-dreaming songs, tragically came true. It was immortality garlanded with death, an extra-special kind of immortality.

9) Ian Curtis, dead name, dead stop, dead mysterious, dead success, dead at the moment, dead all the time, a close relation of the unknown, as withdrawn as it gets, yet in some ways more alive than when he was alive. You can still hear him breathe as he sings his songs.

10) Joy Division, as lovely as a dream in stone, had everything going for them as rock and roll myths. It was just as their record sleeves always cried and whispered, as if they were implicitly predicting in their abstraction the fate of the group and their singer. A fate that was beyond everyone's wildest dreams, even those of the extra-dreamy Wilson at the dreamy Factory. His dreams, thought, were pretty wild. Dreams based on thought. The thought of a wonderful tomorrow.

He thought in the extra time Curtis's death gave this once upon a time group: 'A myth of myths can be built upon this short fast fractured life that was rendered psychedelically breathless by a messy midnight death.' He thought exactly those words, whether he

44

knew it or not. He thought this as a fan of rock and roll corniness, as a fan of rock and roll seriousness, as a fan of fans and the power of their worship.

11) The seriousness of Joy Division was left hanging in space, and violently rocking.

12) What might have been was left viciously disturbed. And so now Joy Division were disturbing the future because a suicide, whatever the circumstance, whatever the pointlessness, must never be forgotten. Because a suicide is two incredible things. It's the waste of a life and it's the making of a life. Suicide is where the point of life gets all mixed up with the pointlessness of it, and there's a shiver that races down the spine of the universe, and beyond, out into eternity, creating shock waves that never ever stop vibrating from one end of the end to the other. And when you think about it a suicide is unforgettable.

TWELVE

Somewhere before or after the middle of a book called before or after it was written *Death in the Family*, I abruptly interrupted a chapter I was writing about the suicide of Ian Curtis with a memory that had just jumped into my head. I don't know where the memory jumped from, apart from the fact it was the past, or what we know as the past. In one way, it jumped from one place to another within my head, which leads me to believe that all of the past and all of the present are pressed tightly inside my brain, which makes it no wonder that I know nothing about the future. There isn't enough room for the future.

A memory jumped out of the shadows and into the light. I'm not sure whether 'jump' is actually the right verb to describe what a memory does, or at least what this memory did. This memory, and I'm very familiar with this memory, sort of sidled into view. It eased into position. It drifted back into the foreground of my imagination. I'm used to this memory, and I'm used to the way it just appears suddenly in front of my mind's eye. Sometimes I think this memory has a personality, and a big part of this personality is its sense of humour. In that case, perhaps it is right for me to say that, this time, the memory jumped into place.

45

It was very aware that here I am writing about some memories, about things that happened, and appeared to happen, about things that need arranging in order to create a picture of events that connect the past with a certain present. And this memory couldn't bear to be left out. It's a star memory, and it wasn't going to let me write for very long without wanting to be heard, to be savoured, to be used. It fancies itself, this memory. It thinks of itself as a major clue in the chain of events that led from a life to a death. It clings to its place in the past in my head even if I've decided it's a red herring, something misleading, just one of those things. It won't let me dismiss it, it won't run away and hide like a lot of memories do. It's not shy like a lot of memories. It's not disguised. It's bold, it's blunt, and it's big-headed enough to twist and turn its way into my mind even as I'm miles away, years away, dreams away, thinking of something else entirely. It likes to take me by surprise, to spite the feeling that I have that this memory can never take me by surprise. I know it so well. I wish I could marry it off, but it stays stubbornly single. I wish I could laugh it off, but it won't completely turn into something funny. It won't completely turn into anything. It's a memory of something strange that happened when I was eleven or twelve and I can talk about it and it can be an odd little anecdote to tell friends, but I never really understand what happened, what the memory is trying to tell me happened. The memory acts all important, but won't give anything clear away. I suppose it's ever present in the top ten list of memories that I have of my father, and inside this impish memory I see him with his self showing the most. But the self on show is as indistinct as it is vivid, it's obviously him, but one I cannot bring myself to recognise. It's a version of my father that unnerves me and yet somehow fills me with an extreme respect. If I am telling people about my father, it is a memory I will tell them about. It is something that happened that I make sure people know, and I look to their reaction to see if it helps me work out who he was and what he was like.

This memory has nudged me and elbowed me and watched me and puzzled me for as many years as it is since the event that happened turned into the memory of the event. This memory is so vivid to me, it almost has a face. I can almost hear it talk. I can touch it. I can smell it.

It smells of a bus. The top deck of a bus. So it's stale and smoky.

It's winter, so it's cold, and the smokiness has that smell I can only describe as a Bonfire Night edge to it. The top of the bus is full. Every seat is filled. My father and I are sitting on a double seat towards the front of the bus. I remember that it is down the left side as you face forwards. There are only a couple of rows in front of us. The bus is packed with Manchester City supporters. City have just played at home, and I presume they must have lost, or not played very well. The memory won't let me budge either side of the events on the bus – it won't let me remember the match, or what happened when me and my father got home. It is too selfish. It just wants to be a memory of these moments, it doesn't want to be sullied with other weakening details. The memory lets me know that we are on a bus driving from Maine Road, the City ground, towards Reddish in Stockport, but it only gives me enough details to conclude that we could be driving through the middle of nowhere and the only important thing about this memory is what my father is about to do.

City must have played badly because the bus is one droning moan of disappointment and annoyance. City fans are notorious for loving a good moan, and they love wallowing in the glory and self-pity of being the self-chosen ones who live in Manchester but do not support their mighty neighbours Manchester United. They love their team and want to show off that they love their team to the point where they feel that they and they alone are in a position to be able to nag about City. They give so much to their team – if only by not supporting United – that they consider themselves licensed to lay into them when they perform below par.

On this journey, every single supporter seemed to be talking at the same time about how useless and pathetic City had been. Between the lines of such complaints always lies this element of weariness, that enough is enough, I sacrificed the possibility of supporting a team that won the European Cup so as to watch City and I want something back in return. Every single supporter on the top deck of the bus was whinging about their team, because they expected something back for their uncompromising commitment. Everyone on the top deck of the bus nagged until the sound of the nagging reached the volume of a road drill. Everyone on the top deck of the bus nagged and niggled and cursed except me and my father. My father sat in stony-faced silence, dead still, staring straight ahead. He might have been wearing a mask of self-hate, but

I'm not sure. I was miles away, looking out of the window, only dimly aware that my father was being put under some kind of pressure by something, not really tuned in to the cacophony of whine and irritation that was raging behind me.

Such annoyance always seemed to be fairly light-hearted to me. It wasn't to be taken that seriously. If you supported Manchester City, and suffered as your bloody-red neighbours constantly outdid your team, outplayed you, and were loved around the world, you were allowed to let off steam. Sometimes you just had to get it out of your system. And here on the top deck of the bus there was a pissed-off gaggle of City supporters loudly getting their frustration out of their systems, making as much noise as they wanted to, because they supported City. Perhaps one reason they did so was that it allowed them to fling the shit of their lives at a convenient target. They liked having a good moan. They liked having this massive chip on their shoulders. Deep down, part of their love for City was because it enabled them to have a damned good moan on regular occasions. It helped them to build up strength. They enjoyed being underdogs, they relished their role. Complaining was part of the whole enterprise.

The nagging reached a quite impressive crescendo. It was surely about to reach some kind of climax that might well have shattered all the windows on the bus. The moaning was so intense it just had to erupt. My father got there first. The sound of the City fans criticising their team non-stop for fifteen minutes as we crept through the traffic leaving City's ground had wound him up until he could bear it no more. The noise he suddenly made on the top deck of the bus made the sound of the nagging seem very weak. Out of nowhere but the provoked depths of his tender soul he roared with an anger that seemed completely inappropriate to everyone but him. He turned round and he just screamed at the passengers. Pent-up fury was unpent in one colossal go. The fury whipped around the top deck of the bus like a gale-force wind. The bus seemed to rock on its wheels. The windows shook with the impact. So did the passengers.

The nagging stopped in an instant. Collective breath was held. Sentences were sliced off in mid-whine. Criticisms were savagely ceased. The moaning of thirty fans was easily absorbed by the anger of one man. The atmosphere on the bus changed in a second from genial bitterness to one of near fear. My father's resentment of what he saw as the supporters' inane pettiness was lacerating. He

48

shouted at them like they were a bunch of naughty children. He'd had enough and he damned well wasn't going to take it any more. Next to him, I was appalled and fascinated as he burst his lungs and stretched and reddened the skin on his face with his contempt and disapproval: 'WILL YOU SHUT UP FOR PITY'S SAKE HAVE YOU GOT NOTHING BETTER TO DO MOANING AND MOANING ON ABOUT THE SAME OLD RUBBISH You're PATHETIC JUST SHUT UP SHUT UP FOR God's SAKE SHUT UP SHUT UP Can't WE JUST HAVE SOME QUIET . . .'

I don't remember him swearing, but he said it with as much hostility as if every word was a 'fuck' or a 'shit'. The effect was as if every word was a 'fuck' or a 'shit'. But even as he very loudly stated his demands, there was something about him that was very much in control. There was something oddly reasonable about the catastrophic loss of temper. He didn't have to swear, and even in whatever far-out place he'd been compelled to reach, he wasn't going to swear in front of his son.

There was a pause as the passengers got used to the fact that they could no longer have their own way. Everyone worked out very quickly that this man at the front of the bus was not messing about. He really meant it. His face was contorted with a commitment to his cause that made theirs look pretty feeble. Everyone followed the orders issued by someone who clearly had more to get out of his system than everyone on that bus combined. More to get out of his system than the thirty thousand who had just watched City play at Maine Road.

My father waited to be sure that the bus had fallen in line with his wishes, and then he said, slightly lowering the volume of his voice but with violence of some sort still a distinct possibility . . . 'Thank you . . .'

The bus trundled on away from Maine Road. The passengers on the top deck had been seriously disciplined. No one dared utter a word. I could sense no relief coming from my father. He just stared ahead as impassively as he had before his spectacular outburst. I felt relieved – relieved that such a level of anger hadn't in any way been directed at me. Behind me, I could feel a wave of sympathy being generated on my behalf because I had such an unstable and potentially crazy father. I didn't care for this sympathy. I just marvelled at the level of my father's hatred for the people on the bus, and felt a grudging respect for his ability to do such a thing in public. I wasn't really sure if this meant he was mad or anything, but I think after that I found it more and more difficult to look him in the eyes. After all, such an occasion made me consider that there was much more to my father than met the eye. Such a performance took a kind of greatness. It took a kind of seriousness. And, yes, maybe madness.

Brave, foolhardy whispering and gently belligerent muttering tentatively returned to the bus from the passengers behind us who had been mortified into an unsteady silence. All the whispering was undoubtedly directed towards my father. For someone who had just abused a busful of strangers with no direct provocation, he took this whispering behind his back rather well. He sat in his seat with a straight back and he looked straight ahead. He assumed a stern but relaxed look as if nothing out of the ordinary had happened. He tried to hide his loneliness, but didn't really succeed. His son next to him was slightly shocked by everything that had happened but did the best he could to exhibit a kind of solidarity with his father.

The bus arrived at its destination and everyone, except my father, quietly trooped off as if something had happened that doesn't happen every day. I wonder how many of the passengers talked about this day for years to come. How many of them turned this mad day into a star memory, just like I have. My father never mentioned what had happened. I can't imagine what kind of memory he made out of the bus journey. What had he been thinking? Was he taking out his feelings on those behind him, or himself?

As far as I could tell, he got on with his life and I was never able to work out just how important or unimportant this jagged rage had been in the race his life was following from day to day from life to death. Was it a life-changing moment, or was he just particularly fed up that day? The memory doesn't really help me. It just reminds me of the day my father went berserk sitting right next to me and acted as if nothing had happened.

In a book I was writing called *The Influence of the Letter J on My Immediate Life* I would then move back into a section I was writing about the rock group Joy Division and the suicide of Ian Curtis. The memory had achieved its aim, and had made its point. It skulked off back to its hideaway with a little smirk on its face smelling as always of the top deck of a 1970s double-decker bus.

13) There was the early death of the man who produced, with an ear that could hear the moon circle the earth, all of the songs of Joy Division. His name was Martin Hannett, and apart from anything else I remember that he was the first person I ever saw smoke a joint. Sometime in the mid-70s, somewhere in an office down Manchester's Oxford Road, near the University. I don't remember what I was doing there or why I was meeting him but I remember this man talking to me as if he knew all about the reasons Captain Beefheart and Tim Buckley and Iggy Pop made the music the way they made it, as if he'd been to their world, and back. And there was something about the way he smoked the thing he held loosely in his hand that suggested it was the secret to visiting the worlds of Frank Zappa and Neil Young and Love. I remember feeling a little unnerved in his presence, not because he was scary, but because he seemed to know things I only knew that I didn't know, and as he smoked the thing in his hand he sank further and further into his own brand of knowledge, further and further away from me. Eventually, he got so far away from me he appeared quite motionless. I guess he was motionless in relation to the stars.

His knowledge as inspired by the thing he held seriously but lethargically in his hand seemed more romantic and unreasonable than any knowledge of mine. Eventually I would get to hear a soundtrack to his reality-curling knowledge when I heard the music of Joy Division. I would hear a hint of his take on reality, a take that could be taken as ever so slightly, but prettily, mistaken, with how he framed, and softened, and toughened, the songs of Joy Division. He set them into landscapes he'd learnt about by visiting imagined other worlds. He created sound effects copied from sounds he'd heard experiencing the weather in imagined other worlds. I suppose you could say he sort of stoned the songs.

And so Martin Hannett died too. Another death in the Factory family, although by the time he died he was pretty much the black sheep in the family. Or maybe he was the white sheep in a family of black sheep. He didn't kill himself directly. He died from heart failure. His heart broke.

But who's to say that someone who so willingly and regularly visited other worlds – worlds artificially created and/or worlds as real as this one – in the name of discovery, of escape, of courage, of cowardice, wasn't slowly killing himself, and perhaps in the end not so much committing suicide as deciding to visit permanently some other world. A world with new and different possibilities. A world that consisted of sounds and shadows some of which he'd already laid into the close background of some of Joy Division's songs. Sounds that sounded like nothing else but otherness. Sounds that sounded like ghosts sounding out other worlds.

The death of Hannett added more mischief to the myth of Joy Division, more fun and games, more disjointed history, more incidental insubordination, more violence, more degenerate hero-ism, more seriousness. All in all another death added to the gathering components making up Joy Division, with one foot in this world and one foot someplace else, as this big-deal rock and roll illusion trapped inside their very own infinitely variable end-lessly interpreted mystery melodrama. For a fairly obscure northern rock act with a badly botched-up life they were getting bigger than they seemed, on the quiet as big as they come. Their death-festooned myth was becoming noisy and quiet, dazzling and hidden, static and dynamic . . . not quite reaching the level of The Doors, but then the Doors myth is not quite as intriguing as that of Joy Division. And for Wilson there was always the hope of the book, the film, the commercially maximised publicity to help propel Joy Division up another iconic division and into another mythical dimension.

14) Joy Division, after their overnight stop, their collision with fate, neither exist nor do not exist. With the help of a shattered Curtis, the tangle he got his marriage into, the crush his mind squashed into, and a lethal length of clothes line, the group plum-meted a few feet or a few million light years into a rainy limbo where they hang around somewhere between myth and Myth. They hang around somewhere between giants and insects, for everyone to inspect. And sometimes quite a queue builds up. A queue of inspec-tors expecting this group as they sway in breezy limbo to supply them with something you tend to expect from insects and giants.

15) Wonder.

16) I could write – with the intention of a rock writer showered by fall-out – about Joy Division's central role in it all, the it all of rock and roll et al., and yet how they are also so off centre. But then,

to be so central to the story they have to be off centre as well, because the central beauty of rock and roll is that it is off centre. It must never be at the centre. Joy Division had to be off centre to be at the centre of rock and roll, but even when they were at the centre, they were outside the centre. Anything else would be too banal for words. They had to be off centre to be central, to be central in a place that has no centre. At this place, the centre of no-centre, the central place in a centreless place, they could be properly obvious, mysterious, and (in the skipped beat of a missing moment) enigmatic. Here, at this centre that was no centre at all, they would exist in a non-existing way as the greatest rock and roll group ever to be found and ever to go missing.

17) Moving on from the off-centre where we have placed them off centre (to the point of anti-centrality) in the history of rock things, the myth still rises, and obscures and provokes.

18) They said that they were waiting for some guy to come and take them by the hand, and there were these gulping black noises, and these squirming off-white sub-noises, that sounded like they were giving birth or operating on themselves. Noises that had travelled from other worlds and which hovered around the realish-sounding rock like vultures surrounding a body they weren't sure was alive or dead. *Unknown Pleasures* began with music that sounded like it was inside your head nibbling away at your nerve endings and crunching through bone. And so yes, Joy Division's music could form the soundtrack to something very David Lynch-like. It would be no good in a Tarantino setting. Joy Division, like Lynch, never had any intention of wanting to cut the universe down to size. They loved – and hated, but with respect – the size of the universe. The size of the universe is everything.* And the size is in the details. Each detail in the universe carries within it a map of the universe, sometimes to scale. One of the great things about Joy Division was their appreciation of size and their attention to detail, and when to use a map, and when to trust their own instincts about where things were.

It was as if, whether they intended this or not, they were trying to warn us about dangers to avoid. In doing this they alerted us to dangers of which we may not previously have been aware.

* And nothing.

According to Joy Division, whether they knew it or not, nothing is neutral nothing is impotent nothing is next to nothing nothing comes first nothing comes last nothing is at the centre and an atom may ruin all an atom may ransom us all. And so you wake up frightened with the feeling of having overslept. And so they made us think of another separate world that maniacs and exiles invent when the normal everyday world seems impossible.

19) The mood shifts again.

20) There were the writings of Ian Curtis, who was underground by the time he was twenty-three. He wrote these tranquil and delirious autobiographical fragments, these notes and notices from an above-ground underground, images that leapt out of pounded language, and it sounded as if all his senses were being tensed. The words seemed to come from someone who had lived so much more than twenty-odd years. Something was concentrating his mind wonderfully. It was exactly as if he suspected, consciously or not, that it – the all-embracing it, the it of all its, the it you can see in the eyes of a dying man – was coming to an end one way or another sooner rather than later. Even without having all that I've mentioned – their off-centred centrality, their essence-ness, their post-punk zeal, their book of contacts – Curtis's impressions and depressions, his fast-decaying urgency, would have lifted Joy Division into greatness.

He sang from the knife-edge of doubt with a kind of suave sordid middle-of-the-road disconnectedness. He sang about defeat, and a defeated mind, with a dissolved glory, as if there was a kind of triumph in the difficulties of life. He sang suffering with an almost tender listlessness. He put the perfect voice to strangled thoughts. He put this awkward but handsome spin on despair. He crooned anxiety as if he was flirting with the Grim Reaper. He delivered sullen commotion. He expressed his restlessness and soul-sickness with a damaged insouciance. Even when he was charged, and confrontational, he seemed resigned. He sang his sharply apprehensive songs in the spirit of: I'll get this off my chest. And then get this chest off me.

This music that rocked – that could go the distance and bash your brains in – hung inside a sense of sadness and waste and emptiness. And, as more and more of Curtis's life tore through its complications, the music was embraced by a physical and mental exhaustion.

It was as if Curtis was transferring himself into the very body of the music, stumbling over the line from where the music was for him to where he was for the music. The songs weren't helping him deal with or recover from the traumas of his life, they were encouraging a fascination with the speed and danger of the drama. They weren't an escape from the madness; they sent him right into the madness. The music was taking him away, from himself, from others, from life. It was taking him over. It was needing the drama of his life. And so there was more drama. And more madness. And so the sin always rises. And so Ian Curtis – depressed, epileptic, unfaithful, artistic, pressured – was using his songs and being used by his songs to create a map of despair at the end of a life. The map was perfectly to scale. Of course, he didn't have to follow the map. But he'd lost his bearings.

21) Ian Curtis lived his life intensely to such depths. It became a rock and roll life. A poet's life. A madman's life. A sick life. Formerly a real life. You can hear the depth and intensity in the deep, intense pop song 'Love Will Tear Us Apart'. Listening to the song you can tell exactly – around an unknown hard centre – when his life started to end. And you get a hint of when it started to begin. You can even hear when he started to believe in death. It's all there in the details of his voice, as it forms and reforms, as it swells and fades, and in the way it's coated thickly with memory, and regret.

22) There was Ian Curtis leading the group who were all playing their instruments as if they were leading. As if there were three lead instruments. The glass-smashing and capering Bernard Sumner guitars, the cold and splendidly alert Steve Morris drums, the iron-tough and lurid Peter Hook bass. Even the spare and marooned noises off, the phantom implants drafted in from some other blue world by Martin Hannett to gee up, or down, proceedings, these noises acted as if they had an (ectoplasmic) ego all of their own, as if they were actually leading. The circle completed itself with Curtis and his tragic voice and antic geed-up, or -down, dancing – he moved to the music as if he wanted to run on the spot faster than the planet was spinning – and he was leading the group, and us, into his . . . space.

23)

24) The space that exists in the music of Joy Division has always been infinitely bewitching. Somehow – everything still stretched around somehow, stretched as tight as the rope that squeezed the life out of Curtis – the group could leave such emptiness in the middle of their music, and at the edges, without weakening it. It added to the strength, the resonance. Perhaps it came out of the space they were leaving around each other – even as they came together to make this music, and sort of fell in love with each other, they kept themselves to themselves. They stayed trapped inside their own splendid isolation, stuck inside their own young minds. They all played and sang from deep inside their own detailed worlds. Joy Divison was privacy times four.

And so their music is about, finally, isolation. It is about the difficulty of keeping in touch with other human beings as we create for safety's sake a reality around us that works for us as much as it can. A reality we can trust. It's about the mind, as far as my mind is concerned, and the tricks that it plays on itself, the harm it can do itself as it struggles to float in a world containing so much water it can drown you in a second. The songs are about the way the mind can find all sorts of ways to prise apart illusion and reality and then cobble them back together in a way that makes sense if only for the moment.

25) And then there are the songs, again and again, because they just do not wear out whatever you take from them, wherever you take them. Somewhere in there, amidst other more secretive and even more catastrophic narratives, you can make out Ian's feisty, frail battle for self-preservation, a battle he was winning and then he was losing. Perhaps if he hadn't got drunk that night, and hadn't listened to Iggy Pop shrieking for mercy, and hadn't watched a Herzog film, and hadn't thought he'd fucked up his life, he wouldn't have killed himself. Until the next week, or the next month. Perhaps he might have found his bearings and done away with the map.

Even if he had survived, there would still be these songs, and they're not great because he died, they're great because he sang about how close life can be to death. He sang about how the difference between life and death is never more than an instant, a moment, a thought, and he sang about what it's like to get closer and closer to that moment, that thought. He could have got this close to the moment and survived. But the closer you get to such a moment, the more lethal emotions become. Emotions can kill. Emotions kill more people than anything else, one way or another.

26) These songs were lifted beyond themselves by being – as far as it can go, if this isn't too far-fetched – set inside the enclosed, abstract and echoing space of a mind which envelopes the songs from all directions. This is some illusion. And some reality. Ian Curtis's mind somehow – how this is so is always on the tip of my tongue – held the songs in shivering space. And so I suppose I'm saying, this time, that with the music of Joy Division we can see inside a mind. And we hear him beginning to think ideas he only has so much time to formulate, ideas and thoughts that are about, with such boyish bravado and such adult cynicism, everything and then nothing. He was beginning to think and his early thoughts were the end. The thoughts were just too good. And too bad.

27) And so he re-enters the shadows of living night, disappears into the overnight that strangled his everything and then nothing. And so his ideas, they're forgotten, abandoned, miscarried, before he ever really knew he was having them. Carried away by the twists and turns of his own life, startled by responsibility, adrift in the turmoil of extended adolescence, he thought for a moment he could escape. He thought he could fly. But he didn't fly. He slumped with a vicious snap into the infinitely minuscule gap between life and death. A life that had weakened him beyond measure also conspired to give him the uncanny strength to lift life right out of his body and hurl it into the dark side of the dark.

28) His empty and empty-handed body survived him a few days and was laid to rest one afternoon in a chapel in his home town, Macclesfield, for friends and relatives to pay their respects.

29) Ian Curtis gave Joy Division their life and their death. He gave Joy Division his life and his death. He gave them their perverted specialness. He actually risked his neck. He was under crisis and he passed this sense of crisis – real and imagined, and in the end what's the difference? – right into the bloody unstable body of the music. Right into its heart and soul. He was fighting mad, he'd given up, and you can sense the tension between wanting life and wanting death in the turbulence of the music. You can hear the fight that went on between the steady common sense that stabilises this life in this time, and the ferocious senselessness that constantly threatens the balance of life, that wobbles life, and wobbles it, and rocks it,

and rolls it, until it shakes itself apart. The epilepsy that came late in his life seemed to symbolise the way his life was shaking itself to bits, pulling itself apart at the seams, dragging Curtis and his very being into another state of mind, a sleepless unconsciousness. He danced with controlled uncontrollability as if he wanted to outstrip the speed of the planet. His epileptic fits sickly emphasised his need to move faster than the world. His emotions moved him faster than the earth as it hurtles through space. His soul was vibrating like a demonic hummingbird. It all added up to an acceleration, a momentum, that saw him leave the third planet from the sun far, far behind.

30) He was frightened, and his music was frightening. He was in love with the wrong woman at the wrong time. He was hurtling down a tunnel of love and hate wondering why there was no light at the end. He was a father a lifetime before he was ready. He was depressed because he was sick. He was sick because he was depressed. And so he was lonely. That he and his friends – who were just as lonely in their own lost ways – could turn these thoughts and confusions so magically into sounds – gentle, pure, heartbreaking and lacerating sounds – is but a hint of the alchemical extravagance of the strangely intelligent, ridiculously burdened, youthfully defiant, magnificently doomed, glooming and blooming, old-style, avant-garde, anonymous and famous rock and roll group.

If I may be so bold at such an exact time, covered with the fall-out of a series of big and little explosions in my past, to say the following: Joy Division locate us in the gently smouldering nowhere solid hell* of communal remembering, of mutual awareness, never exact, never erased.

And so, mind you, there we have it.†

In the middle of a book – page 78 out of 143, so I think we can call it the middle – called *Drinking Ourselves to Death*, I was talking

---

* The word 'hell' stems from the Germanic root meaning 'concealed' and originally, like Hades of Sheol, had less to do with punishment than simple bleak survival in a vague netherworld.
† Another end, another day, another doldrum, another beginning, another way of seeing things when there is nothing and everything to see. And so, on. And on. And so on. Until it, or something very like it, comes.

with my father over a drink in a pub about this essay I had written on Joy Division. I don't know what he was drinking. I never knew what his favourite drink was, but I'll guess at a pint of bitter. I was drinking whisky and Coke. He was lost for words when I asked him if he'd read the Joy Division essay, and what he thought of it. This is not surprising, as he had died before Joy Division had formed, and anyway he didn't have much interest in pop music. He was never really used to the fact that I was a writer – published, paid, national – when he died.

I remember him reading the first major feature I ever had published in the *New Musical Express*. I had interviewed my teenage hero, Marc Bolan, in London. It had been a traumatic journey for me, only the second I had ever made by train to London. I had bought a brand new pair of jeans for the interview, and my mum had washed them the day before I travelled down to do the interview. The blue denim had streaked badly and she had ironed a crease into them. So I interviewed someone who had brought magic and glamour into my life wearing a pathetic pair of trousers and I just couldn't take my mind off these awful trousers. My mind was wrapped up in this streaky, pressed denim. The denim blocked out the light. I felt stupid, and could barely concentrate on the unbelievable fact that I was actually talking to someone who had so beautifully changed my life. I felt I had failed him by wearing such dreadful trousers, even though he probably never even noticed them in much the same way I didn't to be honest even notice his. If he had noticed them, he might have thought they were some arcane northern fashion. He might have quite respected the crease down the front and the streaky mottled effect. As someone who was wearing them, though, I can say that the very thought of them, hanging around in front of me, the very sensation of them hugging my poor legs, castrated my soul. I had let the whole wonderful world of pop music down by wearing such crap trousers as I interviewed a pop god.

My first journey had been a few months before when I went down to the offices of the *New Musical Express* by the River Thames in London to be interviewed for a job. I had sent the paper a copy of a fanzine I had written called *Out There* with a note to the editor, Nick Logan, that simply claimed: 'I can do better than you.' I neglected to give a telephone number, as it never occurred to me anything would become of my communication. A communication that was so terse and arrogant because just recently punk with its attendant values had entered my life. In the fanzine you can detect the change that there had been in my passions and beliefs. There were articles I had written on the jazz drummer John Stevens, on the singer Bettina Jonic, on Brian Eno, on Aerosmith, and there were little stories friends had done for me on Ted Nugent and Bob Dylan. Dylan was actually on the cover. But I had by then seen The Sex Pistols, and Patti Smith, and the Stranglers, and Buzzcocks, and The Ramones, and the excitement I felt watching these bizarre-looking alien beings change the entire fabric of rock music poured into my fanzine. I inserted a little editorial imploring Mick Jagger to quit. I imagined a love affair between Patti Smith and Marc Bolan.

Luckily, the formality I had learnt at school about how to lay out a letter had not been rinsed away by my new enthusiasm for punk rebellion. Even though I had sent to the *NME* a small scrap of torn paper with my assertion of superiority scrawled in irritated biro, I had neatly written out my address in the top right-hand corner of the letter. A few days later, causing as much emotion as if we had won the pools, a telegram arrived from Nick Logan, expressing interest in my fanzine, and interest in me writing for the paper. I had never seen my father so happy as when that telegram arrived. At the time I was working part-time in a Stockport bookshop, and my father was convinced that, having left school at sixteen, with no real interest in any career, and just an idealistic determination to be a writer, I would drift off into a future of uncertainty always on the edge of unemployment. Probably, he was thinking that I would follow his footsteps into a life made shapeless by lack of steady employment. The telegram from Logan at the *NME* caused unusual joy in our household. I had been given a chance to achieve something.

I had been asked to bring something I had written to show Logan. I hadn't really got anything, but a couple of days earlier I had seen Buzzcocks, one of the original Manchester punk-inspired pop groups, play in front of a handful of people in a hall in Deansgate, in the city centre. My father gave me a lift to Stockport station to catch an early-morning InterCity train. I planned to write a review of the Buzzcocks performance on my way to London. The train was packed, and I was forced to travel backwards squashed into a seat next to another passenger. Somehow on the three-hour early-morning journey I managed to write the review. Nick Logan politely accepted the handwritten article, talked to me about me, and pop music, and the *NME*. Then I returned home, not sure what to expect. The next Thursday, the day the *NME* came into my local newsagent, I rushed out to buy a copy. This was something I had done for four years. The only thing I could think that I wanted to do with my life was write for the *New Musical Express*. I'd thought this since I was fourteen. It was my equivalent of playing football for England. It was my equivalent of going to university. It seemed, placed as I was in Stockport, which was a long way from the centre of everything, and a long way outside pop music, and writing, and a future, that it was an impossible dream. I hadn't really planned on my review actually being in the paper. I hadn't dared believe that the few pages handwritten as I travelled backwards on a 7.30 InterCity train to London would actually be treated with such professional respect that they would be printed in the pages of my beloved *New Musical Express*. I had accepted that they were just a test.

There was still enough hope inside me that somehow the words about Buzzcocks were good enough to make the paper. I got my copy, and turned to the live review pages. The review had been printed. It looked so real and proper and I read it over and over again as I walked back home. It was hypnotic. I was a writer. I could call myself that now without anybody sniggering.

I don't remember my father's response to that review being printed. I do remember how pleased he was a few months later when my article about Marc Bolan was published, taking up two whole pages of the *NME*. And I remember how embarrassed I was as he read it in front of me. In the article about Bolan I had lied. Not by pretending that I was wearing a great pair of trousers as I did the interview, but by saying that I had lost my virginity to a girl with corkscrew hair after a concert by Bolan and his group T. Rex. My father didn't mention this part. We never ever talked about sex. As far as he was concerned, I didn't have a sex life. The truth was, I didn't. I'd made it up about losing my virginity, in an attempt to come across in the article like some experienced and otherworldly punk reporter. The truth was, when my father died, I was a virgin. I think he knew. But what did he care?

He died a few months after I wrote the Marc Bolan piece. So did Marc Bolan. Before he died, I met Marc Bolan a couple more times, and was even beginning to get to know him. I was beginning to get to know him better than my father. Which, what with one thing and another, wouldn't have been hard. I think that my father died first, although I can't be certain. I do remember how I found out about the death of Marc Bolan. Early one morning my mother woke me up with the news that he had perished in a car crash. I woke up with a start with my mother's face about two inches away from me and she all but shouted, 'Marc Bolan's dead!' What with the news and the way she told me the news she might as well have handed me a Brillo pad and some rubber gloves and told me to go and clean the cooker.

This in-my-face way of informing me about the death of people soon became a habit. Soon she was within an inch of my face waking me up to loudly inform me: 'Elvis Presley's dead.' This run was completed on Christmas morning of what I'm sure was the same year as the death of Bolan, Presley and my father – Bolan representing the time of my life, Presley representing the time of my father's life. In my memory, they all seemed to have died in the same month.

At about six o'clock on Christmas morning, there was my mother's face again, pushed into mine, stricken with a look I now knew was because she had just found out someone had died. In the instant before she shrieked the news at me, I wondered who on earth it could be this time. Someone who represented the time of my mum's life? Who could that be? Doris Day? Pat Phoenix, Elsie Tanner in *Coronation Street*? My mum's favourite singer, Johnny Cash?

'Your grandma Morley has died!' she cried, in a voice that would have stopped Father Christmas from visiting our house that year even if he existed. Blearily I tried to work out if this news made me feel the way I had felt when Bolan died, Presley died, my Woodwork teacher at school died, or when my father died. None of them, really. It just made me feel that just lately I had had a lot of death to get used to, and I seemed to be getting used to it. And so the second funeral I ever went to was the funeral of my father's mother.

Right in the middle of a book I'd called *The Riddle of the Middle*, which was all about middles and contained a variety of middles to books I'd really written or nearly written, I imagined a series of comments I might want to make in the middle of a book called *A Matter of Life and Death*. These included:

1) As Epicurus assured us two millennia ago, death is 'nothing'.

2) The brain's speciality is the active storage and control of information, just as the heart specialises in pumping and controlling the flow of blood. The vitality of both these organs is essential to life. Thanks to medical science, should the heart fail, we can now transplant it. Not so with the brain. The brain is who we are; when the brain dies, we are pronounced dead, even if the heart is still beating. It is the working brain, the subjective activity of which we call 'mind' that determines the self.

3) Do you really wish that without further delay I draw you into a more or less madcap story, that I present you with more or less well-rendered stock characters caught up in more or less plausible conflicts? That will come soon enough, if that is to come.

4) Literature is full of characters who drop dead from the effects of overpowering emotion. Shakespeare's King Lear, for example, dies of a broken heart when his favourite daughter Cordelia is cruelly murdered shortly after Lear is reconciled with her. On discovering Cordelia's body, Lear gives vent to crushing grief:

> Howl, howl, howl, howl! O! you are men of stones:
> Had I your tongue and eyes, I'd use them so
> That heaven's vaults should crack. She's gone for ever!

Then Lear drops down dead.

5) Anhedonia means in literal translation 'the absence of pleasure', but in fact in its most severe form anhedonia becomes an absence of feeling, a profound blunting of emotion such that life itself loses meaning. Anhedonia can accompany morbid grief, as when Hamlet, stricken by the brutal murder of his father, questions the meaning of life: 'How weary, stale, flat, and unprofitable / Seem to me all the uses of this world.'

But this lack of feeling, especially of pleasure, is most frequently present in melancholia. Melancholia lies on a continuum with depression, extending the illness to its most disabling and frightening form. It is a depression that has taken root and grown independent, distorting and choking the accustomed feeling of being alive.

6) What I write today I will not write in a year's time. I will not write it tomorrow. I will not write about my father's funeral now. I won't even write about it in a year's time. I will write about it when

I remember enough or dream about the funeral to make it a very different account from what it would be if I wrote it now. I will put the moment off. I will wait until later. I will think about it another time. Anyway, funerals don't belong in the middle. They belong at the end. At least, in this book they do. I will save the funeral for the end. For after I have thought up a little bit more life. For now, my father remains stuck in the middle of his life, and lost in the middle of this book.

7) Meanwhile, what with one thing and another.

8) It was twenty-eight years after he had been born – he had been born a couple of years before the toothbrush had been invented – and he had got very used to this life.

9) But you never get entirely used to life.

10) He vaguely wondered who had condemned him to it. To this life which was allegedly, his life. He sat on a very old, very soft, very scruffy sofa. The sofa was fat and battered. It even looked a little bruised. It didn't have the look of a style that was older than him, but it looked older than he was just because of the faded covers and the dust and crumbs and the old stains ground into the arms. It looked ancient. It slumped in the living room as if it was exhausted after centuries of travels. It was the shape of resignation, which is a shape you could describe as shapeless. It was worn out. And he was sitting on it, worn out.

It wasn't much of a colour. Whatever colour it was, something that might once have been brown, was now the colour of a sludge that had existed since the Middle Ages. There was an argument for saying that every atom and molecule that made up this dumb apology for a settee had been around since the birth of the universe, that it was just another physical manifestation of an explosion that was still in the process of exploding. The settee was just another particle of the Big Bang. Another example of the miraculous debris that had exploded into being out of the nonsense of nothing. It was a torn shred of the miracle of life. It was a part of the fall-out of the Big Bang as ultimately awe-inspiring as Saturn or Marilyn Monroe or a cabbage. It existed. It was mind-boggling. The stuffing that stuck out of ripped seams existed. It was an uncanny if very local example of how, what with one thing and another, what with the way things turned out, something had come from nothing. It was an object that was as grotty and as beautiful as anything big or small in the universe could be, now that the universe had been expanding for a few billion years. Everything is a detail of this expansion, a part of this expansion, the expansion itself – everything is just an effect of a commotion-driven motion – and this settee, old, broken and soggy as it was, existed as a detail of the expanding universe. A detail made up of other details, and some of those details, some of the details that had gathered in this place to help make the shape of the settee were stunning. They were little miracles. They were the absolute essence of the universe. In some ways, the aged and ugly settee was the perfect centre of the universe. There was also an argument for saying that the settee was a waste of space, a mistake, and the universe wanted no part of it.

He hated the settee. As far as he was concerned it was a piece of junk. But he put up with it and he sat on it. What else could he do? It had been handed on to him by his mother-in-law. In the way that your family often gives you furniture when you cannot afford considering that the furniture might not be to taste, it might be falling apart, it might be useless. But they hand it on, because they want to help, and it's difficult to reject this help. And so this settee now dominated a small lounge in a small two-up and two-down in an anonymous little side street in a nondescript town to the south of Manchester and the east of Stockport. It was far too large for the room, but again this was a practical detail that was little help in the situation. He and his wife needed a settee, his wife's mother had one that was no use to her, and so into the house it came, too big, too old, too soft, but something you had to say thank you for and look grateful about.

He sat on a second-hand settee and he had the look of a man who had outlived certain desires. The settee wasn't entirely responsible for this, but it didn't help. It smelt old, as if it spent a large amount of the day belching out stale wind. It was bloated enough for you to feel that it had a problem with gas, not necessarily the kind of gas you find swirling enigmatically through the fibres of the universe, but the gas you get from eating too many baked beans. The settee had experienced years and years of intimate human touching, it had been crushed by selfish arse after wriggling arse, undermined by an eternity of fatigue and laziness. It was silent but if it had been able to make a noise it would have been a very tired noise, a sad, sighing noise, a noise that never ended. Perhaps that's the noise the universe makes as it continues expanding to the point where it can only expand some more.

The settee was part of some grand mysterious plan as orchestrated by the endlessly expanding universe. It has to be said though that within that plan, the settee had resigned itself to its flabby fate. It had given up. It let the universe get on with things. When the universe had made up its mind what was up and what was down and what was next and what was before it would let the settee in on the joke. The settee was pretty sure about this. It had the weary look of something resigned to the possibility that the universe was leading us all towards some cosmic joke, that perhaps the universe itself was the cosmic joke.

The young man sat on the settee and felt a long way off from ever being let in on any cosmic joke. He would have quite happily blown up the settee in the way that he would have quite sadly blown up himself. All that would happen would be a couple of very minor changes in the shape of two very very small details of a very very small part of a very indifferent universe. He could never muster the energy to blow himself and the settee into kingdom come. He could barely muster the energy to think such a thought.

His world was drained of emotion. All sense of perspective had disappeared. Strangers, friends, family and lovers were all held in equal affection. The events of the day had no obvious priority. There was no guide to tell him which task was most important, what to wear, what food to eat. Life was without meaning and with meaning had gone motivation. His whole being felt colourless. The emotion that had drained away seemed replaced by a liquid void. The settee seemed perched on the edge of this void.

He sat on the settee. His hair was very straight, black, and tightly slicked back with a couple of ear-lobe-sized knobs of Brylcreem. He always kept his hair slicked back, and it was just long enough to brush over the top of his shirt collar. When he washed his hair, and he occasionally did, although not many people had ever seen him do it, it was long enough for his fringe to hang over his eyes. His sideboards were mid-Presley long, and potentially a little bushy. This created a kind of seedy attractiveness. His skin was quite leathery, and he had difficulty achieving a close shave. It would only be for a few hours at a time that he would appear moderately clean-shaven. He preferred to shave before he went to bed. Shaving first thing in the morning was one of those things that really annoyed him. One of those things guaranteed to keep him in bed. It took an awful lot to get him out of bed, and the thought of having to get up to shave made staying in bed and disappearing under the covers even more comforting. He tended to draw the bedclothes over his head as if he was avoiding the blinding light of life. Getting out of bed meant having to deal with the glare. He preferred not to make the decision to get out of bed, because making that decision only led to having to make a series of other, more important decisions. Getting out of bed meant becoming a decision-maker. Making decisions made him tired. Even decisions about what colour tie to wear.

He sat on the settee at the centre of the universe thinking some of the thoughts a nearly thirty-year-old man with two kids living on the grey wet edges of Manchester might think in 1965. He thought some other thoughts too. Thoughts that only he owned. Thoughts nothing to do with who and what he was as he lived a 1965 kind of life in 1965 clothes with 1965 ideas. Thoughts that had everything to do with nothing: a nothing that seemed to make more sense to him than where he lived and when he lived.

He sat on the settee eating a dry Weetabix biscuit spread thickly with Stork margarine. It must have been the weekend because he wasn't at work.

He hated work. There must be more to life than work. More to life than this settee. But he had his doubts. He certainly had his doubts. If you were to ask him what he had in life, he would have replied, 'Doubts.'

It must have been a Sunday. It didn't seem like any other day. Only a Sunday seems like a Sunday. Sunday was the day when he could leave behind his work and the daily doldrums of mundane decision-making knowing that it would all have to start again the very next day. He could step off the conveyor belt for a moment but be tormented by the realisation that he would have to step straight back on. The potential peace of a Sunday was a torture because really it only showed up the lack of peace in the rest of his life. He could drift off into something that resembled himself, only to be cruelly dragged back into routine by the monster that was Monday. Sunday was an airy existential illusion of coherence and relaxation perpetually compromised by the growing shadow of Monday. Monday the miserable. There was always melancholy Monday.

He sat on the settee and thought of Monday morning. Sunday led nowhere else. Always to another Monday, when you had to pick your life up, a life that just got heavier and heavier, and carry it through the week. He would reach the end of the week as if it was the end of his life. Then it would all begin again. It was as if he was stuck in some time loop. Things appeared to change, there were slightly different things to do, slightly different things to say, but essentially he was just repeating himself. Life was just repeating itself. In this local corner of the universe in this local time everything was always the same in spite of the illusion of appearance, in spite of the apparent changes that went on around a young man living in England in 1965. Any differences that there seemed to be in life provoked exactly the same emotional responses, exactly the same feeling that he'd felt this before, and felt that before, and this, and that. Nothing was new as far as he could feel. There were just different ways of getting to the same old feelings. Different ways of reaching the same old point where he just wanted to fall to his knees and weep. There was the same way of coming back to Monday morning. There was the same way of sitting on the settee feeling as dull as a lump of lead.

There was little to look forward to but this mandatory journey from Monday to Monday. From one end to another without end.

Sitting on this settee he forever sighed and stretched and yawned. Out of the corner of his eye he caught sight of his children, a girl and a boy, who must have been in the room all along. He had thought he was alone, but then sometimes he could sink so far into his blasted thoughts he could be in a crowd of thirty thousand people and feel he was alone.

The children surprised him. He was surprised that he had found the life in him to muster up yet more life. He dimly remembered that once upon a time before the Monday mornings had piled up on top of him and begun to bury him alive he'd had plenty of life. Nothing was too much for him. Gradually, nothing had got on top of him.

He looked at his children. There was a part of him in them, he supposed. Perhaps they had taken a lot of his life out of him, leaving him feeling lifeless. They drained the life out of him. They'd taken him away from his part, from his future. Mean thoughts, but sometimes he felt mean, mean because of the lack of meaning in his life. He felt so apart from himself, so apart from who he was meant to be, apart from everything and a part of nothing, that he knew deep down he was being mean but the mean thoughts seemed no different from positive thoughts, or kind thoughts. They were just thoughts he had, and it was difficult for him to see that there could be any difference in the impact on the outside world of a nice thought or a nasty thought. He was slipping back into a kind of formlessness. He felt he was becoming invisible. It was hard work to hold on to routine, normal notions of decency and discrimination, things he'd spent all his life finding out about. It was becoming difficult for him to understand what difference there was between good and bad. His instincts were deserting him. They were leaking out of him into the fabric of the settee. It wasn't the children sucking the life out of him. It was the settee. The settee hated him as much as he hated the settee.

He sat on the settee feeling irritated with himself for finding the world so irritating. He felt that his skin was covered with thorns. He had this urge to scratch some part of his body that didn't exist – as if once there had been an extra limb that had been amputated, leaving behind the apparent sensation of a living part that had once existed. There was a terrible itch just in front of his forehead, as if a horn had been there, and then sliced off. In the end, he felt he would be better off without his body altogether. Perhaps that was why he liked being in his bed so much. Half asleep in between the covers he could achieve a feeling of weightlessness, as if he was leaving his body behind, and all the problems that came with it. The key was to leave his mind behind, and all the problems that came with that. Sleep helped him leave the mind behind, but then came waking, returning to the world, and the mind, as if life was some grand, grotesque version of Monday morning.

He would lie in bed for as long as he could, putting off the moment when he would have to return to his body, and feel his body return to him.

He would lie in bed dipped in sleep wondering who made up the mind-sapping maniac known as Monday morning. He bet it was the settee in some previous life.

He would lie in bed wondering why his father had not donated any of his life to his son. There seemed to be no part of his father inside him. He couldn't feel his father. Unless that unspecified fear he always felt, a fear of the unknown and yet also the known, was something to do with his father. It was a fear that you could also describe as a kind of grief. Grief for something that was missing in his life, grief for the lack of a father figure, for the lack of a guiding light, for the lack of someone close to him, someone he could believe in. Someone who could show him, rightly or wrongly, how maybe to make the next move, and come to the next decision. This grief had turned over the years into fear. He was on his own, he had been left behind. The man who had made him wasn't around to help him, to finish off what he had begun when he brought this life, his life, into the world. He had no immediate precedent that suggested how to move through life, whether or not he followed this precedent or ignored it. He had nothing to rebel against or agree with. He was the oldest man in his family, had been for some time, and this made him feel adrift. It made him feel alone. It meant that every single one of his nerve endings shivered with insecurity.

His father had died during the Second World War. The son wasn't even ten years old. They had never got to know each other. The son would lie in bed thinking of some questions that he wanted to ask his father. But the father couldn't answer. The father had disappeared leaving a little boy behind who in lots of ways would always be that little boy. A little boy without a father, wondering which way to turn next. The little boy never really got to find out what a father was for. Eventually, he could barely remember that he had even had a father.

It made him feel as if the whole universe was relying on him to create coherence and stability. The grief and the fear that were the same thing filled the vacuum left by his father and produced in him a kind of numbed hypersensitivity. He felt things too much, but nothing seemed real. He would get trapped inside his own thoughts and lose interest in the outside world. The future seemed absurd and something that would never happen. The past was as real as a dream and had probably never happened. The present was best spent asleep. Then, at another extreme, he would get trapped in the outside world, and every problem, big or little, seemed to stab at him, every manoeuvre was a torment. He lost touch with his thoughts, he was a prisoner outside his own mind. Life forced him on against his will. The future was too real. The past was a mess. The present crowded around him. The present crushed him.

He would lie in bed losing track of the past, present and future.

He sat on the settee and his children made some daft, scary noise to the left of him, trying to attract his attention. They were demanding something from him, calling back to him from his future. Sometimes he found it so hard to concentrate on his children. If the universe ever let him in on the nature of the cosmic joke of it all, he was sure that the fact that he had children would form some part of the punchline. They treated him as if he was at the centre of their fresh, stunning universe. They did so with such loving energy. This vaguely annoyed him. Didn't they understand that this settee he was sitting on had greater claims to be at the centre of their universe?

He would lie in bed feeling lonely in the world and feeling the loneliness of the world.

He sat on the settee and realised that his son was now as old as he had been when his father disappeared out of his life.

He would lie in bed and feel a strange restlessness take root inside him like sadness.

He sat on the settee and thought to himself, he was a son, and he needed a father. He almost felt jealous that his son had a father, until he remembered that the father was him. His son needed a father to show him the way through life.

He would lie in bed and there was something inside him that had accepted that there are some people in life who are destined to go mad.

He sat on the settee and thought, My father was only around to show me life up to the age of eight.

He would lie in bed and wonder what it would be like to know nothing of himself and this world.

He sat on the settee and looked at his son looking at him as if he was the only thing that really mattered in his life. He had created life and now this life wanted something from him.

He would lie in bed and wonder if he was now older than his father had ever been.

He would sit on the settee and wonder if he was now older than his father had ever been.

He would lie in bed and think that he could never get up.

He sat on the settee and looked at his son who was looking at him looking for meaning and answers.

He would lie in bed and feel that he had run out of answers.

He sat on the settee and he had no answers to whatever it was his son wanted to know. So he would lie as best he could. He would make up the answers. He lied the way he supposed a father always lied to his son. With great regard for the subtleties of reality.

He would lie in bed and feel that everyone in the world even his son was a stranger to him.

He would sit on the settee and wish that he was asleep.

He would lie in bed and go back to sleep.

11) I feel I must mention the Marquis de Sade, Jean-Paul Sartre, scenarios, scepticism, Scheherazade, Arthur Schopenhauer, science, scientific attitudes, seasonal affective disorder, *Season in Hell, A*, secrets, self; and death, self-awareness, self-conception and self-conceptualisation, self-concern, self-conscious emotions, self-consciousness, self-direction, self-disclosure, self-help, selfishness, self-knowledge, self-liberation, self-presentation, self-preservation, self-realisation, self-recognition, self-reflection, senses, effect of stress on, serotonin, severe depression, sexuality, Mary Shelley, shyness, si (death), skeleton, skull, sickness, sleep, sleep deprivation, smoking, social environment, social fragmentation, social isolation, social pressures, social relationships, sociology, Socrates, solidarity in death, solipsism, solitary living, Susan Sontag, soul, Edmund Spenser, Benedict de Spinoza, spiritual development, stigma, stimulants, mood disorders and, Stoicism, Tom Stoppard, *Stranger, The* (Camus), subjectivity, suffering, suicide (dysthymia and, mania and, manic depression and, melancholic depression and, parental loss and depression and, predictors of, seasonal prevalence and, serotonin and), surgery, surrealism, survival, suspension of disbelief, suspicious thinking and mania, syphilis – because I think that any book about death should have such things in its index. And now this book will.

12) I am, of course, a bit late in joining the realm of those who make the book the subject of their books, who make writing the theme of what they have written, who draw attention to the fact that there is attention to be drawn to how or if or why you get from the beginning to the end when you are writing. What can I do about it? I couldn't help the fact that I was born at the time I was born. I cannot help the fact that I arrived a little later than others who were so inclined. I'd like to believe that if I had arrived before others who had similar inclinations I would still have been bent towards writing about a self-consciousness about writing. I would always have

found myself in the position of needing to adopt a position during the writing about the writing.

Yes, this theme has, for at least a generation, been the delight, the joy, the madness of a hundred different literary types. I myself have been worked up about this genre of works and the commentaries they elicit to the point of swearing that I would never get in on the act. I would write a straightforward book that would reveal its sense simply and immediately, and I would be well hidden, politely invisible. I would purely narrate with no hint of an appearance by any part of a fictional or real me that was outside or on top of the flow of things. There would be no mirror held up to other mirrors, no shiny reflections throwing back an image in reverse, no rooms within rooms, no doors leading nowhere, no windows overlooking other windows, no lists leading to other lists leading in a back-to-front way back to the front of a house of words.

But I couldn't resist slipping between the words, the sentences, the paragraphs, and commenting on the writing, crawling over the sequence of events, and breaking up the narrative, throwing it up in the air and letting it land wherever. I couldn't resist popping up in the middle of the book to point out that this indeed was the middle of the book. I couldn't avoid the dreaminess of piling inconclusion upon inconclusion in order to reach a conclusion. I couldn't resist pointing out that what you are reading isn't truth. It's writing. It was just too tempting. I couldn't restrain myself. I was born to do this. I suppose you could blame my father, or perhaps the death of my father. You see, there's something about me that just has to tell you where the blame lies, what the problem is. I'm doing that now, and there probably wasn't even a problem.

Time to disappear back into the narrative, until we meet again. Which, knowing my luck, or yours, will be sooner rather than later.

13) But not this soon. (Damn – it was just too tempting.) And so, meanwhile, in the middle of a book I was writing called *Death in the Family*, I was being as straightforward as I could possibly be under the circumstances, and I was transparently writing:

FOURTEEN

A few days before my fortieth birthday, I got a terrible headache. There was a steady throb behind my left ear, just at the bottom by the lobe. There was no moment when I suddenly felt it happen. I was just gradually aware of a dull constant pain, as if somebody was pressing their finger into the pressure point. I took some pain-killers, and thought it was probably a headache that would soon disappear. A good night's sleep, and there would be no more pain. I mentioned it to my fiancée, Elizabeth, because I didn't think much of it. It was worthy only of a small moan.

The next day, the pain was still there. It hadn't got any worse, and because I was getting used to it the pain didn't seem to be as definite. But it persisted. The ache was starting to get on my nerves. I was beginning to begin to think that there might be something wrong. By now, a regular headache would have gone away. This headache was acting as if it was determined to stay. By now, I didn't want to mention it to Elizabeth in case she made me take it more seriously than I wanted to. The more serious the ache became, the less I wanted to talk about it. To talk about it was to acknowledge it head-on. I thought if I kept the ache to myself, I could somehow manage it, and swallow it up inside. I could keep the ache between me and the back of my mind. If I didn't make a fuss about it, then it would just fade away. This was the superstition I usually followed when some ache or twinge interfered with my generally vague well-being.

Gradually, the pain went from being something lurking at the back of my mind, and it crossed over to the front of my conscious-ness. I was being forced to concentrate on it. This buzzy little ache was demanding my full attention. It was starting to displace my thoughts. It was starting to taunt me.

The merciless ache was now complemented by my increasing anxiety about what it was and what it was doing, and this mean union of ache and anxiety was completely preoccupying me. It was forcing me down into myself, and as far as Elizabeth was concerned, looking at me from the outside, I was retreating into a black and edgy mood. I tried to hide my concern, but I had nothing to hide behind but my concern.

I wanted the ache to go away, to prove to me that it was harmless, just one of those pointless aches you get now and then that you forget as soon as it's gone. After twenty-four hours of this pressure making its motions to move in with me for ever I was getting desperate. I pleaded with the ache to leave me alone. It was now so much part of me I was beginning to have conversations with it.

I was even entertaining thoughts of going to see a doctor, something that I was reluctant to do. I thought I was one of those people who would still be uneasy about going to a doctor even if their arm dropped off. I still wasn't saying anything to Elizabeth, because by keeping it to myself I thought I was making it less real, and if I didn't take the pain seriously then it would just give up and go and try somewhere else. The best thing I could do was ignore the ache. Unfortunately, this didn't seem to be persuading the ache to mooch off in a sulk. It was persuading the ache to get stuck in.

I rolled my jaw around, as if the action would somehow crack open the ache, like it was the pain you get after a too-rapid descent in a plane. I exercised my jaw, pushing my face here and there, frantically trying to find some way of relieving the throb. I fingered the area, delicately and then roughly, as if this might make a difference. I really wanted to punch it, but by now I guessed that even if I knocked my head off, the ache would remain. At the end of all this grimacing and prodding, I began a slow-motion yawn. It didn't seem to be me yawning. Maybe it was the ache, demonstrating its mocking indifference to my futile attempts to get rid of it.

The yawn was coming at me from a long way off, and it was clearly going to be an unusual yawn. I was caught halfway between suppressing the yawn, and letting it become a beautiful thing with a life of its own. I held on to the yawn, and at the same time I let go. It was a strange tight and loose yawn, and at the end of it I felt strange, tight and loose. Something had happened to me. I noticed the ache had gone, but I didn't feel good about it. The ache had been replaced by something more abstract, something more worrying, and something that was going to demand much more of my attention.

The yawn had flung me through a barrier. I landed on the other side feeling dazed. I was nervous about something, but I wasn't sure what. There were butterflies in my stomach, but I wasn't sure why. It was as if time had ever so slightly slowed down. There was a tiny draining of colour from the soft surfaces of my immediate surroundings. The hard surfaces were enriched with colour. Sound was a touch muffled. I could taste my tongue, and it wasn't pleasant. It tasted burnt and slimy. Saliva fizzed in my mouth like ancient space dust. My legs seemed a couple of feet further away from me than before I had yawned. My face felt remotely like it had split into two. I was much more aware of my heartbeat than usual. When I stood up, I felt giddy. All in all, I felt funny. Funny peculiar, funny ha-ha – it was as if my soul was suddenly ticklish – funny squared. I casually mentioned to Elizabeth that something odd had happened to my face, but I kept it as light as I could and said it with a bit of a laugh, as if I'd just yawned too hard and locked my jaw. As if it was stupid of me that I'd done something stupid and there was nothing to worry about. Anyway, the ache had apparently gone.

I was hiding the full extent of what had happened to me, and trying to work out for myself what on earth was going on. One side of my face was very stiff, but I just presumed, and hoped, that this was because of the strain of the big yawn. I thought that perhaps I had pulled a muscle in my face, or at least badly yanked one. Nothing serious, I convinced myself. Everything would be fine in a moment. I went into the kitchen and opened myself a can of Coke. I'd always found a can of Coke very comforting when I felt troubled. I believed with all of my heart that it was the real thing. Funnily enough, this was the last can of Coke I ever drank. It will remain the last can of Coke I ever drank. The Coke turned out to be too real.

I drank it very quickly, even though it tasted of burnt toffee, and immediately realised that instead of soothing me, instead of calming me into a satisfying quickness, the Coke seemed to be encouraging my body to squeeze itself from the inside. It must have been the caffeine agitating my symptoms, but suddenly I felt dizzier, and my ears were humming. My tongue was rudely swelling, my heart seemed to be pounding inside my skull, my legs were running away with themselves, I felt funny cubed, and one side of my face seemed to be setting like concrete. The yawn had broken me like it was an earthquake and I was a planet. It had ripped cracks into my entire being. It was the ache yawning after all, the ache having its revenge on my determination to kill it off as if it were nothing.

The nervousness I had felt quickly transformed into straight fear. I was scared, and one side of my face felt literally scared stiff. By now Elizabeth had picked up on my strange and withdrawn behaviour, and I couldn't hide it any more that there was something clearly wrong with me. As I feared, she encouraged me to go straight to hospital. I couldn't face it, still clinging to the hope that everything would slip back to normal if I just carried on as normal and ignored the fact that something had happened that wasn't normal. I kept moving around the house, kidding myself that I was just overreacting to the headache, and that if I just found things to do, places to move to, everything would settle down. I couldn't think straight because my body wasn't straight, but I clung to the belief that whatever had just wobbled in my world would very quickly straighten itself. There was nothing seriously wrong with me, because nothing seriously wrong ever happened to me. Then again, I reasoned to myself as if I was being reasonable even though I was being spun around by lack of reason, I seem to be racing around the house with a speeding mind and a funny face as if there was something seriously wrong. I began to think that there was something wrong with me if I didn't think there was something wrong with me, even if there wasn't something wrong with me. Or something.

Thinking that I was having a panic attack of some kind, I marched out into the night with the wild hope that I might walk it all off. There was a trapped part of me that realised I might actually have to go to hospital, even though I still had both arms. But I tore into the fresh air and started to walk nowhere in particular with some mad aim to outstrip the weird new feelings that were dry-drowning me. I told Elizabeth I was feeling better, just a little woozy, and that I just needed a walk to clear my head. I was lying because I felt that the truth might be enough to kill me. Somehow, I thought that if I kept lying, to Elizabeth, and to myself, eventually the lies would become truth.

By now, even though I still wasn't going to let on, it was clear even inside the crumpled shock of haze surrounding me that there was something badly wrong with one side of my face. It had got stuck. It was locked into an expression – of horror, I felt. Maybe I was turning into an insect.

When I smiled, only one side of my mouth moved. If I ate, I couldn't keep the food in my mouth. When I drank my final unrefreshing Coke, a lot of it dribbled out of the corner of my mouth. I couldn't even blink my left eyelid. One side of my face had become as immobile as rock. This wasn't meant to happen. Your face was meant to move like a face all the time it was a face.

77

I couldn't face up to this appalling loss of face.

I walked very fast towards nowhere as if this would take me away from my panic. The usual balance of power between brain and body that I feel there is inside me without really thinking about it was shifting. There was a battle going on between my brain and body, and it was this battle that was releasing tons of butterflies into my central nervous system. Some butterflies escaped into other areas of my body, and fluttered around, making my legs, my arms, my chest feel queasy inside and out. The butterflies raced around my bloodstream, bursting past my heart, coursing down my arms and crashing into the ends of my fingers. Butterflies found their way into my brain and started to interfere with any possible clarity of thought. Butterflies carried alarm around my body with them. The only place in my body where the butterflies couldn't reach was the left side of my face. It was completely sealed off, inside and out. It was cut off from the rest of my body. Cut off from reality. It seemed dead to life. One side of my face had completely forgotten how to be a face. It was as if it had never even known.

As I walked, my bones turned to butterflies, my nerves a nest for butterflies, my mind messed up by all this brand new internal chaos, I was thinking in a way that seemed very quick and very slow. It was dawning on me just how real all this was. One side of my face really was frozen. Often when these things happen, at first you think you are mistaken, that what is happening isn't that serious, and soon everything will return to normal. By now everything should have returned to normal, and everything hadn't. I pinched and slapped and rubbed my face. Nothing. I walked on towards nowhere feeling nothing in one side of my face, and feeling sick with worry everywhere else. I wanted to vomit up this worry it was making me feel so dizzy and nauseous. I wanted to sweat it out. I wanted to sleep it off, lose it, outrun it, forget it, waste it. Then I realised that the worry, what felt like worry, was so much part of me that if I got rid of it I would be getting rid of myself. What felt like worry was actually my body in revolt, against my mind's confusion, against the stupid caffeine in its system, against the change in circumstances. It was making me feel that I was going to have to do something about this. It was overruling the dreadful caution of my mind, demanding that I head towards a hospital and help it. It wasn't interested in any fears I might have that by going to a hospital and being seen to by a doctor would mean that I would learn the worst. This already was the worst. Something had actually happened to my body and my body was trying to regain control.

I walked towards nowhere but began to realise that there was a hospital on the fringes of this nowhere I was marching towards. I rang Elizabeth to tell her I was feeling all right, but in the end perhaps to admit that I needed to go to hospital. I only let the phone ring a couple of times and then lost my nerve. I kept walking. The walking made me feel I was doing something, that I was tackling the problem through some kind of action.

As I walked, I began to think that I was going to die and yet I felt incredibly alive. There was no way I could stop moving. To sit still for a moment made me more aware of the part of my body that had stopped moving and the rest of my body that was trying to make up for it by moving faster. I thought I had suffered a stroke, and that the paralysis there was in my face was going to spread down the whole left side of my body. I was sure I could feel it slipping down my neck towards my heart. The left side of my body was definitely starting to stiffen. My left arm was sluggish, my hand felt awkward, the chest around my heart seemed to be on fire but there was no pain, just a tightening, a slow inexorable squeezing.

I walked on, slightly changing direction, becoming gradually more grown-up and responsible in my choice of destination, and imagined the worst. I'd had a stroke and the entire left side of my body was going to be paralysed. I would forget how to talk, how to read, how to walk, and I would have to learn everything again. There was something in me that started to accept this amidst all the panic. I knew that whatever it was that had happened had happened, and there was nothing I could do to stop it. There was no use pretending to myself that I was one of those people who was going to coast through life escaping the possibility of anything serious happening to their bodies. Up to this point, there had never been anything badly wrong with me. I'd broken a toe once. I got flu now and then. But the big things never seemed to bother me. I was fairly healthy. So here I was, a few days short of my fortieth birthday, and middle age had smashed me and my quiet smugness around the face.

I rang Elizabeth and told her that I was going to have to go to hospital. I needed her to help me get there. When she had told me to go to hospital earlier, I felt that she was being far too premature.

79

I was scared enough and stubborn enough to feel that she was forcing me to do something against my will, and I didn't want to waste the hospital's time. I wanted to be able to mention an ache, a dizzy spell, without it leading to a visit to hospital.

I left the phone box and walked almost at a run towards the hospital to meet Elizabeth, having been forced to admit that there was a real problem. Middle age had left me with half a face, and was now heading swiftly and surely with lethal intent down the whole left side of my body. Middle age was sending me on an adventure to hospital. My body had sent me a present. Was it turning me into a cockroach from the inside?

As a middle-aged man with something shattering on my mind and a body in new ruin I headed with scared but now resigned determination towards the hospital. If I was going to lose half my body I might as well be told why and how I was going to lose half my body.

In the middle of all this transforming panic and desperation, there was a flicker of a memory trying to make its way through the cascading butterflies and the unfastening fear. A twitch of a memory that was just enough to offer a little hope that all was not paralysis and a fate as dull as death. It was a memory that had always been waiting for such a thing to happen so that it could make itself known and alert me to the fact that this was always bound to happen. It runs in the family. It was a little time bomb waiting to go off. You didn't want to worry about it all the time, but the chances were that eventually this was going to happen.

I remembered my mother telling me that my father had lost the feeling down one side of his face. I had never really wanted to consider this as a possibility for me, because she had said that it was a tough thing for him to deal with, that it took a long time for the feeling to come back, and he never really recovered. But now, faced with the choice as I saw it between a full bodily paralysis and a nasty but hopefully temporary facial freeze, I was choosing the stiff face above the stiff body. I was hoping that I had received a little gift in the genes from my father. Received with love and fear just in time for my fortieth birthday.

I met up with Elizabeth and held her hand very tightly. She held my hand very tightly. I had been so exiled in my terror I had completely failed to see how, as far as she was concerned, within a few hours I had turned into a different person. I had complained about a headache, said that it had gone, more or less stopped talking, become extremely restless, and then raced out into the cold night claiming I needed some fresh air. I felt that I had managed to maintain an air of normality. I thought I'd managed to hide how upset I was. The only thing I'd managed to hide was my old self. To Elizabeth I had become somebody who didn't want to talk, who when he did talk spoke with a tremble in his voice. I had become somebody who was making a very bad job of pretending that I was fine. Compared to my old self, the self there was before the ache and the yawn, I had gone a little mad. I was so wrapped up in myself I wasn't noticing, or caring, that to the outside world I appeared completely wrapped up in myself.

I walked into the Casualty department of the hospital feeling almost high with the altered state of my existence. One big yawn, my very own big bang, had sent me off into a very different world. I must have been a changed person just to have walked into the hospital. I tended to think that once you entered such a place, you were destined to be embraced by the medical world and never fully recover from your ailment. New ailments would join in, and you would become the type of person who was a regular visitor to doctors and hospitals. Medical maintenance would become part of the fabric of your life. The walk to nowhere, though, had taken me beyond the point of no return. I could even imagine dying if I didn't go to hospital. However much the visit to the hospital changed me, it would never change me as much as what had happened to the left side of my body.

At the lowest point of my walk into a wilderness of fear, as I stopped off at panic station, I was all but convinced that I was going to die. And I wasn't going to die with a smile on my face. I couldn't die with a smile on my face even if I had felt like it. At best I would have died with half a smile on my face. It was because there was only half a smile on my face that I didn't feel like dying with a smile on my face. My death mask would not be serene and peaceful. It would look exactly like I'd died. I would look scared stiff. I would look like I was screaming for help through one side of my mouth.

I could feel death creeping down my neck, down my upper chest and shoulder, creeping towards my heart. Death was going to grab my heart and stop it as definitively as the left side of my face had been stopped. Death was going to snatch life out from underneath me. My last words were more or less a giant yawn. A yawn that had come to symbolise only too horribly the gaping jaws of death. The thought of death coming straight at me along with a million frantic butterflies through the back door of a yawn in the end made me walk very briskly away from nowhere and towards a hospital.

I walked up to the reception desk knowing that in a few seconds I would learn whether I had suffered a stroke or whether I had (only!) inherited the curse of my father. Simply having a paralysed face suddenly seemed like an attractive proposition next to the alternatives of the left side of my body being paralysed or my whole body, mind and soul being paralysed to the ultimate paralysing point of death. I explained to the receptionist what had happened and she asked me a few questions. My answers were awkwardly spoken through a mouth that mostly couldn't move. I sounded like I had stuffed my mouth with a whole bag of cheese and onion crisps. I sounded punch-drunk. From what I said, about the ache behind my ear, the colossal yawn, the way my face had frozen, she was fairly sure I had an attack of Bell's palsy, and that it wasn't a stroke. I had to wait for as many hours as it took for a doctor to be free to see me, but the fact that it didn't seem to be a stroke, or life-threatening, and strangely even the fact that I hadn't wasted the hospital's time, made me sigh with relief through the odd-shaped gap I could muster with my mouth. Along with the sigh, a billion half-crazed butterflies shot out of my cubist mouth and swooped into the night air.

My brush with death was over. It had left me with a fight to save my face.

Eventually I found out that Bell's palsy is caused by a severing of the seventh facial nerve, a nerve which controls all the facial muscles except those involved in chewing. Damage to the protective sheath of insulating material around the nerve fibres reduces their ability to transmit electrical signals from the brain to the muscles of the face. The ache that I'd had a couple of days before is a warning that this small but vital nerve is being put under severe pressure and is about to snap. The warning was useless to me, and I don't know what you can do even if you do know what the ache means. The severing of the nerve can be caused by something as simple as a cold draught, it can be caused by emotional pressure, and it is highly likely to be hereditary. There is some thought that the nerve inflammation may be due to a virus – perhaps the same virus that causes cold sores and fever blisters.

The way that the hospital receptionist had been able to tell so quickly that it was Bell's palsy was because the paralysis of my face was so straight and clean down the middle. By looking at my forehead, you could see that any movement stopped dead in the middle of my forehead. There was a totally vertical break. If there had been a slight overlap, if I could still move one side of my forehead just a little, then it might have been a stroke. A fortieth-birthday stroke.

I was also slightly lucky that my face had paralysed into the position it had – deadpan, but moderately straight. For some people, the face droops, it sags downwards. It looks as if it has collapsed. Around the mouth, my face had frozen into a position of mild sadness, which some people said was no different from usual. Around the eye, which stayed wide open because the lid was unable to blink, my face had stuck in a state of mild surprise. Perhaps this was the surprise I'd felt as I yawned and felt the vibration of the wings of a billion butterflies rush into my body.

The next day, I called my mother. 'I've got what my father had,' I blurted out in much the same manner she used when informing me of someone's death. 'What,' she said, sounding worried, 'melancholic depression?'

My mother had often told me that after my father had suffered from his Bell's palsy, his face had never entirely recovered, and nor had his state of mind. I now understood why he had been so rattled. Having any kind of paralysis opens up a number of doors to a whole host of potential demons. While you have the paralysis you're never completely convinced that it will go away. My face seemed so hard, so immobile – and yet oddly soft to touch – that I could never imagine it returning to how it had been. And as it recovers, it does so in such a gradual, invisible way, you never feel any moments of triumph, of breakthrough. Medical advice is worryingly vague – no one is quite sure how it happens in the first place, no one is quite sure about how well you and your face will recover, no one is sure how long it will take for the paralysis to ebb away, and no one is quite sure whether or not the Bell's palsy will recur. It will take a mixture of drugs, physiotherapy and luck for your face to begin moving again, and then more physiotherapy and luck for there to be a chance your face will return to its old shape and mobility. And all of this will take time. But no one knows how much time. In fact, in the end, the main advice is just that . . . it will get better. You're given a course of steroids to reduce the swelling, a physiotherapy regime to follow, but no one really knows whether these have any benefit at all, other than the latter perhaps being psychologically important. It just gets better, it just repairs itself, like a cut or a bruise. But this 'cut' or 'bruise' happens to be disfiguring and frightening.

My mother tried hard to tell me that actually, after all, my father made a quick and amazing recovery, and he was never bothered again, either emotionally or by another attack. If this was one of those things that she felt had been a trigger that set him off towards his deep and chronic depression, she did a good job of hiding it. She explained that my father had never looked like a gargoyle during his paralysis, and I hadn't been terrified by his face at all. I could have sworn she had once told me these things, but clearly her job was now to persuade me that I would make a complete recovery. Elizabeth also recognised the need for her to direct positive feelings right into my face, a face that was clogged up with negativity. The last thing you want to hear after the realism of diagnosis and the realism of the condition is any more realism. Cheerfulness and encouragement seem surreal in the state you're in, but you prefer that to anything else because your state – in mind and body – is surreal.

My father was in his early twenties when he was smashed around the face by Bell's palsy. It must have been terrifying. When you have it, you cannot eat or drink properly, you cannot sleep properly and you cannot talk properly. Because you cannot blink, there's a chance that you might scratch your eyeball. The tear duct has also been damaged, so you are not producing any moisture to protect the eye. You feel ugly, awkward, and the whole of your being seems centred on the side of your face that has set into stone. Your whole body comes out in sympathy with your face and you feel weakened. You feel weakened in body and spirit and far too tired to raise the energy you feel you need to recover. For the first few days there seems to be no change in your face. You start to think about the possibility of your face never recovering. Not being able to move what once was moved without you even thinking about it can get very frustrating, even claustrophobic. Just to get the smallest twitch out of a nostril, or the thinnest line on one side of your forehead, or any kind of movement in that part of your mouth that has locked into a grimace seems as impossible as changing shape. One side of your face has completely seized up, and it seems to affect your mind and imagination as well.*

* the you that is you is split right down the middle you are ripped in two your heart is sliced down the middle reality is prized apart there's two parts of everything two sides to life to reality to your self sensation doubles up your hearing is torn your taste is ransacked your touch is out of focus there's a line right down the middle of reality on one side it's full colour on the other side it's black and white you have to balance two sides that are completely different weights the fingers on your left hand seem thicker or softer than the fingers on your right hand the left side of your body is the thin end of the wedge one side of your mind is all interference the other side is pure clarity your skin seems too tight on the left side and too loose on the right side your imagination is dreaming of two things simultaneously your dreams are separated within themselves images are bisected sensation is sucking on one side blowing on the other there's nothing much to the left of you nothing special to the right of you you're neither here nor there to one side and stuck in space to the other side you're pinned down to the left and pinned up to the right and the left side of your life is floating and the right side of your life is bubbling and on the left hand reality is turning itself inside out and on the right hand reality is settling down for the night fragments shapes like grief on this side fragments shaped like meaning on that far as the left side of death goes it's etc, etc. and as for the right side of life it's and so on and so on.

I was talking to my father in a pub and he was drinking beer and I'm drinking let's say mead I wasn't that used to pubs my father never got to introduce me to the mysterious ways of the pub and I asked him about his Bell's palsy but he was on a roll and still answering something else but the answer could still apply all answers ultimately answer all questions he said 'the feeling that you cannot survive such whirlwinds arises from a consummation on a purely inner flame the flames of life burn in a closed oven from which the heat cannot escape. Those who live on an external plane are saved from the outset: but do they have anything to save when they are not aware of any danger? the parxoysm of interior experience leads you to regions where danger is absolute, because life which self-consciously actualises its roots in experience can only negate itself. Life is too limited and fragmentary to endure great tensions. Did not all the mystics feel that they could not live after all their great ecstasies? What could they expect from this world, and as those who sense, beyond the normal limits, life, loneliness, despair, and death, and so on and on and so on. so on and so on, etc.'

85

You also feel slightly embarrassed.† You feel a little foolish, as if it was something that you did that caused this ghastly accident. It's a stupid little affliction. It can be caused by just a simple blast of cold air. There's no way you can see what causes it. It might just be your mind playing mean-spirited tricks on you. Really, it's just a bloody cold sore. You might be able to glorify it as a metaphysical cold sore. In the end, however invisible and mysterious it is, it's just an internal cold sore.

You eventually recover, after what seems like a lot of waiting time, a lot of will-power and an awful lot of worry. You feel that you can help the recovery, but you cannot speed it up. A corner of you tightens up and then very gradually loosens up. It's not as

---

† It was an embarrassing thing to have speaking purely as a writer. All around me writers were compiling memoirs based on their strokes, their cancer, their paralysis, even their death. These were big subjects, make no mistake. They couldn't really get any bigger. All around there were life-and-death struggles and such movement of emotion. And here was I, looking for a subject that would lend itself to pure narrative, looking for a story that would touch people's hearts, looking for a way to perfectly blend my intense self-awareness with some easy-going self-effacement, and all that happened to me was that a tiny nerve serving my face gave up the ghost. I was told not to worry, there's nothing we can do really, it'll get better in a few weeks, you probably won't be able to tell the difference, it's probably best you just carry on with your life as normal. It's just not fair. Writers were having subjects handed to them on a hospital plate, they were lumbered with conditions the size of a continent, they were having to finish their books with poignant and pointed speed before they died. They were profoundly compelled to meet their deadlines in more ways than one. Their deadline was often death or the threat of death. I had no such luck. My condition was the size of a small cul-de-sac. I didn't know where to half-look. I hid the half of my face that was capable of showing shame.

But I shouldn't complain. I already had my subject, and even though it was nothing special, even though it was nothing really, I had worked out the beginning, middle and the end. And funnily enough, the Bell's palsy fitted quite neatly, if not as dramatically and appropriately as, well, my death, into the story. And, and this is even funnier, eventually, but perhaps not as quickly or as devastatingly as I might like for the sake of the book, I would die. Perhaps in its own little way the Bell's palsy was the first clear warning of my incoming death.

That cheers me up.

cataclysmic as a stroke, and it doesn't take as much to recover as it would if it was a stroke. But you feel hard-done-by. You feel that you are going through as much as you can bear, even though you know that you are only going through a fraction of what you suffer when you have a stroke, or break your back. There's been enough damage to the face and the psyche to make you feel you are suffering hell, especially considering the tiny and you would have thought inconsequential nature of the nerve. There doesn't appear to be an awful lot wrong with you, there's just the slightly slumped and deadened face, but you are going through a crisis out of all proportion to the relatively small size of the problem. You feel that the headache would have been enough.

The after-effects of the headache propel you inside a world where you glimpse what it's like to experience profound paralysis, you understand enough to know how scary and extreme such a thing would be, you get a sighting of something dark and nasty. A sudden little snap in a minuscule part of your body and you plunge into blackness. The blackness isn't bottomless. There is a bottom. You hit it hard. For a few weeks you're existentially concussed. Your senses are all out of sync with each other. You're not sure which way is up, which way is down. Somehow, you start to make your way towards what you hope is the clearness of well-being. It's a struggle, and you can understand why it can leave a lasting mark on the soul.

I was older than my father had been when I contracted Bell's palsy. There was a part of me that was perhaps waiting for it to happen. Even though it had shocked me to the core, it hadn't really come out of the blue. For my father, as far as I know, it came out of nowhere. And it left him covered with bits and pieces of nowhere. It left him with a bitter appreciation of nowhere. It left him with a trace of facial stiffness that would always be there to remind him that, out of cold thin air, it could happen again, or that something worse could happen. It left him, in his early twenties, with the constant apprehension that through some slight accident of movement you can swing with utter completeness from brightness to blackness, from everydayness to strangeness. In the blink of an eye – which then you cannot blink – you can cross over from a position where you feel you're pushing life out of the way into a place where life is pushing you back. You're not in control of life: life is in control of you.

87

Bell's palsy,* the spiteful little irritant, cuts into your life and makes you appreciate that you must take nothing for granted. At any minute some part of you is ready to collapse, to break, to tear. There is always something lurking around you ready to leap up out of nothing and drag you back down with it. There's just a cracking split second between something and nothing, and my father found that out early on in his life. His seventh facial nerve was severed by nothing that you could see with the naked eye and then there was nothing holding the nerve together. The nerve gradually repaired itself, but the nothing that cut the nerve up, the nothing you cannot touch or smell or taste or hear, leaked into his body and stayed there for the rest of his life, slowly leaking into his system. Nothing filled him out until he burst and all his nerves were severed.

I was nearly forty when it happened to me, old enough to be the father of someone who was my father's age when it happened to him. There's a part of time that froze along with my father's face. My father with his frozen face is frozen inside this stopped time, waiting with suspended breath, patiently, impatiently, for his life to advance once more. When my face froze I jerked into this stopped time, and I was my father's father. He was young and sad and scared. I was middle-aged and podgy and greying. He probably wouldn't have recognised me. As far as he was concerned, I was only three.

There was nothing I could do to help him. I knew his future, and it was a future that led exactly into the nowhere he feared precisely because his face had jammed. I wish I could have give him some advice based on my reactions to the Bell's palsy, reactions that were based on the help I'd received across time because I knew my father had been through it. I knew what to watch out for, what to avoid. At forty, it didn't seem such a momentous thing. Life, because there is such a thing spreading all around you as you get older, has prepared you for these things. You expect them to happen. It's part of the obstacle course. The obstacle course is filled with more

* Named after the surgeon who discovered it Bell's palsy is a benign weakness of the infratemporal portion of the facial nerve. It is typically a self-limiting process which is not life-threatening. It typically improves in 2–6 months and almost always in twelve. Some experts say there is very little chance of recurrence: some statistics report that in about ten per cent of cases there is recurrence.
Eighty-six per cent of patients make a complete recovery.

challenges and problems as you get older, and you tend to see them coming, even if they're not quite in the form you expected. Something is bound to happen. Life is not that smooth a spread. It's filled with lumps. When you're not that much older than a teenager, you don't want to have to waste time dealing with the lumps. You just want to spit them out, ignore them. I wish I could have told my father that this was just one of those things, a silly little lump in life. It wasn't the end of the world, or even the beginning of the end of the world. It was just a pathetic accident of nature, of birth, of the weather. It wasn't personal. You hadn't been singled out by some mysterious force and dumped into the dark because you were who you were and you'd done something to provoke fate. In a way, you'd just sneezed, dislodged a bit of dust, you'd had an itch and you'd scratched it. You'd cut your finger on a tin can. The body needed to heal. That was all. It didn't have to get inside your mind and make you distrust life, it didn't have to change your whole outlook on things. It should never have maimed your emotions.

We were both frozen in time and I couldn't get to tell my father any of this. We would recover in our own ways in our own times. My father would never even get to know that one day I would suffer the same bleak little curse. Bell's palsy shook him badly as a metaphor for all the terror that lurks just out of sight at the end of the next second, the next sentence, the next breath. It was an abrupt introduction to the existence of this ever-ready and random hostility. Bell's palsy merely (merely!) confirmed to me the alertness and agility of the terror that hovers around all of us as we head towards our certain fate. My father had prepared me for Bell's palsy, even though I didn't really know it. Because of where his Bell's palsy eventually led, to nowhere special, to nothing much in paralysing particular, he had also prepared me for how darkness surrounds life just as the universe surrounds the planet. I really knew that.

I ground out my recovery. I learnt how to eat without biting too many times the lifeless slimy lump that was the left side of my tongue. I adjusted to the tiredness that spread through my body as if my face was trying to infect the rest of me with its chronic indifference.

I had to do my facial massaging and exercises into a mirror, to ensure that I was tackling the right problem area. I had to repeat stretching and pulling movements thirty times all around my face: forehead, eyes, nose, mouth, cheeks, chin. Looking into the mirror was looking right into the face of half a fool. It was like looking at someone who hadn't been finished off. I had to get used to the sight of half of me trying to smile again and again, as if my mouth actually existed. I could see the left side of my face, but it felt like a figment of my imagination.

I would try and lift up my left nostril. The effort it took seemed more than if I was trying to lift a ton weight with my little finger. I would try and close my eyelid. It was like trying to shut a door that was already shut. To raise my left eyebrow was as absurd a proposition as trying to elevate my body off the floor. I would regularly do my exercises in the mirror and be rewarded with absolutely no response in any areas of my face. There was a complete lack of interest. The left side of my face was treating me with utter coldness. The left side of my face was a waste of skin.

I would feel movement in my mind, I would will movement. In the mirror, I could see on the right side of my face too much movement. Grotesque movement. That side of my face was overloaded with features. It was a frenetic parade of Jerry Lewis grimaces. On the left side of my face, no movement whatsoever. This side of my face was intrinsically featureless. Cryptic unmovement. It was a marble slab of Buster Keaton deadpan. The left side of my face was just tragi-comically stuck onto the right side of my face: visual noise slapped next to visual silence. I had to work constantly to fit the two sides of my face back together, to rediscover the natural balance that I'd had all my life. It seemed a very complicated puzzle, and it took a lot of thought, and a lot of will-power – to keep going, to keep putting an infinity of things back together in order just to match the two sides of my face.

I found the will-power I needed because I didn't want Elizabeth to have to see a lopsided face for the rest of her life, because I didn't want my mother to feel that I was heading into the same narrowing tunnel as my father. And because I didn't want to betray the pain and confusion that my father had gone through when Bell's palsy cut his face in two, and tried to cut his personality in two. I wanted to beat it, for my father, with my father.

Then, out of the quiet, out of the stillness, out of the distance, there was a tiny spark of energy. Something approaching a hint of warmth. The thick ice that was masking my face was showing signs of cracking.

I could feel if not pins and needles then certainly a pin and a needle pricking my lifeless face. With almost exquisite slowness the left side of my face began to return to life. Rock-hard muscles imperceptibly melted into something softer and more human. The corner of my lips weakly flickered as if they were finally beginning to see the funny side. Weeks of pulling the right side of my face into all sorts of ridiculous positions, as if to show the left side what to do, as if to shame the left side into action, were finally paying off.

I never thought I could be made so happy by the sight of my nostril twitching. If I could have smiled properly I would have smiled with delight now that I could move my eye, cheek and chin enough to manage what was almost an expression. My features started to return, first as a kind of rough sketch, but then very quickly the sketch got more and more lifelike. My taste buds were coming back to life. My tongue became less and less of an alien rotting away in my mouth. Soon it actually resembled a tongue. This seemed like a miracle – the fact that there was a tongue where a tongue should be was magical. I wanted to kiss my tongue, so I did, sort of, from the inside. What a kiss it was, with loads of tongue.

Lines and wrinkles reappeared on my forehead, on my nose, around my mouth. They'd been flattened out by the paralysis, but I was pleased to see them back. Nice, healthy forty-year-old wrinkles, wrinkles that showed off feeling, and experience, and life. Wrinkles that existed out of respect for the complicated action of life. I could crinkle up my nose, if I wanted to. It's not something I find myself doing a lot, but the point was, I could. My face came back together again, bit by bit, piece by piece, one expression after another. It was a buckled piece of metal that after much manipulation popped back into shape.

I looked like myself again. It wasn't an exact fit, the face had sunk a little bit to the left, but it could have been worse. While I'd had it somebody, trying to make me feel better, had mentioned that Bell's palsy was the cause of Sylvester Stallone's collapsed face and thick, drugged voice. I think another contribution to the will-power I needed to get my face back to normal was the thought of Sylvester Stallone's squashed, irregular face and his dozy voice.*

From the ache behind the ear to full facial recovery took about six weeks. It seemed longer, it seemed shorter. Time was frozen, time

* Thanks, Sly. I owe you one.

was raging. I can still feel the fact that my face suddenly went AWOL, there's still a sense of strangeness that can rise up when I feel tired or under stress, and occasionally I notice a non-specific, even imaginary, stiffness down the left side of my face. It's like an aftershock, a flashback. It reminds me that another reaction could happen again. I feel that my face is very vulnerable, and I imagine that my father felt this vulnerability even more.

In the way that the separation of the left side of my face from my body separated me from the rest of reality I am aware of how you need completeness in mind and body to complete the comforting apparentness of reality. Eventually, perhaps, if my face had stayed partially paralysed, I would have got used to it, it would have formed its own mental and physical completeness, and another reality in turn would have been completed. But it would have been in a new less comforting way. It would not have been the reality that forty years of living had drummed into me was all that there was. I would have had to get used to a different reality, and that would only have been the half of it. When I get a flashback I see reality ever so slightly shimmer and I feel the early stages of panic well up inside me. I relax, I calm down, I believe in the reality that's all around me like it's a god, and I cling on for dear life in the way some people would compare to praying.

What I don't do is drink a Coke.*

---

* My name is Paul Morley and I'm a Coke addict. I was a four-can-a-day man. I believed in Coca-cola. I believed in the magic of the ingredients, I believed in the mystical nature of the refreshment, I believed in the kick, I believed in the taste, I believed it was the real thing. And then I didn't. I had a Coke just at that moment when the swelling in my nerve metamorphosed into a muscle paralysis, and the drink sent me spiralling off into a kind of hallucination of the spirit. It took the panic that was spreading through the body and it emphasised it, underlined it, exaggerated it, nourished it. I could suddenly understand that the Coke inside me was bad for me. It was the kind of liquid that could dissolve coins and rot bones and eat through tissue, it was the acid of capitalism streaming through my blood, it was burning my soul, it was nothing but sugar in gory disguise, it was hypnotising me from the inside to believe in the black fizz of evil. It wasn't the real thing. It was just a thing. And it had possessed me.

And then I was free. I lost the taste for it. I saw through the illusion. A near-death experience had left me with this gift to see the demonic Coca-cola for what it really was. Coloured carbonated sugar-water with a

Towards the end of a book I was slowly writing about time called *Slow Motion in Stockport*, I found myself considering sugar. Sugar and time have a lot in common. They both sweeten the universe, what with one thing or another, and if you try and hold a lot of sugar or time in your hands, it just runs through your fingers. Eternity is in love with the productions of time, and sugar. As Shakespeare said, Be not coy, but use your time, and sugar.

You can buy sugar, and you can buy time, though not at the supermarket. Sugar runs out, and so does time. You can see through time, and you can see through sugar. On the other hand sugar is opaque, and so is time. You can explain time, and you can explain sugar. On the other hand . . .

You can leave footprints on the sands of time: you can leave footprints in a pile of sugar. You waste time: you waste sugar. If you leave time or sugar alone in a cupboard that isn't airtight, then the sugar and the time get all lumped together and turn rock-hard. Boil time or sugar, and it turns to liquid. Freeze sugar or time, and not a lot happens. In the end, in their own way, time and sugar rot us to death. We are destroyed by time's – and sugar's – devouring hand.

My father used to put three teaspoonfuls of sugar in his tea. Three teaspoons overflowing with sugar. Because my father used to have his tea so sweet, so did I. Like father, like son, in much the same way as like sugar, like time. The three sugars made the tea intensely sweet, and it meant that you weren't drinking a cup of tea, you were drinking a cup of tea-flavoured syrup. When my father had a cup of tea, it wasn't teatime. It was sugartime.

---

chemically contrived taste. The revelation was the most refreshing thing that has ever happened to me because of Coca-cola. I now have as much interest in drinking Coke as I do in drinking the urine of a skunk.
I spent my fortieth birthday with one side of my face as smooth and impassive as a glacier, and without, for the first time in twenty-five years, any Coke or chocolate. The Bell's palsy was escorting me into a brave new world where sugar in all its most insidious disguises wasn't going to be of any real or imaginary use to me. For better or worse, I had grown up, with a sugar-free crave-crushing body-squeezing sense-trembling face-halving soul-wrenching nut-cracking bang.
Ouch.

My father drank a lot of tea. I can't remember him ever drinking anything else. I think his favourite was Brooke Bond PG Tips, but it was hard for any flavour to really conquer the high heaps of white sugar that were shovelled into the tea. When I think of my father, I instantly think of four things: cups of tea filled with three peaked points of sugar – because of displacement, when the cup was filled with tea there had to be quite a gap at the top so that when the sugar was poured in the liquid didn't spill out over the rim; the *Daily* and *Sunday Express* – in their broadsheet days, when the newspapers were large and unwieldy but with a tabloid lightness, with a gossipy, simplistic kind of caged Toryism; Guards cigarettes – a brand now defunct that comes out of an era when cigarettes were considered to be a harmless, glamorous and essential prop to modern living; and then there was more sugar, the sugar he would pour all over his salad – a post-war salad of limp lettuce, hard tomatoes, beetroot and cucumber that he would coat with snowy layers of sugar. I know of no one else who used such a dressing, but then you should have seen the amount of sugar he poured on his cornflakes.

It was only the sugar-soaked tea that I really inherited from my father. From the age of five or six, more or less until he died, this was how I thought you drank tea. Very strong and very sweet. Not only could you stand a spoon in this tea, you could stand a cricket bat in it. Once my father had died, the amount of sugar I put in my tea gradually lessened. So did the amount of tea I drank. Eventually, I would put no sugar into my tea. And then no milk. Finally, no tea, not in the way my father would recognise. He would be horrified to see me drink camomile tea, peppermint tea, even fruit-flavoured teas. He would have thought I'd gone mad. But then, growing up is a kind of madness. You have to be a little mad to survive the fact that there is no survival, a fact that gets more and more factual the older you get.

I think he would be surprised how much I've changed my habits. For my father, habits were habits and they didn't change. If you were pushed in any way to move reluctantly with the times, then your habits went with you. The sugar, the cigarettes, the *Express*, these were his things, his comforts, his life. Right up to his death.

Towards the end of a book I was weightlessly writing about space called *The Gravity of Grammar School*, I found myself considering bread. My father was as solid a white bread man as you could imagine. Bread was meant to be white like sugar was meant to be white. I remember him eating white bread sandwiches spread with Stork margarine and smeared thickly with red jam. I remember the white bread toasted under the grill in such a way that it weakened the fibres of the bread and turned it almost transparent. I remember this toast smeared with the off-yellow Stork and smothered with off-amber clumps of Robinson's marmalade that had thick slivers of off-orange peel suspended inside it. The marmalade looked like infected frogspawn. It looked like something that, if you put it into the water supply, could kill half of Greater Manchester. Thick spills of it used to coagulate around the rim of the jar, irregular shapes of rancid jelly that you swore would glow in the dark. If you ever got a drop of this marmalade on your clothes, it was as difficult to get off as superglue. My father used to love it.

Much to his disgust, from a very early age, I took against white bread. I developed a fondness for Hovis from about the age of six. The local baker sold mini-sized Hovis, for two old pence, and I could eat one of those on its own, like a cake. My father resented what he saw as fussiness, but in the end even he had to yield to the fact that I would not, even could not, eat white bread. There had to be a special unsliced Hovis bought especially for me. This frustrated my father, who viewed it as some terrible fad, as a waste of money, and as an early sign that I was perhaps some kind of troublemaker. I postponed becoming a complete vegetarian until after he had died. He was a very meaty man.

And then, towards the end of a book I was not writing about the death of my father called *Oh How Far Off the Skies Are, and All That*, I began to consider how I was going to conclude this near autobiographical story. I had thought of a number of ways to finish the book, and these included:

1) I would apologise for neglecting to give my mother a name.

2) I would compose a small essay on the soft and easygoing fig roll, my favourite biscuit, as if to say that, after all that, what with one thing and another, life goes on.

3) I would somehow, against all the odds, wrap things up with a fantasy that I was the sole survivor of the species. This ending seemed to be a bitingly bitter-sweet blend of hope and hopelessness.

4) I would metaphorically burst into tears. Or maybe meta-

phorically break into song. Or metaphorically forget to finish altogether.

5) I would end with a joke. There was the one the writer and comedian Robert Newman told about suicide. He said that in Sweden, a country notorious for its high suicide rate, when you buy a Volvo it comes with a special attachment. A custom-built airtight tube that stretches from the exhaust pipe into the driver's seat.

Then there was the Jerry Seinfeld routine, about how you might want to kill yourself because you felt that you were useless at everything. So you tried to kill yourself and you failed and so you just confirmed that you were useless at everything. You were so useless you couldn't even kill yourself! And where did that get you? Nowhere! It didn't help at all! And so you'd want to kill yourself . . .

And what about the suicide joke as told by the American talk-show host Jay Leno? That would finish the book on a strange downward-spiralling up-note.

A guy hanged himself with a phone cord because he didn't get the Christmas present that he wanted.

The present he wanted was a cordless phone.

6) My father was the only person I've ever known who didn't find Basil Fawlty funny. He could watch an entire episode of *Fawlty Towers* with a straight face. He didn't think that the trouble that Basil found himself in was anything to laugh at. He saw a kind of truth. My mother would actually fall off her chair with hysterics. My father would stare intently at Basil as he tripped from one mentally crippling crisis to another. I think he identified with Basil Fawlty. He understood the earthly trap that Basil was in, the scrapes he got himself into, the suppressed rage, the panic, the deep, drawn sadness. He appreciated the way Basil battled the odds that were stacked against him because he cared so much about life, and doing the right thing, that in the end it all went wrong, and he couldn't find it in himself to care any more.

Fawlty Towers was a real-life tragedy to my father. It was no laughing matter. He watched Basil slump down after yet another desolate blow to his pride and ego, and sigh to himself. 'Phhtttt. What was that? That was your life, mate. Oh. Do I get another? Afraid not . . .' My father would look very thoughtful and as his wife uncontrollably shook with laughter there was perhaps a very gentle nodding of his head.

7) I would finish with my father's funeral. At the end of a book, a funeral. It had to go at the end of the book, because I kept putting off the moment when I would write it. In the end, it wasn't the last thing that I would write, although I would pretend that it was.

My mother and I travelled down to Stroud the day before. What with one thing and another, my father was cremated in Stroud, in Gloucestershire. I don't remember how we travelled to Stroud. I remember that my sisters were considered too young to attend the funeral.

The night before the funeral my mother and I stayed in a bed-and-breakfast guest house. I remember that everyone there was very nice to us. I don't remember any conversation with my mother during that whole day. I do remember that she went to bed early and that I stayed up. In the television lounge, alone, I watched the Clint Eastwood movie *Play Misty for Me*. I concentrated very hard, using it to take my mind off things. It seemed so real, as if the story had actually happened and somehow I was part of it. I can quote much of it off by heart. Whenever it's shown on television, I watch it, and I feel intensely removed from the moment, I feel hollowed out, and I feel passionately sad.

The mingling of the film and my father's funeral means that to this day Clint Eastwood reminds me of my father. There's something about the masculinity of Eastwood's image that I think resembles the strict masculinity of my father, who for all my early life was the most masculine thing I knew. They were physically nothing like each other, but they both brooded, and they both kept things to themselves, and they could both materialise in given situations as a man without a name. And they both, in real life and in fiction, had a hell of a temper. And as much as, when I think of my father, I see a lot of Basil Fawlty, tense, shattered, with a type of wrecked loneliness, I also see hints of Eastwood, proud, erect, with his type of quiet, loner loneliness.*

Mr Spock, the Vulcan science officer from *Star Trek*, also has something in his bearing and appearance that reminds me of my

* I now watch the sure, manly Clint Eastwood get older in a way my father never will. I see him shrink and bend and squint, and note a touch of fear in his eyes, and I see death pick at him bit by bit. Death picked off my father in one big go, and there was no time to fade away, and change shape, and slowly stop.

father. The sense of being an alien lost amongst humans with their confusing ways, their soft touches, their wild hearts. The sense of keeping his feelings hidden away, only for them to explode into view in the most abrupt ways. The meticulousness, the superiority and yet the inferiority, somehow even the physical strength, because I think of my father as being so strong because he was always so much stronger than me. The unorthodox cleverness, because I always think of my father as being a lot cleverer than he let on, or was allowed to let on.

I think of Spock not always trying to do the right thing, but really believing that he was doing the right thing, and that reminds me of my father. Even the lines on his forehead, and his gaze, and his nose – it all reminds me of my father. Perhaps I have just turned Spock, one of my favourite fictional figures, into a virtual father figure. Or perhaps I liked Spock so much because he reminded me of my father.

I went to bed after *Play Misty for Me*, but I don't remember if I went to sleep quickly, or slowly, easily, or with difficulty. The next day was the funeral of my father, this lost mixture of himself, not himself, Clint Eastwood, Basil Fawlty and Mr Spock, although actually he most resembled the 1950s actor Michael Rennie. There was also something of Tommy Steele's goofiness around the mouth, and Tony Hancock's despair around the soul, and, if I searched hard enough, the doomed heroism of Jim Clarke, the racing-car driver who died in his own race against time.

The only pair of black trousers I possessed were corduroy. I remember that they were quite faded and a bit baggy. I don't remember what shoes I wore, or what jacket. It wouldn't have been a suit that I wore. I didn't own one. I don't remember owning a tie and I don't remember wearing one. Maybe I wore one of my father's. I don't remember going to bed. I don't remember getting up in the morning. I don't remember washing my face or cleaning my teeth or shaving or getting dressed. I don't remember eating breakfast.

I kept putting off the moment when I would write about the funeral hoping that if I kept it to last, I would remember things. But most of it is a blank. I remember something about the guest house – that it looked like someone's house – but that's about all.

I remember waiting outside the chapel where there was to be a brief ceremony before my father was, as they say, laid to rest. Family arrived. There was my mum's sister Sally, my father's brother-in-law Michael, his son and my father's nephew Stephen, my Auntie Jill and her husband Graham, and that's all I can remember. There must have been more people, but I just can't remember. I keep wanting to ask my mother who else was there, but I can never quite find the right moment. I greeted everyone a little over-exuberantly, as if I was trying to communicate that my father's death was just one of those things, and today was just one of those days.

The ceremony was wet through. That's the only way I can think of describing it. We were all underwater. We were all at sea. We all held our breath. My mother was next to me, shrivelled up what with all the water and everything. Cousins and uncles and aunties were behind me with faces as expressionless as fishes staring straight ahead into a very soaked nowhere. An Irish vicar, about three foot six tall with eyes like a haddock and webbed feet, spoke some watery words that sounded as if they were in a language that disappeared with Atlantis. As he spoke, a shoal of po-faced angel fish seemed to shimmer past his face. My father's coffin was at the front of the chapel indifferent to the world, as blithe and lethargic as a beached walrus. Something inside me wanted to go up to the coffin and open the lid and see for myself my father lying in the coffin as believable as death. But I couldn't move. It was like there was a current in the chapel, not pushing me back, but too strong to push against. And because of all the water in the chapel, I couldn't cry. I was underwater hearing strangled sounds and seeing bizarre shapes and I couldn't cry. The water wasn't going to let the tears form. All the pressure in the chapel was just too much. Too much to allow tears, or movement, or even thought and emotion. The haddock vicar began what resembled a fishy version of the Lord's Prayer and I got the sensation that we were all in a submarine a thousand feet under the surface of the sea. There was nothing around the chapel but hundreds and hundreds of miles of deep, dark sea, and we were drifting through it, slowly sinking, opening our mouths and making no sound as we pretended to know the words to the Lord's Prayer. The submarine was leaking, letting in water and fish and coral and sea vegetable, and this catastrophic recital of the Twenty-third Psalm seemed to open up more holes and let more water into the chapel. Then my father's coffin slowly began to move as organ music was played that sounded like the sound of whales in pain. The coffin with, as far as we could tell, my father inside it floated down a conveyor belt towards a small porthole. We were all saturated and we'd held our breath for too long and the submarine was attempting to rise to the surface and return to land and my father's coffin disappeared through the porthole into such nothingness the nothingness you find below the ground that you find at the bottom of the sea on this planet the nothingness you find below the ground that you find at the bottom of the sea on a planet a billion light years away from ours. I held my breath for just a little bit longer, and then I breathed out in a rush, and hundreds of little bubbles surged out of my mouth and raced above my head and above a passing mermaid up, up and away towards outer space where there is nothing. And then my father, who I hadn't seen for a few days, was burnt to dust.

We all filed out into the oddly bright afternoon light of Stroud, in Gloucestershire, where my father died for some reason or another. We all shook ourselves dry and started to breathe again. My mother thanked the haddock vicar for the service, which struck me at the time – and I remember this – as being a little surprising, as he had no idea who my father was, or who we were, and had conducted the service with as much sensitivity as a frozen fish finger. But what did I know? I had water on the brain. And my mother would have thanked him if he'd said goodbye to my father wearing pink pyjamas and singing 'We All Live in a Yellow Submarine'. My mother was in no mood for discrimination.

I remember that afterwards we all went into Stroud town centre to have a meal. I didn't have the fish. We all got drunk. I don't think I'd ever been as drunk.

Maybe that's why I can't remember much of what happened the day my father was, to all intents and purposes, cremated.

8) I have never been back to Stroud since.

9) I would end with the answer to Heidegger's fundamental philosophical question: 'Why is there something rather than nothing?' Imagine the surprise! What a happy ending that would be.

I could also end by considering the idea that suicide is an experiment. It is a question which man puts to nature. Namely, what change will death produce in a man's existence, and in his insight into the nature of things? It is a clumsy experiment to make – for it involves the destruction of the very consciousness which put the question and awaits the answer. That might be too confusing an ending, but then what is death if it is not confusing? There is nothing in life that is as confusing as death, except perhaps the filling in a Jaffa cake and Mickey Mouse's feet.

10) Before I finish, I shouldn't forget a few more things that should be under 's' in the index of a book written about death. I could finish with this list: Sceptic, sceptical theory, self-deception, self-responsibility, self-understanding, 'semiotic self', spiritual dimension, split-brain personality, Storr, A., suffering, symbiotic-annihilation. This would mean that the book would end with the word 'annihilation', but then it would also end with the word 'annihilation' if I finished the book with the answer to Heidegger's most basic and most blatant question.

11) I would finish in the pub, where I have been talking to my father over a drink. I suppose you could say I have been interviewing him, as there are a lot of questions I was never able to ask him. He died before we ever really had a proper, lengthy conversation about anything other than football, or television, or nothing much. This imaginary conversation in a pub somewhere between Stroud and Stockport is a chance for me to get to know him, to get to know him as a man who took one hell of a risk at the very end of his life, as a man who had such a lot on his mind. In a way, he had two minds. You could say of him that for a lot of the time he was in two minds. He had such a lot on one mind, and next to nothing on the other. He would switch from mind to mind, and then one day he made a mistake and fucked up the switch from one mind to another and ended up somewhere else. He ended up mindless. I ask him the answer to a question, maybe the Heidegger one about nothing and something. 'Ask a question and you'll get an answer. But it won't tell you much!'

He's on his second pack of cigarettes. I don't smoke. I think I don't smoke because I was rebelling against my father. It was something he did and therefore it was not going to be something that I did. I also made a decision that I would never wear as much brown as him.

And so the book would end with my dad speaking in a voice I can't remember, smoking a last cigarette, meekly answering a question I can't remember, except that it had something to do with annihilation.

'The ebb and flow of the outside is like a distant monotonous murmur unable to stir interest or curiosity. After having struggled madly to solve all problems, after having suffered on the heights of despair, in the supreme hour of revelation, you will find that the only answer, the only reality, is silence.'

Do you know that there are over two hundred bones in a skeleton? 'No.'

12) I could finish by asking my father, What's the matter? What's wrong with you?

And he would reply, 'Nothing. Nothing's the matter with me. I've merely taken a leap outside my fate, and now I don't know where to turn, what to run for . . .'

13) Have I mentioned that when a would-be suicide hooks up one end of a hose to a car exhaust pipe and inhales at the other, he is taking advantage of the affinity that haemoglobin has for carbon monoxide, which it prefers by a factor of 200 to 300 over its lifegiving competitor, oxygen? The patient dies because his brain and heart are deprived of an adequate oxygen supply. The colour imparted to the blood by the carboxyhaemoglobin makes it significantly brighter and paradoxically even more vibrant than its normal state, with the result that the skin and the mucous membranes of a person who dies by carbon monoxide have a remarkable cherry-red tinge. The absence of the typical bluish discoloration of asphyxia may deceive those who discover what appears to be a pink-cheeked body in the bloom of health, but dead nevertheless.

14) The End.*

16) It was Steve Martin – or was it E. M. Cioran? – who said you cannot overstress the importance of a finishing sentence.

17) But there's still some time to go before the finishing sentence. For all this talk of death, we're nowhere near the end. We haven't yet reached the death that is the point, the hard centre, the reason for this book. For all this talk of death, we've only really had one death. To prove it, we've seen his body.

Here lies the body of Ian Curtis, singer with the rock group Joy Division. It lies in front of me telling the terrible truth about its state of health. It is there but not there in front of me, shockingly representing a person that no longer exists, very clearly announcing in its

15) *Nothing could be further from the truth.

present non-existence that a corpse is no more a person than a house is a home.

Why am I in a position to see the post-ultimate position of this young man who, in his songs, announced that we only have convictions if we study nothing thoroughly? Why am I staring through and past and over and around and at and not at this courageous coward? How did I ever get to see the body of Ian Curtis?

I didn't know his family. I only knew him from a distance. My invitation, if that is the word, came from the boss of Ian's record company, the restless, chronically anti-reticent Tony Wilson. The death of Ian Curtis has not stilled the fast-beating heart of his ambition for Joy Division, and he is very keen that I view the body, and not-the-body, of Ian Curtis. He clearly thinks it is important that I experience a last sighting of Ian, even if it is just this simplistic physical echo of Ian, before there is no Ian, no visual echo, to see. He wants me to have this sight so that I can connect it with all my other sightings of Ian, on stage, off stage, on form, off form, full of life, lost in life. He wants me to use these sightings to make up some pattern of sense, some trail of meaning, about the life of Ian Curtis. Wilson insists, as if it's any of his business, that I must have this final glimpse, this badly broken souvenir. To be honest, I was baffled about what I was doing there looking at the body of Ian Curtis. I felt that I was badly intruding on something very private. Wilson was fussing around me like a mother hen, and creating a little drama out of someone's awful death that seemed purely for his own interests. He acted like he owned the body, and I felt that I wasn't doing anything as proper, as reasonable, as paying respects, but that I was being dragged into some dark game that had rules I knew nothing about. I felt like I was taking part in some scam.

Years later, Wilson would tell me that he took me along to see the body because he wanted me to have some inside knowledge, some exclusive journalistic details, about the death of Ian Curtis for when I came to write the book that he assumed I would write about Joy Division. A book that would be called *Who Killed Ian Curtis?* and which would help turn Joy Division into the monsters of myth that he dearly wanted them to be. I never wrote the book, and so the details were wasted. Me seeing the body was a waste of waste.

In this book that I never wrote, towards the end I explained how embarrassed I had been to be in this small room with what strangely remained of Ian Curtis. I was embarrassed for a lot of reasons. I was embarrassed in front of Ian, embarrassed that he would be thinking, What the fuck are you doing here? I was embarrassed that Wilson was pulling me into some frivolous façade without the knowledge of Ian's family. Mostly, on the day, I was embarrassed about the flimsy bunch of flowers that I had brought with me, and the flimsy message that I had attached to the bouquet. I remember Wilson's greedy searching eyes looking at the card, no doubt hoping to see these wonderful words of commiseration and commemoration that would be apt coming from the mind of the one he had chosen to write the book about Joy Division that would seal their unearthly glory. I remember, even though he tried to hide it, his disappointment when he saw that all I had written, blocked by death and embarrassment and bewilderment, was: 'Sadly missed.'

I think Wilson was hoping to see on the card: 'Man should stop being – or becoming – a rational animal. He should become a lunatic, risking everything for the sake of his dangerous fantasies, capable of exaltations, ready to die for all that the world has as well as for what it has not. Each man's ideal should be to stop being a man. This can only be attained through absolute arbitrariness ... all important things bear the sign of death ...'

The situation was too real, though, to be this real.

The situation was too unreal, though, to be this unreal.

Eventually it would occur to me, it would come into focus, it would seem odd, that I had seen the dead body of Ian Curtis but not of my father, and that this might form part of a book I was going to write called *Death in the Family*. At some point in this book, right about now in fact, nowhere near the end, but nowhere near the beginning either, just exactly in its own place, I would explain why I never got to see the dead body of my father.

18) I think it was the day after my father died, my Uncle Graham – the husband of my mother's sister, Jill – drove me down to Stroud, the town where my father had been found dead. I was still in a state of shock, and would have happily spent the entire journey scrubbing away at a cooker. I remember that I was putting a brave face on things, and putting off reactions to the death of my father, some of which I am still putting off.

19) I suppose the journey I took with Uncle Graham in his big shiny executive car from Stockport to Stroud was the same journey

as the last journey my father took. Perhaps the service station where we stopped off for lunch was the same service station my father stopped at, for a meal, and a think. It was a sunny day, and in a funny sinking sort of way a very pleasant journey.

Uncle Graham was a bank manager, and he very practically decided to use the journey to explain to me the level of my new responsibilities. He probed me on my future prospects like a combination of careers master and prospective father-in-law. I was intoxicated with maximum-proof grief, and couldn't really concentrate on his survey of my family's brand-new situation. I remember being a little annoyed that he considered my desire to be a writer as being impractical. I protested that I was already writing for the *New Musical Express*, but with courteous persistence he dismissed this as a venture with little future. He recommended that I use the four O levels that I had somehow mustered to get a job in a bank. He could help me. The thought of this made me feel even thicker in the head. Not only had my father died, but now I was going to have to go and work in a bank. Things had changed around an awful lot in the last couple of days.

We arrived in Stroud, and went to a police station. Everyone there was very nice to me. It was the first time I had ever spoken to a policeman. Or was it the second time? I was asked a few questions about my father, and I answered as if I knew what I was talking about. It was decided out of my earshot that, as a teenager, I was too young to be the one who would formally identify the body of my father. My Uncle Graham disappeared to look at the dead body of my father and I was given a cup of tea with three sugars to drink. It was good and strong and you could have stood my shock upright in it.

Apparently, my father looked very peaceful, and I believed my Uncle Graham when he told me this. I also totally trusted him that he had got it right in identifying my father. Somewhere near me in some room in this building lay something that according to Uncle Graham would remind me of my father, but for some reason I had absolutely no urge to go and search for him, in all his new him-lessness. Maybe it was because I was just letting the authority of the police, and the precise maturity of Uncle Graham, dictate the terms of my visit to Stroud, or maybe it was because I was putting off the moment when I would believe that my father had died. Perhaps I just didn't think of it, because my thoughts had been interfered with, until it was too late. Now, I can't understand why I didn't want to see him, dead. To have seen him, dead, would have helped complete the shape of his life, put a kind of lid on it, so that everything would be kept in place, memories, feelings, emotion. By not seeing his body, there was no shape, no lid, and everything just spilled out. That last sight of my father might have pulled his life together for me, made him more real. In the way that death concentrates the mind, seeing his body might have concentrated my mind into remembering him much more vividly than I do. The shock I felt needed some kind of focus, a direction, and having no sight of my dead father allowed some of the shock to wander off in all sorts of directions, and some of it to stick where it was. Stuck to the roof of my imagination, like dried-up marmalade.

Without that final sighting, the memory of my father – and to me all my father became is memory – has tended to drift off, to disperse into a faraway nowhere, and his life has turned out as vague as his death. By never seeing his dead body, I've never felt that my father has been completely finished. Even though he is finished with life. At least, I think he's finished with life.

There's a part of me, a part that occasionally from its dark, placeless corner composes some of my dreams, that feels, despite all the evidence, and all the reality, that my father is still alive. He adopted another identity. He has another life which he's getting on with in mute parallel to mine, and one day he reappears, much to everyone's surprise, more alive than I ever knew he ever was. I have dreamt this now and then: the return of my dead father from some wonderful adventure, and then life carries on, as before, but different, with my father, warmer and wiser, weirdly himself, back at the centre of our family things.

He has appeared in my dreams as if his life never stopped, and he's just popped in for a chat. We go to a pub, and we have a drink, and I ask him questions, and he answers as if he is some mystical philosopher living under the constraints of suicidal insomnia, meditating on the absurdity of existence and the agony of consciousness. But he's only joking. He's going to live for ever!

I don't suppose I would have these dreams if I had seen the dead body of my father. I would have different dreams. I would dream of his dead body, and his beautiful ruddy complexion. I would dream of him in heaven, or in hell. I would dream of him living his life before he died. But I wouldn't dream that he is still alive, up to date with *Coronation Street* and Manchester City, smoking a new brand now that Guards are no more, sugaring his tea as emphatically as ever, a mystery man with a hidden past and an unbelievable future.

As I drove home with Uncle Graham, making the journey from Stroud to Stockport that my father never got to make, we were both fairly quiet. We had our own thoughts to consider. Mine had lost all sense of order, and my uncle's were covered by the shadow of the dead body he had just seen. I didn't ask him any questions about what he had just seen. I would see him over the years at funerals, always funerals. My mother's father died, my mother's mother died, and at the funerals there would be Graham, reliable and mature like I remembered him, surefooted, distant, and with his own apparently unfazed thoughts. I remember him saying to me, as we drove down to Stroud so that he could see my father's body and I couldn't, that he just couldn't understand the depths that someone had to sink to in order to kill themselves. He said it in such a way that suggested he did understand, after all.

I never asked him about my father's dead body. And then one day, it must have been twenty years after my father died, I suddenly got the urge to ask Uncle Graham what he had seen that day, and what he had felt like. Just as I was seriously starting to think about calling him up and talking to him, I got one of those calls from my mother. 'Your Uncle Graham has died,' she told me, with the usual abruptness. What with one thing and another, it turned out that he had died two years earlier, and my mother had only just found out. So I never went to the funeral of the man who saw the body of my dead father.

20) I wonder when I will start dreaming about my Uncle Graham.

SIXTEEN

My father disappeared. It was 1970, and he was in his early thirties, with a wife, three kids and a nine-to-five job. Everything had been going along as normally as you imagine it to be, when one day my father didn't return home from work. I knew next to nothing about my father, his work, his life, he was just my dad, a bit strained, a bit edgy, but he was always there, or thereabouts, living in the same house as me, running our lives in a way that seemed the best he could. We lived in quite a nice house, and he drove quite a nice car, and I was going to the local grammar school, which filled him with hopes for my future, and he and my mum seemed to be getting on all right, as much as most of their lives together was conducted in secrecy and privacy. My two sisters seemed to be what you'd expect from two young girls living in Stockport in the early 70s. Everything did seem pretty normal. But I must have been living in a dream world. How wrong could I be? Behind the normal curtains of our normal semi-detached house in this normal street, something had been brewing. I had been noticing my own life too much to notice.

My father had, after years of struggle, found himself quite a good job working at the north-west Shell/BP headquarters in Wythenshawe, a few miles outside Manchester city centre. As far as I could tell from what he said about his job, it was some sort of clerical work, and it was going well enough for him to have been promoted a couple of times. I never knew exactly what it was he did. I remember at school a teacher once asked each boy in my class what it was their fathers did for a living. All the boys alphabetically in front of me replied that their fathers were doctors, lawyers, accountants, all very specific occupations. I couldn't think what it was my father did. He didn't actually seem to have a profession. I toyed with making something up, but this seemed a terrible thing to have to do. When it came to my turn, I had managed to come up with an answer. I said that he was a clerk.

'A clerk?' asked the teacher, raising his eyebrows in a polite quest for more information.

'Yes, you know, an office clerk . . .' I didn't really have a clue what that was, or even if that was what my father did, but at least I'd thought of an answer. Even if the answer did crush me slightly, and selfishly, as the rest of the class reeled off their engineers and scientists and bank managers.

I was in the back garden of our house playing football. My mother and two sisters were inside the house doing whatever it was they did inside the house while I was in the background playing football. Every day after school, and for a large part of the weekends, I would play football in the back garden. I spent a lot of my early years thinking that football was something you played on your own, with the back of a garage as a goal, and rocks and cans and shrubbery as your opponents. On my own in the back garden I was a great player, and would spend hours playing imaginary games, dreaming that I was playing for imaginary teams and, bizarrely, for Scotland. So there I was in my dream life in the background when my mother rather casually came out to tell me that Dad was late home from work.

I don't know whether my mother was making anything out of this, but I certainly wasn't. I had a lot else on my mind. While I was playing some imaginary match in the back garden, three or four gardens down the sexiest thing that lived near me, Hilary Angel, and three of her friends were mucking around and beginning to flirt with me. They were asking that I come over and join them in their mucking around. The thought was so exciting and tempting to a young boy who had never been kissed and whose sex life was between him and his fingers that I seized up into an acute form of adolescent paralysis. As the girls teased me and made inviting moves for me to go and play with them, something that was stretching my imagination out into a flesh-toned beyond, my mother would keep coming out to tell me that there was no sign of my dad. I really didn't care about this, as I was working myself up into a state where I would go and visit these girls. For someone who went to a boys' school, these girls were just so girlish, and exotic, and there, that it felt like heaven was opening up for me just a few gardens away from where I was. The girls kept waving and giggling. For all I knew, they might have been making fun of me – they were my age, but with their make-up and miniskirts and feathered haircuts and budding breasts they looked like women to me, and I would have found them taking the mickey out of me much more of a real-life turn-on than anything I'd ever known.

It started to get dark, and there was still no sign of my dad. By now, it was clear in the gathering murk that there was something seriously wrong. My mother was frantic, and I had to resist the allure of the garden girls and join her and my sisters inside to face up to the empty space that was growing where my father should have been. The fantasy of Hilary and her friends and a possible first kiss disappeared in a puff of smoke. I allow the thirteen-year-old that I was to say 'shit' to himself in response to this appalling frustration.

My father had disappeared.

Here was a new situation to get used to – your father goes missing – and I think I adapted pretty quickly, if a little moodily. The first day he was gone, I had a day off school. I don't remember what happened over the next few days, or weeks, but I carried on at school, and the family Dad had left behind adjusted to their new circumstances, waiting for good news, waiting for bad news, just waiting. I suppose I drifted through these days with a little premonition of much greater later shock. I remember the same feelings of trying to be brave, of being embarrassed if I had to tell anybody what had happened in case they were embarrassed.

Then, I think, we actually gave up hope.

And then he turned up in a mental hospital in Chichester, Sussex. He had suffered some kind of breakdown. He had tried to kill himself. A few days later he returned home, not so much a shadow of his former self, more a reflection. He then tried to put his life back together again, and behind our normal curtains we tried hard to be a normal family. But we were aware that there was something about Dad that wasn't normal. Perhaps I could have spotted it earlier. Perhaps my mother already had. But now the something-other-than-normal-ness of my father hung in the atmosphere. We became self-conscious about it. We had to move around it. We didn't acknowledge it.

My father had to deal with it. Sometimes he could, and sometimes he couldn't. When he could, he would just about hold on to habit and routine. When he couldn't, he would slip further and further away from any kind of normal, from the kind of normal where you have a wife, three kids, a mortgage, and a nine-to-five job.

For a few years, I got used to the fact that my father seemed to make a more and more erratic series of appearances in my life, and quite a few disappearances. He would run away quite regularly. Once, during one of his disappearing acts, my mother's brother David saw him in a bank in Derby. 'Hello,' he said, 'what a surprise seeing you here.' My father looked him right in the eyes, said, 'I have no idea who you are,' and walked off.

I grew up dismally unaware that my father was a much more complicated and tormented man than I could ever have imagined. The weight of life put so much pressure on him that in the end he preferred what he predicted would be the lightness of death, the ease, the relief. He was wrestling with demons, losing his grip, running out of answers, climbing the mountain of his despair, and filling with emptiness.

Meanwhile, dreamily oblivious to the secret tragedies and blackened melancholy of my disappearing father, I just wanted my first kiss. I was waiting for my life to start.

PART TWO

Some things you wait for all your life, and some things you don't. Some things you see coming, and some things you don't. Some things make you think, and some things don't. Some things make you start, and some things . . . don't.

Some things do, and some things don't. Some things carefully pierce your skin, and some things don't.

Then again, some things start with a kiss, and some things don't.

The first girl I ever kissed was an angel. Hilary Angel, to be precise. That was the name of the first girl I ever kissed. She tasted of grass and spit and muddy beauty.

Peter Shelley. That was the name of the first boy I ever kissed. And the last. He tasted roughly speaking like his mouth was watering at the very thought of writing pop songs about love that were as sweet and intense and transitory as infatuation.

I thought, and still do, that Hilary had a face like Mick Jagger and legs like Tina Turner. She was all lip and leg and female muscle. She was a girl, and something else. A girl in real life and a girl in my imagination, which tended to stretch the point of her girliness to an erect hilt. She seemed to me as alien as an animal, and as trendy as a pin-up in *Fab 208* magazine. The boutique skirts she wore usually stopped dead or alive a randy dozen go-go inches above her serious and fluid knees, high up these moving thighs that had a way of leading me into a dark wood of desire as I lay in bed at night, fourteen years old and destined to deal flat out with constantly stiffening emotionally frayed lust.

I remember her once walking down Arlington Drive, the road in Woodsmoor, Stockport, where we both lived, a few doors apart, and she wasn't wearing a miniskirt. She was wearing a deeply fashionably deep purple maxiskirt with nerve-tingling aplomb. I stiffened on the spot. She may have been hiding her legs, but really she was showing them off. They were nowhere to be seen but everywhere to be imagined. She was walking with her mum, but she wasn't really with her. She was sex on the street where I lived, and she put one foot in front of the other like she knew it. There was something about her swollen mouth and her lizard eyes that gave away everything about why any of us are on the planet, and I was being fiercely urged as a boy pinned down on this planet by strange changes in mind and body to find out the exact nature of the connection between her mouth, her eyes, and the reasons for existence.

She was a tough and tender thirteen years old, and as far as I could tell from the shy safe distance I kept away from her, spying on her from inside a swaying fantasy, she went out with thick scowling sixteen-year-old skinhead Stockport County fans who had skulls like tanks. These boys seemed to me to have achieved a kind of perfection of appearance, right down to the laces in their shoes, and their heads and eyes and skin shone with certainty. They were clean deadly wild animals and the neat correctly measured turn-ups on their jeans seemed to clearly suggest that they intuitively appreciated the flash relationship between Hilary's lips and the essence of existence. I couldn't imagine the animal world that Hilary and her shrewd, unburdened skinheads inhabited, but the thought of them stalking through it and setting off all manner of sparks was a faint, dangerous turn-on.

I was fourteen, but looked and acted six years younger and thirty years older, with a face, if you could pick it out through the fresh acne and stubborn blackheads and freaky bumfluff, like a sore Stan Laurel, and a body like a baby bambi. I felt generally broke, and felt that I looked broken. Hilary and her skinheads, her uniformed tribe of strong, loyal followers, seemed unbreakable, to belong to each other, to belong in a real world that from the weak outside seemed complete and sure. They always looked as if they knew what they were doing and where they were going. They had no doubts, their clothes fitted their sure bodies, and fitted the times. They were fashionably fashionable. I didn't belong anywhere and could never muster up the difficult will-power and still presence of mind required to choose clothes that would represent me properly as a teenager set inside a town called Stockport in a year made out as 1971. I didn't know what I was doing. I didn't know where I was going. Hilary and her rock-hard skinheads seemed to have it all worked out, just by wearing the right trousers, the right skirt, and they had this tremendous physical sense of being. There was nothing physical about me. Everything was just mental. The thought and the sight and the impossibility of Hilary intensified the sticky tension that there was in me between the physical and the mental and mocked it from fantasy afar, and the pushy thought of her swollen mouth swelled up inside me until I was mentally fit to physically burst.

I'd paid fantasy attention to the unreal Hilary, angel of temptation, for months as she patrolled Arlington Drive, her sexual territory, wearing short skirts, and hanging around street corners with inscrutable beefed-up bovver boys in button-down tartan shirts and highly polished Oxford shoes. She was as blonde as my dream of her, she was all of the women in the world dressed up in one thirteen-year-old go, she was the absolute conducting target of my adolescent sexual madness. Because I felt twice removed from the world and as transparent as a thought, it never occurred to me that she was aware that I even existed. We were in different dimensions. She was a party girl, and I was a bookshop boy. She was a good-time girl, and I was a sad-time boy. Her boyfriends were rough and tough Stockport County fans and they beat up grannies and Rochdale fans, and I wanted to be a romantic poet from the nineteenth century. Once as we passed each other on the street, me just thinking without aim, her just wearing a short skirt aimed at my heart and groin and weakness, I thought that she smiled at me, with a kind of catty hunger, but the flaming blush that instantly flushed through me as our eyes made contact across the dimensions obliterated from the moment any sense of reality and left behind merely the disappearing edges of the illusion I might have that we shared the same neighbourhood, let alone the same planet. The decayed dream of her never-never smile helped one or two of my thoughts take aim and brought a kind of rubbed collapsed pleasure into my life for a night-time moment or two. In my night-time thoughts we were a perfect partnership – she didn't exist, not for me, and I didn't exist either, not for sure.

Once, again, I swear she said hello to me, but I didn't believe it enough for me to say hello back, or perhaps I just figured she was just teasing me. Even if she was aware that I existed, maybe because her mum and mine were neighbours and knew each other, I couldn't possibly be anything that she could be interested in. She liked her boys real and stuffed with presence, with their hair shaved to the tumultuous scalp and skin that glowed for England, and preferably with tattoos on their menacing forearms. Presence leaked out of me every night, my skin was the colour and texture of misery, my hair slid greasily down my ears and neck, and if you had tried to tattoo my arm it would have disintegrated. But then one day something of my fantasy of her spilled over into the real life of Woodsmoor, Stockport, 1971, helping in its way to prove that sometimes there's not a lot of difference between reality as it's spun by the world and what you think reality is inside your own spinning head. Although sometimes there is.

She was wearing bright clothes that framed her lips and legs so they pulsated with driven visibility, and I was drabbed down to the point of invisibility, and with sudden realness she tartly accosted me as I drifted outside my house. I spent a lot of time just standing around my house doing nothing that I can recall but just standing around. Realities and dimensions and dreams and days of the week and my mind and her body clashed in epic surprise as she told me with blonde force that she had always fancied me and could we meet later that evening down at the nearby sports ground. Her ripened, vulgar lips chewed gum with life-affirmative vigour and I dumbly stared at her for ever as if I was about to inherit the earth.

I said, or I thought, I wasn't your type. Wrong hair. Wrong clothes. Wrong face. Wrong body. Wrong mind. Wrong everything.

She said, seizing the moment using her lips and gum with such mouthy agility I thought my trousers might fall down, I like the way you dress. It had never occurred to me before that I did in fact in any sense dress. All she ever saw me wear was a bright-orange nylon shirt from C&A, flared jeans that flopped on behalf of my general sense of ill-being, and a tatty knitted maroon waistcoat that had belonged to somebody's grandfather if not mine. These clothes were my uniform when I wasn't in my school uniform, quite fashionable in 1899, or 1967, or even 1994, but definitely not in 1971. I have no idea how or if these clothes ever got washed.

I said, or I thought, something along the lines of, I am not a skinhead. This shows how experienced I was in the art of the chat-up. It's a sure winner – stand in front of a girl with a mouth as marvellous as the Atlantic Ocean and announce into eyes made up so as to turn a girl into a woman in the blink of an eye that you are not a skinhead.

She said, almost kindly, with a gummy giggle, I know you're not a skinhead. That doesn't matter. She looked at me like I was weird or something. But not *weird* weird. Weird good. To her, the fact that I appeared, just, at the edges of vision, to mooch my way through life living off my dreams was mysterious, or something. It was exotic.

My mother, who I vaguely knew as my mother, and who was married to my father, who vaguely knew me as his son, thought that
I was too strange to live. She occasionally nervously asked me
questions that I realise in hindsight were asked to prise the truth
from me about my heroin habit, and she didn't so much consider
me mysterious as simply missing.

I should say that I didn't take heroin. In fact, I don't remember
taking anything during 1971, no food, no drink, nothing. My
mother assumed I took heroin because for her it was the only way to
explain my behaviour, which was usually located at an odd point
between quite quiet and peculiarly quiet.

I can't be sure, because it was an odd year as years go, as oddness
goes, but I think I washed my hair once in 1971. I don't remember
the actual act of my washing it, but for the sake of common decency
I'm going to say that I did wash it, once. I remember reading in a
magazine that an efficient way to get rid of grease in your hair when
you didn't have time to wash it – and I had so much time I had no
time – was to warm some salt in the oven and then brush it through
your hair. I tried this, and for a couple of weeks you couldn't tell the
dandruff in my still-greasy hair from the salt. My usual remedy for
cleaning my greasy hair, because washing it seemed to be as great a
task as climbing Mount Everest, was to brush talcum powder
through it, like a form of dry-cleaning. The effect the talc had on my
hair was to leave the area around my middle parting white and
dusty, then elsewhere produce brittle bursts of static, so that my
hair flew out in electric wisps in erratic places around my head.
Because of my complexion, I looked half dead, and because of my
hair, I looked in a state of shock, and because of my diet, I looked as
if my next trip would be to a gas chamber. So you could forgive my
mother for thinking that I was taking heroin, although if I had been
I think I would have looked healthier, and my hair wouldn't have
looked as though it was lagging behind the rest of time.

I suppose for Hilary I was some kind of light relief amidst her
heavy diet of skinheads.

I brushed some talcum powder through my hair and left the
house for my unexpected meeting with the girl of my dirty dreams.
Because of the way I felt about myself – guilty, innocent, stupid,
desperate, secretive – and because of the way I felt about Hilary – I
felt disgusting about her – I didn't want my parents to know what

was about to happen. Something made me feel that my father, who I knew little about other than what I guessed, who spent a lot of time in his life which was somewhere other than mine, and who I felt in a way had a sense of superiority about the rest of the world, would consider Hilary, with her feathered hair and glossy lips, a little common. It was her common-ness, what I thought of as her gorgeous everyday-ness, her now-ness, her near-ness, that led me to believe that sex, and having sex, was the key to understanding and ordering the torturing randomness of existence. Somewhere between the lips of Hilary Angel, as I saw it as a fourteen-year-old boy tense with dense urges, lay all the answers to all the questions which squeezed my mind and stretched my body.

I said to my parents, who must have been in the room as I said it, that I was going for a ride on my bike. This must have aroused their suspicions that something was up because I hadn't ridden my bike in months, hadn't really left my room for weeks – even when I went to school, I sort of left most of myself behind in my little bedroom, thinking thoughts of thinking and associated chaos – hadn't really said anything to them for a few days. In many ways they were still waiting for my first words. They would have probably been quite relieved that I was off to do something relatively normal like meet a girl.

Even if it was Hilary Angel. As common as chewing-gum.

I had never kissed a girl before, and this embarrassed me, even though nobody really knew that I hadn't and nobody really cared. Everything in life embarrassed me, as far as I could tell, and I kept my whole life secret, as far as I could be bothered, even from myself. I left the house as inconspicuously as I could, covered in shame and talcum powder, shimmering with indefinite nervousness, yet somehow with a feeling of unusual power, as I was quite sure I was heading towards a certain first kiss. The way the miniskirted mascaraed Hilary had asked me for a walk as she chewed her gum and smacked her lips and moved her mouth in a flirtatious parody of the way she moved her legs promised me nothing less than the earth in the shape of a kiss.

My life was about to change. A kiss would make sense of the changes my mind and body were itching and twisting through and propel me into a future man made by a man no other than myself. I said goodbye as normally and politely as I could, another thing that must have slightly alarmed my parents as I didn't normally go in for that sort of thing.

I imagine them watching me go, me pretty convinced that I had convinced them that I had decided to rediscover the delights of my bicycle and go for an early-evening ride around the block, and they must have thought, Well, he's about to have his first ever kiss, with that common Hilary Angel. I don't imagine what my two sisters thought about all this, as I don't remember them at this time, as for some reason they didn't seem to be in my life, in my reality, in 1971. Mostly, they seemed suspended, or lost in their own time, which wasn't running in time with my time.

The lovely ugly common uncommon lippy leggy scary skingirl Hilary was a little put off to see me arrive for our meeting and my first kiss rolling my bicycle, but then I was mysterious, and I clearly had strange habits, some of them were actually sprinkled into my hair, and she wasn't going to let my Claude Butler put her off. I'm sure that she knew it was my first kiss. I didn't walk like a boy who had ever kissed anyone, especially when I was pushing a five-gear drop-handled bicycle. I guessed that it was her thirty-seventh kiss, just by looking at the cheap but classic sin-red lipstick that had been pushed onto her mighty mouth. The words 'kiss me' seemed etched into the pattern of lines on her lips, and even the words 'fuck me' seemed all but fully formed. She was something to fear and desire all at once. Her eyes sent out a fluctuating blue signal of clued-up tease. I thought, Whatever it is that she is about to do is written all over her ever so slightly flared navy-blue miniskirt, a skirt that was up to here, or thereabouts, and that was surely up to no good. She eyed the bike as if she was plotting ways to get rid of it, so that it didn't come between us. Maybe she was thinking, God, do I have to kiss that as well? The adult in me that was yet to form, yet to remember, yet to be so sophisticated and expectant, the adult in me that was there but not there, a long way off but buried in time, the adult that led me on from present to present so that the past became the future, the adult in me that was awakening faster than it ever had as I smelt the fastness on her skin, hoped that she was wondering what to sit on first – me or the bike.

With what I hoped was irresistible lyrical finesse I expressed my dream-deep affection for the exposed glamour of her long living legs. The three of us, me loaded with anticipation, Hilary as curved and full as the sky, the bike a chained, mute witness, made our way across the playing fields near Arlington Drive, Woodsmoor, Stockport, Cheshire, 1971. I have no idea what we talked about, but whatever it was we talked about was simply a cover for what we really had on our minds. Hilary expertly manoeuvred me over to a wooden bench set at the side of a football pitch and swiftly separated me from my security bicycle. The bike went crashing to the floor in front of where we sat, wheels and pedals stuck in the air looking as awkward as I felt. She sat next to me up close and crossed her legs so that the skirt she had on shrank to the size of a belt and the world was full of her thighs as far as my eye could see. I really like your legs, I said again, because at that moment this was all the conversation I could think of. I really like your legs. This was something of an underestimation. She crossed her legs again, and kicked me in the groin and heart and mind and eyes, and the way the knee of the top leg bent over the bottom leg seemed somehow to sum up the sensation of sex which was now possibly as close to me as it had ever been. Between those crossed legs was sex, and she knew it in a fundamentally female way that was thirteen years old and thirteen thousand years old. I really like your legs, I repeated, stuck in the moment, stuck in my frustration, stuck in my apprehension. She smiled. For now it seemed that whatever I said or did simply confirmed my dopy charms.

It was a cold evening and quite windy, or it could have been a warm night and fairly still. I don't remember really. It was all as real as anything but just as much in my mind then as I remember it now.

I had never been so close before to such a creature.

I kept looking at her legs, the way they crossed and curved, the way they were tight and loose, the way they changed shape from thigh to ankle, the way they revealed everything and concealed much more. It all made me go hard and soft at the same time.

She had that hungry look on her face like she could have eaten me and then the rest of the man world in a snapped instant.

The coarse streaked extravagance of her crudely applied make-up created a bruised parody of beauty that made me think I was about to sink into the quicksand of sin.

She smelled mixed up like the future.

She could change the orbit of the planet with a single pout.

I like your legs.

Her knees made me go weak at the knees.

The nail varnish on her bitten fingernails had chipped off leaving little pink pearl insect patterns.

There's a pink beetle on her fingernail.

I wonder what she was thinking when she painted on her nail varnish.

I like your legs.

There was no one around for miles.

For centuries.

Her styled hair was stiff with lacquer like it was the most natural thing in the world.

She didn't say a word.

She wasn't designed to.

There's a pink patch painted onto her thumbnail in the erratic shape of desire.

I really like your . . .

Her swollen little big blue-purple mouth suddenly swooped, her face filled my world instead of her considerable legs, and her mostly moist plump lips stuck themselves almost dead centre on my pure dry kid-thin lips.

We kissed.

Drily, wetly, most definitely, quite quickly, mouth to mouth, nose to nose.

More nerves lead directly from the brain to the lip than lead anywhere else. Kissing someone else is like falling into their mind. If you do it right.

It was brilliant.

But.

I didn't know what to do with my hands but very nearly knew what to do with my tongue, like it was natural.

I stopped breathing . . .

I remember as we instantly kissed for ever with little thrilling hints of something that I was learning was tongue, which was suddenly the most mysterious part of the body, a wriggling symbol of the hidden strangeness of life and everything, as I dived into the deep end of physical contact and touched someone for what seemed like the very first non-accidental time, as I tried desperately yet calmly to freeze the shooting moment, I looked past her bare ear beyond her stiff yellow curls over the playing fields out towards the Pennine Hills darkly moaning in the distance and wonderfully taking the shape of the squirming flesh in my arms, and I frantically screamed to myself at a pitch of self-consciousness in flaming capital letters that shot out from my tongue right through her body and back into my brain: THIS IS IT!

This is it. I was kissing a girl. Something in me made me promise that if I ever wrote a book I would record this moment. Something in me already knew that I would write a book and that over a quarter of a century later I would be recording the moment. There was already the future me inside me looking at the moment, remembering it from afar as it happened, working at the details, making them up, sealing them, certifying them, holding them in place. There were other mes inside the me as I kissed this girl full of her own hers, there was baby me, past me, unformed me, kid me, now me, future me, formed me, stunned me, controlled me, the me for whom this was so new, the me for whom this was something I'd been waiting for all my life, the me who was still waiting, the me who had never kissed anyone, the me who kept on kissing. There was the me who was somehow aware that everything happens all at once and the future happens at the same time as the past and the present, and inside this kissing moment, time, which mostly seems to move forwards and to be made of consecutive overlapped moments, collapses into itself. As I kissed I was everything I ever was and everything I will ever be. I was remembering the moment as it happened. I was anticipating the moment as it happened. I was right inside the moment as it happened. Me, me, me, a tangle of time, egos, dreams, hopes and memories.

And then I was on my own. It all stopped happening and the fourteen-year-old me was separated from a whole lot of other mes, flung back into an ordinary, uncomplicated present, landing with a bump of raw hope that I was now a man, and that the next logical step after such a kiss was sex, with all its turning, eternal secrets.

After, oh, devastating seconds, we unstuck ourselves. From the outside I suppose the kiss had looked very awkward and pretty unspectacular. From the inside it seemed as special as birth. I was a changed boy, experienced as such, although by the look on Hilary's straight face she didn't seem a changed girl. It was my best ever kiss.

It was clearly her thirty-seventh best kiss. She looked at me, wiping herself down with a scowl, and seemed to notice the talcum powder in my hair and the wild infatuation in my eyes for the first time.

Carried away with confidence, another first in my life, I asked straight out if we could lie on the ground in front of the bench. I don't know what came over me. Well, I do actually, the kiss came over me, like a dark cloud of lust and desire clouding all reason, like a spell that made me see into the future and know, really know, that one day I would actually have sex, so why not now.

I really like your . . .

I didn't know for present sure what I would do once I'd got her on the floor, although there was something inside me that seemed once to have known, or that seemed that eventually it would know. I didn't know what to do, although the lick of her lips had made the lure of her legs even more irresistible, and I very vaguely felt that this girl who in my own disobedient private masturbatory cosmos, or chaos, had been so distinctly yielding, would let me put my hand up her skirt. Because I really liked her legs.

I was on my own.

She said something along the unyielding lines of, Ugh, what on earth do we want to lie on the ground for? and she looked at the ground as if it was covered in dog shit, which come to think of it it was. But I had just kissed an angel and felt the future and to me the ground looked like an inviting fluffy white cloud.

I thought, What for? What for? Why do we want to lie on the ground?

For urgent relief.

For rhymes and reasons shooting up the towers and whistling along the tunnels of innate unruly biological imperativeness way beyond my or anyone's immediate control.

Oh, come on, Hilary, I sort of begged, shouted, cried, panicked, quickly losing all the cool that a few seconds of kissing had graced me with. Cool, I would eventually realise, is the ability to draw on a lifetime of experiences from the past and the future and compress them into the present moment so that you can be still and elegant or move through the time around you with transcendent fluency. Cool is quick thinking in slow motion. Cool is slowing the planet down. I'd glimpsed the epiphanic glories of cool as I kissed the lips of time, today represented by a thirteen-year-old from Arlington Drive,

Woodsmoor, Stockport, but as soon as the kiss was over, I reverted to my standard clumsiness. I was on my own. The planet speeded up. I had trouble maintaining my position on it as it hurtled through space.

I really love your . . .

I'm not a skinhead . . .

The look on Hilary's face was savage. Without speaking, keeping those essential lips shut tight, the look on her face was saying, or sneering, A kiss is just a kiss. It was saying, You creep. It was saying, You should be put to sleep. It was saying, Wash your mouth out with soap. It was saying, Wash your hair. And clean your teeth. And fuck off. Her face was saying a lot of things, it had the features to do that. It was saying a lot of things very quickly, and yet very slowly, because time had stood still, even as the planet accelerated. The discrepancy between the frozen time and the speeding planet added to the way Hilary was reviewing our kiss with such evident horror was making me feel sick. So I was sick and dizzy and clumsy in the moment it took to reach the moment after I had asked Hilary to lie on the ground, and in this moment existence, here represented by the Chorus of Pain, was now performing in my spinning head a full production song-and-trance version of that old adolescent classic, 'Embarrassment':

First verse: *What is marvellous*
               Is that each day
               Brings a new reason
               For the earth to swallow you up
               And for you to disappear

Chorus: *Stay flat on your back*
               And moan
               Shame!
               Remorse!
               Indignity!
               You will always be alone . . .

In this particular version of 'Embarrassment', as the Chorus of Pain left the stage, they whispered a little refrain, in the key of taunt:

               The angel only kissed you for a bet
               One of her skinheads is hiding
               in a nearby bush

Watching
Sniggering
He owes her a pound.

This version was a big hit in hell.

As the Chorus of Pain floated back to their dressing room at the back of my mind to change costumes for their next appearance – coming soon – Hilary said, suddenly all prim and proper, that she didn't think lying on the ground was a very good idea. A few minutes before she seemed about to eat me alive, to lip me apart. Now, the lips had lost their rudeness, their Jagger danger, her eyes had lost their appetite, and she didn't fancy me any more. If she ever had. She had gone from being body-hot to being as cold as only a thirteen-year-old girl can be when she just doesn't want to be on the same planet as you. I wasn't mysterious any more. I was a freak. Her make-up now seemed very subtle and skilfully applied, and her skirt coyly brushed past her knees, and her virgin body was illuminated with angelic innocence.

I was the animal.

She got up and left, taking her dream legs and my first kiss with her. I wonder what she did with it.

I was alone with my bike. I didn't feel like kissing it.

It was red and blue and it had five gears, but I never worked out how to use them properly. The trouble I had with the gears is one reason why, over a quarter of a century later, I still can't drive. I never kissed a girl in the back seat of my car.

I got the bike for my fourteenth birthday. I had wanted a Raleigh Chopper, the fashionable bike of the time, but my father had ruled that I was too old for such a gimmick. Instead he bought me a second-hand bicycle with drop handlebars and two-tone tyres.

I started to ride my bike a lot in the daze after I had kissed Hilary.

A few years later I saw a photograph of Hilary in the local newspaper. She had got married. She can't have been more than seventeen. Her new husband, who was about nineteen, wore a hungry look all of his own. He had a full, neat, footballer's curly head of hair, but I guess that he had been one of her rock-hard skinheads. Perhaps he was the thirty-eighth boy she had ever kissed, a rebound from the revolting adventure she'd had with me. He didn't look like he had a Chorus of Pain in his head. Hilary was wearing wedding-white, she was covered in netting and lace and satin, but she didn't look like an Angel. That was probably because she was now an O'Shaughnessy. I'm glad the first girl I ever kissed wasn't an O'Shaughnessy.

I never kissed anyone again until I was seventeen, not for real, not outside my fantasies, which doomed me as much as they liberated me. My fantasies fuelled my frustrations, which fuelled my fantasies, which fuelled my frustrations, which fuelled my frustrations, which fuelled my fantasies, until you get the picture, and all this effing about gave the Chorus of Pain a few epic numbers to compose and perform, plus a few extravagant costumes to wear. 'I'm the Ghost of Sadness', 'A Ship Is Sailing out of My Brain and Cutting the World in Two', 'Your Mind Doesn't Upset You the Way My Mind Upsets Me' – these were all big Pain hits inside my head in Woodsmoor, 1971.

After the angel turned devil-woman on me, with evil on her mind in the shape of a pink penis painted onto the nail of her middle finger, I decided that kissing was dangerous. It hurt. And I never asked anyone again to lie on the ground so that I could put my hand up their skirt. Not until I was, oh, at least thirty-six. Asking someone to lie on the ground so that you could put your hand up their skirt was very dangerous indeed, but I timed it better the second time.

One thing you learn as you grow up is timing, for better or worse.

I wonder where and when my father first kissed a girl. I would guess for the sake of this aside, Cliftonville, Margate, 1949. This leads me to wonder when he last kissed a girl, or a woman. What was his last proper kiss, not a peck on the cheek, like before he died? Did the way two tongues twisted inside time inside mouths tell him something about his future, or lack of it? Did he pay much attention to the way two sets of lips found ways, as old as time and as new as now, to touch? Was he aware that this was his last kiss, and did he compare it with his first? Did he think that his first kiss made him think that life was just beginning, and his last kiss made him think it was all over? Because it was so different from the first. Was he aware during his first kiss that sometime somewhere there would be a last kiss? Did he feel the last kiss even as he was inside the first kiss?

Was it his wife he kissed last? My mother, who I knew more than him.

As I kissed Hilary locked in 1971 I think I felt far away amidst the smacked high of the moment that this was something that led to an end, that every time you do something for the first time means you are setting up a chain of events that will have an end. Doing something for the first time means that you will do that thing for the last time. As soon as you have breathed your first breath, something inside you knows that eventually, before you can really gather your thoughts, there will be a last breath. This thought, tiny and massive as the kiss started and finished within its own unique life span, made me snatch at the moment too much, rush into it so that really I was only rushing out of it. And then it was over. The end of the kiss.

Back at the house at Arlington Drive, Woodsmoor, my father had no idea that I was rushing through a kiss with Hilary Angel, but I think he had a sort of idea that, what with one thing and another, he didn't have long to live.

You kiss life hello and then you kiss it goodbye. You start to breathe and then you stop.

Every life is the story of a collapse. If biographies are so fascinating, it is because the heroes, and the cowards quite as much, strive to innovate in the art of the debacle.

Most of the big and little things that I did and said and felt and thought for the very first time were done and said and felt and thought, at an educated guess, before and during my teens when I lived in Stockport, a typically fourth-division sad town sunk six miles to the south of Manchester, to the north of the Derbyshire Moors, on the dud edges of rich Cheshire. It had some pretty parts, some interesting history, but I remember it as being a place trying to catch up with the modern world wobbling on the border between nowhere and somewhere.

The River Mersey flowed right through its middle, for some reason, thirty miles before it reached Liverpool, the city you think of as its home. I never considered going to look for the source of the Mersey, although it can't be that much outside Stockport. I don't recall ever actually seeing the river, but I knew it was there, some-where, coming into town, under the town, going out of town. Someone I knew once fell into it when he was drunk, but he beat the river and lived to tell the funny tale. The centre of Stockport, the activity centre of my life for most of my drifting teens, is named after the river. Mersey Square is the home of the Mersey Shopping Centre, which, unless I'm making it up, was the first-ever shopping centre built in Britain, an open-air mall in miniature, shaped out of dense optimism and inscrutable concrete, an experiment in social engineering and civic planning that somehow worked. The centre, marked out by a tall flat-acked modernist clock, is one of those architectural arrangements that must have looked very cute and space-age as a model, and that was probably very cute on the day it opened, and that was not so cute from the day it was used. Thirty-five years after it opened, it's still standing. It used to look like a lump that had landed from the future. It now looks like a lump that has landed from the past. Sometime around 1971 I suppose it was as contemporary as anything.

I started thinking about Stockport and the shopping centre, the station and the chalky, pigeon-shitty bluster of the Town Hall, the bricks and the despair, the old roads and the new orange and white buses bussed in from the same flattened future as the shopping centre, as I was finishing my first near-enough novel. The book was called at various times *Various, Times, Exactly*, 1971, *A Wondering We Will Go*, *Fucking Nerve*, *Shit, Everybody Knows Someone Who Is Dead*, *The Man Who Killed Himself*, and *A Book with Nine Titles Not Including This One*. It started out with the lines, 'I'm on my way, on my endless way. I've started out on my endless way, my endless way will convince me of its endlessness.' In many ways, some of them quite fascinating, it went downhill from there. Just like Stockport, in fact, which in an Escheristic sense was all down-hill. Wherever you walked you seemed to be going downhill. Even though you must occasionally have been going uphill so that you could turn round and come downhill, all of the time you were trav-elling downhill. Down into the bus pit of Mersey Square, down into the compound of the Mersey Shopping Centre, down into the dusted and ashed hollow ache at the very bottom of the world.

I loved and hated Stockport like it was a member of the family.

*

Stockport was where it all began for me, it was where it was at, as far as I knew to be concerned, and there was plenty of Stockport in the book. In one sense the book was about people and their bags. In another sense it was about someone, maybe me, walking for two hours through wet countryside with no particular destination in mind. And then it was about Stockport and the way its greyness tried to turn the green of the surrounding hills into something as miserable and expressionless as its grey sodden self, the way Stockport believed in concrete and bus stops, the way that at the bottom of everything was the Mersey Shopping Centre, with its conspicuous tiling and its cemented functionalism. Stockport was a major character in my always nearly finished book, and if there was a murder in the book, and there sort of was, then I'm not giving anything away, except the end, to say that Stockport did it. A lump of concrete was the murder weapon.

I began wondering more and more as I nearly finished this numbhumming murder mystery what made up the writer of this book, who was also a central character, and who, just like me, once lived up to his neck in sensitivity, who once lived up to his past in Stockport, and who suffered a kind of monthly cycle where the 'period' was, every four weeks, feeling the tranquillising, descending, cursed sensation that I was going to vanish for ever into thin grey Stockport 1971 air. What helped produce and reproduce this splitting, fretting, remote, extremely delicate boy creature constantly infatuated by ideas, ideals and idols? What influenced this sabotaged man mind of mine, what forces of nature and culture and environment had created this character, real and unreal, who spent his days and nights on the life edge of introspection, and who ended up writing sentences that finished like this (there's one exactly the same as this one on page 129 of my not-a-novel)? How had it happened that this dispossessed, defeated 1971 Stockport teenager had come to be writing in such a free uneasy way a not-real novel concerned with such things as the superiority of music over life and death, the melancholy of impotence, modesty, solitude, changes of heart, handbags, the distance between the self and the self, the tolerance of ambiguities, and the history of the knowing world from 1957 to whatever the present is from your present point of view? And what had inspired a being to ask such questions?

What am I like?

131

The answer to this question, and many of the others, lies in the ancient stone, soft soil and hard soul of Stockport, may even be Stockport itself. Stockport – the colour of nausea, standing there with a bloody piece of concrete, guilty as pock-marked skin, as stagnant as a dead stag, all bottom, unwashable, home shit home. Stockport – motto: Is suicide a solution?

Once I was deep inside the book, the book where Stockport calmly shot itself through the heart using a pillow to muffle the sound and a ruler in order that it would not miss its heart, I began to understand that before I finished, before the last sentence, the possible mirror image of the first sentence, I was obliged to make a visit back to Stockport. There were some details I needed to check. When you write about a town killing itself, with a gun, bang, you have to be sure you've got the facts right, you have to be certain it really was a suicide, and not a murder in disguise. You have to look at the dead body, and examine it for tell-tale signs.

Stockport. The town that shut on a Wednesday afternoon, but who could tell the difference? The town run down by shadows of men who never appeared in daylight. The town at the bottom of the world. As ponderous as a hippopotamus. The town that had the wrinkled buckled shape of something that had been sat on by a giant mythical hippopotamus. The town scarred by its own shopping-centre face-lift. The town I couldn't wait to escape from, the town where I didn't want to die.

I left Stockport a few months after my father died. I think I fled on his behalf.

I lived in Stockport because my father and mother lived there. I'm not sure how they found it, and there was something about my father's relationship with the town that suggested he had no choice about landing there. Life had conspired to place him in this position. He was abandoned there by a very indifferent fate, and he put up a little resistance, and then he didn't.

Despite the number of years he lived there, from the mid-60s to the late 70s, he always seemed an outsider, someone looking for the way out. He moved his family three times, but never got out, always moving inside the small grit and grind of Stockport. The town must have been something of a maze to him. A maze always heading downhill. He finally found an amazing way to escape Stockport. He died. It was the only way he could find the exit. He used his own dead body to smuggle himself out of the place that always puzzled him, because it always seemed to lead back to itself. He spent his final years in Stockport and then I suppose he found a better place.

As a child creeping and crawling into my insect teens the time we spent there, thirteen or fourteen or so years, seemed a lot longer. A lot longer. But it never quite seemed a prison sentence. But I think for my father, who knew all about prison sentences, it became one. A life sentence. Which can become a death sentence.

It could have been anywhere, but it happened to be Stockport, that I started to think too much about, you know, what the fuck's going on, although I don't know whether I phrased it like that. I'm not sure when I first started to use the word 'fuck'. It would have been in Stockport, but I can't recall the first time I ever said the word out loud. I wonder if I felt that it was a big deal. Felt the exciting power of the word. Spat it out like an incantation that might change, for better or worse, the circumstances of my life. I seem to have known the word since before I was born. The word is as familiar to me as my skin in a way that say the word 'conclusion' isn't. I could easily imagine 'fuck' being the first word I ever spoke. The first real word. The rest were just words I used to pass the time, to convince my parents that I was normal, growing up as you'd expect a pale young boy who smiled a bit who found himself in Stockport, near Manchester, in the 1960s. I suppose I said 'fuck' to myself, and then one day I said it aloud, and even though I didn't know it this would have been as much a breakthrough, an adjustment in individual sensibility, as my first kiss. 'Fuck,' you get to say in your life, and then you get to say, 'fuck the world'. You get to say anything you want, until it's made clear you can't say anything you want. Once I'd said my fuck, I'd condemned myself. Someday, somewhere, I would say it for the very last time, and then I would die. What the fuck's going on?

I saw, in Stockport 1969/70/71/72, that life was not just life, complete and self-explaining with proper rules and smooth order, but a purposeless matter of life and death, cloaked in chaos, a hugely contagious absence. Stockport takes the responsibility for introducing me to the feeling that life was something to lose yourself in, and the town must have accepted the responsibility for introducing this feeling to lots of other people as well, because all this responsibility seemed to hang grey and low over the town like a storm about to break.

I left Stockport in the late 70s. It's still to leave me. Over the years, as I lived well away from it, in body and spirit, I have as part of some healing process or as some darkly enjoyed self-punishment, turned Stockport and my teen time there into a bad parody of adolescent hardship. I've rubbed out details of real life and everyday straightness, leaving just a tangled trails of trials, confusions, humiliations, inadequacies, disappointments, regrets, despairs, and think of myself, rightly or wrongly, as an emotionally pulverised boy whose favourite state was solitude, and whose state of mind was a state.

I think that's what I was like, although looking back I only see a ghost of myself, in a family of ghosts, ghosting through their present, vivid to themselves, somewhere other to everyone else. I think of myself as being one of life's little sufferers. An enthusiast of stupor. Coming alive in my fantasies of what could be if I wasn't so much me. Maybe everybody feels like this, more or less, in their teens, and I was quite ordinary, or maybe I felt like this because I was an accident of birth surviving and fidgeting through this place called Stockport, which was good for nothing, and I was having trouble with the truth, and I was quite unordinary.

One day, before I finished my book about the dead-end streets that tripped Stockport up on its way to the end of time, I went back to see and smell Stockport, just for the day, just to see how guilty the town looked, or how innocent. Just to see how cowed the place was by the responsibility it had for all those people who had to spend their lives circling its impassive 1960s/1970s/1980s/1990s shopping centre.

I left Stockport station and naturally walked down the hill towards Mersey Square. There were plenty of people walking around, catching buses, pouring into the shopping centre, just as they did in my days, twenty years before. They all seemed to be taking it for granted that they lived in Stockport. Stockport seemed to be taking it for granted that all these people were where they were. The

134

general atmosphere was one of mundane plausibility. People were raising their children and burying their dead.

I noticed that Stockport had passively crept into its future and seemed very able at passing the time of day. New motorway bypasses had appeared, the kind of highways that swept around the town in and out of Manchester and over the hills and far away. The kind of roads where rich famous Manchester United footballers would be stopped for speeding.

The shops and the cars and the clothes that people wore and the clouds in the sky seemed to connect the town with the rest of Britain and indeed the civilised world. Inches and yards were well on their way to turning into centimetres and metres. This seemed moderately surprising. Everything seemed normal, and although I tried my best to excavate something sinister out of the walls, out of the concrete, out of the streets, I couldn't really manage it. The town seemed too boring to be evil.

Everyone seemed to be getting on with their lives and Stockport seemed to let them, within reason. Everyone seemed to accept that this was where they were. And so did Stockport. The overriding sense of the place was that this is where it was, it had been here for centuries, it was comfortable where it was, and nothing was going to change that.

I decided that when I lived here I must have been disconcerted by the solid old straightness of the place. Straightness that I saw as strangeness.

Buses left the square and buses arrived. People waited for buses and people got off buses. It was like this when I lived here. People lived in Stockport and most of them never really thought about it. Not like me.

Not like my father.

My parents, wriggling inside the sticky web of Stockport, apparently feeling no inclination to find any exit, or just stuck fast, had moved from Woodsmoor – Angeltown – to another neat and staid Stockport village, Offerton. Going back after twenty years, as a ghost writer, I am touched by how green and pleasant these parts of town are. These parts of town must have escaped being crushed by the bottom of the mythical hippo when it crashed down on the town.

The house where we lived in Woodsmoor, number 4 Arlington Drive, is a polite, compact semi-detached on the outskirts of miles of countryside. The area hums with suburban well-being. You would have to be pretty miserable in the head to consider that this was a miserable place to live. In my memory I had passed dark thieving shadows over this house, as if its roof was grazed by a low dense cloud of geographical responsibility, as if the house was about to be sat on by a monstrous hippo. In fact, the area looks as if it has been wrapped in cotton wool for decades, but then it is sunny the day I visit.

I wander round the corner to the place, near enough, where I tasted my first kiss, and what I remember as a fairly featureless wasteland surrounded by squat ugly buildings is actually a sweeping mixture of meadow and heath called Flowery Fields, wild and intensely green, with large trees generously shielding the surrounding houses. I had thought of it as scrappy and half-hearted, an inner-city scrub of grey-green, but the fresh open countryside seems to spill into Woodsmoor. I remember it as a small and banal little place, and feel almost cheated by the pleasantness of the area. It was as if someone had programmed my memory but had missed out lots of vital information. Or perhaps my memory was ruptured by the fact that it was from 4 Arlington Drive that my father first disappeared. My mind had rationalised the place as grim, or else why had my father run away? Perhaps, though, it was the very mocking niceness of the place, the illusion of peace that it created inside the collapsed Stockport, that eventually split my father's head in two. I look at the house where we lived for a few years, and imagine that my parents are still living there. The houses round there certainly look as if people stay in them for twenty-five years and more, settle down into a kind of domestic bliss. There are people round there, and you can sense it, that make this place more than their home. They make it their life, and then, ultimately, their death. Maybe this is what my father was trying to flee – the sense that the future was homing in on you and trying to keep you in your place, one place, a little house in a nice area where you would stay for all of your life, looking at the same view, the same walls, the same people. As attractive as it seemed, for someone who knew the inside of a prison, who had seen what staying in one place for twenty-five years does to a man, even the trees and the gardens and the surrounding countryside didn't make up for this kind of doomed permanence.

I look at number 4 Arlington Drive, and the little window on the right above the front door. This was the window to my small bedroom, a room where I played the first record I ever bought, 'Ride a White Swan' by T. Rex, a song that was to me the equivalent of the wardrobe in *The Lion, the Witch and the Wardrobe*. I played this magical seven-inch single on a Phillips stereo sound system that my father had bought me at the Co-op in the Mersey Shopping Centre. It cost about £30. It was the greatest thing he ever bought me. Maybe that was my wardrobe really, and Marc Bolan, who sang 'Ride a White Swan' as if only to me, was my Lion, my Aslan.

I stop looking at number 4, and stop vaguely wishing that my parents were still there, growing old, comfortably, softly, sadly, happily, with comparative peace of mind, proud of their house, its contents, its garden, pleased that their children view it as a kind of sanctuary where they may escape for a while the pressures of their own life. I let slip the dreamy feeling that this is where I go when I want to come home. I stop thinking that this is the house where my father lives, and that it is some kind of castle of domestic ease, the place I will bring my children to see their grandparents clearly fixed in time and space, the place where my parents will die having made it so much their own, having improved it and maintained it and loved it. For my father, after a while, a place became too much his own. He recognised himself in the hall, in the kitchen, on the stairs, and he chased himself away, too restless to commit to what takes a kind of courage. Stillness. Acceptance. He resigned himself to keep moving. He never resigned himself to settling back and letting himself be at one with where he was, wherever it was. He kept moving until he died.

Number 4 Arlington Drive, Woodsmoor, Stockport, Cheshire, 1968–71 never became our family skin. It was just another place my father passed through as he searched for a way out from Stockport, or the world, or himself. Another place the rest of us passed through with him, childishly taking it for granted that this is where we lived for ever, until we didn't any more. Other people have taken over this home, passed through, believed that it is everything, loved and lost and perhaps sensed a troubled past that was nothing to do with them.

The house in Offerton, two or three miles across the southern reaches of Stockport, closer to the Pennines, also surprises me. 14 Dovedale Road is a quaint mock-chalet semi-detached nestled in a settlement of similar houses arranged around a patch of cheerful grass. I could see why a teenager beginning to exercise his muscles of alienation and discover the arts of self-affliction might find such cosiness pretty irritating, but not why he might plant in his memory the idea that the house was damned and claustrophobic. But, then, appearances can be deceptive. As a teenager, blank and lanky, I couldn't have cared less that we lived in a nice house, with nice neighbours, in a nice area, and so I had no inclination to remember it as a nice house. I remember it as a dingy place, with a rough little garden dotted with a sad little swing, where pet rabbits met horrible long lingering deaths, where the atmosphere was edgy with anticipation over whether my father would disappear for a few days with no warning whatsoever.

I stand outside and look at the house where I first shaved. It was here that my dad and I had our one nearly intimate conversation. I plucked up the courage over a few days to ask him not about sex, but how high on my cheek I should shave. Was there a place to stop? We enjoyed a couple of minutes of man talk and he explained to me what he did. I felt it was something of a breakthrough to be talking with my father like this, but we never really built on the conversation. Other things got in the way, things that were ultimately more a matter of life and death than how you shaved.

14 Dovedale Road, which does look like it sounds, is another house where I could imagine my mother and father still living, heading towards well-earned retirement, known around the neighbourhood as a decent, loving couple, a pair you can rely on. You could definitely imagine people moving into these houses and staying there for ever, wrapping their homes around them like a protective shell, sinking into this part of Stockport with relief and discreet bravery. Working in the same job for thirty years and retiring with a pat on the back and something for the house, the house you'd lived in since the 1970s. Such a thought must have put my father in a rage, scared him to death, worried him something rotten, made him race out of the door for a few days of escape and, perhaps, a blissful change of identity. As soon as my father moved into such a house, pleased with himself that he could afford such a place, home his family, he would

look around, and see his future all mapped out. Mapped out in the living room, in the bedroom, in the garden. This was it. It was all over. Thirty years from now I'll be retired, still here, Stockport through and through, as dead in life as you are when you're dead in death. I take a last look at 14 Dovedale Road, Offerton, Stockport, Cheshire, 1971–75, and see a future for my father that could never have been. I see the static gloom of responsibility.

I also see the place where I kissed a girl for the second time. I see the place where I first seriously started to think about death. I see the place where I wanted to kill myself. I remember this peaceful-looking house with its wooden frontage and gay porch and its glad little front garden with its mock wishing-well as the place where I started to seriously appreciate death and where, for a moment that still repeats itself, I wanted to die. As I stand in Offerton, a place I'll never visit again because it was another place, another place in Stockport, that my father was passing through, closely followed by his family, I begin to realise that it wasn't only Stockport that changed the way I lived and thought and edged into the future. There was school. My equivalent of the witch.

The way things turned out I wanted to die because of the school I went to.

I suffered so intensely, what with one thing and another, because of the school I went to, which, wouldn't you just know it, happened to be in Stockport.

The sheer ill luck of existence. I noticed that ill luck between the ages of thirteen and fourteen. I may have noticed it before then, between the ages of twelve and thirteen, or between the ages of nothing and twelve. I was just noticing it again between the ages of thirteen and fourteen, with much more clarity, with much more feeling, with a real sense that I could actually do something about it. As I noticed it when I was living in Offerton, Stockport, faced with the prospect of yet another Monday at school, the Chorus of Pain, dressed all in black and blue with little pointed hats and long false noses, sang me a song. They sang, cheerfully:

> *Panic*
> *Panic*

139

Panic in the face of everything
Of presence
Of the void
Panic
Oh, and you have to go to school.

The song was called 'Panic', taken from the musical *Panic*, which was a great success in Panic, the capital of Panic, which is next to nowhere.

For vast stretches of my life, for amounts of time that seemed longer than a long life, there was nothing worse than having to go to school. And for reasons that were beyond me at the time, I had to go to school. I had to go to one school in particular.

At the age of eleven, before I really began to understand that thinking could get you into trouble, when life and everything just seemed to open up around me for ever and hadn't really begun to close in, I was one of fifteen boys in the County of Cheshire to win a scholarship via the eleven-plus to Stockport Grammar School. I don't know how this happened. I must have been cleverer than I seemed to myself. I have reason to believe that sheer stupid childlike love of life carried me through this test, and it was stupid, because I really didn't want to go to Stockport Grammar School. Its reputation preceded it.

It was second or third to Manchester Grammar School in the area in terms of scholarly reputation and its steady reliability when it came to channelling pupils into Cambridge or Oxford, places which from where I was, aged eleven, seemed as remote and alien as Jupiter and Mars. This feeling has never really changed.

My father must have been ambitious for me, or seen something or other in me, along with the teachers at my primary school, because I was put in for the entrance exams to Manchester Grammar School. I don't remember much about the experience, except that my visit to the school to take the exams seemed to me a lot like what it would be to visit the House of Lords. As luck would have it, I wasn't all that clever, and I failed. The thought of going to Manchester Grammar School seemed like travelling back a couple of hundred years in time. It was a place that I would be sent to, a place where I would disappear and become somebody else. I half thought my father's eagerness to have me go there was his way of trying to get rid of me.

If I did medium well in my eleven-plus examinations I would go to Stockport School, a second-level grammar school that seemed as modern and neutral as the Mersey Shopping Centre. If I did fairly poorly, I would go to Stockport Technical College, which worried me slightly, as it seemed to be a school where you would learn to be a car mechanic and little else. I had no real idea who I was or what I wanted to do at eleven, but I knew I didn't want to be a car mechanic. I knew that I didn't want to go to a school where, as far as I could tell, you did nothing much but use drills and bang nails.

If I did really shit, and couldn't even spell my name, I would go to Reddish Vale, the local secondary modern school, which, from my point of view, influenced by my mother and father to be oddly snobby, was the equivalent of going to a Borstal. Feeling very average, very ordinary, encouraged by the school and I suppose my dad to think of myself as brighter than some, I complacently assumed that, exams done, I would be going to Stockport School, with most of my friends from school. Life would just sort of carry on as inevitably as it had always done, very slightly downhill towards an average, ordinary future.

We lived then in dingy Reddish, the first place we found in Stockport. The first place we had found in Manchester when we moved up from the Isle of Wight was Eccles, which has a cake named after it, or is named after a cake, a cake that appears to be stuffed with dead flies. It had a Goon named after it, a Goon played by Spike Milligan, the most savagely depressed of the Goons. Some areas of Manchester were used to contain a population that was spilling out of the centre of the city. Nobody spilled over into Eccles. You sort of spat into it. For all that, Eccles just wasn't Stockport enough.

Reddish was a part of Stockport that was at the bruised and scratched edges of rundown war-ruined Manchester, full of small houses made up out of a dark mournful red that I assumed gave the place its name. The lids of these houses were routine sad grey. If there is a middle of nowhere, then Reddish is just down the road from there. It was one of those places that just seemed to be fading away, and you have no idea how that can ever change, how the place will ever be rejuvenated, so you imagine that in a couple of hundred years, it will have disappeared altogether. It would leave behind nothing but ghosts, and ghost bricks, and ghost slates, and ghost shops.

We lived in a tiny two-up and two-down semi-detached house in a small street opposite the local Essoldo cinema. At the end of the street there was the local Conservative Association, which was a building of rotten grandeur that looked like it had never had a hey-day. I used to use its gateway as goal-posts. Opposite the Conservative Association was a shop that sold bicycles and a few sad toys. There was a rumour that the owner was related to Davy Jones of The Monkees, which gave the shop a thin glamour it didn't really deserve. Round the corner there was a big brickworks with a towering old brick chimney that boasted a kind of pathetic poignancy, as a local landmark of uselessness that stood guard over very little.

I think 12 Westbourne Grove was the first house that my parents owned. They must have been in their late twenties when they bought it, and in the back garden it had a huge rock-solid redbrick bomb shelter that my father eventually demolished himself, brick by brick. The concrete base always remained, and would become the penalty area in my fantasy games of back-garden football. A rusty old single bed base would be the goal.

It was in this house, on my bed in the coffin-sized box room at the front of the house, at about age nine, imagining that I was being tied down by a bunch of warrior women dancing out of some deep deep past, some long-lost future, that I masturbated for the first time.

I rubbed bits of my body fantasising for all I was worth, stretching the limits of my mental vocabulary, rubbed and rubbed until my arm and then my leg and then my tummy felt all warm and fuzzy. And then I rubbed my penis, looking to make that as warm and fuzzy as my leg and arm. I thought to myself not in words but through instinct that it must be nice to have pins and needles in my penis. But as I rubbed my penis I felt something different. A burning sensation near my belly. A white flame of almost pain dissolved into itself inside my groin. It brought tears to my eyes. It smeared my mind with an intensity that kept me very quiet. It plummeted me whirling through a feeling of melted distance. It was unbearably bearable. It was like I had a funny bone in my penis. I'd scooped the world! I'd found out something for myself. I wonder if anyone else knows about this? I was a lucky prince in an enchanted wood summoning summer with a whistle and banishing winter with a nod. It made me shiver and screw up my eyes. It made me laugh out loud to myself. I rubbed myself into a state of fleshed and warped happiness. I instantly gave myself something of a reputation. All my head was jellyfish. I wheeled into oblivion and spun straight out again. I scattered some semen. I stretched my legs. Rimbaud's verse whistled past my head. Flags proudly flew embroidered with my initials. I sped through a tremendous contraction of debauchery. My innocence was abstractly devastated. Something in me didn't understand but knew only too well that this way the madness of creation lies. I was very curious about what had happened and I did it again as soon as I could. I was not yet aware of the habit this could become. It never occurred to me that now there was a first time, there would, one day, be a last time. In the dark in the black cocoon of the room I had realised the essential extent of pleasure, and I still realise it, and will, to a point, until the last time I masturbate.

I did it again as soon as I could.
You've got lovely . . .
I handed it to myself.
I was very pleased with myself.
I was wonderful.
Wonderful!
I've handed the feeling on down the years.
I am wonderful.

Once upon a time, feeling wonderful, I sat down to write my autobiography. I named it *Masturbation* and it began:
I wasn't physically born in Reddish, Stockport. Mentally, approximately, I was. Reddish was a standard hemmed-in working-class district full of red little boxes, and later in my life I always tended to describe myself as coming from that particular background rather than the blander lower-middle-class heights we as a family climbed towards later on. Defining myself as specifically working class, Stockport grey, rather than something above working but lower than middle, this added to my sense of suffering, embellished the feeling that I had struggled against the odds – and yet all I had done was escape Stockport, something you can do quite easily by moving, or dying, which are sometimes the same thing.
Feeling working class, feeling part of some union of people at the bottom of the pile, gave me some kind of identity, some

protection, when I unexpectedly and to my bitter frustration earned a place at Stockport Grammar School. I knew of nobody for miles around who went to such a school, a school in Stockport that seemed on the other side of the world. Only the rich, the privileged or the strangely, sadly gifted went to such an ancient, bricked-up place. I didn't feel gifted. Strange, yes. Sad, certainly. But not gifted. If I had been so gifted I would have somehow organised it that I avoided qualifying for a scholarship to a school that seemed from where I breathed so strict, so serious, so stiff, so stuffy. And so full of boys.

I cried when I heard the news that I had won a free place at the grammar school. It felt like a real failure in my life. To my parents it was an absolute triumph. My mother was ecstatic when she received the letter informing us of my achievement, and you didn't often see my father as visibly delighted with something. I felt the walls of life, a boundary I never knew existed before, scrape in closer to me. I wanted to go into hiding. I didn't feel so wonderful. Surely it was an error? Perhaps I would confess to cheating . . . My parents' enthusiasm squashed my will to fight back. To make an appeal against this alleged success seem completely ridiculous. Why couldn't I have come sixteenth?

I vainly hoped that my parents in a moment of madness might turn down my place so that I could join all my primary-school friends who had, as nature intended, won places at the shiny new Stockport School. They were bright, but not too bright, or not too whatever it was that plunged you into the Gothic hell of Stockport Grammar School, and in my books that was plenty bright enough.

All through the long summer holidays that needed to be a thousand years longer, chewed up by misery, the intimidating defects of Stockport Grammar School weighed against my mind. Things that had previously only been rumours turned into sick truths as I found out more and more about the dreadful new school. It felt as if I was about to join the army.

The school didn't play football, the love of my life, because that was a culturally and socially inferior sport. It was common, and probably too beautiful. It played Rugby Union, the sport of mental and physical strength, the gentleman's game, which built character and appetite. It wasn't only the 'ug' in rugby that made me think of it as a hard, nasty, ugly sport. It wasn't sport. It was fighting. I didn't like fighting. The alternative winter sport was lacrosse, which I knew nothing about, but which I'd heard involved a long wooden stick that you used to try and chop your opponent's arm off. Both sports seemed based on bruises. For the rest of my schooldays sport was going to consist of black eyes and cracked ribs.

There was school on Saturday morning, just to remind you at the weekend how disciplined you needed to be, how organised, how committed to the school. The weekend was no escape. The school chased you into the weekend.

School rules demanded that you wore shorts in the first form. Just at that liberating moment when you thought you were going to be allowed to grow up and be allowed to wear long trousers, the damned school dragged you back by the scruff of the neck and insisted that you remain junior and inferior and freezing for a whole year more.

To finish off the horror, there was the school uniform. Black and yellow, like something out of those Billy Bunter books I'd read, about a school that seemed to belong in the last century. Tie, blazer, V-necked sweater, a whole corset of humiliation, topped off with an item that was surely as dated as a penny-farthing bicycle. A cap. A fucking cap. Round where I lived wearing a cap was akin to wearing a skirt. But then in my shorts it would look like I was wearing a skirt. Going to school I would look like a girl, bare-legged and shamefully behatted, and then at school I would be required to beat the shit out of other boys, or more likely have the shit beaten out of me, all for the sake of some kind of sporting integrity. As far as I could tell there were no consolations for any of this. And there were no girls.

A few weeks before school began, my mother and I went to the school to buy me my uniform. The school was large and forbidding, the oldest thing I'd ever seen. It was like the prison my dad had worked at on the Isle of Wight. It felt like a place where the best thing to do for your sanity was surrender. Close your mind and surrender.

The funny thing is, it was even worse than I could ever imagine.

During the summer holidays, racing past like someone had greased them, I thought long and hard about this school, for which I could see absolutely no justification. As I thought, I began to glimpse some sort of inner otherness which I'd not paid too much attention to before, something weakly specific to myself that flickered at the back of the beyond of me. It was my self, and I was about to become very conscious of it.

The first day of school arrived. There was just me and my self to face it. I had tried very hard to plan for this first day, and had developed a scheme to get me to school smoothly and painlessly. We lived a few miles away from the school, and the journey generally meant catching two buses. One from north Reddish down into Mersey Square, the number 17 which came every ten minutes, and then one out of the square up the hill towards Hazel Grove. The whole journey took about forty-five minutes. There was one less regular bus, the 17x, that did the journey in one go, with no need to change. It stopped at the top of the road by the Conservative Association at exactly 7.55, and then it would take about half an hour to drop me right outside the school. I never stopped to wonder why.

I left the house encased in apprehension, feeling like a Dickens of a character all trussed up in my stiff new uniform. Slate-grey mid-thigh flannel shorts, lad-red bony knees, knee-length woollen socks, shiny black shoes biting into my heel, and my pert little fop cap which I wore even in the gloomy early-morning wilds of north Reddish with catatonic obedience. Strangely and sadly gifted, with a waft of parental pride from behind me, I marched bravely towards the bus stop to catch the 17x, the bus that would deliver me unto misery in one fell swoop. My black and yellow cap, so new it glowed in the dark, felt like a crown of daffodils. A couple of paper-boys riding past gave me a wolf whistle. Ha.

What I presumed was the 17x arrived and I clambered on board. It was oddly empty. By rights this bus on its special route should have been packed. I didn't really notice, I was miles away, wondering what on earth was in store for me, clutching my brand-new shiny executive fake-leather briefcase with its shiny fake-brass buckle, feeling strangled by my idiotic black and yellow school tie, sleepily furious that I was about to spend five years of my precious life at a school that was founded in 1487.

Inside my brand new shiny executive fake-leather briefcase with its shiny fake-brass buckle: a pencil case bought from WH Smith in the Mersey Shopping Centre for six shillings and elevenpence.

Inside my pencil case bought from WH Smith in the Mersey

146

Shopping Centre for six shillings and elevenpence: a cheap fountain pen, a pencil, a compass, a set square, a rubber.

At Mersey Square I stayed on board the bus, even though the other two passengers got off and no one else got on. I wasn't really thinking. I was school-sick, fraught with first-day nerves, dry in the mouth at the injustice of it all. It was me all alone at the back of the top deck of this ghostly 17x which was carrying me to my doom, up against the rest of the world.

The bus started up again, but instead of taking a left out of Mersey Square and twisting round to head up the hill past the Town Hall towards the grammar school, it turned right, and took the road alongside the shopping centre, heading back towards Reddish. As it hit me full in my morning-dulled mind what had happened – I had caught the wrong bloody bus – I charged down the stairs. The bus picked up speed and travelled further and further in the wrong direction. A sleepy bus conductor registered bored surprise that there was anybody still on the bus. As the bus aggressively sailed past the first stop outside the square, he said, This bus is out of service, it's going back to the garage. I pleaded with him to stop the bus. He rang the bell a few times and the bus came to something like an emergency stop. It felt like an emergency to me. I was going the wrong way and running out of time. Getting to the school I didn't even want to go to suddenly seemed like a real race against time. I was getting further and further away from the school I didn't want to go to, which deep down I may have willed to happen, and now I had to force myself to go back in the right direction. For a split second I thought about giving it all up and running away. But, no doubt because I was in the uniform, the pull of the school was too much for me to match. I started to run the half-mile back to the square, puffing along deserted back streets at the side of the shopping centre, tearfully clutching my brand-new briefcase with its pompous corner protectors. I imagined what would happen if I was late – on my first day at such a ruled and regulated school as Stockport Grammar. They would probably permanently seal the cap to my head, make me write a thousand lines in blood, and force me to drive a number 17x bus as a career when I left school.

As I sprinted back to the relative civilisation of Mersey Square, where I could catch the right bus, I felt hopelessly lost, even though I knew where I was. I was trapped between two bus stops running through thick syrup as if I was in a dream, running backwards, the other way from where I needed to be. As I ran, the real 17x, the one I thought I'd been on – clearly I had been on a phantom – sailed past me with smooth and painless ease. It was full, like I always knew it would be. Sitting downstairs, four seats from the front, was the only other boy from my primary school that had won a scholarship to Stockport Grammar.

Duncan Ellams, the registered school swot, had, naturally, caught the right bus. He noticed me running like a maniac alongside the bus, as I desperately tried to keep up with it so that I might catch it in the square, and he flicked me a cool smug smile. He looked at me like he expected nothing more or less of me than that I should be running six miles to school on the very first day. I tried to look casual, as if I was completely in control of my actions however unlikely they looked, as if I knew exactly what I was doing, and sent him back a comradely wave with all the nonchalance I could muster, as if to say, Funny old thing, this first day at a new school business. The bus accelerated away from me, taking the healthy and efficient Duncan Ellams with it. I stopped to catch my breath, and I wept silently to myself for humanity. I took deep painful breaths, wiped the sweat out from beneath my hard new shirt collar, slightly loosened my absurd school tie, and stared miserably at the back of the disappearing 17x. All this and I still had to get to school. All this and I still had five years of school ahead of me. All this and I was still alive.

As I limped towards Mersey Square, stranded somewhere between simple resignation and a fearful survivalist's determination not to get into trouble, I heard the very first murmurs and chantings of a noise I was to get very used to during my teens. It was the Chorus of Pain, sneaking into my head wearing monstrous yellow and black caps and barbed-wire shorts and camel-hair shirts with clip-on ties made out of fake leather and fake brass. I was in quiet delirium and they were singing me a song, unlike anything I had ever known before. It was called 'An Existence Constantly Transfigured by Failure (to Look Forward To)', and the first line went 'To live is to lose ground (ooh, ooh, ooh).'

Somehow I found the strength to get to school on time.

I never again attempted to catch the 17x to school. I got one bus down into Mersey Square and I got one bus out of the square up the hill to school.

I can't remember what happened that first day at school. I must have survived it in a state of delayed shock: shock from getting into the school, shock from the journey that morning, shock from hearing the Chorus of Pain serenade me with such jolly sarcasm. The next thing I remember is the journey home, where the adventure continued.

I remember catching the 17 from Mersey Square to north Reddish, feeling more and more stupid in my uniform the further I travelled away from the place where it might make relative sense. On this bus I found that there was one other pupil who lived in Reddish apart from the perfect Duncan amongst the 450 who went to the grammar school. He was a few years older than me, a fourth-former probably, and when you're eleven a fifteen-year-old seems so much stronger and bigger. This boy, who looked to me like a grinning rat, was obviously after four years deeply embittered by his tragic years at the school, years which lay ahead of me like great shadows of doom.

We sat next to each other and he acted all friendly until the bus reached my stop in north Reddish outside the Essoldo. I was sitting on the inside of the seat, next to the window, and while he grinned rattishly and his eyes flashed with wicked intent he trapped me there as the bus stopped and then pulled away. I tried to push past him, struggling with my stupid briefcase, now filled with other things than my pencil case. He wasn't having any of it, and pinned me into my seat. No one tried to help me, no doubt because I was wearing that idiotic cap, a cap that seemed to be draining all of my strength, pulling it up into its stitched sections and dispersing it through its cruel peak. A peak that made me feel as noble as a worm. My consummately indifferent opponent wasn't wearing his cap. He had learnt over the years that the grammar school didn't have any spies operating in Reddish. He blankly continued to squeeze me into my seat, taking great pains to keep me in my place with an elbow and a kicking leg as I lashed out trying to get past him. He was representing at the end of my first day some of the intense pointlessness that was ahead of me at Stockport Grammar School. He was making a very good job of it. I started to whimper, perhaps not so much because I was now a couple of stops past the Essoldo, but because I was eleven years old and wearing shorts. Suddenly, he took pity on me, or got bored, and he let me off, just like that, as if we had just been having a friendly chat about our wonderful school. He politely moved his legs out of my way, replaced a thin sneer with a smile somehow thinner, and I raced down the stairs of the bus as chased as I had been a few hours earlier on another bus in another world. I was a mile past my stop. I didn't dare get another bus back, and I slowly walked back through Reddish, past the dismal library, the swimming pool, home of some of my worst pre-teen disasters, and eventually turned the corner into Westbourne Grove. Here I was greeted with the inevitable finale to a first day at school that would go down in my history. Some kids from Reddish Vale, the local comprehensive, nicked my stupid cap. They were defiantly wearing their anti-uniform clothes right in my face, seeming to move much faster than me, able to make noises however inarticulate whereas I was reduced to a fastened silence that matched my briefcase. They ran off with my cap, chucking it over my head to each other, jeering madly as if it really mattered. I had no real desire to, but I followed the script, and made a few pathetic lunging attempts to get it back, knowing really that in this situation someone in my position never ever won. You were always doomed to be the Hunchback of Notre Dame. The Reddish Vale kids in red-and-black-striped sweaters and the Stockport Grammar boy in short shorts and monocle went through the dancing motions of taunt and chase. I imagined that if I turned up for my second day at school without a cap they would sew one to my genitals. The cap was dropped into the gutter. It looked like it belonged there. It was already gathering creases and scratches and dirt marks, just like my soul.

When I got home, surely looking like an eleven-year-old who had been on a day of misadventures that no eleven-year-old ever feels they should ever have to suffer, my mother excitedly asked me how my day at school had been. It was OK, I lied, because I was already quite good at lying to my parents, and very quickly, as I suffered more days at Stockport Grammar School, as I went on many more epic-seeming journeys to and from the school, as I retreated further and further into my own private life, I was to get even better.

We – that's our family, mother, father, son, two daughters, kept together by name, blood and body weight – moved from Reddish to

Woodsmoor, a journey by moving van and car that would take you pretty much the same route as the route from Reddish to my school. The crammed-together little boxes of Reddish replaced by the less crammed-together slightly bigger boxes of Woodsmoor. I think we were about the same number of feet above sea level in Woodsmoor as we were in Offerton – it was all downhill from both locations to Mersey Square and its concrete grotto.

I would be just a morning walk away to school from our house in Woodsmoor. This cut down on the possible traumas on the way to school, at least, and in Woodsmoor, the crappy cap was a little more appropriate. And then we – that's our family, man, woman, boy, two girls, lost in space, found always in parts of Stockport – moved to Offerton, two miles away, still a walk to my school, just a little longer than the one from Woodsmoor. Four years later, in Offerton, in a house with a model of a wishing-well in the front garden, I still owned the same cap that in my mind had become the laughing stock of Reddish. It had become, in ways still symbolising the state of my soul, a battered clutch of dirty cloth, the yellow almost as black as the black, that I wore perched defiantly on the top of a head far too big for it only within sight of the school gates. The cap and I had come to an understanding over the years. I could cope with the cap. It no longer sucked the energy out of my body. It kept itself to itself, and I did the same. It spent most of its time folded up and stuffed into the pocket of my derelict blazer, and within a certain distance from the school, I would whip it out and plop it on my head, where I would ignore it, and let it ignore me. The battle for which of us would wear the other out first was over. There had been enough wearing out.

Some boys of my age had immaculate stiff caps that were replaced every year and which they wore with the sprightly eager-ness of adolescent Beau Brummels, or the easy maturity of England cricket players. Their caps were natural extensions of their stiff upper lips and their stuck-up noses, and, I supposed, natural exten-sions of their stiff, stuck-up souls. I wore mine, which was due never to be replaced, with exhausted cheek. Other boys had crisp blazers that seemed to have been made to measure, with yellow lapel braid that was the colour of the morning sun over Barbados. My blazer was a size or two too small, made to give a tailor a fit, and there were angry ink doodles scratched into the yellow-the-colour-of-cow-dung braiding that would have given a psychologist much to consider. At the time, if I had been shown a Rorschach pattern and asked what it made me think of I would have said, My school, or, My cap flattened out, or, The ink marks that I splatter onto the yellow parts of my school blazer when I am bored, or, The hair that is growing above my penis. I mustn't jump to conclusions, but I like to think that this response would have meant that I was entirely sane. Other boys had immaculate briefcases that shone with order and self-belief. Their textbooks and exercise books were beautifully organised inside. My briefcase, the same briefcase that I'd had on the first day of school, as empty as my hopes, was now torn and split, stuffed to bursting point with all manner of scholarly, and unscholarly, debris. You could see that the case was made up out of coated layers of cardboard. It was so full of stuff and nonsense, textbooks and exercise books treated over the years as a tissue of lies, that it could barely be fastened shut. There were things at the bottom of this case that hadn't seen the light of day for months, even years. I had no intention of ever emptying this case. I would just keep stuffing things into it, until it exploded, or I did. For all I knew, at the bottom of the case, burrowing away under a mound of paper, books, crumbs, old pens, miscellaneous waste paper, leaking ink bottles, rusting bits of metal, old tennis balls, cracked set squares, general staleness, rancid handkerchiefs and discarded socks, was a small family of field mice living off the leftover biscuits and Penguin bars that I would leave in the case. Or maybe a whole new breed of yellow and black creatures were swiftly evolving deep down in the enclosed dark, getting closer and closer to the day they would nibble through the bottom of the case and scamper off down the hill towards the shopping centre, where they would built nests inside the concrete forest and eventually prove as durable as the cockroach in surviving a nuclear blast.

The fat, fetid case was perfectly coordinated with the shapeless blazer and the half-crazed cap. I was indisputably a classic victim of school shock, and as a result I had absentmindedly developed a wretched male scruffiness that would take decades to control. I had no idea, or couldn't care less, that your appearance explained to the outside world the state of your mind. Or maybe I understood this perfectly, and wanted the outside world to appreciate with absolute clarity what I was going through. A journey of such floating awkwardness, casual chaos and monotonous tension that you could measure the level of moral strength I needed to endure this trip by observing the state of my clothes. I looked like I had been fighting. With myself. With the school. With the creatures at the bottom of my briefcase.

It was a different dreamier sharper thicker wearier stronger weaker long-trousered boy that reluctantly walked from Offerton to Stockport Grammar School compared to the startled scared basic short-trousered kid who would anxiously catch two buses to the school from north Reddish. I was the same but totally changed, I was the filling out same, I was the same multiplied, I was the same heading towards more spreading sameness, I was the same split into a million differences.

I don't remember my mother or father changing at all during this time. But then I don't remember them changing at all during any time. I didn't think of my parents as growing, evolving individuals who had problems, fears and weariness all of their own. They seemed like impediments to my own personal growth, as abstract forces located somewhere in the atmosphere of my life that had this strange control over me. They were not separate people, they were one unit, that existed purely and simply to embellish and complicate my very own problems, fears and weariness. I never considered how they fed and clothed and watered and nurtured me. I took them for granted, with total teenage indifference. They weren't people. They were my parents.

I wonder if, after four demoralising, very unsatisfactory school years, they had lost heart in me, as I had. They were so thrilled when I passed into the grammar school, because I was then all set up to live the special life they never had, a life where university and other best things in life were located. They were parents built in the image of parents, wanting me to have the things and opportunities that they thought that they had never had.

Very quickly, pretty much from that very first day, I had slumped. Exam results came twice a year, at Christmas, at the beginning of summer, and they were constant knocks to my fragile esteem. Annual reports, blue-backed board folded into two, were a nightmare for everybody concerned. I was increasingly judged in these reports as academically mediocre, temperamentally unsound, lacking in discipline, and a general all-round no-hoper. If somebody somewhere is at all interested in creating a possible hell for me, then an eternity made up of that hanging, shaming moment just before my father read my 2b report card, filled with those cutting, damning, eerie one-liners scored in different deathless shades of harsh blue and black ink, would do just fine, thank you. My father would be filled with the rage of a sergeant major and emptied with the disappointment of a father as he read how pitifully I was doing. If these masters were being cruel to be kind with their merciless observations of my ability and character, then they were killing me with kindness.

After being at the very top of the 'a' class at primary school, after getting a hundred per cent in some subjects, at the grammar school, I skidded in one massive motion to the bottom of the 'b' form, occasionally getting nought per cent in some subjects. This being Stockport, this being Stockport Grammar School, I was going downhill all the way. Another made-to-measure all-time hell would be made up of that wide-pen bared-teeth moment when the creepy, meta-methodical Physics master was reading out in grindingly relentless order the results of a Physics examination. There were thirty-two boys in my form. The master with monkish care has gravely intoned his way down to the thirty-first boy, who got a solid seven per cent, and he has still to get to my name. It seems an hour ago that the top boy was personally graced with a mystical eighty-three per cent.

You sit there waiting to the left of the centre of the middle of a grey-day drift, feeling the dead weight of some kind of quantum misery mixed in with cosmic spite. You swear you can hear something give birth at the bottom of your briefcase. You sigh a sigh of sighs, a sigh of such stretching size you can't believe that you managed to keep it yourself.

One of those sighs that stretches throughout the rest of your life.

The classroom quietens to a mesmerised hush.

The master, a master of technique when it comes to delivering such deathless information, pauses for extravagant and nauseating effect:

Morley . . .

He unloads the word in a way that is both absently underplayed and appallingly dramatic. I stare nowhere as helpless as a foetus and take the time to consider how dearly we must pay for the invention of speech.

The whole class holds their breath. I hold mine and then I drop it. Maybe I'll get three per cent.

Maybe the Physics master will black out at the moment of tragic delivery.

Your whole life had been flung onto a dungheap. Everything has been flung onto a dungheap and is beginning to stink, fouling everyone's air.

Oh, yes, my wasted imagination, nonsense, babble, all these many long, difficult years, have deceived me, have tricked me, are making fun of me, spitting on me, the way you fling some stinking scrap onto the dungheap, the cataloguing of a loner's misdeeds, with absolute murderous intention, with absolute irresponsibility, reconstructing and subtracting and grafting and feeling no compunction, piling them up and rolling them together and turning them into some ridiculous object.

There is not the slightest trace of reality anywhere – except in the overwhelming feeling of unreality.

Thirty-second.

I knew as bloody much.

I vomit into my briefcase.

I sometimes wonder how I manage to get from one minute to the next, from one day to the next.

Nought per cent.

Hallelujah.

The bastard announced it with relish. And indeed sauce. And a drop of vinegar.

The whole class joins together in a warm snigger of snide approval and condescending respect.

When I was flopping through the third form, the English master read out the results of the year-end English exam, and my name arrived on the list unexpectedly early. I came fourth with sixty-seven per cent. For a cool, caressing few moments, I felt quite wonderful, a hint of the pure pleasure of what it must be like to be successful at such a school. The nagging pressure of failure was rooted out of me. I was instantly reminded of the invulnerable feelings I had regularly felt at my previous school. I thought, a little buoyantly, Perhaps I'm going to do all right at this cruel school after all. Perhaps I'd turned some psychological corner, without really knowing why or how. I'd cracked it. I luxuriated in the sudden ease of fine achievement.

And then I didn't. After he had announced the result, the master mumbled something under his breath, and then seemed a little unsure. He scratched his head. To himself, but I could hear him, the whole class could hear him, he said, Oh, that must be a mistake, that can't be right. After all, I was usually down near the bottom.

It wasn't a mistake, but it might as well have been. It was my best result in any subject, but my reputation as a no-hoper had meant that I felt like an impostor at the top end of the class, an illegal immigrant into the sunny lands of the sixty per cent. I had done well, and no one believed it, so I might as well have done as badly as usual.

It became a lowering drifting circle of failure. The poorer my results, the more I sank into the gloopy mud of mediocrity, the more I would be viewed by the treacherous pride of teachers as difficult, in difficulty, and a furtive troublemaker, and the more I would veer that way anyway. Anyone at the grammar school who wasn't, from the very first day they arrived, after whatever kind of journey, destined for a place at a plum good university, preferably Oxford or Cambridge, just slipped through the rough black and yellow holes in their rigidly traditional and narrow-minded system. You became invisible, unrescuable, useful only as a grubby example to be loosely callously picked on of how not to be, as an example of the great messed-up loser. This was a school explicitly split into two distinct camps. The boys that would and the boys that wouldn't.

I wouldn't.

Duncan Ellams would, though. He was doing well, and fitting neatly into the prudent and rigorous education machine, swot bang in the middle of the 'a' form. Always correctly turned out to the point of campness, he sported a pristine cap that was connected to his head with sinister precision. His briefcase was as shapely as a Rolls Royce. His blazer blazed with creaseless splendour. Perhaps the fact that he was fitting in so smartly and I was sticking out all over the place could be traced back to the time when he caught the 17x with such timely flair and I, hampered by freshly minted haplessness, didn't.

Then again, perhaps I was never going to stand a chance at a private school, called with classic English perversity a public school, where the teachers religiously called the pupils by their hard formal surnames. Your friendly tender first name, not called a Christian name for nothing, was simply ignored, wiped from scholarly sight, at best left as just a solitary cold initial. Your first name was considered too soft, too familiar, and barely existed inside the school boundaries.

Every time that I was called or branded or derided or checked out by the bald name MORLEY by one bullying, baiting master or another, I would wilt a little more. Especially in the first form, after a few years of being treated quite kindly, like a child in fact, at primary school. Nicknames that classmates hastily and nastily concocted early on out of a distortion of name, personality and/or potential deviancy didn't help either. It was as if using the first name was somehow a sign of effeminate weakness, a vulgar compromise that suggested life was going to be easy. The blunt use of your surname by a master and the mean application of a crude nickname by your friends – your enemies could think of much worse – meant that you were transformed into a new version of yourself. A version of you that was more it, more object, more specific a target, than if you were just called by the name that you had spent eleven years getting used to. Which you were now very used to. It fitted you. You had become it. And then it was snatched away from you, and replaced with new names, new yous, to adjust to. Life was not easy. Life was going to get harder. You couldn't even rely on the name you had been called all your life. And you realised that what's in a name is not security, not order, but something temporary, and unstable. A name is just a great pretence that things are what they seem.

I was given the nickname, within days of arriving at the school, of 'Moggers'. I'm not sure how this name was coined. Nicknames were handed around very quickly. No one had much choice. Was there some kind of committee that handed out nicknames? Did one boy take one look at me, think it up, and then it was considered such a brilliantly appropriate and hilarious name that it could only be mine? Was there a shortlist? Perhaps some boy with raw first-form wit figured I had catlike qualities.

I didn't feel very catlike. Mouselike more like. I didn't feel like I looked like a Moggers, who I felt would look hard and aggressive. I get the 'M', and then I lose it. But I never lost the nickname. Where did the 'g's come from? Was I given such a weak, banal kind of nickname because the highly secretive committee decided that I was a weak banal kind of boy not worth giving too much thought to when it came to my nickname? Did I just get a nickname plucked out of a list of boring names to give boys who didn't really lend themselves to interesting nicknames? It stuck to my back for years, despite a valiant third-form attempt to change it to 'Ziggy', which seemed particularly glamorous and enigmatic and much more suited to how I saw my self. But no one was having that. At school, I was Moggers. Or, more dreadfully, Morley.

MORLEY!

It made me hate the name, think of it as damp and creepy, something lacking flair, and for a while, as I was dismissed as Morley by the masters and stamped as Moggers by my classmates, pretty much lose touch with Paul. Paul had been split into three.

After a couple of years I got quite blasé about the teachers turning me into Morley, although the echoes were still there of the shock I felt as an eleven-year-old to be so fixed into position by the use of his surname. As Paul, I felt free. As Morley, I felt trapped. As Moggers, I didn't know who or what I was.

MORLEY!

They might as well have called me number 34526 . . .

MORLEY!

Even when it was said gently it sounded harsh and unforgiving.

MORLEY!

It stripped away layers of protective innocence, and hardened me up.

MORLEY!

The teachers called me Morley and I called them sir.

It really didn't seem right, and yet it did. It was the way it was. It was written somewhere. There was nothing you could do about it.

Sometimes I would think, as a Morley, that my father must hate me for making me go to this school, where Paul wasn't allowed. But I supposed as far as he was concerned he loved me because he wanted me to go to that school. Although he never told me that he loved me. Perhaps if he had, then I could have dealt with the way that I was now a Morley, a Moggers, and treated it with smooth disdain. But he never told me that he loved me, not that I can remember, and if he had I'm sure it would have been something that I would remember. Because it would have been such a shock, such an embarrassment, to both of us. If it had happened, and I can't even pretend that it did, I can't even pretend that I might have forgotten, or that he did and then he stopped, he just didn't, then it would perhaps change the whole way that I remember my father. Because he never did, and he didn't, I know that, even if he felt it, and he did, I'm sure, behind himself, behind his feelings, his mid-twentieth-century grim English stiffness, then I think of him at a distance. I think of him somewhere over there. I think of him as someone playing my dad, going through the motions, which isn't fair, on both of us, because in a way all he was in life was my father, and all I was in life was his son. And if he was going through the motions, then so was I. And yet it was our destiny to be so close. We were made that way. But because he never told me that he loved me, because he always seemed a long way off from intimacy with me, I never think of us as being close. There was always something separating us from appreciating the unique realness of the absolute drama that made us father and son. It was too much for us to take in.

We never really grasped the strange affinity that existed between us. We kept apart from the very thing that made us so uniquely ourselves as father and son. We never talked about being father and son. We never acknowledged it. We never owned up to it. We just accepted it, lived with it, and because he never told me that he loved me, then I never told him that I loved him. I know I didn't. Because if I had done then the moment would have ripped through my being, it would have been so out of character, a character built after his character, and it would be a vital part of me now, as part of what makes me me, as my heart, or my lungs. Or my soul. But I never told him I loved him. I never said, 'I love you too.'

And this makes me think of my father as somebody who was loving me as I loved him beyond reason and beyond words, who was one day going to tell me that he loved me, in a moment, what a moment, after all these years, but because he knew so much that he loved me, like a father loves a son, he assumed that I must know. But he never said that he loved me, I know he didn't, it's not something you make up, and it would have changed things if he had. I would remember him differently, I would remember him a little clearer, I could hear his voice, I would feel a little freer than I do, and I would have been prompted and led and influenced to think of telling him that I loved him. But there was no chance of this happening, because he died. I can't remember the sound of his voice. The sound of him saying 'I love you' or 'Do you want a cup of tea?'

doesn't linger in my mind. I don't remember him ever asking me if I wanted a cup of tea. He must have, but I've forgotten. But I'm sure I would remember. I would remember the sound of his voice saying it. But I don't. His voice is beyond my thoughts. I can't make him say things in my mind because I don't know what his voice was like. I never thought that I would have to remember it. I thought that I would always be hearing it. Deep down, in the part of me that was receiving the future and letting it make my mind up about myself, I felt that eventually he would get around to saying that he loved me. Or some male equivalent.

I wonder what else he never got around to saying. I wonder what else he never got around to feeling.

And now I think of him as too cold, too anxious, too confused to tell me that he loved me. I think of him as anxious, cold and confused, and I have some of that in me, whatever that stuff is that makes life seem strewn with emotional obstacles that are entirely of your own making, with some help from your father. And his father before him. Etc.

I think of him as more Morley than anything else. Even more than Dad, which I must have called him all the time. I think of him as fastened in time as Morley, voiceless and vague and pained and gone.

As I was turned by the slow grind of the school into one flat blocked Morley I wondered if he thought of me as Morley. He called me Paul, but then what with one thing and another he had to. I wonder if I hated being called Morley so much because it made me think that I was like my father. Just another Morley. And I didn't want to be like him. Not then, anyway. Not in that way. Not in a way where you were trapped by your name. Not in a way that it stopped you feeling. And took away your voice.

MORLEY!

I would jump out of my skin when they first called me Morley, stung to the point of disorientation, and then slowly I crawled back inside my skin, and found ways to hide there. Eventually, to be called Morley was just one of those sick dull reminders of the dead heavy ways of the school. The name became something of an abstraction loosely connected with the me that was also, at school, becoming an abstraction.

As I was being beaten back and down by this nagging school harassment and their wicked indifferent way with the word and the meaning of Morley, there was something inside me that didn't want to get lost. I wanted to hide from others, but not from myself. As every day at school became a variation on the same hallucination, something separate from what I hoped was reality, outside of the school, I worked up my own sense of reality. I tuned in to myself. I learned for myself. Talked to myself. I started to turn into myself.

Outside of school, somewhere in the air, somewhere in the time that stretched around me, somewhere right where I found myself, a long way from the pre-existing void, a little way on from those days when the me in me was formed and forming, I found pop music.

Or pop music found me, right where I was. I happened to be there. Waiting. Hallucinating. Looking for something. Needing something. It was all quite a coincidence. Quite a twentieth-century coincidence.

Pop music loved me, and it told me so, in oh so many different ways. I said 'I love you too' in my own particular way. A way that mixed up the religious and the sexual and the sisterly and the brotherly and the unnatural. It sang me love songs. I wrote it love letters.

I fell head-over-feelings in love with the sounds and images and words and moments and beats and spaces and secrets and it seemed all mine all mind and it all pinpointed and outlined the sensitivities and crises of my most radically transitional years and the noise of the code words defined my passions and developed my needs and discharged all manner of inner tension and outer confusion and the energy the power the subtlety concentrated into itself an over-whelming sense of life. Life as it should be lived. As it could be lived. As it can be lived. I was hooked by the hooks of the pop song in the way that pop hooks are meant to hook you. Right through the heart.

The coincidence never ceases to amaze me. Just at that age when I was beginning to feel that loss and frustration is everything, and so too is desire and dreaming, pop music pops up, pulling faces, throw-ing daggers, walking tightropes, exploiting the antic circumstances of your proto-psyche, glamorously celebrating the psycho-sexual complications of life, sweetly demonstrating the psychic implication of differing world structures, sounding like dreams look, lifting the weight off your crushed spirit, teaching you about a mood beyond time and space. Pop shows up to show off the volatile multiversity of a cunning, crowded, confusing world where you're all on your own and surrounded at all times.

So there was pop, peeling away layers of the dull grey world and revealing new colours and new possibilities, and it arrived just in the nick of time. You couldn't have planned it better. I was born at just the right moment in the dicey vastness of all the moments there will ever be just so that I could connect with the time when pop exploded in a bit of time to make accidental sense of nonsense. Who'd have thought.

Pop music, making the mystery of the world something to marvel at rather than fear and deny, helped take my mind off school. It helped dull the pain. It helped replace it with pleasure.

It was because of pop that, sometime between forms 2b and 3b, in the standard way, I started to visibly rebel against the dark dreary ways of the school. I started to fight back. The temperamental outburst of pop music and the alien physicality of its exponents seemed just as valid a reality as, if not more valid than, the trancelike traditionalism of my grammar school. Before pop music fully gave me something all of my own, and created a kind of welfare of the self, a world that seemed for me and not against me, to rebel meant rebelling against parents and school and, for better or worse, that's all I had in the world. I had football, and Manchester City, but this fantasy, this conversion of the truth, didn't inspire feelings of rebellion or psychological restlessness. It was football that pulled the two Morleys, Dad and me, as close as we could ever be, but it was a closeness that never spilled over into the rest of our lives.

Football was a comfort that soothed. Pop music was a comfort that inspired. Pop music as a magic spell provoked me to challenge the inextricably bound conventions of school and parents, the limits of my world, and this seemed exciting. It also seemed a threat to whatever security there was in my life, and that was scary. But this scariness seemed to intensify the excitement. Out on my own I had found something of my own. School didn't know about it. It wasn't something I could share with my father or my mother. Or even my sisters. Or, in a way, anybody. It was my secret. It made me feel very wonderful.

You could say that the beginning of this story – the story of a death that meant something to me – really began the moment I heard the song 'Ride a White Swan' by T. Rex. Something strange with a halo of fantastical out-of-focus tenderness pounced on me. Hearing this stylised, sinister, soothing pop song, a fantasy of grace crushed into two minutes of warped beat and fated motion, a succulent noise pulsing in time with space dust dispersed on the far side of the galaxy, changed everything. I wasn't sure why. I didn't understand it. I couldn't work out if it had blurred its way from the sixteenth century, or divined itself from the distant future. I felt something, though, and perhaps it was hearing 'Ride a White Swan' that made me start feeling deeper and darker as an individual. I felt its gaudiness, its confidence, its transformative sorcery. I felt, I sensed, I dreamt ultrafabulous things about life and death and sex and wonder that I am still trying to work out – still trying to find.

This innocent, primitive, lethargic little pop song. This cunning, smart, effervescent little pop song. It didn't so much awake my imagination as help spin it over from being a childlike imagination to being an adult imagination. The song completed some kind of emotional circuit. It sent me out into a grown-up future. It increased my heartbeat. It helped me leap up the steps from immaturity to maturity.

A few days after I heard 'Ride a White Swan' on the radio, I saw T. Rex on the television. The sight finished me off. And then it started me all over again. Two tentatively hashed creatures as inhuman as glass dressed to the membranes in soft velvets marble swirls and shiny satins sat hunched over electric instruments creating an atmosphere all of their own and singing their song as if to Alice in Wonderland. Seeing them didn't help at all in working out what unknown dialect they were singing in. I still had no idea what they were singing about, although I got the feeling, although I couldn't articulate it, I couldn't actually catch any of the symbolism, that it was some distorted fairy tale, and penile feet were slipping into vaginal slippers, honey represented sperm, and there were enchanted pools where one could see one's reflection, and there were descriptions of transformation in a flutter of wings. It was all over in a couple of incomprehensible, vivid minutes. I wanted more.

Their hair was everywhere. It formed the magical forest they sang from within. Marc Bolan, singing as if he was being strangled by the big bad wolf, posing like he could kill the wolf with a lash of his tongue, had tumultuous black curly hair that tumbled up and over and through his beautiful, tenacious face like silk barbed wire. Mickey Finn, skinny and dead still, pale to the point of transparency, had eerie flat brown hair that hung down over his shoulders and hugged the contours of his frail body. You could have used his hair to climb up a beanstalk. Mickey Finn seemed miles away, Bolan a little closer, and yet further out. I suppose it was my first real sighting of 60s-styled freaks, but they shocked into my mind with swift, abrupt ritualistic intensity.

I think this moment was the beginning of this story. It meant that eventually I could tell this story. It's where everything began that means I am now writing this story the way I am writing it. I wanted to be Marc Bolan, but I also wanted to be able to explain why I wanted to be Marc Bolan, I wanted to describe the feelings I had when I saw and heard him. I wanted to chase the dreams he was having, match them with my own. I wanted to find other things like him, and write about them, write about how they made me think and feel and lust. From the moment I saw and heard Marc Bolan celebrate the mysteries of the unconscious with a sensational combination of narcotic pop and nursery rhyme, male and female urges, sense and nonsense, precision and suspense, I wanted to be a writer.

I became a writer. More Paul than Morley. More Paul Morley than Moggers.

I wanted to grow my hair. Not ear-lappingly long. Mickey Finn long. Marc Bolan long. As long as my fantasies.

And, what with one thing and another, the growing of my hair set me off on an adventure that would end with the knowledge of death. The knowledge of death is, one way or another, the subject of this book. So the beginning of this book, even though it doesn't need to go at the beginning, actually starts with 'Ride a White Swan' and Marc Bolan, and the way my mind grew because I found out through two minutes of flickering pop how strange and wonderful the world could be.

I started to grow my hair. It grew longer than the normal school regulations allowed, not that this was much to get excited about. The school decreed from up on high that your hair must not touch the ears or come anywhere near the collar of your shirt. At first, my hair tickled my ears, grazed my collar. But then it grew longer. I was fighting back against the school in my own way. Marc Bolan had shown me that the world was much more than facts and figures. It was a kind of fiction, a fiction you could turn into reality, your own kind of reality, if you believed enough.

Representing this new belief, my hair began to reach over my ears, the collar of my shirt, stretch down my forehead over my eyebrows, every scraggy talcumed quarter of an inch a blow for independence. It grew an inch over my blazer collar, half an inch over my ears. Nothing seemed to stop it. My father, whose own hair was 1961 rock and roll long and Brylcreemed well beyond convention, didn't seem to care. I suppose even as it crept over ears and collar it still wasn't as long as his.

But I started to feel like a revolutionary. Even in the early 70s, long hair hadn't made its way into the stuffy, deeply militarised, tyrannical world of Stockport Grammar School. I started to feel I was gaining strength, my hair representing the power of my imagination, the development of my individuality.

Feeling very sure of myself, in a roundabout way, because every moment at school I would feel I was trapped inside a nameless dilemma, I would turn up for morning school assembly where we would sing hymns that drove with maniacal monotony towards a single point of futility. Four hundred pupils and a ragbag of masters would drone the Lord's Prayer, some sullenly, some with desperate enthusiasm. We were confirming in our own sagged way how Christianity gives a special disturbing weight to the world.

Morning assembly was presided over by the wildly intimidating headmaster F. W. Scott, Adolf Hitler as played by the manic comedian Ken Dodd. Rumour had it that he was barking mad, half man, half rabid monkey, because years before he had killed his own son by driving over him accidentally as he was backing out of his garage. The first major obstacle of the day was to avoid his schizoid glare as he scanned the assembled pupils searching out for boys who were blatantly breaking the hair commandment. This wasn't made easy because I would usually stand next to my friend Jonathan Edelstein, a Jewish boy with carrot-red hair cut into tousled layers. He was very tall for his age and seemed to have been shaving all of his life so that even at the age of twelve he had a five o'clock shadow at nine in the morning. His sideboards had achieved a 70s Engelbert Humperdinck bushiness by the time of his bar mitzvah. I was trying to hide from the dangerous F. W. Scott standing next to a giraffe in a false beard. An orange false beard.

Jonathan and I had devised what seemed a perfect way to fool Scott and his batty staff about the true length of our hair. We would push the sides of our hair back behind our ears and slip the back of it tightly underneath the collars of our blazers. For weeks at a time we would attend assembly and lessons pretty confident that this would fool teachers in their forties and fifties who knew every trick in the book. Perhaps we thought that with long hair being such a new thing, this was a new trick, one the teachers were clueless about. As far as we could tell, it seemed to work, although maybe the teachers, even the insane Scott, took pity on us in our idiocy. We walked around the school as stiff as boards, and could make no sudden movements in case this dislodged our hair. Basically, we could just look straight ahead, and swivel awkwardly from side to side. This took some concentration, but it seemed to work. Until it didn't.

MORLEY!

Sometimes the name was exclaimed with a little more vigour than other times.

I was confused when one day, as I was sitting minding my own business during some lesson or another, my hair as superbly tucked into its disguised position as it ever was, the teacher threw a blackboard cleaner at me.

What are those rat-tails you wear on your head? he demanded to know, with menace.

Boys in front of me in the class swung around to enjoy my predicament in the way that boys at such a school did. To enjoy my suffering, and to relish the relief that attention had been taken away from whatever problem they were experiencing. They swung around in a way that I couldn't have, because my hair was deeply rooted down the back of my blazer. I had the mobility of a Thunderbird puppet.

But, I bravely protested, as if it were true, which in one odd sense it was, my hair is above my ears and above my collar.

He expelled a definitive Stockport Grammar School teacher's snort.

Just get it cut, he breathed, with a hint of fire.

Tears stung my eyes. It had taken a long time to grow it this long. A thirteenth of my life.

I had almost managed to convince myself that I had a regulation haircut, even though it was almost long enough for me to chew the ends, my immediate goal.

I got it cut, and it hurt.

For the first couple of years, whenever a teacher got fed up with my transparent ways of disguising my long hair, I would easily give in, fearful of the consequences. For a while the gathering strength of my rebellion would be curtailed and, wearing a raw bristling army service haircut, I sang dried hymns to an early-morning God who seemed colder and less likely than he used to and not as long-haired as I imagined when I was six.

Jonathan once asked me if I wanted to go to a Black Sabbath concert with him at the Manchester Free Trade Hall. The thought mesmerised me. I had never been to a pop concert before. I wouldn't go with him, because it was a few days after I had been forced to have my hair taken away from me. It was so short that I thought everybody at the concert, and no doubt Black Sabbath themselves, and the support act Curved Air, especially Darryl Way the violinist, would laugh at me. I was sure you couldn't go to a Black Sabbath concert with short hair. You weren't allowed to.

For some reason, Jonathan never seemed to get told to cut his hair as often as me. Maybe the teachers thought his long hair, feathered and ruffled in the mad mod style of Rod Stewart, was some sort of religious thing.

I once had a direct encounter with the stark raving F. W. Scott concerning my hair. He stalked the narrow corridors of the school like a fanatic, but only rarely made supernatural appearances outside his wretched nest of an office so usually it was quite easy to avoid him. Especially if you avoided the corridor where his office was. But, late for a History period in an area of the school he had no right to be in, as far as I could work out, I sauntered around a corner and there he was, charging towards me. Scott at full speed was a terrible sight. Scott at slow speed was a terrible sight, but at least then you might get the chance to run away. This time there was no way we could avoid each other. He almost ran right into me. A large part of my heart stopped and the rest of it leapt into my mouth. He peered at me as if I was a specimen of vomit offered up to him for unspecified inspection. Then he stared at my hair like I was waving my penis in his face.

I must have been in the fifth form, nearing the end of my time at the school, as it had become clear to everyone concerned that the sixth form was no concern of mine. By then I had become so self-ishly, imaginatively insistent on growing my hair to what could be called progressive rock lengths that if I had stuck it down the collar of my blazer it would have stuck out of the bottom. Neither of us said anything to the other. I don't suppose he knew my name and I had lost the power of speech. He silently, impatiently gestured for me to follow him. He raced off down the corridor at the speed of dark and I had to jog just to keep up with him.

I thought at speed, I am about to be expelled, and I felt liberated and nauseous all at the same time. He took me into his gloomy wood-panelled office, lined with old photographs and trophies and plaques. It seemed a place that hadn't seen natural daylight for centuries. I had been in this office only once before, a couple of years previous to this new emergency. That time I had been ordered to report to him by a young Physics master who cracked after the class had been humming non-stop throughout his lesson for forty minutes. He picked on me as the representative of the class, and off I went for my date with destiny. The headmaster, in an indulgent mood, tried to engage me in a little chat about my future before he punished me. What do you want to be when you leave school? he asked, unnerving me by staring at me with these eyes that seemed to roll around in their sockets and then back inside his head and then out again. The two eyes when they did settle seemed to stare in different directions. He stooped forward all the time, tight into my precious space, with gnarled haughtiness.

I want to be a journalist, I said, figuring this was an intelligent, honest answer that might provoke a productive conversation about how to achieve this ambition.

His eyes swivelled in amusement and his shoulders hunched over even more. Oh no, he smirked. Oh no, he shook his head. Oh no, and he almost looked sorry for me. No, no, no, he tried to explain, I don't think you're really up to that. You need very good qualifica-tions to be a journalist, and it's a very tough business. No, no, no, you should think of another career. He didn't say like driving a bus, but he might as well have.

That little chat probably inspired me as much as anything, as much as hearing 'Ride a White Swan', to become a journalist.

And here I was again. If anything his eyes were crankier than the last time, and he was now stooped so low Groucho Marx would have been jealous. After some swirling silence as he sized me up and eyed my long greasy hair with puzzled contempt, he finally asked me, surprisingly in a language I could understand, to look at a large shiny brass plaque that was hanging on the wall of his office. He roughly pushed me right up to it. Look at that, he breathed. What do you see?

Sarcasm swilled up to the back of my throat. I forced it back down. I didn't really know what he was talking about. I saw a shield-shaped plaque with some dates and names on it.

Come on, boy, he snapped.

Er . . .

Yes, he rasped.

I prayed hard that a swan might swoop down and carry me off.

Look, he huffed. Can't you see? he puffed.

Is that a plaque I see before me?

His eyes bulged. I admitted defeat. I didn't know what I was supposed to see.

He started to swoop towards me, as if he might want to pass right through me and take my heart in his bony fingers.

The Chorus of Pain found time to enter my mind, stage left, hair spiked on crazed end up to the clouds, noses underbrushed with Groucho moustaches, snarly mouths biting down on yard-long Marxist cigars, singing at the tops of their voices a neglected classic from the light opera *You Shall Never Get out of This* entitled 'He Was Sure to Catch You Sooner or Later'.

I felt comprehensively sullen, and yet there was a hysterical part of me that was irrationally enjoying this cheerless occasion. Sick mist seemed to waft around the creepy Scott as he hovered next to me like a great grey vulture. I was closer than I ever thought possible to this near-mythical head beast. I could lividly appreciate how his right forearm poked stiffly out from his body at a forty-five-degree angle, and how his right hand seemed frozen into a gnarled claw. I could see and near-enough feel how his barmy eyes watered with bleary scepticism. Scorpions appeared to crawl through his thorned hair. Tufts of stiff black hair dripped from his nose like vile insects in a state of advanced rigor mortis. His buckled teeth were rotten and brown as if they had once been set on fire. He seemed to be talking to me without moving his lips.

169

What do you see, boy? he hissed.

I saw the plaque.

And behind that the wall.

And beyond that . . . eternity.

He was so angry his mouth was watering with some dark-green liquid that miserably leaked down his chin. The decayed skin on his face glistened with annoyance.

I wish I could have given him the answer he wanted, just to move proceedings on a bit, but I didn't have a clue what he was urging me to see, if not the bloody plaque.

It became a battle of wills.

Would I see what I was supposed to see before the joke or what-ever it was turned too sour for either of us to bear and he had to ruin the whole occasion by telling me what it was I was supposed to see?

I saw the plaque and behind that I saw the wall and behind that I saw . . . the end.

Something had to give.

He did. This only succeeded in annoying him even more.

He revolved on the spot and seemed to levitate a few inches off the ground in total headmasterly disgust that I had ruined a cherished set piece.

He sat behind his immense desk with a melodramatic display of self-control and with meticulously phrased exasperation explained to me what the point was of this ritual.

Look in the plaque.

Pause for punchline.

At your reflection, boy!

Canned laughter filled his office. Wasn't I the stupid one?

I focused on a blurred yellow image of my face.

I was meant to be using the plaque as a mirror and looking at my reflection.

What a gag.

Look at the length of your hair, boy!

Ah.

My hair was so long that not only could I have chewed it but I could have swallowed it as well.

I wanted to swallow it, along with the rest of me, as Scott scowled at me across his bleak office, jarred by the state of my hair, infuri-ated by my blasé obstinacy in the face of his little piece of theatre.

I stood there feeling foolish because I still couldn't remember my lines. I wasn't sure if I should laugh at his little joke or keep a serious expression of considered respect. I sort of did both at once, which resulted in a short series of nervous snorts, an increasing heartbeat, intense irregular blinking, an inarticulate stutter, a minimal raising of the eyebrows, a shrug of the shoulders, a fumbling with the hands, much sweat on the palms, a loss of feeling in the legs and an overall feeling that I was sinking to the centre of the earth. All this seemed pretty camp to me, but it clearly wasn't theatrical enough for Scott. He prepared for his grand finale as I twitched with sloppy bewilderment.

He opened a drawer in his desk and pulled out a large pair of shiny silver scissors. He floated towards me.

Fucking hell.

He's going to stab me.

He creaked a smile.

He said, There is no place at my school for a boy with hair like that. Your hair is far too long. You are a disgrace.

I don't think I had any lines at this stage.

And as you seem incapable of getting it cut yourself.

Yes, there was no doubt this was his scene.

He paused with the timing he must have learnt from watching a lot of Alistair Sim films.

The life of my hair flashed before my eyes.

He lifted the scissors into the air.

He grabbed hold of my hair.

I am going to cut it myself.

He said this as if he was suddenly enjoying himself again.

The thought of having my hair cut by a man who was clearly off his rocker and imagined life was a West End play written by Agatha Christie jolted me into recovering my power of speech. At last, I remembered my lines.

It's OK, sir, I said, I was planning to have it cut this week anyway.

He lowered his claw.

Why haven't you had it cut before?

According to the script, I was to say something about my mum not being able to afford a haircut for me. He clearly didn't believe me, but our time was almost over.

He went back to his desk.

He put the scissors back into the drawer.

He came back towards me and with a look on his face that was somewhere between murderous and magnanimous handed me twenty-five new pence.

There, he preened, enunciating the words with magnificent care, now you can get your hair cut. A small smile of triumph twitched weirdly at the corner of his mouth.

The curtain came down. The applause was deafening. Scott received a standing ovation, and I withdrew as meekly and as unobtrusively as possible. As I left his office the cheers were ringing out and the tears were flowing freely from his broken eyes. I shut the door and supposed that the next item on his agenda was the ritual sacrificing of a white swan.

F. W. Scott, despite his best efforts, didn't give me my worst moments at the corrupting grammar school. Encounters with him were rare, specialist treats that had a different quality, a different set of textures, from the daily, hourly, engagements you strained through with the masters he delegated everyday duties to. He generously shared the power of life and death teachers had over you with a coven of pulseless, withered creatures each with his own gnarled brand of eccentricity. Each master had his own oppressive style of commanding bland respect and blind obedience, of forcing his personality down the throats of young teenage boys.

There were the odd friendly, pleasant, even young masters who had somehow made their way into the school without experience of the nineteenth century, but you always tended to distrust their motives. They wouldn't last anyway. They'd leave, as meekly as they arrived. Or they would be converted. Possessed by the school. Absorbed into its black system.

There was the Art master, the big, hearty Mr Stanley, nicknamed 'Baxter', as in 'Backs to the Wall'. He taught me Art for four years, and everything I learnt from him about art can be placed between the last word of this sentence, 'follows', and the full stop that follows.

There was the Woodwork teacher, Mr Bromley, who rumour had it had been sacked in the 1950s for throwing a chisel at a boy. The chisel had stuck in the boy's hand. The teacher was let go but inexplicably rehired a couple of years later. When he got angry with a boy, which happened a few times every period, he would splutter and choke with such fury his whole head would turn blood-purple. At the beginning of every dismal two-hour period he would hurl a piece of carpentry at any boys he had developed a particular antipathy towards. You would never have any suspicions that this man could develop a wayward fondness towards young boys. He hated them with brain-purpling passion. He taught me for four years, and I never got to finish my Woodwork exercises off and thus move on with the other boys to make toast racks and picture frames. I spent four years trying to saw a neat dovetail in a block of wood, while having chunks of wood chucked at me.

There was the Music teacher, Mr Steele, who also played the organ in assembly in the style of a silent movie Phantom of the Opera. He would sit the boys in lines on benches and every period for about two minutes ask us a question or two about music. He would wander up and down behind us, and when he asked a question he would knee the boy who happened to be in front of him in the base of the spine, which was the signal that he must give the answer. Maybe this process was some subtle satire on the fact we weren't, in Music, actually facing the music, whereas in every other period, during each and every day, in the rest of the school we were constantly, what with one thing and another, facing the music. For the rest of the period we all read Superman comics. I did this for four years, to the extent that if I now see a piece of sheet music I can only think that Superman is very vulnerable to kryptonite.

Mr Gosling was the Religious Knowledge teacher, and all I can remember of the time I studied with him – apart from the rather strange end result – is that I was once so bored, so exquisitely dead from the body out, so tired of his repetitive drone, so convinced that God was being slowly killed by the monotony within the class, so stunned by all the tedium that appeared to be issuing from the Bible via the grey mouth of the tireless Gosling, a mouth that never did anything unusual, that during one majestic yawn my jaw locked wide open and for the life of me I couldn't shut it. Gosling moaned on about the Lord stirring up the spirit of Cyrus the King of Persia, and I experienced a panic exceptional even by the usual standards of panic at the school. Desperately trying to shut my mouth, I wondered if my ignorance of Gosling and his way of featuring God had been looked upon unkindly, had incurred the wrath of God, who, after all that, actually did exist, and right now was in the school having a cup of tea with F. W. Scott, and sharing old memories. And now the devil himself had swooped through my mouth, left it wide open in a position of gremlin deformation, and was now beavering away inside my brain ready to snatch my mind to hell. After a couple of minutes of frantic struggle and true fear, I managed to clamp my mouth shut. I could breathe again. As my jaw slammed shut, as I felt the thrilling feeling of my tongue touching the roof of my mouth, as I experienced the miracle of being able to tap the top row of my teeth on the bottom row, as I found a wonderful variety of ways to open and close my mouth, I knew for sure that God was dead. Gosling's God was as dead as Gosling's delivery. Hallelujah.

After four years of studying Music, Art, Woodwork and Religious Knowledge, you were then meant to choose, or have chosen for you, one subject from the four that you would take during the fifth form, the subject you would take your GCE O level in. Those without any noticeable art or craft or inspirational flair, those who had failed to crack the malicious mysteries of Stanley, Steele and Bromley, were doomed to endure another year of Religious Knowledge. Another year of the plain Gosling and his way of pursuing the mysteries of existence in a tone of voice that suggested he was merely interested in the weight of a loaf of white bread.

Consigned to the group generally considered to be the losers, those that lacked, I spent another slack year slowly drowning in the 774,746 words of the Bible. Nagged by the 593,493 words in the Old Testament, niggled by the 181,253 words in the New Testament, I sat inside Gosling's Spartan classroom feeling as if I was being buried alive by emptiness. Every period, as one second turned over into another second with drowsy slowness, I felt apathy as a kind of unbreakable energy, and the Chorus of Pain would staidly perform their early classic 'A Dingy Kind of Deprivation'. The Chorus were all in grey, the sky was grey, the scenery was grey, the music was grey, the voices were grey, greyly mocking the arid monody of the ever grave Gosling with his grey, grey eyes and his grey, grey skin.

Another Chorus of Pain classic was named after the one biblical verse I could remember after my extra year studying Religious Knowledge, which made five years in all apparently studying the

Bible, and its associated paraphernalia. I can still remember this verse today, as it has often come in useful over the years as I have had not only to face the music in life, but the woodwork, the art, and indeed the religious knowledge. John Chapter 11, verse 35: 'Jesus wept.'

I said it when I received my O level results. Due to some miracle that suggested God actually did exist, or some accident that confirmed that he really didn't, or some joke engineered by Gosling who after all that was some kind of discreet surrealist, I passed Religious Knowledge. Grade 4: my three other O levels, English, English Literature and History, were grade 6, the lowest pass grade of all. I'm still amazed by this result.

I vaguely remember the examination. The questions meant very little to me. There was one that asked about the relationship between Jonah and the Whale, and because I had spent a few years writing, for my own secret pleasure, about such things as Marc Bolan's white swan and Captain Beefheart's jumbo grasshoppers, I pressed on with wild confidence, writing an essay that was full of words that must have convinced the marker that whatever they were about, they were certainly in an order, and made you think. Not necessarily about Jonah and the Whale, but, what with one biblical thing and religiously another, a metaphor's a metaphor, and I was clearly having a whale of a time putting words together into a certain energetic order, and that was enough to do with the whale to see me through.

Having a whale of a time with words, splashing them all over the page, didn't really help in my Biology, or Physics, or French examinations. I failed them all. The teachers never really helped me appreciate which words to splash, in what order, so I tended to splash my own, in my own order, but having a whale of a time wasn't as impressive or, apparently, relevant in Chemistry as it was in Religious Knowledge.

I also failed Geography. This was because, when it came to Geography, I was inside the whale, and had no chance of getting out.

The Geography master was called Mr Dunnel, and he was the worst of the lot. He was The Master. A worse temper than the Biology teacher. Meaner than the French teacher. Odder than the Latin teacher. (I studied Latin for five years, and the only thing I can remember is that . . . Superman is vulnerable to kryptonite.)

Dunnel was grotesquely wedded to the school. He was probably born in 1485. He had the school running in fluid form through his veins. If he ever stepped outside the boundaries of the school, he would turn to ash.

There must have been a coffin in his classroom, apparently built by Lucifer in the Middle Ages, where he rested when he wasn't, in a manner of speaking, teaching. He taught me everything I don't know about geography. He must have been F. W. Scott's favourite. They were probably related in some ancient incestuous way. All the masters at the school were their children, some more successfully fucked-up than others.

During the day I revisit the slopes and backhills of Stockport, I go back to the school, emblazoned with lack of sentiment, feeling the weary nothing I felt the day I left the school. I'm mildly interested as I approach the school whether walking around the building might make me feel safely, distantly fond of the place, or if the corridors and rooms and quadrangle will merely echo the steady dread and resentment I felt during the thousand days the place rained on me. Perhaps, the writer in me thinks, The school will help me find the last line of the book I'm writing, featuring Stockport, and how all its hills lead away from God, and salvation, and tomorrow.

A line that is something along the last lines of: If we manage to last in spite of anything, it is because our infirmities are so many and so contradictory that they cancel each other out.

Or: I now calculate my adolescence to be from the age of thirteen to my late thirties.

Or: It was the Geography teacher who did it. He buried his victim in Stockholm, which is the capital of Sweden.

It is a school holiday as I roam around the school. It is very empty, and so small. It doesn't look like the mean labyrinth I remember, or thought I remembered. Its Gothic shapes and flourishes seemed more toy-town than menacing. There's much more to the school than there was in my day, a quarter of a century before. New buildings as modern and as neutral as the Mersey Shopping Centre, full of glass and concrete, are arranged around the old building at the centre, which makes the nineteenth-century heart of the school seem less dominant than it used to. The twentieth century has arrived, in a way that it had only barely when I was a pupil.

I pass through in a thousand seconds. I don't really want to stick around. I feel no warm, or even cold, nostalgia, just little stabs of barely remembered tension, little spasms of trepidation. It's church-like in its stillness, its stone pathways and serious corridors echoey with decades of fraught school history. It seems unexpectedly quaint for an environment where the fittest survived and the weak-est were sacrificed, but it retains the quality it always had, of being supremely indifferent to my presence. It couldn't care less about me. I didn't really belong there, and the school knew, the school had a way of turning its back on me, keeping at a long distance. I can't believe I was ever there, that I ever even half-belonged, that there are any traces of my presence. Of the five years I spent trying to find a way out.

And then, as I get ready to leave after one more last time, after spending the amount of time there I would have liked to have spent there the first time – five minutes – I walk down the corridor that used to house the staff room. This corridor contained the concen-trated essence of the horror that lurked inside the school. Not only was there the staff room where the gorgon masters congregated to prepare for their next assaults on the soft souls of their charges, and also the headmaster's office, guarded by burnt-black ravens, but also the classroom where Mr Dunnel would teach, or preach, Geo-graphy in a way that could make mountains tremble. This was a corridor that John Carpenter should make films about.

Lining this stagnant corridor were school photographs, long thin wood-framed oblongs containing photographs of a year's entire pupils fronted by a nightmare gaggle of masters. For suspicious reasons that I've never quite understood, there are no photographs of me as a teenager, except for one taken on Scarborough beach in 1972. It was taken by my father. I am slumped into a deckchair wearing yellow loon pants and a turquoise T-shirt with the words 'Mott the Hoople' written on it. My head from the nose up is not in the photograph. You can't tell from what's left of my expression what I'm thinking or feeling, but in all sorts of ways it is a photo-graph of someone who can't quite see where he's going. His eyes and his mind aren't connected to the rest of his body. They're somewhere else, presumably in another photo, possibly in another dimension.

177

I don't have much of a picture of what I looked like as a teenager, but there in this corridor of hell I find myself losing myself in two school photographs. Odd evidence that I did once pass through this place.

I recognise myself in the photographs because it is as if the crushed stunned boys in the photos have been waiting all these years for me to come back and find them so that they can reach out to me and tell me what a bastard of a time they are having, so that they can once and for all escape from this place. We can leave together.

In the 1970 school photograph, there is Morley, trying hard to be Paul. I pout at the edge of tears, my face puffy, baby-boyish, looking like one very shaky thirteen-year-old, as if I am trapped on a bus, or in a school, going in the wrong direction, as if I am saying, as if I am sending a pleading message to the outside world, Get me out of this place NOW. I want to take this young boy away with me, but I suppose I already have.

Three years later, in a 1973 school photograph, there is Moggers. I am the very embodiment of a lost cause, from the point of view of the school. A lot has happened to me in three years. There is an aggression, an indifference about me that there wasn't three years before. I look like I know more about Iggy and the Stooges than the French Revolution.

At thirteen, I could see no way out. At sixteen, it looks as though my heart and mind have already left the school, and only my skin and bones and, last but not least, my hair remain. I am dreary on the back row, quietly tucked into my feelings of hostility for the whole idea of this photograph, the whole idea of this school, and I stare past the camera as unsmiling as the day I was born. It's funny how morbid, and miserable, and sly I look, not obviously spoiling the photograph, but just staining a small part of it with a defeated contempt entirely at odds with the commemorative point of such an occasion. Anyone scanning through the faces of the 400-odd boys in the photograph would stub their gaze on me. They might also be taken aback by the grinning giraffe in the orange false beard standing next to me. And apart from anything else, they would wonder why I am wearing a wig in the style of the 1970s Francis Rossi of Status Quo. Was it some kind of school-photo-day practical joke? I sometimes thought I might be exaggerating to myself how long my hair grew during that final year, but there it hangs with dour lopsided defiance way past shoulders, fringe hanging with Mickey Finn flatness over my face. It must have been a mere few days after the photo was taken that Scott, sitting in front of the assembled school as if he is Sir Michael Redgrave playing Sir Matt Busby, tried to cut it all off with a pair of scissors.

In both photographs, one boy is captured on both the left side of the back row and the right side, having sprinted from one side of the pose of pupils to the other side as the camera was slowly panning along to create its elongated panoramic effect. He looks very happy, with himself, and school, and life in general. He probably, then and now, wouldn't recognise the school of my pummelled memories. For him, and a lot of the other boys reverently smiling in the photos behind the overacting Scott, their school days were in a rough and tumble every schoolday sort of way the best of their lives. But then, I don't suppose the school ever really threatened their lives.

It is fitting that the photographs holding these miniature miser-ablist images of a heavily schooled me should be so lifelessly hanging in the corridor by the quadrangle that contains the classroom of Mr Dunnel. On one side of the heavy oak door to Dunnel's class-room is the younger Morley, pale but clinging on because he didn't know any better or worse, and over on the other side of the door of doom is the older Morley, paler and unclung because he knew better and he knew worse. Dunnel's trapdoor separates the two boys. It is what happened in Dunnel's intensely atmospheric Geo-graphy room that helped metaphysically and emotionally separate the two boys and their lives so completely.

Mr Dunnel changed the shape of my life by helping to open up the door, the floor, the roof, the walls to the piercing, dizzying, oceanically motionless vastness of death.

At the beginning of the fourth form, as another sign of pop-driven life stirring within me, I had managed to convince my mother, who looked after such matters, that I would be allowed in the new school year to wear flared loon pants to school, as long as they were black. This was not true, the school allowed no such thing, but I wanted to get back at the school for making me wear short trousers when I was twelve, and I thought that I would get away with wearing flared trousers as long as they were not too flared, and inconspicu-ously black. At the time, loon pants had considerable cultural significance, they set you in the present, even the future, and demonstrated your feelings about school, parents, rules. In my deeply private life, where I made fantasy rules up for myself to compete with the strict binding rules made up by my school and my parents, I calculated that the meaty combination of my potentially flowing pretty chewable life-affirming hair and a pair of beautifully flared loon pants would adequately compensate for the inevitable inhuman horror of another year of Stockport Grammar School. It never entered my calculations that this combination might turn out to be an aggravation, to all parts of my life, known and unknown.

Unfortunately, as far as I could tell when I went out looking for the precious loons, in the whole of Stockport, and even Manchester, every single shop that would sell this kind of trouser had run out. These shops took a lot of courage to enter, because they all looked like drug dens from where I was imagining. Loon pants were spectacularly available in orange, turquoise or violet, but not at all available in sober school black. 'Black' and 'loon pants' seemed a contradiction in terms. I did toy with the idea of a two-tone purple pair with lime-green stars on the back pockets, but I could see even in my summer holiday madness that this would be insane. I had to be relatively sensible. After a determined search, because there was no putting me off, I found a pair that seemed to reasonably flirt with my set requirements. They were black. Mostly. They had white stitching around all the seams, up and down the leg, across the hem, around the pockets, but carried away by the sensible blackness I didn't consider the stitching too obtrusive. And they were cotton. Sort of. Actually, they were heavy-duty canvas that would probably have made a good hold-all, or even a quite practical tent, but, I reasoned, at least they're not satin or velvet. The only flaw I could immediately see was the size of the flare. They were so flared, so Dumbo-flappingly huge at the bottoms, they would have tested the fashion mettle of Jimi Hendrix himself.

Perhaps the only person who could have worn them with any degree of suitability in the entire twentieth century would have been Sammy Davis, Jr, singing 'Candy Man' at the Las Vegas Sahara Sands Hotel in 1972.

Maybe Ru Paul could have handled them at the Grammy's in 1994.

I fell in love with them.

My mother was appalled by my purchase. I swore to her that they would be OK. The teachers are getting used to the new fashions, I appallingly lied. I'm sure that as I told this lie the flares on my trousers grew even larger. Reluctantly she agreed, but she warned me that it would have to be allowed, because there was no more money for new trousers. They'd cost five pounds, a good quid more than a school-regulation pair would have cost. My father would have forced me to take them back and get an ordinary pair if he had found out what was going on, but I think by the fourth form he had lost touch a little with what and how I was doing at school.

On the first day of the new term I walked down from Offerton towards the grammar school looking like one of those mixed-up creatures you can create using those books that have top and bottom halves of animals cut into two. The top half of me had a scarecrow resemblance to a fourth-form Stockport Grammar School boy in standard uniform. The bottom half of me looked like an off-duty exotic dancer.

I felt wonderful.

On top of some world or another.

As if I was squeezing how wonderful and myself I could feel in the dreamy, wanky ebbs and flows of my self-made private life of fantasies out through some barrier into the so-called real world.

I thought, School, thou art no match for me!

It's great to be young.

To make me feel even better, I somehow managed to survive the first couple of hours at school, assembly and all, despite looking like an apprentice Brian Jones, from The Rolling Stones. All the other boys were specially combed, scrubbed and mummied for the new term. I was ready to play bass for the Edgar Broughton Band, and no one could come within three yards of me because of the offensive reach of my flares. All my schoolmates were enviously dazzled by my geared-up white stitching, and none of the teachers had seemed to be bothered, and I felt good and ready for anything.

I was ready for anything, except a Geography lesson.

Guess what, coo-crooned the Chorus of Pain, with frogs in their throats and snakes in their eyes, wearing Afghan coats and trousers the size of Afghanistan:

Geography

Geography
There's no light at the end of the tunnel
Geography
Geography
With the most bittom bottom Mr Dunnel.

Mr Dunnel was ready for me, as if it was the culmination of his life's work. As soon as I entered his haunted classroom, the one that made me feel instantly seasick because of all the maps on the wall with their masses of blue water, I was surrounded by boys who looked ever more groomed and correct, fresh and alert after their long holidays. Dunnel pounced on me from behind. He had been standing behind the door scrutinising the class as they took up their seats. He emitted a huge roar as he spotted me trying to hide behind the giraffe, who, it must be said, had left his false beard at home in honour of the new school year.

Up until that moment I had never known what it meant when people said that their heart sank.

But my heart sank.

I knew what they meant.

I felt it drop to the bottom of my trousers.

Even my heart was alarmed at the size of my flares.

Dunnel was a big-chested brashing boar of a man who could have crossed the Pacific Ocean with one step. He had a death-defying nose that looked like it could easily commit a bit of casual violence and hooded bloodshot eyes that could buckle your soul. His titanic body was always draped in a massive multi-pleated dusty black gown. He seemed two sizes too big for the fixtures and fittings in the room. He bellowed at me as if I had got the words 'FUCK DUNNEL' self-tattooed in Quink ink on my forehead.

He was the hunter.

I was the prey.

Bolts of lightning crackled out of his nostrils.

His nostrils were flared as wide as my trousers.

Green steam pissed out of his ears.

I didn't know what to do.

Pray, I suppose.

To the godhead of loon pants.

I prayed.

He didn't answer.

Maybe he didn't exist.

What a time to find out.

The Geography monster made his move. He made it out of bits of broken hell. He made it very well.

The rest of the class sat still in their chairs, contrite on my behalf. I cowered in front of this terribly crossed master who was meta-morphosing in front of my teary eyes into a Judge of everything in life that would wear drug addicts' trousers on the first day of school.

And executor of the aforementioned.

Fuck, even Jim Morrisson would have changed his leather trousers faced with such wrath.

He boomed with devil-winged scorn: Are those trousers that you are wearing?

This was not as easy a question as it seemed.

Technically, I was wearing trousers.

But in his eyes, I predicted, I was wearing the permissive society in canvas form and you just had to take one look at his shiny tan brogues and one-and-a-half-inch trouser turn-ups to realise that here was a man not in favour of any kind of world that had been given any kind of permission to do anything not ratified by Stockport Grammar School, God, or Robert Baden-Powell.

Bing Crosby was a bit racy for him.

I was stuck.

If I said, yes, I was wearing trousers, he might view this as gross mutiny.

If I said, no, I wasn't wearing trousers, he might view this as hallucinatory cheek.

I whimpered instead.

That way it wasn't clear if I had said yes or no.

He looked at me as if the solution to the problem as he saw it was to amputate my legs.

He snarled at me across the century: Or are you wearing some kind of blanket?

I tried a weak smile, because perhaps he was telling some kind of joke, but he viewed this as obscene insolence.

He focused on the white stitching scattered all over my loon pants. Called loon pants, it was dawning on me, because you had to be a lunatic to wear them.

He double-took a couple of times.

Have you got bird droppings on your trousers?

This was another one of those questions that didn't have an easy answer.

I'd come out in a rash, so I took a rash stab at answering.

No, sir.

Wrong answer. As would have been: Yes, sir.

I think the correct answer to all of these questions would have been to have never existed in the first place.

He snapped: Wipe that expression off your face.

This is one of those requests that are made to you at a certain age, a bit like 'Pull up your socks.'

The key is: don't wipe, don't pull.

Whatever you do just don't.

He breathed heavily.

I noticed that his greying hair was sealed to his scalp with neurotic amounts of brilliantine.

He noticed that my hair was long enough to eat, and seemed dusted with icing sugar for extra taste.

He said with diabolical dismay: Have you got talcum powder in your hair?

I think he really wanted an answer to this question. I think he felt that by asking this question, a question he never thought he would get to ask in his teaching career, his entire life had been made the subject of some kind of mockery.

It was an accident, sir, I lied, hoping my flares wouldn't expand any more.

You are the accident, Morley.

There was a brief burst of canned laughter from F. W. Scott's office next door.

My hair was the final straw.

It was lots of final straws, actually.

He'd had enough of toying with me.

He laid out his terms.

He dumped me in shit.

It's great to be young.

The frown marks on his clifflike forehead quivered with cranked-up contempt as he read out the judgment of his court.

The rest of the class sucked in their collective breath as sharply as they dared without attracting the attention of the dangerously provoked Dunnel.

The Chorus of Pain lamented:

> *This body*
> *This body*
> *What use is it*
> *If not to make you understand*
> *The meaning of the word*
> *TORTURER?*

I was to return home that minute. I was not to return to the school until I was wearing unequivocally normal plain-grey trousers with no stitches of silliness and that hugged my ankles and my hair was cut off so that I was a few whiskers away from being pretty much bald.

I was not to attend school until I looked exactly like a boy who deserved to go to such a fine school.

As far as I could tell, this meant I had to replace my entire self.

Mr Dunnel thinly smiled down at me from a position of enormous strength, as if to say, All right, Morley, sort yourself out, and we'll say no more about it. He dismissed me with a snide snap of his tree-trunk-thick fingers.

I left the classroom.

The rest of the class got down to learning how to spot an Anglican Church on an Ordnance Survey map.

The heavy door of the classroom banged shut around me and echoed around an empty corridor. There was no sign of life in the school. The life was dispersed into classrooms, behind closed doors. Anyone the wrong side of one of these closed doors was clearly in trouble.

I was on my own. Dropped from a great height into the ancient shit of time.

I didn't go home for a few hours, because my mother would want to know why I was home so early.

I hoped no one would call to officially inform her. I suppose any official suspension was suspended pending me returning with short hair and conventional trousers.

Dunnel would probably have preferred me in short hair and short trousers.

Cutting my hair was no problem, much as it would break my heart.

How to replace my trousers seemed to black out my future.

I sat in a park, floating between an intoxicating lightheadedness because whatever the vicious circumstances I wasn't at school when I should have been, and a compressed, chilling pessimism because I hadn't got a clue what I was going to tell my mother and, worse, my father about my current predicament.

I decided to make a crude attempt to do something about my trousers.

How on Dunnel's earth had I ever thought I would get away with them?

I sat on a park bench and for hours I tried to fill in every single white stitch within reach with ink from my Platignum fountain pen, as if that might make them less luminous.

The Chorus of Pain had a mental song-and-askance routine for every mocking white stitch.

There were thousands of them.

They were tiny.

I inked and inked. I inked until I was blue in the fingers.

It was hopeless.

I now had a pair of gigantically flared loon pants that were comprehensively smudged with blue ink.

At home I slipped into my bedroom before my mother saw me, before she spotted my trousers, which after just one day's wear were as battered and distressed as I was after my historical encounter with the Geography master in Stockport, Cheshire, England, Great Britain, Europe, The World, The Milky Way, The Universe.

My room at Offerton was the biggest bedroom I had had so far in my life. Every square inch of wall space was covered with posters and pictures and reviews of pop stars. It had all started with Marc Bolan, and now there was David Bowie, Roxy Music, Mott the Hoople, Pink Floyd, Lou Reed, Sparks, New York Dolls, Free, Iggy Pop, Alice Cooper, Jimi Hendrix. Every week new faces and new poses would be cut out of my beloved *New Musical Express* and sellotaped onto any available wall space. My bedroom walls were a starlight mosaic of fabulous pop life. The walls were an image-crammed sign of what was beginning to line my imagination.

I would spend all my spare time in this room. I would let the worlds out there that I wanted to know about come to me. Pop worlds coming through my little transistor radio and the sound system my father had bought for me. Dreams, forms, shadows, glamour, strange tongues, dazzling lust, hidden treasures, secret calls, chaos, love, marvellous things I hadn't yet learned about, fizzed and powered out of the small black speakers and mystically pressed themselves into the texture of my life.

I would shut the curtains that could easily hold out the immediate outside world, that could keep out Stockport, and black out school, and I would hold a tennis racket as if it was an electric guitar and I would mime to my collection of T. Rex records, as if I was in the messiah-marvellous skin of Marc Bolan, as if I was performing to an audience of screaming girls. This made me feel as wonderful as when I masturbated. This was my method for recovering and intensifying my enthusiasm for life and the future, for rekindling vital elemental enthusiasm for the sheer fact of being that my school seemed committed to squandering on my behalf. In this room, through pop music and the way it thrust my imagination beyond reality, I found the energy to re-enter the limited and limiting outside world, of Stockport, of Stockport Grammar School.

The worlds I was finding for myself in my room were bigger and better than the world I was being presented with out there.

I was special in this room.

I could make myself special.

Out there I was nobody.

A few hours after Mr Dunnel had ordered me to change as much of me as I could I sat flat out in my room, as effervescent as a slug. I pondered the exceptional plight that had plastered me into a state of general paralysis.

I couldn't go back to school until I had a new pair of trousers, or Mr Dunnel would destroy me. I couldn't tell my mother, because she had trusted me when I said that I knew what I was doing. She would tell my father, and I felt that there was something about my father that made me think that, if pushed, he could be as furious as Dunnel and Scott combined. A latent anger that I didn't really want to have directed towards me.

The alien might of the school clashed with the domestic might of my father.

I tried my usual ways of escaping into myself.

I tried masturbating.

I was an old hand at it by now.

For the first time in my life it didn't work.

Perhaps wearing the trousers had rendered me temporarily, or Marc help me, permanently impotent.

I tried miming to some T. Rex and pretending to be Marc Bolan. Nothing.

I felt a bit of a fool, to be honest.

The tennis racket seemed like a tennis racket.

The outside world had seeped into my space.

My room had been invaded. I had been invaded.

I wonder what my mother and father made of my actions that night.

I must have avoided any contact with them, and if our paths did accidentally cross, I must have appeared petrified, in a dejected sort of way.

But then, perhaps that wasn't so unusual.

I wonder what they thought I did up in my pop-smeared room that I wanted no one to enter, sealed behind closed doors, and with the curtains shut even during the day, playing the same song, usually by T. Rex, again and again and again.

Feel wonderful?

This night, the black loon pants crumpled in the middle of the room ready to be burned, I went to bed, and I cried, again and again and again, soaked with self-pity.

There is a theory that when you are drowning your entire life will rapidly flash through your mind because your adrenalin-energised brain is travelling in an intense channelled panic through everything you have done in your life searching for something that might once have happened to you that could supply some sort of solution to your predicament. Somewhere, your brain reasons, embedded in a scrap memory, there might be a clue that could save your life.

Cocooned in my submerged bed-world late at anonymous night under heavy-wrapping blankets plagued by thorny thoughts chased by wild beats of unreason a bottomlessly ominous next day advances in the meantime confining me to dread and the world spins round ever so slowly and darkness proceeds on its way into nowhere and I feel like I'm drowning in the sweat of a monster.

Get out of that without moving.

I was drowning close to myself but my life wasn't so much flashing before my eyes as drizzling past in fits and bursts and this wasn't so much suggesting clues as to how I might get out of the situation as pointing out the reasons I had got into it in the first place.

How did I end up feeling that the world didn't know that I existed and yet was out to get me?

This reminded the Chorus of Pain of one of their favourite numbers, 'Persecution,' track five of their *Fated Hits* collection.

This song scoffed at the notion that I wasn't completely fucked-up.

They often sang it when I least needed it, accompanied by a mass tap-dance on a stage set that appeared to be a large lumpy model of my testicles.

Because of the circumstances arising from the day of the trousers the Chorus of Pain tapped quite vigorously and I thought, No wonder I am having trouble getting an erection.

Ouch.

I lay in bed morosely fingering my private parts and I cringed at the singeing thought of what the peevish Dunnel would do to me and my balls and everything else of the outcast me if I turned up at school the next day in my blasphemous trousers.

It's so unfair, I lamented with myself under the bedclothes.

I'm a model pupil as dunces go.

It's not as if I miss days at school.

I didn't have the guts.

Now and then I would feign illness and scrape a few precious days off but that was about it. However much I hated the school I so believed in it as a force of nature that it never occurred to me that I even had the choice to be late or skive off.

I didn't take drugs, although once during a dried-up Maths class I saw some boys surreptitiously passing around some interesting little white tablets. I cadged one, and thought that I hallucinated that I was sharing eternity with Andy Pandy, in order to make it transitory.

It turned out that what I was swallowing was a tic-tac mint.

I didn't smoke.

I didn't beat up any of the other pupils.

I didn't climb over the wall into the girls' convent school next door and get caught with my hand up a girl's skirt in the tool shed.

When I walked home to my house when I lived in Woodsmoor,

which took me past the glass-encased stairway of the convent school, a part of the convent school that was as modern as the Mersey Shopping Centre, I never stood outside and looked at the girls climbing up and down the stairs so that I could see up their skirts.

I wasn't a bad boy, just a bit faint. And getting fainter.

I was just a bit soft. And getting softer.

I sank back into my life vaguely searching for the source of all my straining aimlessness, my intrusive contrariness, my steep desire for everybody to just leave me alone, my haphazard inadequacy, my soaking self-pity. Did it start with me, in me, before I was even born, or thought of, or did it all just join up with me the moment I was born? It was in the air in the space around me and I passed through it and became it.

I thought to myself, What is it about me?

The Chorus of Pain, performing a longer version of 'Persecuted' than usual, introduced their special guest, the well-known all-round entertainer Mr Roy Castle, who was to attempt a world tap-dancing record.

28 taps a second. On my testicles.

Ouch.

I thought about the time at North Reddish Primary School when I was about seven or eight. Tuesday morning was swimming day. Before nine o'clock in the dark and cold our class had to congregate at North Reddish baths for our swimming lesson. The baths were wet and old and chilly and the water in the pool was cold and smelly. One of the hardest parts of my early life was having to lower my white transparent body into the sick iciness of the one-metre end of the pool. It took a lot out of me and my life plucking up the mortal courage to force my upper body into this lapping wet hell. I would then spend many blinding minutes gripping a polystyrene oblong splashing my legs and screwing up my eyes pretending that there was any kind of chance that I would one day learn to swim.

Eventually, after a freezing soaking spluttering pruning eternity of months, I received my 17-yard swimming certificate. This was for swimming one width of the pool. I nearly didn't make it. By the time I'd spent half an hour frantically kicking and sinking I was more or less on the floor of the pool, and I'd only made it halfway across. I don't think they gave certificates for eight and a half yards. I walked the rest of the way.

Getting out of the pool, slopping along the wet stone surround, my tight sopping maroon trunks stuck to my body with saturated vigilance, the damp chilled air snaring my shivering wet skin, my hair frozen into shocked little quirks, my teeth chattering a delirious beat of burden, I would feel very sorry indeed.

For myself.

For a world covered with so much water.

And then I would have to get changed.

This would mean sharing a cramped cubicle with another boy, trying to dry a wet-through and almost decomposing body with an old scrap of rough towelling, and then pulling on coarse clothes over a still damp and resistant skin. When I am in hell I will be wearing a greying white Bri-Nylon shirt that is sticking to a sticky back that is never going to dry.

I would often share my cubicle with David Scholes. One day he noticed something that I very much hoped he wouldn't notice over the months we had spent sharing a cubicle and getting changed in a mixture of exalted relief and remembered misery. He noticed that my white underpants were very dirty indeed. I thought everybody had underpants like that. Grubby and splattered with yellow and streaked with brown. Apparently not. Now that I came to look at David's, they were so white they glowed in the grim dimness of the cubicle. He thought that my underpants were revolting and hilarious. I wanted him to forget all about them, but he was having none of that, and I got the feeling, which added new wetness to the dampness of my skin, that he couldn't wait to tell the rest of the class.

I begged him to keep my underpants to himself, but he was having none of that.

This was hot news on a freezing cold day.

As the boys and girls waited in the small entrance hall to the baths for our teacher to lead us back to the school, David, bursting with pride, revealed his scoop: Paul Morley had pooed in his pants.

I stood there looking like an eight-year-old boy who had pooed in his pants, and the whole class was absolutely delighted.

There was so much laughter the moment could easily have inspired a career in comedy.

If I hadn't felt so sorry.

For myself.

For a world covered with so much shit.

And piss.

And non-specific dirt just as, in its own way, revolting.

I thought about when I was about five and had gone to the toilet and done a wee and my father was furious with me and shouted at me because I hadn't flushed the toilet. But no one had ever told me that you had to flush the toilet after you'd only done a wee. Only after you'd had a poo. How was I supposed to learn anything in life if nobody ever told me anything?

My father was angry.

So was I.

I thought about when I was seven and my father, rather abruptly and with no fair warning as far as I could tell, told me to make him a cup of tea. He thought it was about time I knew how. I must have been the age he was when he learnt.

I went into the kitchen, a bit worried because I didn't know how to make a cup of tea. My mother tried to help me, but my father said, in a voice that seemed a little too loud for my liking, that I had to find out for myself. I tried desperately to remember how my mum made tea. I must have watched her do it a thousand times. I knew that first of all some water had to be boiled in a kettle. This seemed a good start. Perhaps I would have carried on as well if my father hadn't been standing over me with his arms folded in a way that seemed unnecessarily threatening, my mum behind looking helpless.

The water came to a boil. The kitchen simmered with tension. There was more to all this than met the eye. I knew that there should be a teapot involved somewhere in this process, but I couldn't quite work out where. The pressure was starting to become unbearable. It was reaching boiling point. It was all too much considering that all that was happening was that I was attempting to make a cup of tea.

It seemed quite logical, as I forced myself to concentrate with my father glowering at me, that the way to do it was to put a spoonful of tea in the cup and then pour hot water onto the tea. I suppose you could say that I was ahead of my time. Unfortunately there was no such thing as instant tea in 1964.

As I poured the boiling water onto the tea leaves I knew at once that I had made a mistake. Under the circumstances this mistake bordered on the catastrophic. The tea leaves swirled in shock up to the top of the cup and a drop of milk wasn't going to make much difference. As shocked as the tea, I presented this to my father, hoping that he might make allowances considering this was my first try.

He was beside himself with rage, as if I had just crashed his car or something. He screamed at me for my incompetence. My mother tried to calm him down. No chance. He acted as if the fact that I couldn't make a cup of tea was the end of his world, which I remember thinking was very strange. How was I supposed to know how to make a cup of tea? No one had ever told me. What was I? A mind-reader?

My father was so angry.

So was I.

I burst into tears.

I really didn't deserve any of this. I don't think I ever did make him a proper cup of tea.

I lay under the bedclothes with the shadow of Dunnel all around me and wondered if perhaps I should go downstairs and make my father a cup of tea and ask him for some advice.

As if.

He was only downstairs but he was a long way off.

I thought of how I hadn't kissed any girls since I had kissed Hilary a year before, with the expectancy that I would then be kissing girls on a regular basis.

I thought of how hungry I felt.

For all sorts of things.

It was dark and it was a different dark when I shut my eyes from when they were open.

There was no sound except the faint sound of my breath.

I hold my breath.

There's no sound.

I count to forty-seven.

A record.

I hear my mother and father go to bed.

I have no idea what goes on in their bedroom.

When they go in there they sort of cease to exist.

I lie in my bed and I think that bedrooms are mysterious places. Life can begin there and life can end there and life pauses there and life turns into dreams and nightmares there.

It must be getting late.

I wonder if Mr Dunnel is asleep.

I wonder if he is thinking about me as I am thinking about him.

I wonder what the map reference of his house is.

Or his crypt.

I wonder what he'd look like wearing my loon pants.

I wonder who his heroes were at fourteen. Churchill I suppose.

I wondered.

I really like your legs.

My mind never so active as when my body is inactive.

I thought about how much I hated school.

I thought about how every night since I could remember since I'd gone to this merciless school I had prayed intently to some form of God that I had made up in my mind for the sake of daily emergencies, which may have been THE God for all I knew. A figment of the imagination, the imagination being as true as anything, if less solid. And the last thing God would be is solid.

I couldn't believe in the God we sang hymns for and mumbled the Lord's Prayer to during morning assembly, because he was the school's God, he was the teachers' God, a close personal friend of F. W. Scott. He was a God who believed in caps, short trousers, corporal punishment, Rugby Union and Physics exams. But there was a need for me to believe in some form of God or other because lying in my bed fretful about the needling tedium and unexploded mines of school the next day I had to have some kind of protection. Some kind of psychic help. The thing that helped me sleep was praying very seriously to my form of God for three things that might possibly go in my favour the following day:

Please let me find my Biology exercise book before the teacher notices that it has gone missing and loses his biological temper.

Please let the rugby master believe my forged letter where my mother explains that I am not well enough to play rugby this week after school.

Please let me find a girlfriend.

I didn't try to ask for too much.

It didn't seem too much to ask for a girlfriend.

I just thought that my form of God might help things along a little.

I didn't pray that the school might burn down or that I might replace Mickey Finn as Marc Bolan's partner in T. Rex.

Just things within my form of reason. Little things that might make a difference in a small-time hell.

My form of God sometimes seemed to help me, as far as I could superstitiously tell, and sometimes he didn't help me, and I liked the arrangement as it was. The unwritten deal, the unspoken rule, was that I could never pray for more than three things, however many problems I had, and I could never pray for anything too big, however imposing the potential jeopardy. Nothing that could change the course of big-time history, or anything like that. Nothing that would make me, or my form of God, feel that there was a mocking or undermining of the ritual. I had to be sensible about it. Perhaps I didn't think that my form of God was powerful enough to influence any matter concerning the demonic Dunnel. After all, God is really just a part of yourself, a part you form a belief for, or you unform a belief for. I felt that in this situation, praying wasn't going to help. My form of God was in as much trouble as me, and couldn't help at all. Dunnel had made me doubt my form of God.

The bastard.

All the big and little real and unreal fathomable and unfathomable miseries defined and confined in me because of this cruel school had collapsed as I had collapsed into this single pinpoint of outright despair.

I was adrift.

I didn't see what I could do.

I had no one to turn to.

I had no one to pray to.

My solitude swelled up so much it could have blocked the sun.

Sore tears stiffened my cheeks.

On my back in the dark any relief seemed beyond belief.

It's way past midnight.

The house is still and steady.

Something in my room seems ready.

For something.

Or other.

Deep in the velvet crater of my ear.

Something stirs.

At the discreet edge of my life.

Whispering across my captivity.

Nibbling into my cell.

My cell of cells.

And then my misery and anger suddenly seem articulate.

I might as well be dead.

I'm as good as dead.

Dead.

Good.

I wish I was dead.

Of course.

It seemed so obvious.

And right, its exquisitely tempting sense-dissolving late-night wrongness.

I wish I was dead.

Stop.

I want to be alone.

Stop.

I want to go.

Stop.

I remember the inexact blatant moment that the feeling of the thought of the possibility slipped through me in the bedroom dark.

On my back in my bed under the window.

The trees gently rustling in the wind outside.

The room all tossed in shadows.

My mother and father together in bed in the next-door room.

Living their lives. Sleeping their sleep. Dreaming their dreams. Losing their minds.

My little sisters in their bedroom down the hall.

All unaware of my dismal awares.

All the big bad world unaware of my acute sensitivity.

I am going to kill myself.

I wanted no knowledge of anything.

More than a thought.

More than a feeling.

More than a possibility.

I am going to kill myself.

The words had a life of their own in my imagination.

Words that ignited such resonating self-control.

Words that occupied me voicelessly voiced.

Words that would never have to cry for help.

Words that meant nothing at all but what they were.

I was going to kill myself.

Me!

Who couldn't do anything well but pretend and wank and sleep and worry.

I was going to show them.

The only way out of this mess was to find the only way out and I had found the only way out.

It was right in front of my mind all along.

Mr Dunnel couldn't get to me then.

I'd like to see him try.

He'd be sorry.

My death would show him.

I wouldn't have to tell my mother about the trousers.

I wouldn't have to get my hair cut.

I wouldn't have to sit through two hours of Physics ever again.

I wouldn't have to play rugby again.

I wouldn't ever have to go back to that school.

I wouldn't have to worry about not having a girlfriend.

For a blazing illuminating set of sudden moments I felt secure and preposterously alive.

I wouldn't have any more problems.

I wouldn't.

I wanked.

It worked.

I felt wonderful.

On my back in the dark pulling the bedclothes over my head.

I smelt wonderful.

I was sticky in the way I loved to be sticky. Hot sticky. Cool sticky. Satisfied sticky.

My life began to bleed into my death and it all felt so blackly illicitly stickily unspeakably romantic.

I was going to kill myself.

I believed it.

That was the point.

This would be how I would save myself.

From a fate worse than death.

The Chorus of Pain approved.

They were in their element.

They hugged together with their inscrutable faces, and, placing little black caps on their heads, they sang their biggest hit, 'All Curiosity Spent', from their musical *Brief Future*.

> *You are a god!*
> *And we have heard nothing more divine.*

I started to plan my suicide note. I would request that I be buried in my loon pants. I was dead set on going through with it. This was it.

And then I started to consider how I would actually do it.

Aye, there's the rub.

And then I started to consider what would happen to me.

Aye, there's the rub-a-dub-dub.

I was still sure that I would write myself off and write a note and take everything away from me and take me from everything and I'm still sure and then imperceptibly I'm not so sure any more.

Because you see I was so busy with myself and absorbed in my self thinking about how suicide would pleasingly cease me and release me that perhaps I thought too much about the thought of suicide.

And thus the thought of death therefore.

Of what it was.

And most of all what it wasn't.

And of what it meant.

And most of all what it didn't.

I was OK and as cool as a hero and committed to committing suicide when the idea floated on the ethereal side of an abstraction that I had formed myself.

OK and cool when I thought about how I would do it without hesitation and everybody would be really stunned afterwards and wish they'd been nicer to me but I assumed there would be some form of me around to relish how remorseful and upset everyone was.

I wasn't so OK when the idea wafted over to the practical here and now side of the abstraction I had formed. I started to hesitate about how to do it without hesitating and most of all I hesitated when I failed to find a way to kill myself in such a way that there would be a form of me around afterwards to enjoy the aftermath.

Suicide was a real comfort when I imagined that it would hide me at a time when I most wanted to be hidden. I could hide behind life for a while. I would just turn up somewhere else. Suicide was the ultimate hiding place from stress and the future and the stress of the future.

But then it slowly occurred to me in my suicidal bliss as a creeping revelation that once done there would be no me.

No me.

To acknowlege, appreciate, see, hear, know.

No me.

To congratulate myself on my success.

That I was hidden that I am hiding I am hid.

No me to be aware of my hiding.

No me here.

No me there.

No me then.

No me when.

No me never.

No me coming back to say, to me and everyone else:

Surprise!

And with ancient abruptness a prodigious stab of eruptive harshness the in-glowing negative of an orgasm snatched my breath away and created panic pumping with liquid clarity from my toes to my eyes and there was no comfort any more and I wasn't a child any more and I had to get out of bed after a lifetime spent lying on my back in the dark and I had to move around quick struggling for breath and sense and I was snapped in two and crudely put back together again inside a foaming burst that lasted a nano-second or a billion years snapped by something as light and as insubstantial as a snowflake that had fluttered all the way down to me from the end of time. All being is nowhere. The ground will give way beneath my feet. Nonsense is the outcome of every possible sense. You are held out over nothing at all times. Nothing is always part of the very nature of things. In a flash, here, in a flash, there, before life, nothing, after life, nothing. Death is everything, death is nothing. We dissolve into nothingness the way salt dissolves in a liquid. Under every moment is the eternity of nothingness, of death, and a comet could smash the sun at any moment.

The reality of nothingness, the nothingness of 'reality'.

Reality is really 'reality'.

Reality is '   '.

I must have breathed in the void.

I felt terrible.

I had been encouraged to believe that death was like a hundred-year sleep. It was one of my mother's answers when I innocently raised the question, feeling out what the word 'death' actually meant. The answer seemed less likely to my childish mind as the years passed, but I never had the desire to fully confront the developing unlikeliness of this hundred-year sleep. The idea, the prospect, the fairy-tale absurdity just shaded the back of my mind. There was no death in the family, no death of relatives, to provoke me to think harder about the true nature of this ultimate far-fetched obstinacy.

When I was considering suicide, in all young seriousness, completely believing in the still dark that this form of escape was completely correct, I still cautiously, superstitiously, innocently believed in the funny feeling that it was a sort of deep sleep which was one day, what with one thing and another, over. Eventually, somehow, somewhere, sometime, some me would resurface, and everything would be the same, but better. I would be a better form of myself.

I didn't want to go to any next stage of reasoning, and consider why the whole world wasn't killing themselves when things got rough. Life was all this that was happening to me, and death was just one of those words in life whose meaning hadn't yet begun to fill out. The night I lay on my back, trousers dead crumpled a few feet away from me, withdrawing from life, contemplating a real suicide, was the night the meaning of the word filled out. And filled out. And filled out. Taking its awful shape, its unique placeless shapeless shape, and once the meaning of the word had filled out, was the exact appalling shape of death as I formed it, the thing, not the word, took over, and filled me out, and emptied me out, and I didn't believe that death was a sleep any more. Not even a big sleep. And it was no joke.

It was a limitless disaster area always advancing towards us, always bringing up the rear, a way out that was no way out, inside us, outside us, why we are here, why we aren't here, the undesirable calm after the storm, the utter forgetfulness, and so on and so on, or rather, and not so on, and not so on.

It appeared that death was nothing.

Is nothing.

Will be nothing.

Nothing much more than nothing.

Death will be everything.

I worked it out. The nothing of death was the everything of life minus the everything of life plus the sense of nothing of death from the point of view of life minus all that divided by itself plus the nothing that there was before we were born minus having ever known anything minus itself minus everything minus nothing plus nothing etc., etc., etc.

Or rather, not etc., not etc., not etc.

I had received a quick education in the quickness of all the things that we could see death pointing towards as far as we can tell from where life was always pointing towards.

Pointing towards death pointing towards itself.

Life points towards the point of death.

The pointed point.

The point of everything.

Death was the limit.

I felt terrible.

It was all so sudden.

I had realised how essentially terrifying death is – or what the word covers up, or uncovers – and I still realise it today.

I have hounded on the feeling over the years.

The feeling is like dropping in a lift faster than the speed of light right to the rot bottom of what's known for now as your life.

I zigzagged around my room a couple of times, trying to outrun this new sensation, the sensation of the anticipation of non-sensation. I pushed up against a wall and pushed hard trying to push these new feelings – feelings about no feelings – away. I got back into bed under the blanket in the dark to try and sort out how to begin my new life now that I had died a little, or begun to prepare for death.

I wasn't so sure that I should kill myself now that I had been run through by the showstopping size and texture and weight of death. The absence of size and texture and weight.

But then, I wasn't not so sure.

Death hadn't killed off my suicidal feelings entirely. Death had just made suicide a little more complicated, a touch more intimidating.

There was death ahead of me.

But there was also Mr Dunnel.

As night flattened out into morning there were still yet more spinning calculations.

If I was going to die anyway, and it would happen, I could see that now, it would happen eventually, what with one thing and another, then why not now? Was there any real difference in the great banging scheme of things if I died in a few years or a few moments? Would it make much difference to me, to anything, to space and time?

If I was going to die anyway, and I was quickly getting used to the fact that I would never get used to this, then why not die when I was going to die anyway, whenever that was? Why now?

Unless whenever was now.

But then if I was going to die so that there was no me

not ever

as if never

whenever

if it was all that futile all that pointless what did it matter anyway what Dunnel did to me?

Nothing could be worse than death, as I now saw it from the place where I lived aware of the worst thing of death. Except perhaps the engulfing fire of Mr Dunnel's wrath.

Death versus Dunnel.

The battle rattled around my brain.

I was oddly pleased I had actually dared to think of suicide. It made me seem very sophisticated, me lying in my bed, at three or four in the morning, reducing by my own hand, my own mind, all of space so it only existed inside the four walls of my bedroom. Stopping time outside, so time stood still in Stockport, Cheshire, England, Great Britain, Europe, The World, The Milky Way, The Universe, as I contemplated my fate, and considered my duty. Killing yourself seemed to be the most sophisticated thing in the world. Such a sophisticated state of mind you had to be in to consider such a commitment. A state of mind bordering on its own borders of bewilderment and clarity. A state of mind swallowed by a whale: a whale of a mind. A mind that had grounded on a destination as mysterious as the mind itself.

The sophistication of killing yourself. The sensational sophistication. The icy passion and the sense of superiority that is required to complete the act. The skill and precision. The judgement. The timing.

You have to time it exactly right.

And then it could set you above and beyond the history of everything and set you apart from everyone as if you knew better.

And bury you beneath the history of everything and set you apart from yourself in no time at all.

My timing was out. It was put out by the sudden appreciation that I wouldn't be around to receive the acclaim for my sensational sophistication.

Or, another way of looking at it, I wouldn't be around to take the blame for my sensational sophistication, the blame that might come from those who misunderstood the act, the commitment, as the result of, shall we say, very cloudy judgement.

Whatever, my timing was put right out. The time when I might have, could have, was going to, was thinking, was reaching the point, it passed. It left me behind. I left it behind. Something else happened. I didn't die. I missed the moment and found myself with all the time in the world, at least for now.

I think there was a split second, measured by the abyss between two pulses, when lying on my bed in the dark childishly subtly anticipating that I was going to kill myself, that if I had possessed some black-magic pill that could have wiped me out in an instant, no change of mind no mind to change, then I would have done it, in the last dip before the full deathness of death spread its wings through my mind and body. If my timing hadn't been interrupted by the puzzle of how to kill myself. If there hadn't been this pause that allowed the meaning and non-meaning of death to swamp my consciousness, I would have done, out of spite, joy, and belief that I would escape my fix and yet also be around, in some form, to have the last laugh. I would have done it in a moment of inspired nonsensical action hardly believing it myself and then there would have been no me to believe in anyway. I would have taken myself beyond belief.

If it had been that easy, if some preparation had made it that easy, I would have done it. And that would have been the end of this story just about at the same time as its beginning. And I would have felt very pleased with myself, and very sorry for myself.

I wonder if there is a moment just after you die where the life that was in you gets a last fractured sliver of space and time to register how you, and the new form of you, feel now that you are dead. Some cosmic moment that threads between this life and the next.

Some elemental umbilical cord. You have an instant of consciousness enabling you to register your reaction to the fact you are dead.
And whatever you felt in that flash instant, that's your lot, that's
your heaven or hell, that's how you spend eternity, feeling that way,
locked inside that reaction, kept in that mood: terrified, shocked,
sad, insulted, delighted, appalled, indignant, resigned, confused . . .
a new you in the form of your instantly initial response to an end
that isn't quite the end you thought it would be. You become an
emotion frozen inside infinity.

In those circumstances if you commit suicide you have a chance
of controlling your response. Suicide is the act of taking charge of
how you feel about death at the moment it happens.

My timing was out. I wasn't prepared enough to make this kind of
preparation, and one thing I learnt was that when you decide to
commit suicide, you have to be prepared, what with one thing and
another. It might be a messy, sudden, brutal, sullen, chaotic instant
act, a moment of savage spontaneity, when you're stoned on your
own collapsing mix-up of cowardice courage craziness concern
agony misery madness, but deep down, burning hard and consistent
like a pilot light, you must be prepared. You must be prepared to a
state of well-rehearsed precision, so that whatever the circumstances
you find yourself in at the moment of decision, of release, whatever
state you're in, however smashed, or exhausted, or damned, you slip
through the ultimate pain barrier with spatial ease, with exquisite
end timing, with a kind of specific mortal grace. Nothing holds you
back, because you are prepared. The details of the job at hand are
merely that, details, just a way to unfasten your hold on this life, to
unbuckle the last belted connection to the reality of this world. With
a prepared anticipation of the way ahead, you jump. You are deeply
prepared. The preparation has taken away any possibility of doubt.
Faced with the massed confusion of the imminent rush from life to
death you are toned and balanced and finely contained within your
own desire for death, particularly ready to make a flawless leap of
faith into your own special kind of independence. All the nerves in
your body have combined and centred to produce a single nerve that
is all the nerve you need to progress through the shattered remnants
of your life into black airless emptiness.

You are so prepared that death is prepared for you.

I wasn't prepared for how much you must be ready, even if

your readiness only appeared a second before. You must be so ready that there's a kind of inevitability about the way you slip, snap, swallow, cut, shoot, jump, squeeze away. You must be so prepared that no amount of life-instinct or fear of death or squeamishness or guilt or shame or panic or remorse gets to interfere. All of your life has led to this step, and it's a step you take as easily as if you are walking into another room. You are so ready and so prepared because of your thoughts, because of your life, that you have elevated yourself up above the reasoning attached to this life and are already beginning to understand, appreciate, desire the reasoning associated with the next one, call it death, call it nothing. However sordid the final moments, however planned, however improvised, there's no doubting the outcome as you fall over, and out.

Sometimes you might be more prepared than you thought you were, and kill yourself without meaning to. You reach the moment, make a decision you don't really mean, because you're wanting help, you're needing guidance, and something within you is ready for action, and ready for inaction. Something inside you has prepared itself and therefore you for death, and it only takes the combination of your fleeting harassed pressurised decision and the readiness your body has against all your real wishes to push you right over the edge into dismal edgelessness. The whole push and weight and complexity and moisture and relative certainty of your life can be curtailed in a moment, chopped off at the neck, if there's the right alignment of accidental self-resentment, the means at hand and inner psychic readiness. A readiness somewhere inside you that effortlessly overcomes a forceful natural reluctance and pushes you too hard towards a destination you never really wanted. And then it's too late. A moment later you would have recovered your balance, overcome the urges, checked your self, defended yourself against some strange instinct that rose up within you, and still be alive.

If, what with one thing and another, your timing is out, and death carries on without you, you might appreciate how close life is to death. You get to understand how thin the membrane is between existence and non-existence. It can be measured by a blink of an eye, a flash of inspiration, a single breath. Life is separated from death by nothing at all. By an opaque thin nothing stretched around time that can snap open when you least expect it, or when you most expect it.

A second after you decide that you won't kill yourself, you're alive. You could have decided to kill yourself, and you would have been dead. All the complicated mythiness of routine and blood and reaction and sheer interactive day-to-dayness as dictated by the terms of this current lifetime arrangement smashes to an instant stop. You have no future, and your past collapses into your present. Alive, everything carries on, as if nothing has happened. Dead, nothing carries on, as if everything has happened. Alive, you get to keep changing your mind. Dead, there is no mind to change. Everything stops. Everything carries on. A moment can separate these two issues. A brush with death makes you marvel at the gap between significance and insignificance, a gap that is in itself both significant and insignificant.

The moment after I could have quite easily taken my own life, as long as it had been all over with before I knew it, and if the means had been there in front of me, safe, swift, reliable, I'd weakened. I'd fumbled my timing. I'd underestimated the accuracy of purpose and the amount of preparation required to hit a target that is so massive and so minute. There was still enough anger and bewilderment inside me to have done something savage involving wrists and razors. I was still in the mood to contrive a suicide attempt, the kind that is a dangerously petulant cry for help shrieked for real, Look at me I don't know what the fuck I'm doing.

I might have been more prepared than I knew and I might have sliced my wrists and I might have bled to death not meaning to bleed to death and then it would have been too late I would have splattered through the membrane that thinly stretches between life and death a membrane you can move through only one way. This way to that way. Not the other way round.

Of course I wasn't nearly prepared enough. Not deep down. A moment after the moment when I might have done it if there was a way that was too convenient to exist, I suppose I was just in a state of mind where I thought I would rather bleed from the wrists than have said to my mum, Look, I made a mistake. Can I have a new pair of trousers, please? I'll do the washing-up for a year. Can everything carry on as normal? I couldn't say this to her. I'd rather slash my wrists.

And then it was all over.

I blacked out.

I'd exhausted myself.

Death saved my life that night.

I'd thought about death so much I hadn't found the time to die. Death had interfered with my timing. When you want to die, even though you want to die more than anything in life, it's best not to think about death too much. It can interrupt the flow. It can get in the way. You don't want to think about death. You just want death. Not as something you think about, but as something you don't think about. Because you can't. You're dead.

Life didn't keep me alive that night. Death did.

After that night, I became very interested in death, the deathlessness of it, the closeness, and yet the distance. The distance! There is no longer distance than death. From then on, death was with me daily, along with masturbation, pop music and the next day. I would think about it every day, it was something that limited my vision, and yet somehow also extended it, enriched it. There would be little flashback attacks of the flash-forward panic I'd experienced when I realised the dreadful cut-off point that the word 'death' represented. When things got bad in my life I would play around with the narcissistic idea of suicide, but never as seriously as the first time. The trouser time. The first time was special. Nothing could be as definite, as unrivalled, as precarious, as the first time. The first time is the first link in the chain that leads to the last time, the last link. You realise what death is for a first time, and this means that there will be a last time. The last time you realise what death is is before you die. Perhaps if you never realised what death really was, you would never die. You wouldn't make it happen, you wouldn't create something for yourself to believe in that you get to believe so much, you make come true. There is a first time for everything. And a last time. Except death. The first and the last time happen at the same time.

I developed an attitude towards suicide that a few years later I saw perfectly expressed in a book by the great German philosopher Friedrich Nietzsche – being as interested in death as I now was meant that I was soon reading books by Friedrich Nietzsche.

He wrote: 'The thought of suicide is a great consolation; by means of it one gets successfully through many a bad night.'

If things were that bad, then kill yourself. Be prepared, and kill yourself.

But things could never be that bad. How could it ever be that bad? When things were bad, you lapped up the bitter-sweet taste of suicide, and you thought, Well, I can always kill myself, that will stop the pain, the pressure. There is always suicide because there is always death, and death rules life.

But then, there's always tomorrow. I can kill myself tomorrow, and kill off tomorrow, and spend tonight revelling in my fantastic suicide decision, spend some time enjoying the moment of my own specially planned death.

Then maybe things will sort themselves out and even get better.

And then it would have been a waste of a damned good death, if things got better anyway.

If they don't get better, I can always kill myself.

But let's just wait and see.

What have I got to lose?

I'm going to die anyway. Sooner, later, the difference is almost as tiny as the difference between life and death.

A couple of hours after I'd dropped off to sleep having done a deal with death I got ready for school as if nothing had happened.

Because nothing had happened. And happened hard.

Everything around me seemed to be carrying on the same, so I carried on the same, even though things were different. Things are always different, day in, day out, and you just have to carry on as if everything is the same.

While I was asleep dreaming of the north, east, west and south of death, my mind, or something quite like it, must have kept on fussing, because some kind of decision had been made for me when I woke up. Something had been sorted out. Sleep had calmed me. That's what I needed all along. Sleep, not death. In my sleep my exhausted, frantic mind, or something closely resembling my mind, had come to a solution. Something could be worked out. In my sleep something about me had reached a decision. There was something to be done. Things weren't that bad. I could always kill myself tomorrow.

I had been in such a state the day before that I had missed the obvious. I hadn't considered that I didn't have a Geography period on the second day of school. I should have paid much more attention to the first period of the new term, when we sat down and copied out our new timetable. No Geography. If I kept my dim wits about me, I could easily avoid Dunnel. There was no need to go anywhere near his classroom in the horror corridor. He never ventured very far from its smoking borders. There wasn't a Geography period for a couple of days.

The risk was, could I get through the second school day of the new term without any major mishap and without running into Dunnel. It seemed a risk worth taking after the night I'd just been through, because after such a night everything seemed freshly coated with a filmy layer of absurdity and triviality. Then, after school, I could get my hair cut, and do something about my trousers. Life may have been coated with absurdity, but it wasn't absurd enough that I wanted to tell my mother about the cock-up with the trousers.

The fact that I had been so close to my own death the night before, and I have never felt as close, meant that I felt just a homeopathically tiny amount braver, or more detached, and sleepwalked in a dazed way through the second hell day of the fourth form, trusting that if I didn't pay too much attention to my hair and loon pants, no one else would.

I just hoped that a scornful Dunnel hadn't pinned up a wanted poster in the masters' common room:

WANTED
for grotesque decadence, sullen apathy, horrible hair, pornographic trousers, constant yawning and the inability to interpret the steepness of a hill from an Ordnance Survey map:
MORLEY
Get him.

There were a couple of scares, but then there usually were during a school day, regarding some such silly business. The Biology master, a man nicknamed 'Bug' for reasons of size, nature and his surname, Jermy, threw a freak-out with junior Dunnel distaste because of the length of my hair. I somehow managed to speak despite the lump in my throat, a lump that had swelled up the day before and which was not shrinking very noticeably. I thought as Bug fingered my hair with photosynthetic disdain that Dunnel was telepathically communicating with him. It's all right, sir, I explained, feeling cornered but not cowered, not after what I knew about death and its close relations, I have already been ordered to get it cut.

This could have been a disastrous thing to say to him. I was admitting that, yes, I knew my hair was too long, but also that he wasn't the first master to notice the length of my hair, and I wasn't getting it cut directly because of him. This wasn't good for his ego, which I had realised by now is all masters care about. Luckily, hair wasn't particularly his area of main concern. His interests were very esoteric. He liked to show me up during school dinners. When he was on dinner duty, he would often painstakingly demonstrate to me how to eat properly with a knife and fork. He seemed to enjoy feeding me mashed potatoes and peas in front of my friends. No, Morley, push the peas onto the back of the fork Don't hold it like a shovel.

He finished fingering my hair. Make sure it's cut the next time I see you, he said. Oh, I will, sir, I said, with a brand new tinge of nihilism.

What could he do to me, anyway. Kill me?

The French master looked as though he had forgotten how to speak French and also English when he saw my trousers. They looked as if I had spent the night sleeping rough wearing them. In a way, I had. Everyone in the class braced themselves for a Dunnel-like bust-up as on the day before, but this time it was different. I was different, if the same. I apologised, although in my head it didn't seem to be me speaking the words, and explained that my new school trousers had torn the day before, and that they were being repaired. It never occurred to me as I confidently spun a web of lies that the teachers might communicate with each other. I was performing a dance of death with the truth and my trousers. My answer seemed to help the French master recover a basic understanding of English, if not French, and it seemed acceptable to him as long as the next time he saw me I was wearing regulation school trousers. Yes, sir, of course, sir, I confidently exclaimed. The lesson continued, and I continued on my way towards ending four years of French knowing only that *Je m'appelle* Clark Kent, and I am vulnerable to kryptonite.

I wondered why I hadn't acted the same way in front of Dunnel yesterday. These aren't my regular school trousers. They're a temporary replacement. My real ones – and of course the ones I'm wearing aren't real, they're an utter figment of my imagination – were burnt in an ironing accident, and they will be replaced forthwith. Might have worked, especially with the cunning use of the word 'forthwith'. But then, I didn't know death yesterday. And I'd loved my loon pants yesterday, and dearly wanted to hold on to them. Today, the other side of life and death, I had accepted that they would have to be sacrificed for the greater good.

At home that night, with freshly mown hair, I rifled through the chest of drawers in my room looking for last year's pair of school trousers. My near-death experience had taught me to exhaust all possibilities before giving up. They would be tatty, they would be dirty, but they would be charcoal, and they would respectfully hug the ankle.

I couldn't find them. My mother must have thrown them out. I carried on looking through the old clothes in each drawer. I found a pair of trousers I don't believe I had ever seen before. They were a very pale grey, with fine white stripes about an inch apart from each other. But they were cotton, they were straight-legged, and they were all I had. They didn't have a zip, and when I tried them on, they were a bit too small, and pinched into my waist. But, I shrugged with reason, they were worth a try.

I left for school the next morning, after a night spent getting even more used to the flattening fact I wasn't going to be around some time sooner or later, and I was as ready as I could ever be for my date with Dunnel. The final showdown.

I left home a little earlier than usual. The plan was, apparently, that I would leave my house wearing my battered loon pants, so that my mother wouldn't suspect anything. Inside my briefcase, squashed into a small space amongst all the odds and sods crowded in there, I packed the zipless grey trousers and a large rather ornate safety pin I had found, which I was going to use to fasten the zip together. The safety pin was the size of a knuckleduster.

I had worked out that if I walked in a certain stiff-backed bent-kneed sort of way, my school sweater should just about cover the fly area, which even with the giant safety pin was still bursting to become exposed. I would get to school before most of the pupils and masters arrived and in the toilets I would change into the strange grey trousers. They were tight and very scratchy, but what's a scratch or two between life and death? After school, I would change back into my loon pants, and my mother, and Mr Dunnel, would be none the wiser.

I was extremely satisfied with this plan. For a few months I did this every day. By Christmas I managed to persuade my mother to buy me a new pair of regulation trousers, but the first half of my fourth year at Stockport Grammar School was spent in a trouser-swapping frenzy that bordered on straight farce.

Within a couple of months, when my hair was starting to grow longer, I could be seen walking around school with my hair stuck down the back of my blazer, not able to turn my head, and my legs bent at the knee, so that my sweater might cover up the fact I had no zip. I would be in a terrible state if I had to make any kind of sudden movement. Both pairs of trousers would be constantly creased but somehow I got away with it. Or thought that I did. With English-prisoner-of-war cunning I had managed to get out of the predicament I was in, even though it caused me weeks of anxiety as I had to spend my mornings and afternoons changing from one pair of trousers into another.

Stockport Grammar School taught me that even at the moment of seeming triumph there will be anguish. And that Superman was right not to wear trousers.

Some thoughts that I had and some thoughts that I never had as I lay there thinking about killing myself:

1) There is no kind of place for suicide in an ordered world – it should never be allowed to happen.

2) The recognition of the certainty of death gives us a certainty that nothing else can give us.

3) Suicide isn't an abomination because God forbids it: God forbids it because it is an abomination.

4) Nothing could be further from the truth.

5) I wonder what would happen if I wore a dress to school.

6) A man is a particle inserted in tangled and unstable groups.

7) It's great to be young.

8) When a would-be suicide hooks up one end of a hose to an automobile's exhaust pipe and inhales at the other, he is taking advantage of the affinity that haemoglobin has for carbon monoxide, which it prefers by a factor of 200 to 300 over its life-giving competitor, oxygen. The patient dies because his brain and heart are deprived of an adequate oxygen supply. The colour imparted to the blood by the carboxyhaemoglobin makes it significantly brighter and paradoxically even more vibrant than its normal state, with the

result that the skin and the mucous membranes of a person who dies by carbon monoxide poisoning have a remarkable cherry-red tinge. The absence of the typical bluish discoloration of asphyxia may deceive those who discover what appears to be a pink-cheeked body in the bloom of health, but dead nonetheless.

9) Dad!

10) In the case of death, we do not face something that awaits us in some distant future, but something we bring into the world with us at the moment we are born. Our life runs up against death at its every step: we keep one foot planted in the vale of death at all times. Our life stands poised at the brink of the abyss of nihility, to which it may return at any minute.

I was alive, and the Chorus of Pain creepily and yet almost affectionately performed one of their very few cover versions. 'Happiness', by Ken Dodd. Done, obscurely but fittingly, in the style of the Indian rock band Quintessence, which meant lots of airy flutes and bitter-sweet sitars and toppling drums.

> Happiness, happiness,
> The greatest gift that I possess
> I thank the Lord that I possess
> More than my share of happiness.

Meanwhile, back at school, Mr Dunnel acted as if nothing had happened. The key words in that last sentence are 'acted' and 'nothing' and, come to think of it, 'as' and 'if'. At the beginning of the next Geography class, Dunnel, first name Mister, half-noted that my hair was as it should be, at least as far as he was concerned. As short and feeble as the hair on a baby mouse. He was quietly pleased that I had been struck down like Samson. He also seemed satisfied enough with my trousers, even though to me they seemed wilder and camper than the loon pants. The loon pants that were destined to disappear off the face of the earth. Trousers tend to do this. When you stop wearing them, they disappear. They might hang around for a while, but pretty soon, zip, they're gone.

For the rest of the school year, and the school year after that, Dunnel treated me with standard geographical contempt, in the same way that the Biology master treated me with biological contempt, the Chemistry master with chemical contempt, the Maths master with mathematical contempt, the French master with French contempt. Meanwhile, the Latin master treated me as if I was as dead as his language. (If I was dead, it was because the Latin master kept kryptonite in his desk drawer.)

I don't think that Dunnel and I ever spoke another word to each other again. I turned up to his lessons, sat in anxious silence praying that he wouldn't notice that one of my shoelaces was frayed, or assume that the large safety pin keeping my trousers in one piece was some grotesque phallic joke. I listened as detached as the moon as he dry-droned words about the world as if the world was something he could hold in the palm of his hand, and the moon was something he could swallow whole, and then I would depart. I couldn't be sure, but he never quite seemed the same after the day he sent me home to change my trousers. I wonder if, racked with guilt at treating me so harshly, he had spent a night contemplating his own suicide.

I doubt it. After all, he was already dead. He had killed himself in 1935 because he had torn a hole in his Oxford bags. Sheer will-power ensured that he would, despite his tragic death, teach Geography, gravely from beyond the grave, for the rest of time, or as long as Bucharest was the capital of Romania.

We were not taught Philosophy at school, so I was never treated with philosophical contempt. I think I learnt most about philosophy during my teenage years from the silence in my father's conversation, from the gaps in his sanity. From his inflated remoteness. From his ability to live life as if he was somehow in the middle distance.

His sighs were full of Kant.

I don't know if it was before or after the night of the long trousers, or the long night of the trousers, the night I thought of killing myself, the night I lost my nerve or fumbled my timing, but sometime during our stay at Offerton, my father made another dash for freedom.

During my middle teens, I had a lot to think about, what with school, death, pop music and all-round teenage self-abuse, and my father was slipping away from me – both because I had these new areas of deep concern, and because he also was living more and more inside his head. As well as the usual separation between father and son that might go on during the son's tender teenage years, the average generational tension, there was something else going on. I would be mildly embarrassed by my father, vaguely troubled, a little scared, maybe, in a certain way, in reluctant awe. But this is the time to rebel against the father. It is not healthy at this time to adore your father: that way dullness lies.

All this was perhaps quite ordinary. It's what a fifteen-year-old can easily start to feel about his father, at a time when the natural close-ness of living with another man who has for so long been the voice of authority and the face of your future – the closeness, the authority – all starts to grate, to niggle, to unnerve. A power struggle begins, a game of strength between a younger version and an older version of the same kind of man, separated by time, and hair, and trousers. It's a time when family love can buckle into fizzling resentment.

But above, or below, or to the side of all this, there was a feeling, felt then or later or now, that my father was fading from view. His presence was less and less felt. He would seem to be invisible or reserved for weeks on end, and then there would be a sudden burst of visibility, of life, and then he would dwindle again, run out of breath. It was as if for days at a time he would be reduced to living as a kind of random burst of static, and then normal service would be resumed for a while, and then the interference would return. Sometimes his reception was very clear and steady. And then it would wobble, roll, crackle, break up completely.

I wouldn't say that we consciously avoided each other. The house was too small for that to really work. For physical avoidance, any-way. Mentally, we were definitely keeping in our own space. He didn't seem to want to tell me about what he was doing, and I didn't want to tell him what I was doing. The strangeness of the relation-ship between a father and a son can easily lead towards the father and the son being strangers. We were heading that way.

And then one day he ran away again. When he ran away, up to the time he didn't, this meant that eventually he had to return. When he returned it was awkward all round. My father tried to cling on to the vanishing aura of respectability and reliability that the head of a family should maintain. We pretended that everything was pretty much as it should be and nothing stupid and odd and worrying had happened. Family life would resume, if marginally less stable and solid than before.

The family was more and more in a constant state of recovery. The family was more and more having to repair itself. We were discreetly sorry for him and he was subtly sorry for what he had done and there was just general turbulent sorriness in the air and there was still tomorrow to face. A tomorrow that would be different and exactly the same. A tomorrow that would somehow seem heavier than today.

After each breakdown my father would become incrementally stranger. We didn't really like to acknowledge this, but it was clearly the case. Each time he returned after his secret journey into the outside, his quick trip into the unknown, the interference would get longer and stronger. There was less and less of him that was clear and focused. He was a stranger to the world, a stranger to himself, and consequently a stranger to his family.

It seemed, or we made it seem, all quite normal. Secretly, all of us, mother, father, son, daughter and daughter, in our own special ways, in ways appropriate to our respective ages and experience, were looking around and longing for the normality that there seemed to be in other places.

While I was toying with suicide, shopping it around, licking its lips, fantasising in my Offerton bedroom about sex, pop and death, my father was elsewhere, off my stage, sinking into himself, fighting against life, developing new secrets about his self and his being every single minute of every single day. While I was discovering the ripe, ripped writings of Rimbaud and the brittle, burdened words of Beckett, flirting with the disaster of myself, and the disaster of death, my father was elsewhere, going from his senses, losing touch with his surroundings, thinking about ways out, about changing things. While I was turning the lights out and listening to the scary animal in the night voice of Peter Hammill as he sang about death and, worse, life, listening to the exquisitely mournful voice of Nick Drake sing about life and, worse, death, my father was elsewhere, losing himself in himself, forgetting to be himself, having to become moment by moment a better actor at performing as himself. He was listening to nothing.

As I was reading about the experiences of poets and writers with strong features who used words to climb inside their dreams and emotions and memories and tear them apart, as I was listening to sensitive singers singing sensitively about pain and pleasure and fate and fortune, my father was elsewhere, busy with his own affairs, unaware of Dylan and Baudelaire and Neil Young and Verlaine. As I was obsessed with my life and my school, and my school life, my father was elsewhere, lacking something, always having the feeling that something was lacking.

As I was keeping my alienation moist with adolescent intensity, my father was elsewhere, feeling his life getting colder and colder, and harder and harder. As I was having twisted teenage fun being angry and depressed and frustrated and lonely and anxious, my father was not having any kind of grown-up fun feeling angry and depressed and frustrated and lonely and anxious. As I was living a fantasy of despair and isolation, my father elsewhere was living the real thing. As I was inching towards a life that was all my own, my father was elsewhere, creeping towards a death that was all his own.

As I was in my bedroom, with its blue walls covered with pictures and its white polystyrene tiles on the ceiling, some of which I had punched holes in with the top of my tennis racket as I leapt in the air playing at being Marc Bolan, as I was in my bedroom, thinking I might want to kill myself, my father was elsewhere. He was up to something and paying the bills, or not paying the bills, and he was down in the dumps. As I had my own brief encounter with suicide, as a possibility, as an available and affordable temptation, my father was elsewhere, facing up to nature, and society, and the drive to and from work. As I skidded round the edge of the thought of suicide, my father was elsewhere, holding on to as much of his mind as he could hold on to. As I ate and breathed like an ordinary Stockport teenager, making things up to see what happened, taking things a little too seriously, my father was elsewhere, forcing himself to eat, a man for whom every waking moment leaked terrible seriousness. A man who was searching for an agent who might book him on a motionless journey to the end of, loosely speaking, everything.

As I thought of suicide in the vast smallness of my bedroom, I had no idea that my father might himself have thought of such a thing. No idea that my father in his own way, strangely beside himself, had tried so hard to be so elsewhere. It would never have occurred to me.

In the dark of my bedroom as I edged up to death, I would have thought that dads don't kill themselves. Dads can't kill themselves. Dads keep themselves to themselves. They're a big secret. They're otherwise engaged. They're a law unto themselves. They have a lot on their minds. They're elsewhere. But they don't kill themselves.

For my fifteenth or sixteenth birthday my father bought me Alice Cooper's *Killer* album, the one with the snake's head on the cover. The album was filled with seriously silly songs about death and destruction, hate and fate, flies and nooses. He didn't buy this record for me spontaneously. That would have been particularly impressive, for him to suddenly present me with a record that I really wanted. In another way it would have been really irritating, to feel that he had an understanding of my very own secret world. I gave him a list of records I wanted, and he chose *Killer*. In one way, it is quite impressive that he walked into a shop and asked for an album by Alice Cooper. Unless he got his wife to do it. Or a friend.

I'd like to think he did it. All on his own. I wonder why he chose *Killer* above say *Led Zeppelin I*, Amon Duul II or Loudon Wainwright III. Perhaps he just liked the cover, or got the record shop to play the opening track, 'Under My Wheels', which he oddly discovered gave him ideas. The smug teenager in me wondered if he knew that Alice Cooper was the name of a man, a band, and not a woman.

Years later I met Alice Cooper. He had a forehead just like my dad's. If my father had been alive I would have got Alice's autograph, made out specially to my father: 'To a killer dad, with love from Alice.'

It's a joke, Dad. By the way, Alice is a man. He plays golf with presidents. Nothing ever turns out like you thought it was going to.

I was eleven and then I was sixteen. Though no honours came my way, these were the lovely years. That's one way of looking at it. Certainly, I was eleven and then I was sixteen. Oddly enough, I did leave school with some honours. Not as many or as high and mighty as the school would have liked, if it had cared to like, but enough so that as long as people asked the question how many GCE O levels did you get, and they stopped asking more or less after I was thirty-two, I could decently reply, 'Four.' I became one of those working-class boys from little red houses who pass their eleven-plus with a little too much alacrity and then end up with four sweet little O levels. The 'O' stands for Ordinary, and getting four O levels is the epitome of ordinary, in grammar-school terms. Getting four also means that you get to struggle on with an education, instead of heading straight out into the outside world of work and adulthood. Three O levels, you can just about cling on, two you're counted out. Four, and there are still options. For better and worse. You can stay inside the world of education, a world that is connected to the outside world like a fantasy is connected to a dream.

I can't quite work out what happened, considering I remember the school with such moulded resentment, but I earned the first two of my O levels in the fourth form, when I was fifteen, a year ahead of the usual age you sit these exams. A funny little bubble of near success, a little hint of how it should have gone according to the school, my father, and some script where I might have ended up as a chartered accountant.

The school had some scheme where they encouraged pupils to take two of their O levels a year early, to gauge their potential, to split up some of the workload, and probably just to use the boys to show off, to demonstrate what a fine school they were by displaying all these O levels gathered a year before they should have been.

Rising to the challenge, breaking the habits of a short lifetime, spiting those who might consider me mediocre, I spent time revising for the History O level. I remember taking the thing moderately seriously. I passed with a grade 6. Maybe the examiner misinterpreted my hysterical examination essays as actually being quite historical.

The other O level we took was English Literature. The two set texts we studied were William Shakespeare's *Macbeth* and Thomas Hardy's *The Mayor of Casterbridge*.

I can remember little things about *Macbeth*. Scotland. The three witches. The cauldron. The Thane of Cawdor. Duncan. Lady Macbeth. Banquo. The dagger. The fog. The castle. The blackness. Shakespeare managed to percolate to me through the centuries and through the school walls, even though what I got wasn't directly the original brew. By the time Shakespeare's dream of time had dreamt through time to end up with me, the thing had changed shape, and was, as far as I could tell, something other than a play.

The whole play was like a big block of featureless black ice that was set in front of me, and I was supposed to squeeze dark intricate meaning out of its flat dense surfaces, its smooth cold edges, its epic opaqueness. I never cracked the black ice. It never melted. It didn't seem like it was ever going to melt. Meaning had been frozen into a sense of senselessness by the greatest mind in history in smothered association with my ordinary Stockport mind.

I never saw through the great mind of the writer into the traumatised minds of the characters. At times it seemed like I was expected to swallow in one this huge black block of ice, kept, miraculously, inside the pages of a battered blue textbook. I would lick the black block of ice, and my tongue would stick to the steaming cold, so that if I were asked questions about the play, about its themes, about its mystery, I would be truly tongue-tied. Sometimes I would touch the ice with my hands, to try and work out what it all meant, so that if I was asked to write an essay about the play, my hands were too numb to form any words. I would be paralysed as if in a terrible nightmare.

Occasionally in frustration I would try and stab the big chunk of immense ice with a handy dagger, attempt to chip little fragments of its meaning away so that it would be more manageable, more approachable. But the ice was impenetrable, mighty, dark, hard, endless. It kept the secrets of the play tightly inside its mysterious mass, enclosed the *Macbeth* universe deep within its depthless depths. The ice took on the shape of an abyss of unreality stopping me from getting close to the play's icy articulation of an abyss of unreality. The play itself was in the disguise of itself and was its own obstacle in the way of me understanding its wicked ways. The centreless ice was the essence of inaccessibility and difficulty.

I do have a sense that I finished reading the play. I covered all of its icy solid surface, even if I never managed to get inside it, or get it inside me. I have no recollection of reading even a chapter, a page, a paragraph, a sentence, a word of *The Mayor of Casterbridge*. I must have read at least some of it, it must have been discussed during lessons, I must have had to write essays about the book, but I remember absolutely nothing. This book was black to me like a shadow, a shadow that kept racing away from me, a shadow I could never pin down. A shadow of nothing. If I force myself to remember anything about *The Mayor of Casterbridge*, I would remember that each page was filled with featureless shadows. Each page was filled with shadowy people doing shadowy things, interacting with each other in shadowy ways, eating shadows, drinking shadows, living like shadows on the face of time, dying like shadows when the sun goes down. The meaning of it all was a shadow racing swiftly towards my mind and then completely eclipsing it. The book was a shadow of itself passed over my thoughts. A shadow pressing dully down onto my sense of me. When I think of the book now I just think of a shadow laced over my imagination.

In spite of the monstrous block of dense black ice that froze my mind, I passed English Literature. Perhaps my description of the play as a block of ice within a fog of reason, or my confession that *The Mayor of Casterbridge* was haunted with shadows of people with shadowy motives damned by the shadow of fate, convinced the examiner that I almost knew what I was talking about. At least to the level of grade 6.

One of the consequences of this was that I was comprehensively put off Shakespeare and Hardy, and for years as the eclipsing coldness chased me through my twenties and thirties I would look upon such plays and such books as icy, shadowy things mocking me with their bleak bulk or their sinister closeness. Another consequence was that I had two O levels, and was due to take another batch of seven or eight in a year's time. Perhaps I was going to make a university after all. Not Oxford or Cambridge, but nevertheless a university. I would be the first Morley to go to a university. Maybe this would cheer my father up.

Then again, a year's an eternity at Stockport Grammar School.

The following year, thanks to the God who exists or does not, thanks to my essay on Jonah and the Whale, I sneaked the other two O levels, so that, in this case, two plus two equalled just what it should. There was nothing I could do about it. I like to think that in Mathematics, I got a minus mark. I like to think that if I had retaken my Maths O level, and got another minus mark, this would have meant that, putting the two results together, I would have got a plus mark, and passed. But it was thinking like this that meant I had failed my Maths O level in the first place, with possibly the lowest mark in the history of Maths GCE O level examinations. I think I was in such a state the day I took the exam – not least because the night before I had seen David Bowie at the Manchester Free Trade Hall made up as Aladdin Sane when according to my father I was at my friend's house revising – that if I had been asked the question, what is two plus two, I might well have answered: Nothing. Or, to be more precise, a whale of nothing. Or, to be as exact as a circle

221

measured by Einstein, a whale of nothing, but I'm only dancing. If I had been asked a question about pi, my answer would have begun: 'Time takes a cigarette, puts it in its mouth ... you pull on your finger, then another finger, then your cigarette ... wo oh, wo, oh, oh ... it's a rock'n'roll suicide.'

So I took a good look around me. At all the people passing me by, at the clouds in the sky and the leaves on the trees, at the ground ahead of me and the road behind me, and decided that, what with one thing and another, I could easily do without my Maths O level.

I don't think my father ever understood how I didn't manage to pass my Maths O level. He always thought of me as the boy of six or seven who could already recite the whole of the times table from 2×2 all the way to 12×12. At ten I could add up a single column of figures in near-world-record time. I never got to explain the role David Bowie took in distracting me.

Somewhere during my time at Stockport Grammar School I committed mathematical suicide. I had prepared myself well for this kind of suicide.

At school, there was Hardy and Shakespeare, as seen through a shadow darkly, as positioned imperfectly at the centre of an indistinct block of irreducibly dense ice, and I don't remember ever connecting these transitory shadows and this universe of frozen vitality with my father at home. I don't remember drawing parallels between the spiky coldness and the dogged shadows of the books set before me and the way my father was being chased by his own shadow and freezing himself inside his own growing and enigmatic block of blank and uncrushable ice.

I wasn't alert enough to understand the way my father was slumping under the weight of the frozen shadows that life was dropping down on top of him. Frozen shadows that were penetrating and changing his mind. Frozen shadows that Hardy and Shakespeare knew all about as they made up their fictional realities based on fate and evil and temptation and death.

Because of the state of his life, I think at the time my father would have understood more than me about what was happening inside *Macbeth* and *The Mayor of Casterbridge*, if he had read them. He could have identified with the way that people, individuals stunned and stained by their own consciousness, were being tossed and turned by the fate of the universe and the fate of themselves. He would have understood perfectly that these books are about lone human beings terribly adrift in a universe that consists ultimately of nothing more or less than black cold and fleeting shadows. Everything else is pretty much a mistake and, what with one thing and another, you make do, and watch out, and do the best you can, until you can't.

Despite my unlikely success, I spent the final year at Stockport Grammar School plotting my way out. Even with the two O levels, it was clear to me and to the teachers that I was not the kind of pupil who was going to become a sixth former. I was never destined to wear a prefect's badge. I was 'o' for ordinary, and there was no chance at all of me becoming 'a' for advanced. I don't think my father ever suspected this, and in his own mind I had two more years at Stockport Grammar School.

I was sent along to see a career's adviser in Stockport. I filled in a form he had given me to ascertain my likes and dislikes and work expectations. According to what I had written I wanted a job that paid well, that didn't involve working regular hours, indoors, in an office, that didn't involve working with other people, and that in fact didn't involve me getting up in the morning. I felt that this further confirmed how I was perfectly suited to being a writer.

The careers adviser looked almost as askance as F. W. Scott had back at the school when I'd told him I wanted to be a writer. He rubbed his head, and leafed through a few brochures. He found what he thought was a course that would perhaps make sense of my journalistic ambitions. An Ordinary National Diploma in Business Studies, allegedly the equivalent of doing A levels. The adviser reckoned that because the course had lessons in Law, Computer Studies, Sociology, Economics and Government and also included shorthand and typing, this would be suitable for a budding journalist. In reality, and I think we both knew it, for the kind of writer I wanted to be, I might as well have taken a course in Black Magic or Archery for all the good this OND was going to be. But he needed to tick me off his books, to file me away as dealt with, and I needed a good, persuasive story to tell my father when I explained that I wanted to leave school.

If I could find him.

I was eight, and we lived near Manchester, and at school all of the boys in my class were making the one crucial Manchester choice. They were deciding whether to support City or United, blue or red. At six or seven or eight you make a decision that will stay with you all of your life. You commit yourself. And since the Munich air disaster in 1958, when Manchester United ceased to be simply a football team and were on the way to becoming a world-famous legend, a matter-of-fact footballing myth, choosing between City or United had an extra edge of pathos and complexity. It's a weightier choice than the one between Liverpool or Everton, Arsenal or Tottenham, and not as religiously straightforward and preordained as the choice between Celtic and Rangers. It's a metaphysical choice.

The temptation for a young boy to support the Reds is very powerful. When I was eight, the glamorous swirling red mist of United constantly swept through the playground as we played football with filthy tennis balls. Red and white scarves were flung around the youngest boys, already converted by their fathers as the faith got handed down. Most of the boys in my class, because of their fathers and the redness that there must have been drenching their homes, and heralding their arrival on the planet, had committed to United. They had already joined the red army, as if there was no other choice. But in the end, the choice between City and United can even transcend family loyalty.

You make the choice, as a young boy who has barely learned how to read, who can count just above one hundred, based on your tender, freshly formed instincts, based on the newest of feelings about how things should be in the world. It's a philosophical choice. It very early on in your life demonstrates your approach to life. Do you want to make things easier for yourself, or do you want to make things . . . interesting? Choose red, and you choose ease. You choose certainty. Slick, satisfying certainty. Choose blue, and you choose unease. You choose hope. Constant, exasperating, and yet occasionally quite exhilarating hope.

United, managed by the wise and canny Scottish manager Matt Busby, had recovered from the catastrophic 1958 crash which had ripped the heart out of their young side, and a whole new team had been created, boasting such magical names as George Best, Denis

Law and Bobby Charlton. They were winning league champion-
ships, and FA Cups, and their name made the city of Manchester
famous around the world. They were known for the flamboyance
and efficiency of their football, the scope of their ambition, the
might of their support. A young boy could be easily persuaded to
fall in with this supreme inevitability. To support United in the late
60s – and any time since, give or take a couple of years of re-
adjustment – was an easy way into instant glory, and excitement,
and power. An easy way to belong to a gang that was the strongest
you could find. The instant route to supporting the best team in the
world. History and fate and fortune and strength of numbers were
all on your side when you went red.

In 1965, a few miles across Manchester from where the Old
Trafford ground represented footballing heights and symbolised
irresistible football history, Manchester City were having trouble
living in the shadows of their all-conquering neighbours. Neighbours who, since the Munich crash, since Busby had spun a fantasy
with his new young team, had an aura of hallowed invincibility.
City had sunk into the Second Division, their attendances had
dwindled to under 10,000 compared to the 55,000 who regularly
turned up at Old Trafford. Up to the mid-50s, City could hold
their own against United. After the Munich disaster, United drew
away, as a dream, as a religion, as a business, as a football team.
United were inspired by their unique tragedy, and somehow City
were the ones who suffered. They slumped and shrivelled faced
with the righteousness and fervour that United were generating
from without and within as they made their recovery, as they
inexorably evolved into sporting giants. In 1965 United were
building a team that was destined to conquer Europe, and City
were falling apart. United were turning into a brand name, one of
the most identifiable sporting names in the world, and City were
slipping towards possible extinction. United were as mighty as
America, and City seemed as little as Luxembourg. United were
forced forward by the weight of their history and the modernising
single-mindedness of Busby. City were grinding to a halt, drifting
through a series of faceless managers none of whom seemed able to
stop the steady rot.

Even their history seemed less than it used to be. Simply, none of
their players had died. There had been no magnificent sense of

sacrifice. Nothing had happened that separated so sensationally the team from the common herd.

United were in a position to force the world to see things their way. City were rapidly losing whatever identity they'd had. United were Gods. City were nobodies. United were everything. City were next to nothing.

My father appeared to be waiting for me to make the choice he knew I must make. He didn't influence me at all. As a southerner, from a county that only had one team in the football league, Fourth Division Gillingham, he had never shown an interest in football. He seemed to have had no bias either way, but it would have been hard for him not to hope that I would choose United, and he could take me to see some of the greatest players in the country. I imagine him waiting for the moment when I came home and announced my new affiliation, my new desire to go and see the great Manchester United play top teams, and beat them, just a few miles away. I imagine him looking forward to the day I would demand that we travel across the city and watch George Best be brilliant for the complicated sake of it.

In the cold damp late-autumn months of 1965 I made my choice. There was something about the smugness and noisiness of the United fans at my school that struck me even at the age of eight as off-putting. There was something about the thought of United that seemed slightly grotesque. There was an arrogance even then about the team, or the idea of the team, and their supporters – thirty-five years later, this arrogance was powerful enough to knock holes in the ozone layer. It was as if somehow the Munich disaster gave them this protected feeling of superiority. Red, the harsh, mean red of United, seemed to an eight-year-old coming to his human senses the colour of aggression, cynicism, dogma. The United fans in my class seemed to be the boys I didn't trust. Blue, the comforting, gentle sky-blue of City, seemed the colour of sensitivity and an open mind. The City fans in my class, I sensed inside my forming eight-year-old mind, were full of doubt and hesitancy and curiosity, and this seemed instantly attractive to me. It appeared too easy to support United. Too obvious. To support City was a kind of challenge, it involved risk and unorthodoxy, and all of this appealed to me. At eight, before one thing and another, I was this kind of person. I was lured by the stranger journey, not the most comfortable. The blue way seemed full of intrigue. The red way seemed over-organised and over-subscribed.

I went home one day and told my father that I wanted to go and watch Manchester City play football. He took it very well. Perhaps he was relieved that I hadn't been press-ganged by the evil force of United. Perhaps he too identified with the underdogs of City as they coped with their rampaging neighbours. He too sided with the sensitive ones who took to City because they suffered, because they struggled for life, because they were sky-blue, because they weren't United. Like me, because I was like him, he was the kind of person who rejected the easy success associated with supporting United. Within a matter of days, we had seen our first City match.

He tried to surprise me, saying that we were going on a coach journey to see a friend of his. My mother let it slip before we left the house that in fact I was going to see City play. In an instant, the eight-year-old me, revealing precocious sophistication, worked out that my father would be upset if he thought the surprise was spoilt. I pretended I hadn't heard my mother mention the match, and we walked to Holdsworth Square in Reddish to catch the coach. He thought he was keeping a secret, and I was keeping a secret, the secret that I knew that he was keeping a secret. The coach was full, and we had to sit separately. The elderly man next to me started to talk, and asked me if I had gone to the game the previous Wednesday. This was my cue to turn to my father, and innocently ask him if we were going to see City play. I was pleased that I had managed to keep it to myself that I knew all along we were going to the match, and he was pleased that he was able to surprise me.

Manchester City, sixteenth in the Second Division at the time, beat Crystal Palace that day, 3–1. We stood amongst about 10,000 other spectators scattered around the giant Maine Road ground. We were hooked. We were City fans. For the next six or seven years my father and I had the exact relationship you would expect of a father and son in the late 60s and early 70s connected by their respective love for a battling, at times baffling, football team. Our unspecified unconfirmed love for each other travelled from one to the other via the football team we had found for ourselves in this place we had found ourselves living in, what with one thing and another. Supporting Manchester City brought us together. It was where we could be close. We could share a common dream. We could get excited in each other's company, and for a few years not be embarrassed.

Very quickly, we established a routine, a routine that began in the house at Reddish, survived intact through the move to Woodsmoor, and just about made it to the house in Offerton. We would go to every home match, and even some away matches. These were our easiest, simplest, most straightforward times together, as we found togetherness with each other because we were the type of person who fancied City more than United. Soon, funnily enough, it was apparent that our choice had been the right one. United didn't lose their grip on their power and glory, but City, as if from the very first day my father and I became supporters, staged a recovery.

They appointed a manager who was the dignified, shrewd equivalent of United's Busby. Joe Mercer, an experienced, disciplined ex-England player, brought in a younger, eccentric assistant with modern ideas, Malcolm Allison. Their mixture of perception and energy, calm and ruthlessness, turned City from no-hopers into a team that began to rival United for glamour and success. At school, the City fans were no longer mocked from a position of strength because of their pathetic weakness. City fans were now mocked defensively, because they were a team with their own sense of identity, their own attacking style, their own flowering reputation.

City were promoted from the Second Division into the First. They found players that were just as exciting to watch as the Bests and the Laws – Colin Bell, Mike Summerbee, Neil Young. The City attendances started to grow. Soon, they were nearing 40,000. My father conscientiously made sure we got to every match at least an hour before the kick-off so that we could stand in our favourite spot and I could get a good view.

Nearby, United might have been fulfilling their destiny as written in the sky since the Munich air disaster by winning the European Cup, but City, incredibly, by 1968 were winning the League Championship. They needed to win the last game of the season, away at Newcastle, to push their arch-rivals United back into second place. My father took me all the way to Newcastle to watch this final match of the season. City won 4–3, won the League, and as father and son supporters my father and I were pulled as close as we had ever been, and ever would be. I remember the long journey back to Reddish as a sleepy haze of triumph and gratitude. Gratitude that my father had managed to arrange that we were present when Manchester City became the First Division champions.

The next year, City won the FA Cup. The year after that, they won the European Cup Winners' Cup. They had stared the giant United straight in the eyes, and although United didn't blink, nor did City, David had raised himself to the heights of Goliath, and my father and I had watched it happen inside five years.

Joe Mercer left, and by the early 70s the recent magic of City was beginning to wear off. They were still a team of good players, they were still one of the country's leading teams, but the sheer thrill of those days when they were chasing United down, and winning tournaments, and rewarding those who had chosen blue against all the odds was naturally falling away. Gradually, my father and I went to fewer and fewer games, at least together. By the time I was sixteen, the routine that had meant we spent so much time together joined at the mind watching our chosen team was changing. I was changing. He was changing. These changes interfered with the open purity of our relationship. Once, we'd stood in the Kippax stand urging on our team to catch United, and escape the shadow of their devilish neighbours. Nothing got in the way, my school, his work, my friends, his wife. We had no other real interests, somehow not even ourselves. We invested ourselves in the team. By the time I was sixteen, I was too interested in myself, and had no idea what he was interested in.

We were still City fans. But we were fans in a different way. A less passionate, vital, committed way. We were not in love with City any more. We were just loyal.

Perhaps my father missed the fact that we stopped going to the football together, regretted the way our relationship with each other through City just faded away. Perhaps he just lost interest: other things were concerning him. Perhaps if he had lived we would have renewed this part of our relationship in our later years. When I was beyond teenage awkwardness, when City needed the support again to mount yet another attempt at recovery as the shadow of United and their damned success crept once more across the face of the erratic, weakened City. When City needed yet more hope.

By the time my father died, we had stopped going to the football altogether. City became a part of the distance that had developed between us. A reminder of a past that already seemed too dreamy and ideal to have been real. I don't remember the last match we watched together. I don't remember talking about City much before he died. After he died, City went from bad to worse, they staggered about in the top division, they fell down a couple of divisions. United became the world. City became a small town lost in time. But I stayed blue, even when there seemed to be too much death, too much failure, too much wasted time and too many distractions to maintain the faith. I stayed blue because of the eight-year-old who made that brave individual choice in 1965, because of my father who made the choice with me. Because of Newcastle, when City overcame United, and life obliterated death.

And now I remember my father and I remember that he was such a City fan. I see myself standing next to him in the Kop end at Liverpool, where we had managed to squeeze in during a sell-out top-of-the-division match. There's the thirteen-year-old me decked out in blue and white scarf, blue and white hat, blue and white rosette, and he's right next to me, protecting me from the slightly threatening crush that's all around us. He's wearing his own City scarf and chatting easily with the Liverpool fans pressed into us. He's very comfortable with himself, and all the pushing joshing Liverpudlians surrounding us. We're almost the only City fans amidst a stormy sea of Liverpool red. We're little bits of sky that have dropped into a pool of blood.

City have scored an equaliser, right in front of us, it's Francis Lee, moving faster than the wind, slamming the ball into the net right through two defenders and a goalie, and we hug each other right amidst the silent enemy, stunned and amazed that life can be this good. This fantastically sweet.

My dad loved City. For a few years it made life worth living.

The last line to a book that might or might not be about Stockport as a place, a location, a dislocation, a state of mind, a period of time, a colour, a discoloration, a lostness, a means to an end: In the end, what with one thing and another, because one thing leads to another, he lost interest.

I told my father that I was going to leave school at the end of the fifth form. It was the biggest thing I ever had to tell him. There was still enough of him left, enough strength and personality, for him to be disappointed with me. He wasn't as blazingly disappointed as he would have been five years earlier, when he seemed bigger, and brighter, and touchier. A lot had happened in the meantime.

Or maybe that's how I thought of him when I was younger. That he was louder and more dangerous, because I was smaller and more timid. The reputation of my father was based on the feelings of a seven-year-old who was half his size. He looked huge, and seemed to have a very loud voice. I was seeing my father as a dictator. An emperor. All-powerful. At least within the Morley house. As far as I could tell, he was the man who shouted at me a lot. At the time, I didn't take time to wonder if this was because he cared, or because he didn't care.

I told him in the lounge of our house in Offerton that I was going to leave the grammar school, and he was frustrated and let down. Perhaps he was disappointed with himself. That he had let this happen. Let his son lose grip of his potential and after all those grammar-school years leave school at sixteen just like he would have done if he'd gone to a lesser school. Perhaps he saw this failure of mine as just another failure of his.

I explained about the Business Studies course at Stockport Technical College. It wasn't like I was going to work in a shop at the Mersey Shopping Centre. He accepted the fact that I was going to carry on with my education as a reasonable compromise. I'd been worried that my father was going to shout very loud at me for letting him down, for letting myself down. It was all over in a few fast moments. There was no real loss of temper. He groaned more than shouted. He slumped in front of me more than lunged at me. A little more sadness seemed to seep into him.

Consumed by my own problems, I just felt relief. The final chains linking me to the school had been broken. I was free. School was out completely. My father's final surrender had made it official.

No more school.

No more homework.

No more teachers.

No more kryptonite.

(Although I was beginning to believe that the whole of Stockport was built on a layer of kryptonite that affected anyone who came to the town from outside. Especially from the south.)

*

My father sent his best suit, his favourite jacket and trousers, his two good shirts, just about all his clothes, to the local dry-cleaner. The cleaner's was robbed. His clothes were stolen. He was offered a small amount of compensation, about enough to buy a new pair of trousers. As if whatever else was happening in his life, in his mind, wasn't enough, he had now lost all his clothes.

It helps in this life if you have got something to wear. Now, more or less, my father had nothing to wear. He had been stripped of his clothes. He must have wondered who, or what, was out to get him. What else was in store for him. Some might think, You've got to laugh. Not my father. He'd done all his laughing at the tumbling absurdity of life a long time ago. He must have thought, This is beyond a joke. I imagine him sighing to himself with such inner force you could have felt the vibrations 20,000 leagues under the sea.

Without trousers, standing in his underpants as if he would be like that for ever, he must have thought, Life is such a farce.

Perhaps a few weeks after the theft he saw someone standing at the bus stop by the Strawberry Gardens pub wearing his brown corduroy jacket, and he thought, That's it. Enough is enough.

The last line to a book about death or something after a return to a town that is easily described as being on the borders with death: He imagined quietly slipping out of Stockport into a past where he wouldn't have a care in the world.

The last line to a book about the wonderful act of breathing and some of the ways that breathing comes to an end: He had only himself for company.

Within fifteen months I was telling my father that I was going to leave my Business Studies course and work full-time in the Stockport Bookshop where I was already working part-time. His worst fears were confirmed. I was, after all, going to work in a shop. I had no future. But then, what was the future?

He put up little resistance. He had lost control over me, but then he had lost control over everything, including himself. More than enough was more than enough.

It was time to move. Again. One more time.

*

232

The five us, Mum, Dad, Paul, Jayne and Carol, made one more move inside our little world of Stockport. We moved to the other side of Stockport, across Mersey Square, a little closer towards Manchester. From the airy neatness of Offerton to the darker, more sprawling, Heaton Moor. Offerton was mostly made up of young families, of people trying to better themselves. Heaton Moor was a place of students just beginning their adult lives cramming themselves into big ugly houses, and elderly people coming to the end of their time. The atmosphere was more restless than it had been at Offerton.

14 Hawthorn Grove was a bigger version of the tiny old house in Reddish. It was the biggest house we had lived in, but not the smartest. Whatever the reason was that we'd moved, the fact that in Heaton Moor you could buy more for your money, because of the area, because of the size of the houses, probably had something to do with it. I think the reason we moved so many times within Stockport was always as part of some scheme to improve ourselves, to get on, to keep up, to solve problems, sometimes to move closer to a particular school to make it easier for one or other of us to get there. The moves were also taking us away from the outskirts of the city, and closer to the country.

This last move seemed to have the quality of a last-gasp move, to escape an area that was too expensive, but not to slip back to the narrow streets of Reddish. We were slipping back towards the city, but not back where we started. All the moves up to then had seemed to represent a struggle to improve the quality of the family's life, but this one was clearly an attempt to rescue us, to ensure that we didn't end up where we had started. This move demonstrated that my father had lifted his family as high as he could, and now, what with one thing and another, it was going to be a matter of survival.

The house in Hawthorn Grove was our last Stockport house as a complete family. It was my last Stockport house. It was my father's last house ever. I think of the time we spent there as our Gothic period. I think of it as the house on the hill. I think of it surrounded by fog. I think of it as dilapidated. I think of it as being at the end of the road. I think of it as a house that was made up of waiting rooms, all of them lacking personality, none of them quite connected, and in these rooms we all waited, for something inevitable but not quite specific.

*

The last line of a book that started in one house in Stockport and ended in another house in Stockport and told the story of a life where everything meant what it was meant to mean: There was a rumour that a year after the tragic death of the man at 14 Hawthorn Grove, the next man who moved in went mad and took an axe to the house and chopped it to bits.

The last line or two of a book about my time in Stockport up until I first had sex: In the house in Heaton Moor, up in the attic bedroom, I finally lost my virginity, and very nearly my foreskin. In some ways, I had waited for my father to die before I had sex. In other ways, my father kindly got out of the way, allowing me to have sex without there then having to be some kind of embarrassing meeting after the event.

Everything changed in Hawthorn Grove. Because of sex and because of death nothing was ever the same again.

I spent the months after we moved to Hawthorn Grove concentrating on writing a magazine of my own. The bookshop where I worked sold Xeroxed left-wing agitprop magazines such as *Manchester Free Press* and *Mole Express*, and because of punk there were already the first punk fanzines being produced. I decided that I would do one of my own. I called it *Out There* because that's where I wanted to be, and because that's where I thought of my favourite music as being. I wrote essays about Brian Eno and Patti Smith, and filled it with stuff on Bob Dylan, attacks on Mick Jagger, flights of fancy about Marc Bolan. I showed off my liking for the English free jazz of John Stevens and Keith Tippett. I also started to write about the punk music that was for the moment changing everything – The Ramones, The Stranglers, The Sex Pistols. The magazine was loaded with my bedroom-nurtured imagination It was a combination of my bedroom enthusiasm for the avant-garde, for pop, for poetry, for the mysterious and for the provocative – symbolised by the adoring essay I wrote about Patti Smith.

My father lent me the money to get it typeset and professionally printed, and after months of planning and preparation I finally had a glossy little black and white A3-sized magazine. This was my way of saying, I am a writer. Even if nothing else had happened in my life to make me be a writer, this magazine would have made me feel I had done something. It was also my way of saying to my father that I was not a failure. This was what I wanted to do. This was how I wanted to tell the world that I had something to say, something different, and that I was not intent on giving up so early in life, and disappearing into a Stockport future that was never much different from the past. I had my own kind of knowledge, and it was as valid as any.

The review of The Sex Pistols in *Out There* that revealed a kind of belief in something that my father never had as far as I knew a kind of belief in something that went beyond belief a kind of belief in something that can save your life when you come to think about it a kind of belief in belief itself a kind of belief that I believe was as alien to my father as a belief in himself and after all my father in the end only believed in nothing:

So there we were. Priding ourselves on attractive elitism upwards of seventy or so cross-sectioned furry freaks and plastic poseurs politely settled in the quaintly draped hitherto mysterious Lesser Free Trade Hall. There to see a youthful contemporary quartet play the street avant garde music of the 60s in its properly repressed 70s setting. The Sex Pistols. Plenty of ripe 's's in the name, the surging s* rock very much inbred into the Pistols' controlled chaotic punk muzak. Acceptably stylised, thankfully few traces of commonplace modern ill posturing, the sound owes not a little to two of the few genuine geniuses in rock, Iggy Pop and Ray Davies. Visually, without the purposeful powerful musical support, they falter. Mild mannered fresh faced youths, perhaps uncouth, on leave from their self-imposed army sentence. Johnny Rotten, lead singer, possesses a cute carrot coloured overgrown crew cut† and

---

* At the time, the name of this new music was not yet quite sanctified. 'Punk' to me made it sound stupid, and American, whereas from where I was looking, listening, learning, the music was, in fact, anything but stupid, and was uniquely if newly English, at least when played by the likes of Buzzcocks, the Pistols, The Fall, The Stranglers. In my world I named it 's' rock. 'S' for sex, for surge, for sensation, for sarcastic, for space, for stun, for significance, for sly . . .

And ultimately, what with one thing another, in some form or another, to all intents and purposes, 's' for suicide.

† When I saw The Sex Pistols play at the Lesser Free Trade Hall, a couple of years after I had left school, my hair was possibly longer than any man's

commences the set with a nice pair of small oblong stamp-sized
shades that place him at about grade two menace-punk. When he
whips them off, he shrinks alarmingly, we see the whites of his
beady eyes, and he's a grade two weed. No matter. The rough, raw
tidal surge transforms the quartet into one neat unit of aloof intimi-
dating punks. Guitar, bass, adopt suitably respectable easy-split
stances. Rotten plays Frankenstein playing Lionel Blair with a hint
of the forced mechanism of Bowie, Ferry and Bygraves. Technically,

---

hair in the world apart from the Texas albino rhythm and blues guitar
player Johnny Winter's. I had not cut it since F. W. Scott had threatened to
cut it himself. I was now looking like the kind of person who would not
only fit seamlessly into the audience at a Black Sabbath concert, but also the
kind of person who would be allowed to join on bass the hippy support
group Curved Air. The trouble was, at a Sex Pistols concert, I looked like
the enemy, and one of the points about punk was that there was now a kind
of war going on. A war between the now of the future, the then of the past,
between a new way of doing things, and the old way of holding things back.
Hippies were indulgent failures. Punks were idealistic schemers and
dreamers. The Pistols, and their weird and wonderful entourage, were
breaking from all insipid pasts through their noises, their looks, their
clothes, their haircuts. Long hair now suggested that you were old, behind,
lost. The times were speeding up, and at nineteen or twenty, by having long
hair, I was suggesting that I believed in the dried-up past, in the yesterday of
yesterday. There was a change in the air, and those who believed in the new
sound of the future, the new ideas that came with those sounds, were
ridding themselves of the accessories and styles that were associated with
even the immediate past. This wasn't a matter of fashion – it was a matter
of belief.

My father never liked the length of my hair when it went beyond the
merely scruffy and entered the really long phase. The majestically long
phase. The length of my hair demonstrated that I had reached a level of
independence he never achieved. It symbolised that I was freer than he had
ever been, first because of his overbearing mother, and then because he had
a family to support. He made half-hearted attempts to persuade me to cut
it, but he soon gave up, knowing that the more I was told to cut it, the more
I would keep it long. As far as I could tell, now that the horror school was
behind me, I had no intention of ever cutting it again.

The day after I had seen The Sex Pistols for the third time, the day after I
had managed to get into the Pistols' dressing room and get within spitting
distance of Johnny Rotten himself, whose hair was getting madder and
more cropped by the month, I went into the bathroom in the house at
Hawthorn Grove. I started hacking with a blunt pair of scissors at my long

they're accomplished. Defined limits, but they're disciplined and don't stray. Hard, loud, clean, brisk, and as relentless and as guiltless as a zipless fuck. Their harmonies are spot off. If one of their songs ventures past the 200-second mark, they contentedly sustain the nifty moronic monotonous peak they initially attained. They plagiarise admirably. The Stooges' 'No Fun', The Monkees' 'I'm Not Your Stepping Stone', ' Substitude' by The Who (an obscure 60s sub-cult who now do cabaret and dated 'freaky' films). The Pistols' own songs are London mirror takes of Verlaine's New York violent rejections and sexual rebuttals. They're excellent. Aggression through repression. Get on with it.

I was at home one day. It was about twelve o'clock. My father came home. I don't know what he had been doing. I don't know if he had a job at the time. He seemed to be at a loose end. So did I. My sisters were at school. My mum was out, I'm not sure doing what.

My father and I talked about something, and we decided that we'd have something to eat from the fish and chip shop around the corner. He went and got some fish and chips for himself, and a cheese and onion pie for me. We ate it on our knees in the front room of the house. There didn't seem to be anything out of the ordinary. Did we have a cup of tea? My father must have made it. He could make tea in his sleep.

After we had finished our meal, my father fell asleep and I went upstairs to my room to play some records.

---

hair. Rotten had mockingly refused to talk to me, because, he sneered, I looked like a hippy. An hour later I came out of the bathroom with a very bad haircut. A very short haircut. As far as I was concerned I now looked as dangerous and current as Richard Hell, the New York punk writer and singer who had inspired Rotten's look. There was no way I would now be allowed to join Curved Air.

My father couldn't believe it. To be honest, it made him laugh. I suppose it was one of his last laughs. I also suppose it was a hollow laugh. I'd willingly cut my hair not because of the school's authority, or his authority, but because of the authority of someone called Johnny Rotten. The world was clearly beyond him.

My father lived to see me crop my hair and get rid of my flared trousers. When he died, he had a punk son. When he died, his hair was longer than mine, and he was the one wearing the flared trousers.

I was upstairs playing, say, Henry Cow and Roxy Music, and my father was downstairs, asleep. Perhaps he was making another cup of tea. A few days later he was dead. At times like this you tend to ask yourself, What the hell happened?

Was I expected to cry?

The last paragraph to a book about my mind as created up to a point by the shape and shapelessness of Stockport: I left school, and I took the Chorus of Pain, whose time was up, and I put them on a boat, and I watched them sail down the Mersey towards Liverpool, and the Irish Sea. And as they floated away, to the end of time, to the ends of my mind, I heard their voices get softer and softer as they sang their final song:

> For the soul has a long, long journey after death
> To the sweet home of pure oblivion
> Each needs a little ship, a little ship
> And the proper store of meal for the longest journey.

The last line to a book that might or might not be about going back to Stockport to have a look around and pass through the past to help think up the last line to a book that is about or is not about Stockport, my father, the past, the present and a number of other things that do and don't end where they begin:

When you're dead, you can't remember your name.

PART THREE

ON: ONE MORNING

One morning, it must have been the earliest a day can be so that it can formally be called a morning, some sorry place between five and six, there was a knock on the door of our house in Heaton Moor. It was a bad-news knock: there's no such thing as a good-news knock at that time of the morning. I opened the door in a trance that was significantly not sleepiness expecting worse than the worst. Two pale, stricken, pinched police constables, a boy and a girl, as old and as young as I was, way out of sight of being a man and a woman but they couldn't admit it, stood in front of me as if they were both about to faint and weakly established who I was. They were at the right place.

They acted exactly as if they were bringing very bad news indeed and didn't have the first idea how to bring this very bad news. Even before they said anything, standing on the doorstep as flat as pancakes transparent as glass lonely as clouds clichéd as cops, I couldn't help wondering in a strict moment of clarity what they had felt back at their police station when they were handed this terrible assignment.

At this time of the morning. At this stage in their lives.

There was an extremely delicate, tricky, veiled pause . . .

ON: PAUSING

Behind them the rest of the world was elsewhere. Some of it was awake and some of it was asleep. Grass was growing.

ON: DELAY

. . . as they looked at me and I looked at them and it was a perfectly passive, quite peaceful moment, all things considered, that sank into itself and protected itself and shrieked in silence with exemplary lack of irony.

This was going to be hard for everybody concerned, I could really tell.

They didn't have to say what they were going to have to say because I knew what they were going to say and I knew that they knew that I knew but they were going to have to say it anyway. It couldn't be any other way. The life everybody involved in this little drama had lived up to this point had led unerringly to this point, and we all knew it like we had been following a script. Everything that was happening had been expected, even the news itself, the heart of the matter, news that could only be so dense and absurd because it was, essentially, in the greater scheme of things, unexpected.

They were too young to have been given the responsibility of delivering the ice-old black-hot information that they were about to deliver, and absolutely nothing to do with the given situation, and I was too young to listen to the information, and absolutely everything to do with the given situation. Incidentally, the given situation was loaded with such obviousness, obscurity, and strangeness you couldn't help but feel that life, or something quite like it, moves in mysterious ways. Soon, the given situation would perceptibly change shape, and become loaded with further obviousness, obscurity and strangeness, and then you couldn't help but feel that death is motionless in mysterious ways.

Meanwhile, behind the police constables, who were as white as icebergs about to sink a family, the rest of the world was still massively somewhere else. We all understood as we stood in our assigned positions that we didn't understand what was going on, and mucked in as best as we could. Actually, in a faraway way, there was a part of me that didn't really listen to what they had to say. Some part of me got stuck in the pause and would perhaps stay there for a long unidentified time. That part of me may well be still stuck in the pause, delaying things to such an extent it's beyond a joke.

My father is alive in that pause. To leave that pause behind was to leave my father behind.

A part of me – you could call that part of me 'I' – just knew it.

I just knew it.

Inside this pause he was still alive.

I remember that my father killed himself. I suppose that means that I must have a good memory.

I remember that my father asphyxiated himself. His breathing squeezed to an extreme stop, his brain caved in, his senses cracked up and perpetually ceased, his self fell off its hinges, his memories forgot themselves and scattered themselves at high speed into a jammed null and void, his leftover body was useless to anybody, he passed into a past where nothing happens at all. A past that is so empty, so unobtrusive, the only way we can connect it to now, our present, is by making up truths to explain it that are as fragile and impertinent as lies.

My father has been and gone. He was born, lived a life, looked for truth, told some lies, maintained a staggered dignity, and he died.

I remember that my father, thinking something about a past beyond him and an emptied present, annihilated himself, so that there was nothing to think of in the future. He was so interested in himself that he killed himself.

I remember . . . obliteration.

I remember . . . because I have a good memory.

He disappeared, finally.

Just you try and get me to forget that he killed himself. Believe me, I've tried. How I've tried. I remember that my father killed himself like I might remember someone shooting me through the head, or chopping off my hand, or cutting out my tongue, or choking me with barbed wire. Or operating on my heart without an anaesthetic. I remember it like it really happened. But I've tried so hard to forget that my father killed himself that I don't remember when he killed himself.

I don't remember it in time, as a time, as a date. The flawed memory I have of my father's sick, stunning death, along with all the beaten memories that closely accompany that original memory of his original act, the eccentric offspring of that original memory, it all seems too essential and sensational, too big and moving, to ever put a date on. These memories and sub-memories and kid memories and false memories cannot be dated. They are like shadows of time. They are like echoes of reality. They cannot be pinned down. They cannot be fixed. Not from where I've been flung. Not from where I hang, upside down in relation to the memory I have of my father, the memory I have of him killing himself, with apparent ease, the memory I have of him turning his life inside out, and turning mine upside down.

Death, our greatest fixation, cannot be fixed. Death cannot be dated. It never dates. It is nothing to be nostalgic about. Death hasn't happened yet, not to us, not for us. It is nothing that we know of. Yet death is always happening around us, near us, because of us, on behalf of us, through us. It is all that we know of. It packs life in between its great folds of blankness. It's everywhere we look, just out of sight, just beyond the horizon, just beyond the light of the sun. It's between our breaths, between our heartbeats, between our legs. It's in the spaces between our dreams.

Death is always fresh and original. It's the greatest find in life, and it will take us all our lives to find it. It's the most exclusive and experimental thing that any of us will ever do, and yet the most common and banal. The most everyday. Life can be predictable, it can follow a path of mundane destiny, it can be monotonous, repetitive, but it can never touch death for depths and shallows of predictability, mundanity, monotony, repetition. Life can be an alarming sequence of astonishing moments, but it can never be as alarming or as astonishing as death. All of the changes that there can be in a life, changes in physique, mind, circumstances, mood, fortune, don't mean a thing compared to the single change of death. Death is so original it overshadows in one blank movement all of the millions of changes that are happening a million times a second during every day of every life. Death from where we see it: death as we see it from life.

But original as death is, how original is suicide? How very original. The most original way of doing death. And how very individual. The most individual way of doing death. The most incredible way of changing your mind about things. Fed up with your own mind, you swap it for the overwhelming mind of death. When you kill yourself, you are choosing to stop time, to date your own death, to fix it, to outwit it, or at least to control it. You make a controlled entrance into the profoundly controlled universe of death – death is a location where consciousness is controlled to such an extent it does not even exist.

I don't know if, when my father killed himself, he was aware of the date, and if it was a special day. Something special he had alighted on with the sole intention of using it as his last-ever day. A useful day. I suppose he made it special by deciding to select it as his day of action, or commitment, even if I can't remember the day. The dearly suicidal can make that choice: the exact time of their departure. It's one of the bonuses of taking your own life.

I don't know how specifically my father timed his death, if there was some kind of countdown. All I know is that, after all these years, time spent living at an acute angle to his death, I can't remember when he killed himself. The time of his death escapes me. I have as little idea of the day he killed himself, or the month, as he has. I don't remember when. I remember where, approximately. I remember how, more or less. I don't remember why, give or take a few vague guesses. My memory is good for some things. Not so good for other things.

ON: TIME

It's as if he didn't kill himself inside time. He stepped outside time, as I remember it, and don't remember it. Time stopped whenever it was that he stepped outside it, whenever it was that he disappeared in the mean act of finding himself, whenever it was that he performed something so utterly unique it was hopelessly banal, whenever it was that irritated to hell and tempted beyond belief he not so much called it a day as called it an instant.

But then, since, if it is since, my father killed himself, and a lot of the evidence muddying my mind suggests that he did just that, just like that, if perhaps slightly slower, since my father went and went, it becomes clearer and clearer that time doesn't move. I don't know whether it has got anything to do with my father's great leap onwards, backwards, inwards, nonewards, downwards, or whether it's something to do with the time of my life I've been having, and I would have thought the same even if he had still been living, but I'm pretty sure that time is still.

Time is still all the time. Still, now. Still, is. Still, a pure and empty form. Still, a centre of things from which we proceed. Time, always similar to itself and always unmovable.

Mostly, we act out our lives, we make up our lives, by pretending,

245

very well, that time isn't still. Time never stops. What would we do without ourselves if we admitted that time has stopped? As far as we can tell the only way to stop time is by doing something excessively, insanely original. Like dying. Death stops time. Every day so many people die and so much time stops. The tension in the universe between existence and non-existence is created from the great relationship between the way the dead stop time and the way the living pretend to keep it going as a spectacular illusion.

Life and reality and human nature and all that we make of it is just our desperate, distracted, conversational way of make-believing that time moves forward, continually, inevitably, of make-believing and accepting that there are things to do, battles to be won, corners to be turned, alarms to be set, dates to be recorded, songs to be sung, chances to be taken, own ends to be pursued, nerves to be got on, loves to be loved, memories to be manufactured, images to be processed and possessed, and sentences to be finished.

And, remembering the need for punchlines in life, death sentences to be carried out.

ON: WHAT WOULD COME WITHOUT ARRIVING

I had spent the night on the settee in the front room, feeling impartially funny, woozy with thick thoughtfulness, my insides a fist of struggling butterflies, my outsides not to be depended on for doing much more than keeping my insides in, knowing, as much as you can ever know anything the way you know something for the first time but it's like you always knew it, it's like it was with you when you were born, that something was not right.

My father had been missing for a while. I can't remember how long. A few days I suppose. I had got used to him disappearing for a short while. It was just part of my life. He disappeared. He came back. He always came back. Ever since his first catastrophic nervous breakdown some years earlier, he would run away, flee, escape, perhaps prepare a whole new life and identity, do things I knew nothing about, sit around, stand around, wait around, lose his memory, lose his marbles, relent under the burden of his life, indulge himself, who knows what, but he would always return, chastened, I think, crushed a little out of shape, a shiver or two more hopeless. But the shape of him always appeared to more or less return, the shadows around his soul became less apparent, he seemed to stop shivering, and somehow he put on the front of being able to pick up most of the pieces of his demolished life. Life went on, in a manner of living. He put on a brave face to cover up who knows what fear and loathing that was straining his soul.

This time, it did not feel as if he was going to come back. I don't know what made me think this, maybe I'd found his brave face tossed in the cupboard under the stairs, but I did.

The strangers with the strange job strangely interrupting my life like it was important or something standing there like two peas in a cuckoo's nest, the young policeman and the young policewoman, white and faceless in black and graceless uniforms, officially confirmed in dreadfully shaky voices the news that my father was never going to come back. I don't know how they phrased it. I don't think they said, Your father is dead, his soul broke down, his body followed soon after; but I can't be sure. Whatever it was they said, it convinced me that my father was dead, and I was now to talk about him in the past tense. Except when I was to tell people that he was dead, as in 'My father is dead.' He is dead in this time and space at the moment. He wasn't dead; he used to be alive. He is dead now. In the present. The miracle of death is such that he is as a dead man in three places at once. He was dead before he was alive. He is dead now. He will be dead in the future. This is perhaps one of the things that makes death somehow more of a miracle than life. Life only happens now and then. Death happens all the time.

I strangely thanked the two strangers for letting me in on this predictable strangeness. I had a hunch the news would make me think. I was nineteen, twenty or twenty-one. You could say I still am. It was 1976, 1977 or 1978. You could say it still is.

ON: THE LATEST NEWS

My father had killed himself. I know that because I remember the moment I was told, even though I don't remember the words which were used to tell me. I only remember the pauses.

ON: ERNEST HEMINGWAY

'Is dying hard, Daddy?'
  'No, I think it's pretty easy, Paul. It all depends.'

ON: MAKING AN EFFORT

My father is killing himself, as I think about it, because I think about it. He is killing himself in his own time, in the midst of things real and imaginary, in his own way, in the 1970s, for his own reasons, creating a mystery all around him and the empty space he leaves behind.

He stopped having faith in the idea that time moves forward and pulls you along with it. He stopped pushing himself in a particular direction. He stopped trusting his memories. He stopped having memories. He tripped up on the possibility of impossibility – and, merely because death is the opposite of everything, the impossibility of possibility. He stopped resisting the all-time powerful spell of death, and he stopped, and he stopped stopping, and he couldn't stop himself. He just wanted to be still.

Movement made him impatient, movement forced him to move along with it in a way he didn't want. All around him, everything and everyone was moving, all the time. Moving in his face, moving in his way, moving him out of the way. All that movement representing a constantly changing world, a world changing for no good purpose, changing in vast preparation for nothing. A changing world full of expectancy, prejudice, consequence, demand, routine. Everyone was changing their mind, changing their position, changing their shape. All this change and movement rained upon him like one big pressure, moving him to despair. He was compelled to keep up, by blemished nature, by force of numbers, and it tired him out. The movement of the planet and its unstoppable people, the earth and its turning ends, the hectic need to move on, it all crowded into him, and bullied him. He craved a kind of permanent solitude where he would be on his own, free from movement, beyond the habits of activity.

The universe as we explain it to ourselves, examine it, experience it, explore it, endure it, is all about momentum. It's on the move. It moves us along. For my father, this restless way of imagining oneself being human, of humouring the mind, of moving inside a moving universe, became fundamentally impossible to live with, and he took to searching for a universe where nothing moves, a universe we can't explain, and can't endure. An inhuman universe, where he could stop being human. A universe where everything stops and never starts and where nothing starts and never stops.

Perhaps suicide is a way of killing everyone and everything else around you so that only you survive, in a manner of surviving. It's getting rid of all life so that you can live beyond living in entirely your own isolated way. You don't exactly want to kill yourself and you're not exactly killing yourself. You're killing everything else. You're destroying everything but you, wiping it all away, the sun, the earth, the moon and everything that goes with it, rubbing out the commotion, annihilating all the fuss and the frenzy of conscious existence that's been offending your mind. You remove everything in your way so that there is nothing in your way. You may have to remove yourself to achieve this extravagant egotistical universal removement, but so be it. It's a small price to pay. At least you've got rid of all that ruining living motion, all that spiralling to-ing and fro-ing, all that spiteful action, all that comic hustle and tragic bustle, all that revolting, base and baseless competition.

You swap your own changing mind, a mind that changes and changes and changes with the world, a mind changed by the world despite all your best efforts, with the mind of death. A mind that never changes. A mind that keeps you well apart from all the confusions and ruses of life. Life only knows how to move. Death isn't interested in movement. It is only interested in itself and its inconsiderable lack of movement.

My father killed himself because he infinitely preferred the uninterrupted, undivided loneliness of lifelessness to the facile, fraudulent community of life.

I have no idea, no way of proving, if any of this is how he felt, or didn't feel. How can I ever really know how he confronted his life and his death? How he dealt with the duty to live and his desire for death. The only clues I have to how he felt about himself, and his fate, are connected to my memories of him, memories that have themselves been infected by his suicide, memories that are the way they are because he killed himself. If he hadn't killed himself, my

249

memories would be different. Clearer, perhaps. Less challenged by the way he was slowly, and then quickly, sucked out of the way. They would have been allowed to form, and take real shape, and support a different kind of story. They would build up to support the man he became, and embellish the relationship we would have had, for better or worse, if he had lived. Or even if he had died, but by another way than suicide. His suicide has stained and shadowed and torn the memories of him that I have, so that when I put together an idea of who he was, and what he was doing with his life, it is a picture put together by someone remembering a father who killed himself, whose memories are biased towards being the tossed, trashed memories of the son of a suicide. Because of this, I build up his death, I lose sight of his life. I can't quite make out his face, I can't quite see his eyes, and therefore I can't look him in the eye. I am guessing about why he killed himself from the point of view of someone affected by the fact he killed himself. This may mean I see things clearly. It may mean I don't see them at all. It may be a combination of those two things, with the added spice of my hopes, and fears, and speculations about why he killed himself. For all I know he didn't want to get rid of the rest of the world. Or the rest of time. He only wanted to get rid of himself. He was fed up with himself. He loved the world. He hated himself. He gave up. He took the easy way out. Then again, perhaps he took the hard way out. He was brave. He was a coward. He was existential action hero bringing his life to an engineered halt with mindful precision. He was a small man defeated by a small life in a small town who could see nothing ahead of him but failure, humiliation, and sadness. He finally emptied a mind that was already almost completely emptied.

Something like some of all that. Something like none of all that.

What I do know, for sure, because I'm thinking it now, is that my father designed his own death, with cunning, with care, and with commitment. And I find that thought impressive, horrifying and a lot more puzzling than I've ever really admitted to myself.

ON: CONFLICTING PIECES OF INFORMATION

He is so uninterested in his life that he is killing himself.

ON: ROUTINE

He always manages to kill himself at exactly the same time. He is never late. He is never early. I don't know what it would take for him to forget. At always the right time, correct down to the second, my father arrives for his death. He is always promptly a condemned man. His death is a constant consistent endless matter of routine. It is what he does for an end of living. He has timed his death down to a split second of infinity. He cannot escape his time. It is always there. Ready for him. And he's ready for it. He's prepared.

And here comes the time when his time is up, once more. And once more he holds his breath.

ON: JULIA KRISTEVA

'The depressed person is a radical, sullen atheist.'

ON: SUSAN SONTAG

'Depression is melancholy without the charms.'

ON: F. SCOTT FITZGERALD

'Of course, all life is a process of breaking down.'

ON: CARL JUNG

My father never completely owned his own shadow.

ON: KURT VONNEGUT

You can inherit from your parents, without knowing it, without knowing how, a real and emphatic sadness, about life, and about living. Sadness is handed on, in the air, in the blood, in the way these things are.

ON: UP NORTH AND DOWN SOUTH

I have always felt that my father never liked the North much. He spent his life up to his national service years in Margate, Kent. The South. He moved far north from one country inside a country to another country inside a country when he was about as young as I was when he died because his wife, my mother, was born and lived in Cheshire. This seems extremely chivalrous and willing of him, but then I believe that he moved up north because he wanted to get as far away as possible from his cold, forbidding mother.

His mother, though born in the first decade of the 1900s, never quite made it into the twentieth century, emotionally or morally. I always think of her as a vaguely threatening, dour, inflexible cross between Queen Victoria and the dragon-lady actress Peggy Mount. A distantly dotty curiously unamused and hard-hearted woman, she took the idea of Methodism to a level of dreary intensity. Life was work, and there was nothing else to it. Work was the only really respectable thing. You worked your way towards heaven, or hell. You worked to keep your head above water. You worked to maintain your place in society.

Her own life, since she was born in 1905, or 6, had been hard. She'd suffered from bad arthritis in her teens, and for the rest of her life walked with a pronounced limp. She'd been through two wars, her husband had left her during the second war, she seemed mournful as if she'd been old all her life, and I am sure she was as kind and gentle to me as any grandmother. But what I remember most is her meanness, the fear my father seemed to have of her, and that she took routine, and her religion, very seriously indeed. I have decided, because it makes sense in the story that I am telling, that she was a witheringly old-fashioned, self-righteous and inhibiting influence to escape.

We used to call her Grandma Morley. Our other grandmother, my mother's mother, was Grandma Young. The words 'Grandma Young' now suggest to me a sweet, slightly silly nursery rhyme. The words 'Grandma Morley' now suggest to me something dark and disturbing by the Brothers Grimm.

ON: *THE FUGITIVE*

I remember that my grandmother owned a television set which seemed to have a nine-inch screen and to have been manufactured in the 1940s. She only usually turned it on a couple of times a week, for *Coronation Street*, and *Songs of Praise*.

When we were at her house for summer holidays, she rationed out hours we could watch TV very stingily indeed. One day in the 60s, I think about 1969, my family were spending their usual two weeks in August at her house. My father's sister Eileen, her husband Michael, and cousin Stephen had come over from their house in Chatham a few miles away, for tea, and to watch the final episode of *The Fugitive*.

The Fugitive was a long-running 60s TV series where a man who had been wrongly convicted of a murder and sentenced to death had escaped from his guards during a train crash. For many years we had watched the man's attempts on the run to prove his innocence and to prove that the murder for which he had been found guilty had actually been committed by a mysterious man with one arm. My father, my mother, me, Eileen, Michael and Stephen were all hooked on this series, and desperate to watch this final episode which would explain everything, and bring years of viewing to a fitting climax.

A few minutes before the final episode was due to begin, an episode we had been looking forward to for weeks, the conclusion of a series we had been watching for years, my grandmother had a visitor. She received the visitor in the tiny lounge, where the television was. We were all told to wait in the even tinier, dingier front parlour room next door. We tried to explain how important it was that we saw the last episode of *The Fugitive*, and she said that she would be finished in time. I wouldn't be surprised if she knew that this visitor was due, had arranged it because she viewed our peculiar addiction to this ridiculous American television programme as entirely frivolous.

We all waited in the next room. And waited. The programme started. It was fifty minutes long, so we resigned ourselves to missing the beginning. After half an hour, we were all getting very agitated, and annoyed. My father was sent into the next room to reason with his mother, but was quickly sent back. The look on his face told us all that we were not going to get the chance to watch the final episode of *The Fugitive*.

It would take some of us years to find out what actually happened to the fugitive, and the one-armed man. Some of us, including my father, would never find out. He spent the rest of that evening looking like a man who had been accused of a crime he never committed.

His mother always seemed to be accusing him of something. Perhaps the fact that her husband left her.

ON: DOWN UNDER

For a while in the early 60s we lived in war-torn and badly patched-up areas to the south of Manchester, areas so quiet in themselves it was like they'd quit bothering with the rest of the world, places that plodded, that would never swing, places that dribbled with spare everydayness. They were places that largely resisted great plot, but they were darkly close in their brooding grimness to the bleak holes and black hills where at the time, glibly perverting the course of nature, the so-called 'moors murderers' Brady and Hindley were torturing and murdering young children as small and as innocent as my father's.

The energy-sapping moors and hills that loom and gloom between dimensions on the eastern rim of Manchester can seep into the consciousness of anyone living nearby like poisonous premonitions of the end of time, the end of the imagination . . . like damned hovering hangovers from the beginning of time, the beginning of the imagination. The moors assume the shape and density of depression, especially in the dark, in the rain, when they become a part of some weary, ferocious storm.

They are responsible, to no one and no thing, for much madness, much mystery and nothing much in particular. They soundlessly moan. They're as still as death. As lethargic as time. As old as the hills.

They must have infected my father, these immense lumps of grainy anxiety watching over him, acting like moody unmoving unliving ever-present symbols of the unloving mother he could never escape from until he finally killed her off by killing himself.

The differences between the raw narrow North and the sweeping sea and spaces of the Isle of Thanet would have been shattering in the English 60s. It must have been like the difference between black and white and colour. Like going back in time. In Margate the roads all sloped down to the impalpable sea, the English Channel, the beautiful sandy bays that swept along the south-eastern coast, from Herne Bay to Dover. All roads sloped down to possibility, to the sea, and the exotic ends of the earth. In Stockport all the roads sloped down to the Mersey Shopping Centre, where sand had been mixed into concrete, where nature had been flattened. All roads sloped down to Boots and WH Smith.

But, there was life to live, so to live, and I suppose he got on with it. As you do. Or don't. I remember that my father's darkish southern complexion and his broad open Kent accent made him seem so alien and exotic in the bereft windswept streets of Eccles and Reddish that locals thought he was Australian.

Stockport became his home, and his end of the world. It's as good and bad a place as anywhere to represent the end of the world in the world championship of the end of the world, tucked into the smug and hostile moors, stuck in the faded middle of a wasted England, sunk under centuries of time and smoke. Some time in the something of his exiled life in Stockport, good old static Stockport, stuffed with a sense of its own lack of importance, he suffered his first nervous breakdown.

He lost a good job he had with Shell and BP after his nervous breakdown, a job that seemed to be his for life, a job that seemed to give his future a glossy film of certainty, even in Stockport. I'm not sure what this job was, although he seemed to enjoy it, and the sense of belonging somewhere, and I'm not sure if the pressure of work helped lead to the breakdown, or if it was a separate issue, triggered by other circumstances. What I do know is after he left this job he never seemed to find one that was as safe, as specific or as long lasting. For a few unsure years after leaving Shell and BP he found and lost a series of boring, bitty jobs, mostly as a salesman, pseudo-work that eventually embarrassed him to death. I remember for a while he was a double-glazing salesman for Everest. The sample of double glazing that was stored in our garage at Offerton seemed to resonate with sadness, and futility. He was not the kind of man who could muster up the enthusiasm to persuade people to spend money on something he didn't believe in. I don't think he could have persuaded people to buy something that he did believe in. He was too sensitive to break into people's lives and try and talk them into buying things. He didn't have the cockiness, the thick skin, the buoyancy, the self-belief. He wasn't double-glazed enough. He may have been once, in the South, the warm, exciting South that faced towards more of the south, France, and, happily, beyond. But not in the North, the cold, tiring North that faced further north, towards the wilds of the Lake District, and wistfully, beyond.

I seem to remember that he didn't last long with Everest. A month or so. The sample stayed in our garage, looking ever more unwanted, and past useless. It looked like it needed to be draped with black curtains.

Beaten down by a regular series of irregular breakdowns, and the after-effects of those breakdowns, he found himself, a self he was close to forgetting, past forty, working in some low form or another for the Singer sewing machine company. One day he was asked to attend to the shop-window display at their retail outfit inside the Mersey Shopping Centre.

I think he felt that he was way above and way past dressing a shop window for a place that sold sewing machines. He'd been a sergeant during his national service, he'd worked inside a prison, he had played chess with murderers and armed robbers, he'd had a team of people working under him at Shell and BP, he had a son in his late teens. Having to go on the road and act as a representative for Singer was bad enough, but having to do menial duties in the shop was a terrible threat to what was left of his self-confidence. There in the Mersey Shopping Centre, at the concrete bottom of the dent pushed into Stockport, he must have felt he'd reached the rock bottom of his life.

ON: THE DEATH OF A SALESMAN

Trying, as I am, to understand the obscure life of this simple, complicated man, who I know little about apart from the fact he was my father and he killed himself, I think that this may have been the last straw. The final dent. If at eighteen, in Kent, the Garden of England, looking forward to a life of fast love and slick success, he felt himself at the top of the world, his move to Stockport, the kidney of the North, set him down at the top of a hill, and the only way forward, this being Stockport, was down. Down, down, down, until there was no place left but down under the ground.

I have got a deadened feeling slowly coming back to life that around the time he was working in a half-waking state for Singer, he was so unhappy and self-immersed that the air around him moaned in close sympathy. He was the very flattened essence of humiliated, a man whose gestures were merely remembered ones from a previous life, a man who had all but faded from view. His shadow was more substantial than he was.

He was a man who only had a few weeks to live. A man who knew he only had a few weeks to live. The decision had been taken for him and by him, the last decision in all those decisions that had made up his life. Decisions taken by him, decisions taken about him. In a lifetime of decisions, there is always going to be a final decision. His final decision was the most decisive of his life. It was the purest decision.

To me, though, whatever he was going through as he was led, or led himself, to this decision, he was just my dad, odder than some dads, a bit awkward. As far as I could tell, he seemed less bad-tempered than he once had been. It is this slender clue that leads me to believe he had given up. There was a hint, just a hint, he only offered hints of hints, whispers of hints, that he had been going through the motions of his life, a life, some life, for days, months, years. He was a very guarded man. He gave little away about himself, although he never hid the fact that he smoked Guards cigarettes. He smoked them up until the day, the hour, the minute that he died, at which time he became impenetrably guarded, guarded by death, the ultimate refuge of a guarded man.

I don't remember at the time directly thinking how much my father was falling apart. I don't remember thinking that he seemed on the verge of anything momentous.

I don't remember the last few weeks, the last few days, in any kind of detail.

I don't remember the last time I saw him.

I don't remember the last time we spoke.

It wasn't like I was ready, thinking, Oh, I'd better make an effort today to communicate with my father, to concentrate on his face, his voice, his eyes, the whole expression of his being. Because it's the last time that I will ever see him. We'd better have a telling conversation, about something deep, and important, something I will remember for ever, in detail. Details that will help me recall the last time I ever saw my father.

I must have been in bed the morning he left for 'work' – or, in his special case, on this special day, for death. So I would probably have seen him, for the last time, the night before. We weren't the type of family that went in for big goodnights, so I don't suppose I ever even said goodnight to him, or, in the language of our family, a small, bony language, that never developed much over the years, 'n'night'. But then, I suppose he knew what he was up to, so I can guess that he went out of his way to make sure he said something to me. I can hope that, anyway. I can say that the last words he ever said to me were 'n'night'.

And I said 'n'night' back. We didn't look into each other's eyes. We didn't kiss. We never kissed.

All but done and gone, already much less than himself, consumed by the low and high complications of being, knowing that something was going to change, he rather curiously laid a brand-new carpet in the front lounge of our house in Heaton Moor. Putting his house in order. Or perhaps he hadn't yet decided that he was going to kill himself. This wasn't his way of finalising his life's business. He fully expected to walk on this carpet for many years. Wear it down with his heel and soul. The decision to kill himself was a spur of the moment decision taken after he had laid the carpet. Maybe he didn't like the colour. It's amazing to consider what can finally put you over the edge.

My father bought the carpet after I had repaid him the money he had lent me to print my magazine. I don't remember the colour of the carpet. Nor does my father.

The day after the carpet was finished, fitted with the care and commitment of a man who didn't immediately appear to have given up on life, he drove the company van, a sky-blue Ford Escort van, towards the South. I remember that it was a van, because after years of slowly and conscientiously moving up through the ranks of car quality, he had slipped back to driving a commercial van. The cars mapped out a part of his life story. From the serious big green Rover he drove at the beginning of his marriage that represented dreams and optimism, through a funny little Mini that took him into the 60s, then a practical Mini estate that suggested his family was growing, a square-looking reliable old pale blue-grey Vauxhall Viva that hinted he was moving into a settled future, and then finally, his pride and joy, a brand-new gold Vauxhall Viva that in its flash lines and bold colour seemed to pick out that part of my father's wide southern personality that had been narrowed and distorted by the North. This was as high as he reached. The car symbolised his ambition, his sense of style, things he clung on to as long as he could before life, that part of it that was, after all that, beyond his control, ripped him apart, and mocked his ambition, and ruined his style, and snatched away the car. The gold Vauxhall Viva, the colour of Shirley Eaton after her body had been painted gold, after she had been suffocated, by James Bond's greatest foe, Goldfinger, disappeared, and took away some of the light in his eye, and the spring in his step, and his belief in a future. For a while he didn't have a car at all. He couldn't afford one. To my father, being carless was a direct threat to the very notion of manhood.

He drove in the opposite direction from the moors, down towards the west of the country. He didn't head towards the south-east, where his mother lurked, counting the pennies in the local church collection box by the front door. He drove hundreds of miles to a place that he didn't appear to have any connection with. He drove to the green, swaying and pleasant countryside around Stroud, near Gloucester, to a positive, bright, open version of the dark satanic moors. He didn't want to die in the North. He didn't want to be buried in Stockport and spend the rest of time there. Perhaps he thought of his family and didn't want to ruin the town for them by polluting it with his suicide. He wanted to die in the South, but he didn't want to die near his mother. The only direction left to him was the south-west.

In a lovers' lane he must have chanced upon he went through the motions of a death he must have planned years ago, months ago, days ago, that morning. He threaded a hosepipe from the exhaust pipe of the Ford van through to the front driver's seat. He shut tight all the windows. He felt the last life in himself. He settled down. And then.

The clouds rushed by. In the silence of the night you could have heard the noise they were making as they sped overhead.

The van engine purred pointlessly.
He did it.
You would have heard nothing.

ON: PAUSING

Or, on those moments when a memory or even less is enough to help you slip out of the world. Grass keeps growing.

ON: THE TIME IT TAKES TO DIE

It would have taken somewhere between a few minutes and a few hours for him to die.

ON: AN ESTIMATE

Let's say it took forty-seven minutes. One for every year of his life, and a few for, in some sense, luck.

ON: STATISTICS

Someone somewhere in Britain had killed themselves two hours before him, and someone somewhere in Britain would kill themselves two hours later.

ON: GOING

The last light was snatched from his eyes.

ON: THE INSIDE OF HIS FATHER

A journey that had begun remarkably inside his distant father and that then shot out at the speed of fuck . . .

ON: THE INSIDE OF HIS MOTHER

A journey that then continued remarkably inside his distant mother for an amount of time that's beyond time and that then squirmed with bloody might out into the gathering light where he was forced to be himself . . .

ON: THE LENGTH OF A LIFE

A journey that then piled the imagination high, with its own timed twists and turns, ups and downs, ifs and buts, firsts and lasts, had come, as if it had never been anywhere, to an end, to this end, this black end. A journey that had gone the struggling sluggish distance.

ON: THOUGHTLESSNESS

A maximum of finality. A demonstration of the undemonstrable. A suffocating climax. There was nothing behind him. Nothing ahead of him. He missed himself. He solved himself. He limited himself. He loved himself. He hated himself. He loved life. He hated life. His life . . . the life his life had become.

All of his life came to nothing. All of his life, filling out his bursting head, filling in his borrowed mind, crushed into his last crushing moments, all of his life, tricking him, leading him astray, shaming him, abandoning him, enshrouding him. All of his life, which he tried to take hold of, until he could take no more, until he could do nothing but take his life, take it away. It was all that was left. He tried to run his life, but his life ran away from him. His life had a life of its own. It wasn't himself that he killed. It was his life. A life that had invaded him, taken him over, altered him. Somewhere amidst his life, there he was, trying to survive as his life ran amok, trying to influence his life from his point of view, trying to out-think it, trying to out-manoeuvre it. In the end, his life won. It possessed him. It took him on a journey he was less and less in control of.

Then, while his life wasn't looking, he got rid of it.

There were enough of his own thoughts left amongst the wreckage of his life for him to think of a way out.

ON: EXHAUSTION

All of his thinking, his non-stop thinking. It was exhausting. And so, he exhausted himself.

He exhausted himself to death.

ON: BEING A LITTLE PRESUMPTUOUS

I don't know. I remember things as I remember them, or as I think they might have happened. I put together some memories I have with some speculation that I have made with some guesses about his state of mind in order to come up with some story that seems to do the job of telling the story of how he died.

I am setting myself up, reaching for a kind of comfort within an uncomfortable situation. I am putting myself at the centre of things. I am constructing a pattern of events out of things hopeful and hopeless, remembered and half-remembered, imagined and dreamt, assumed and presumed. I might even begin to believe that this is how it was. These are the details: I made them up out of truth and thoughts, thoughts which I think are true, or at least in the same area as truth. Not that I'm sure what the area of truth is. Where does it begin, and end? Where is its heart? How near is it to the sea?

But none of what I'm writing is a conscious lie. It's all true, as far as I'm concerned. I'm just not sure what led me to believe that these details are true. I just accept that they are. It seems more convenient to respect the details I have gathered over the years. Details such as:

My father had electroconvulsive therapy. ECT. The 'T' could stand also for 'treatment', 'torture', 'terror', 'torment', 'tearing apart'. I believe that after my father's first nervous breakdown he was given electrical therapy.

Convulsive therapy began in the 1930s as a treatment for severe schizophrenia. It was noticed that schizophrenics seemed in a better state after they had suffered spontaneous seizures. It was as if the weather had cleared. A storm had passed. At first the seizures were induced by medication, and eventually, after the drugs were replaced by small doses of electricity, it was recognised that those who benefited most were those individuals with severe mood disorder.

262

And so ECT became most commonly used in the treatment of those with melancholic depression.

It was said that just as the passage of electricity through the heart can produce a rhythmic pulse, electrical therapy can stabilise the beat of the brain. When you think of electrical therapy as applied to a heart, you think of something that is life-saving. When you think of ECT, and the application of a series of electric shocks to someone's head as they are bound down on a table, shaking, jerking, biting down hard on some object between their teeth, you think of something nasty and barbaric. They are based on the same principles, but one seems to pull someone back from the brink of death by supernatural force, and the other seems to burn out the brains of a helpless subject and send them once broken a step closer to death. ECT seems designed to obliterate the disorder in someone's mind by obliterating the mind.

Of course, modern ECT treatment is one of the safest treatments in psychiatry. Trust me, I read a doctor writing that. Before the use of anaesthesia, the procedure was a dramatic spectacle, and it's that thrashing about, where there are no drugs to relax the body, that we think of when we imagine the treatment. The process is now so controlled that anyone witnessing the administration of ECT will be amazed at how smooth and simple it is, and how far away it is from its reputation.

When I think of my father having the muscle-wrenching head-crunching treatment, I believe he was not under anaesthetic, and that he was virtually attacked, and he flailed around in desperation, having his brains fried, his mind brutally interfered with. If he had been under anaesthetic I still believe he would have had his mind torched and savaged, it just would have appeared, looking at him, that something gentle and medically refreshing was happening. This is what I believe. This is the image I've always had in my head of the few times my father received ECT. That it wasn't a help. The shocks bit deep into his memory and chewed out huge chunks of it and spat them away. When he woke up, I believe, he wasn't the same. He wasn't all of what he had been. Physically, he was identical, except for a little loss of light in his eyes, and a rubbed-out look around his eyes, but mentally, he was a changed man. He had a different mind. He had a different life. You can understand what electricity can do to a heart: somehow you can rationalise that it gives it a surge of much needed energy. But what does electricity do to the soul, which doesn't need that kind of rush of energy, which doesn't want to be assaulted by such concentrated reality? I can only imagine that the soul, after a blast of shock treatment, has been scalded. It is much tenderer after such a confusion of volts. It is weaker.

It is said that there is no evidence that electroconvulsive therapy permanently impairs the memory. Six months after their treatment, the majority of patients' private and public memories all but fully return. But because my father was treated in this way – and how I feel about this can be explained by the fact I want to write treated as 'treated' – I don't believe this. I believe it does impair the memory. I believe it jolts it out of line. Maybe the memories don't all get erased, but they somehow slip out of focus, almost as if they're memories that belong to someone else, but which are inside your head, in your imagination. You need these memories to be as clear, as shapely, as numerous as possible, because you need memories to invent your life, to make it up as you go along. Your whole life is based on your memory of your life up to now. If those memories are tampered with, twisted, scarred, then there isn't as much of you living on as there should be.

And whatever happens to your memory after the treatment, you don't seem to forget the fact that you had it. For someone like my father, who wanted so much to appear to be able to cope, every time he remembered the treatment, it would have been a shock to the system. There was something not right about him. He was wrong. He had been given this treatment, because he was delusional, because he was manic, because he was *mad*. He would have felt ashamed. This is what I believe he would have believed. And it would have scared him. More and more.

There's another detail I remember. He was prescribed anti-depressants to take. They were meant to decrease anxiety and stabilise disturbances of mood. He hated to take them, and eventually he stopped. Perhaps he disliked the side effects of what he was taking, which I can imagine were dry mouth, insomnia, nausea, difficulty with orgasm, stiffness of movement, gastrointestinal difficulty. He wanted to feel normal. These side effects reminded him, sometimes cruelly, that he was not normal. He decided to confront his abnormality head on, without drugs, without help. He decided to believe that how he felt was as normal as anything. He didn't need drugs. He didn't need sedating. There was nothing wrong with him.

There was just something wrong with his life. It didn't fit.

ON: CONFUSION

He picks them up and flings them away. He picks them up again. His poor little deranged head. These thoughts in his head, these splinters of thoughts, these scissors of thoughts, these knives of thoughts, these razors of thoughts . . . cutting his mind to ribbons.

ON: HIS MIND

1) Cut
2) Burnt
3) Dropped
4) Sliced
5) Bruised
6) Stunned
7) Lost
8) Forgotten
9) Improbable
10) Gone

ON: POSSESSIONS

I can think of nothing that he owned that he cherished. He collected nothing. He gathered nothing around him. He had few if any mementoes of his past. A couple of small table-tennis trophies he had won as a teenager. The walls in our houses were largely bare. It was as though he didn't want to get too emotionally attached to things and objects, because he knew, somehow, that sooner rather than later he would have to leave them behind.

There was a framed Chinese drawing of a horse that followed us around from the South to the North, from the Isle of Wight to Stockport: the only picture on the wall. The more we moved, and the more this horse kept coming with us, until it was a part of the family, the more and more ominous it seemed to become. It hung on the walls of our houses, a stark, solitary piece of decoration, as if my mother and father thought it was valuable or something. Forty years after buying the drawing, my mother found an identical drawing in a junk shop. It was priced fifty pence.

There was some Chinese writing down the side of the picture, a handful of Chinese characters. For all we knew the writing said, 'Let us seek death like a horse seeks water.'

ON: SAMUEL BECKETT

My father decided not to hang himself. Presumably he didn't want to end his life with an erection.

ON: MICHEL FOUCAULT

My father decided not to hang himself in the kitchen and leave a blue tongue dangling.

ON: CALCULATIONS

I wonder if he knew as part of his preparation that, if he had decided to hang himself, for the weight and height he was, a shade under six feet, about twelve and a half stone, he would have needed an eight-foot eight-inch drop.

ON: THE UNIVERSE (PAUL VALÉRY SAID IT MIGHT WELL BE HEAD-SHAPED)

There is no back of the mind to put things in. The mind is exactly the same shape as the universe. They map onto each other as gracefully, as perfectly, as surreally as zero goes into zero, and everything in the universe, and everything is in it, if not now then at some time, is in the same place in the mind. There is no back of the universe.

266

Everything is at the centre of the universe. Everything is at the centre of your mind.

Everything you've ever done is there in your mind. It's there in the universe. You can pretend that a memory of your past is not there, you can pretend to kick it out, hide it, rubbish it, suppress it, explode it, deny it, evade it, but it's there. Even if you don't recognise it. Even if it has changed appearance. Or shape. Or entire character. It's there. Everything in the universe, your universe, my universe, our universe, is in the mind. In the end, in a moment, you'll find it, whatever it is that you're looking for, or not looking for. Or it will find you: all memories are tracking you through the universe, following you around, ready to pounce on you and grab you unawares. That's where memories come from. They come from behind. They're behind you. And sometimes, the longer they've been away, in their own world, minding their own business, cloaked in themselves, locked up in themselves, the stronger they are. They've been saving themselves up. Ultimately they'll want a little attention. And they'll bring with them the darkness of having been away for so long, right at the centre of the universe, your mind, but far, far away. They'll bring with them the darkness that fills the mind and the universe, the darkness that separates remembering from not remembering.

ON: THE FUCKING PAST

I heard my father say 'fuck' once.

Just once. I heard him say 'fuck' once. Fuck. I remember thinking as he said it that I had never heard him say that word before, and it was sudden and weird, and I don't remember ever hearing him say it again. He was on the phone. He must have been speaking to a friend, although I never think of my father having friends, men he went out with, men he compared his life with. I was standing where he couldn't see me. He didn't know I was near. This rude disorientating discreetly glamorous 'fuck' of my father must have impressed me enormously at the time, must have crossed my mind instantly to become a memory, and take its place at the centre of the universe.

I remember the impact of the word, as if he'd said it on live TV with the casual force and experienced languor of Kenneth Tynan, and my world changed a little. My father was someone else, he wasn't who I thought he was. I'm not sure how old I was when I heard him say 'fuck', like he said it all the time, but only when it was needed, but I was old enough to know the word. I knew enough to appreciate in that moment, the moment of the 'fuck' that fell out of my father's mouth with such adult ease, what a skilful job my father had been doing in never saying the word or anything like it in my presence. As he said it, 'fuck', he sounded freer, looser, not as stiff and caged as he seemed to be to me. He sounded like somebody else, maybe like somebody I might have got to know if he was still alive. We never reached the stage where we could say 'fuck' in each other's presence. We weren't even at the 'bloody hell' stage.

It slightly scared me, this 'fuck' of my father. It slightly thrilled me. It showed up in four letters how much of my father was hidden from me, how much more there was to him that I never saw. Beyond the word 'fuck' lay the whole life of my father way out of sight, out of my mind. The word 'fuck' was the tip of an immense iceberg of intimacy and secrets that were submerged beneath the sea of our relationship. I only ever saw the surface, the crashing waves, the drifting, the choppiness. We sailed the surface of life. Underneath was a whole murky subterranean world of other, strange, deeply personal adventure. My father swam with the sharks.

My father saying the word 'fuck' with philosophical finesse, with such authority, released the full forbidden dangerous power of the word; its original sin. He said the word 'fuck' as if it was the most natural thing in the world, but to me it was one of the most unnatural things. A word that is just a sound, and yet which leaps with a shifty, shifting history all of its own. I have never heard anyone say the word 'fuck' like my father said it, as if the word really was something awful and dirty and vital. It was as if the Queen had suddenly said it.

I was hearing and sensing a man who had kept himself well away from me, a man who kept certain parts of himself secret from certain people. There was the part I knew, the part his wife knew, the part his workmates knew, the part his sister knew, the part his mother knew. He kept them all separate. He didn't give the whole of himself to anyone, not even himself. Until he died, when he brought all the parts of himself together. Bound together in one unusual mental space, all the parts of him were such a weight he sank to the bottom of the sea, leaving the rest of us bobbing about on the surface, waiting for the inevitable storm to hit.

ON: FROM ONE FUCKING THING TO ANOTHER

Another dark memory moving up out of the darkness of myself. Another phone call. My father speaking to another friend. Suddenly, he seems to have a lot of friends, but I am still convinced that a good way to describe him was as a loner. He was certainly a loner on the day he died, but then, who isn't?

I am overhearing another little part of his secret world. He is talking about me. Perhaps I get a chance to find out what he thinks of me. This might be important to know, in the long term, even in the short term. I never really know what he thinks of me.

I have written something for a local fanzine, a fanzine called *Penetration* that I sold in the bookshop where I worked. A boy as vague as a sigh with eyes not quite in place comes in every two or three months with a handful of magazines he has printed himself about a world that seems to only contain Motorhead, The Pink Fairies, MC5 and Iggy and the Stooges. He's into an underground metal music, the kind that a year or two later would stain the sound of punk. His hair is long and greasy and he always wears placid black. He sometimes comes in with a girl who seems to want to look like a china version of him and who wears a lot of white netting. He's called Paul, he doesn't say much, and I think of him as the weirdest person in Stockport. He and his girlfriend never smile in a way that bares their teeth and it's easy to imagine that this is because there is a strange reason that they don't want to reveal their teeth.

He lets me write something for his fanzine. I have wanted to be a writer for three or four years. Nobody believes that I can be a writer. For Paul's *Penetration* I write about the controversial American comedian Lenny Bruce, someone I have developed a late-teenage infatuation with. I've bought the books. The one with his jokes in, that are not jokes, more a kind of hyper-hip social science. He's a punk philosopher in the sense that William Burroughs is a punk, or Charlie Parker a philosopher. The one about his life, which closed around him until one day he was dead, on the toilet, an early hint of perhaps the true shape of twentieth-century fame. He'd talked himself to death. I've tracked down obscure recordings of his shows, the shows that fell apart the more he was hounded by the police, and the censors, and society. I've seen the film, where Dustin Hoffman as Lenny lethally injects himself with method.

I fell for Lenny Bruce because here was a man who wanted to make things better, to make things fairer, to make things more beautiful, and he was prepared to be ugly, and reviled, and lonely in his pursuit of his dream. He was a cultural revolutionary, using language and the imagination as his weapons of attack. He improvised like a great jazzman, thought like a great novelist, rapped like a great poet, and I thought of him as a modern prophet forging some kind of preposterous but fabulous link between Arthur Rimbaud, Albert Camus and Groucho Marx. He was so funny it soon wasn't funny any more: it was a matter of life and death.

You could say that I did an A level in Lenny Bruce. Back at school, my former classmates were doing A levels in Maths and English and French. I was doing mine on the history of a man who was too hurt, too smart, too honest to be allowed to live. A man who kept saying 'fuck' because it was the only decent thing to do.

The essay I write about Lenny Bruce is the first thing of mine that is ever printed. It is laid out in the wrong order. The paragraphs are all muddled. It's cut up in a way I never intended. Fuck.

My father tells his friend that he has read the piece, which is news to me. I didn't think he would be interested. I don't know if he notices that the piece is all jumbled. I'm a little embarrassed that he has read the piece. It is about Lenny Bruce, but it's just as much about me, about my passions and desires. I'm not sure how I feel about his knowing that this side of me exists, mainly because I've kept it so far from him that I've got used to it that way.

My father, sounding relaxed and different from my dad, is saying how surprised he was by the article. He says it as if he never considered that I could write, but then he also says it as if he is proud of me. He's impressed that it's any kind of writing at all, that it says something, that it has opinions. I wonder if he's ever heard of Lenny Bruce, if he knows what I'm talking about, if he knows what he's talking about. I think of my dad as more of a Ken Dodd man.

He tells his friend in words I can't remember fuck I can't even remember the sound of his voice that I can actually write, that it's sort of proper. I feel a muzzled mixture of resentment and anger, because it's like he's patronising me, and also a kind of emergent superiority, that I am entering a world, of ideas and people, that my father knows nothing about. He can only watch in wonder as I soar off, above him and his fixed place in the scheme of things. Lenny Bruce had given me my wings. I passed my Lenny Bruce A level, even though the words were in the wrong order. The meaning was still there, in between the lines, in whatever order they were. The meaning had something to do with the differences between Lenny Bruce and my father and the differences between me and my father, and yet also with the similarities.

ON: MANCHESTER

After I had finished cleaning the oven, which meant that my father had just killed himself, I went straight into another project, something else calculated to make me forget the immediacy of death. There must have been some days, some activity in between, the drive down to Stroud with my Uncle Graham for instance. But essentially, as far as I can remember, after I finished cleaning the oven, I blanked out for a bit, and then I started writing an article for the *New Musical Express* about the music scene in Manchester, something that was growing by the week because of punk, and two catalysing visits to the city by The Sex Pistols. It was my second feature for the paper, and along with the feature on Marc Bolan it was perhaps my second unofficial A level. 'A' for 'alternative'.

I sat cross-legged on the new carpet in the front room and wrote about who I saw as the leaders of the scene, Buzzcocks, Joy Division, The Fall and Magazine, about bands I saw as the also-rans, such as Slaughter and the Dogs and V2, about the excitement that was at a certain level, for a certain set of people, changing the mood of the city. Punk, and music, and a new attitude, an attitude that was essentially saying, We've had enough of the war, and its shadow, that's still here, shading the present, shrinking the future, thirty years after the war ended. The 60s didn't ultimately shake away the war. There wasn't enough aggression, enough direct action.

I withdrew into the article. It was written with the kind of breathless passion you might expect from someone whose father had killed himself only a few days before. I was seeing in this new music

271

some kind of salvation, from private grief and public frustration. All of my writing for the *New Musical Express* over the next few years was written in direct and indirect response to the suicide of my father. I was writing around his death, through his death, in spite of his death. I was thinking deeply about pop music, the newer the better, to avoid thinking deeply about my father. I was paying more close anxious attention to the suicide of the lead singer of Joy Division than I was to the suicide of my father.

The article, a mythologising mixture of me, Manchester and music, was printed just three weeks after my father had died. A large photograph of the original lead singer of Buzzcocks, Howard Devoto, dominated the two-page spread. He looked all brain and bone, a cross between Franz Kafka and a baby. His songs with Buzzcocks were abbreviated and abstract pop songs that communicated the quick thrills of all kinds of addiction, from sex to shopping, and the quick terrors of mental collapse. They were highly detailed, literate punk outbursts delivered with the abrupt frenzy of an illicit fuck. His new group Magazine would write songs that set Beckett and Dostoevsky to a music that was somewhere between Roxy and Weill. These songs were slower. They slowed down the motion of the mind. They concentrated on the sensations of consciousness, they weren't attempts to actually make a noise that was itself the noise of consciousness. The Buzzcocks songs were a case of lashing out against the world, and the self. The Magazine songs were a case of savouring the precious, pressurising realities of the world, and of the self. I was a big fan of Howard Devoto, and because of the suicide of my father, and because of the type of highly charged, self-conscious songs he wrote, I would briefly get some of the suicidally tangled things out of my system when I wrote about his work.

I remember going to bed the night before the Thursday that the *New Musical Express* was due in the shops. I was sleeping downstairs, something I had started to do since my father had died. About four o'clock in the morning the phone rang. This house was still very much a house of death, and so the sound of the phone sounded more urgent and demanding than it might at another time. I woke up and answered it, half asleep. A strange, strangled voice started ranting at me. Who's this fucking Howard Devoto then? Bloody ponce. Balding git. What you doing writing about him? And what's this bloody blue postage stamp doing up here, this photo of Slaughter and the Dogs? Why didn't you write more about Slaughter and the Dogs? You gave them one line. Why did Howard Devoto get all this space?

I tried to find out who was calling me. A fan, the voice snarled. A fan who'll take a bloody knife to you if you don't pay more attention to Slaughter and the Dogs. I'll be around in the morning with a knife and we'll sort this out. The phone went dead.

Before I'd even seen the article I'd written, somebody to do with Slaughter and the Dogs, a member of the band, or a fan, or their manager, had got hold of a copy a day earlier in London. Before I even knew that there was a giant photograph of Devoto and a tiny photo of Slaughter and the Dogs, I was being threatened at four in the morning by someone who clearly disagreed with my reasoning that Slaughter and the Dogs were corny, and Howard Devoto was enigmatic king of punk.

I went back to bed in the newly dadless death house and felt very insecure indeed. Opinions were dangerous things. I didn't sleep. I thought but didn't think. No one came around in the morning with a knife to sort things out. I never found out who had actually made the call.

I suppose, despite a last-minute scare, a little late, I passed my second A level.

ON: ACHIEVEMENT

Actually, the article on Manchester was my third A level. The second of my A levels was the *Out There* fanzine. I remember my father proudly showed it to his mother, as if it really was an example of my academic achievement. She glanced through it and in front of him tore it up into little pieces. She thought it was obscene. She said to my father that he should be ashamed of himself that his son was responsible for such filth. I think she was particularly needled by the fact she saw the word 'erection'. She might have been annoyed by the fact it was spelt 'errection'.

It was another way for my grandmother to say to my father, Everything about you is useless and wrong. Which was a way of saying everything her husband had done was useless and wrong.

ON: A FUNNY THING HAPPENED ON THE WAY TO MYSELF

These memories of a me that wasn't quite the me that I am now changed me into the me that I am now and I have changed these memories of me by being the me that I am because of these memories and because of the me that I am because of these memories I will make of these memories what I will make of them and they will make of me what they will make of me as long as I remember them. Within reason.

ON: BUZZCOCKS, AS OPPOSED TO 'THE BUZZCOCKS', WHICH TAUGHT ME MORE ABOUT GRAMMAR THAN FIVE YEARS AT GRAMMAR SCHOOL, BECAUSE I LEARNT WHAT THE DEFINITE ARTICLE WAS

I remember that after my father killed himself, I was upset because it meant that I couldn't go to London the following Monday to see Buzzcocks play in Croydon.

My life had been interrupted.

I remember people ringing me about the plans for the London trip. I felt I was letting them down because I couldn't make it, and that my excuse was too much, too big, too ludicrous. Sorry, I can't come to the Buzzcocks gig because my father is dead. He killed himself.

I remember nervously trying to help the people I was telling by acting like it was no big deal. Just one of those things. They sounded very uncomfortable. Well, they didn't sound uncomfortable, because they tended to be quiet after I told them that my father had killed himself. They paused uncomfortably. They had thought they were calling me for a chat that was more or less small. They then realised that they had put a call through to reality, which was huge, and beyond most everyday language. They were suddenly having to talk about death, and they weren't expecting that. So they paused.

It was my fault they had to pause.

It was my father's fault.

I felt a little guilty.

A shade ashamed.

ON: BREAKING THE NEWS

The morning after, over the phone, I told my girlfriend at the time, Pamela, that my father was dead. She was the third girl I had ever kissed, and she had met my father twice. I think they said a few words to each other.

She'd thought my fanzine looked as dull and boring as a university prospectus, and she hated the new punk music, so our time together was already coming to an end. And yet I was having to tell her this information that seemed so dreadfully personal and grotesque. It was peculiar enough that I had to tell her that my father was dead. It got really unnerving when I had to tell her that he had killed himself. I suppose I didn't really want to tell her any of this. It was as if our family had been badly cursed. I wanted to keep it to myself. On the other hand, I wasn't sure how long I could keep up the pretence. It felt like something I had to tell people, especially my girlfriend, even though she wasn't likely to be my girlfriend for much longer. I suppose I had been handed, on a broken plate, a dramatic way of breaking the news to someone that I didn't really want to see for much longer that nothing lasts for ever.

We finished the call as if we had just been talking about nothing in particular. It wouldn't be long before I was kissing the fourth girl in my life.

And so, fatherless, freed, framed, on.

ON: DOROTHY PARKER

My father, though agreeing that razors pain you, rivers are damp, acids stain you, drugs cause cramp, guns aren't lawful and nooses give, mustn't have minded the smell of fumes. And even if he did, he thought it was a small price to pay.

He thought you might as well die.

ON: KURT COBAIN

My father decided not to shoot himself through the head. Presumably he didn't blame his brain for all his problems.

ON: MICHEL FOUCAULT (2)

He didn't want to leave a tiny bit of brain on the pavement for the dogs to sniff.

ON: WHAT HAPPENS NEXT

Whatever has happened to me, I always remember that my father killed himself. And ever since he did it, since he just went and perished like nobody's business, I think I have tried to continue to act as if everything was normal. It was just one of those things. Could have happened to anybody. Run of the mill. Nothing special. But then, I was probably lying to myself. I was keeping things from myself. In chasing frantically, or just quietly tailing, a sense of normality, even though worlds might be crumbling around me, and feelings smashing in on me, I have obstinately set myself at a distance from the others that my father so diabolically abandoned. My mother and two sisters. His wife and two daughters.

We never talk about his suicide. If ever, rarely, the four of us find ourselves in the same room, it is never mentioned. It is a dead thing. It might be in the air. It might be in our thoughts. It might be between the lines of what we say to each other. But nothing is said. Everything is on pause. We try so hard to avoid contact with the issue, to avoid making contact with the dead, that we end up acting, behind ragged politeness, as if we are all completely doomed.

I have never been able to imagine talking to my sisters, or worse, my mother about this grotesque, timeless inconvenience, this definitive curse, this horrific disappointment. This suicide that brought us together in an instant and branded us for life and flung us apart into our own shadowy darkness. For years I have never felt that this situation would change. We go through the motions echoing how my father went through so many motions as he slowed down before death.

I often wondered, despite myself, how they felt, but I tried not to think too hard about it. I never really had a total urge to find out. I thought that if I found out too much about how they really feel I might find out too much about how I really felt. And I've never wanted to know. I've got on with my life as if nothing much happened, and everything's OK, and the death of my father just changed the shape of my family, and that's the shape it is. The death of my father meant that we had no father and there was nothing to be done about it and everything changed and yet nothing changed. It was like some boundary in my life had been removed, some sense of balance, however rickety, and some kind of structure, however messy. My father had gone the way of Father Christmas, and God, and I'd learnt by now that once these things have gone, these things that are a state of mind, a security, then you immediately have to find some kind of replacement. I replaced my father with myself, with my own life, with my writing, with my belief in pop music, with my own needs, and to an extent my father took my family with him.

The shock of his death threw me out into the world. Within five or six or seven years of his death, the force that was impelling me to replace the loss with something else meant that I had become successful as a writer, and was involved with pop records that would become the most commercially successful in all of the 80s. I acted and performed and wrote and created things as if no one was paying attention, because my father wasn't paying attention. I operated as if I was in some kind of void, leaving no traces behind me. At the moment of things happening, I would be aware that something I was part of, something I had written, or made up, had been noticed. After the moment, I felt as if it had all been forgotten, forgotten like my father's death. I am still surprised if someone says to me that they have read something I've written, or listened to some music I was involved with. For me, it disappeared with the past. It disappeared like my father. It was something I had done to race away from the disappearance of my father, and the past. I did things that were sometimes quite notorious, quite public, quite appreciated, but I would later feel as if I had passed through in a state of invisibility, as if I had been cloaked by the death of my father. I felt I had left nothing behind me, like my father. I couldn't see how anybody would be interested in anything I'd done. After all, my father wasn't interested. It was like I had to make myself up new every day.

The shock of his death sent me spinning through the 80s and 90s, through my twenties and thirties, and I never had the strength to talk with my mother and sisters about what had happened. The shock forced me to concentrate on other things. To race away as fast as I could, geographically, emotionally, metaphysically.

After twenty years the power of the shock, the momentum the moment created, is perhaps fading away. The tidal wave of his suicide has washed me up on an island, and as I lie on the beach, soaked to the skin, stunned to the heart, I see around me the washed-up shapes of my mother, and of my two sisters. We get up and brush the sand off our bodies.

ON: THOSE INNER RUMBLINGS WHICH COME TO NOTHING

I think that my mother and sisters have an awful lot to tell me about the life and death of my father, from their point of view. I think they might have an awful lot to tell me about how he felt at various times. I think that, between them, they remember an awful lot about the things I have forgotten. Maybe I remember some things they have forgotten.

For years, I have felt that to hear their stories, to embrace their sadness, would be too much. To suddenly be able to understand the effect of my father's dip into eternity on the four of us, individually and collectively, would be a little too real to cope with. I've tended to prefer my reality a little askew. A dab unreal, as reality goes. I like my reality a touch under the weather.

I forget a lot, where I was, what was happening. Perhaps they don't. They were there. They were witnesses. Perhaps they've retained more information than I have, perhaps the shock that struck them manifested itself in different ways. I get the feeling that to talk to them, to remember with them, would be to live right through my father's death, perhaps for the first real time. The first time it happened it seemed more surreal than anything else. My father's suicide was a fine act of surrealism. To not believe in the

278

reality of this life to such an extent that you bend it right round the edge of eternity and snap it off, and replace it with death, this is something of a surreal re-ordering of life. Suicide is the ultimate surreality, taking you deep and deeper still into a place where nothing is as it seems.

My mother, my sisters and I are washed up on the same island lost amidst the vast unknown sea of my father's life and death. It's not a coincidence that we should all be here on this same beach. Perhaps now is the time to talk, to share and share alike experiences and memories of my father, who he was, what he was, and how he lived his life, and died his death. We've been all at sea for long enough and now perhaps is the time to put back together the family my father ripped apart with his sensational exit, and as we do so, return him to his family. We were a family because of him and then we weren't a family because of him, because he scattered us across a waste of life when he killed himself. If we talk about what happened perhaps I will find my father, who has been hiding from me, who has been lost to me, and find that he is dead, but he is not gone. He is still part of his family. He is still part of me.

Or I could carry on pretending that everything is fine. We could sit here on the beach and silently look out to sea and keep ourselves to ourselves and keep our versions of our husband and father to ourselves.

ON: MY MIND

Self-pity is not so sterile as we suppose. Once we feel it's mere onset, we adopt a thinker's attitude, and come to think of it, we come to think!

ON: FOG

I remember, it must have been in the last few months before he died, that the *New Musical Express* had asked me to write a review of the last ever concert to be played by the Edgar Broughton Band, a wild band of inbred English eccentrics who, if I may be technical for a moment, were on a strange line of rock somewhere around Van Der Graaf Generator, Captain Beefheart and The Pink Fairies.

There was a time when such things as the last ever concert by the Edgar Broughton Band seemed important. The gig was to be held in Oldham, ten or so miles from Stockport. It was one of the first commissions the *NME* had ever given me.

That evening, Stockport, and most of Manchester, were covered with a dense, magnificent fog. You couldn't see more than six feet in front of you. My father, seeing that I had no idea how I could make it all the way to Oldham in such a fog, offered to drive me. He could see how important it was to me. We set off. We drove at less than ten miles an hour, creeping out of Stockport towards Oldham and the last ever concert by the Edgar Broughton Band.

The journey must have taken over an hour, perhaps longer. We would have been on our own, enveloped by eerie fluid grey, suspended in the space beyond Stockport, and we would have had plenty of time to talk. To exchange views. To relate to each other. We would have had some special time together to marvel at the great and strange fact we were father and son.

I can't remember anything we talked about. I don't even remember explaining to him why it was important that this was the last ever concert to be played by the Edgar Broughton Band. I didn't use the opportunity, as far as I can remember, to ask him how he was, how was work. How's life, so to speak. Are you feeling all right?

I remember us in the car, like cardboard cut-outs. Like ghosts. I remember slowly moving along roads that were packed with fog like it was special-effect foam. It was as if the outside world had melted away, as if houses and walls and trees and fields had turned into twisted soft shapes of giant grey.

I remember that somehow we made it to Oldham and we managed to find the venue. I remember saying goodbye to my father. He drove back home. We must have reasoned that the fog would lift later and I could make my own way home. There was never any question of him waiting. I don't remember me saying, You should come and watch the last ever concert by the Edgar Broughton Band.

I don't remember anything about the concert or how I got home.

I wonder about my father driving back through the thick fog, penetrating its soft rolling contours, driving alone surrounded by nothing but nothing. If that had been the night he had disappeared, never to return, somehow that would have seemed appropriate. He disappeared into the fog. He became the fog, and when it fizzled out, so did he. He went with the fog. The fog descended upon Stockport, blanked it out for a night, and took him away.

Perhaps if it had happened that way I would remember more about what we talked about during the journey. As it is, I think of this journey as being something that took place purely so that years later I could use the occasion as a metaphor for how my mind is so fogged up. Everything about the car drive, the talk during it, what my father was wearing, what I was wearing, even what car it was – was it a blue Ford Escort? – the last ever concert by the Edgar Broughton Band – all of it has disappeared, all of it is forgotten. What I remember is the fog.

A fog that seemed alive, a fog that was a metaphor taking shape, a fog that had the shape of time becoming visible. A fog that had descended upon Stockport not to take my father away, but to seep into my brain, to cloud my mind, and shroud my memories.

And then the fog clears and I can make my way home.

ON: COMPLETION

I think I used the money I received for writing about the last ever concert by the Edgar Broughton Band to pay my father back for the money he had lent me to print my magazine.

ON: WHAT GOES AROUND COMES AROUND

Or maybe I used the money I received for the Marc Bolan article to pay back my father.

ON: THE WINDMILLS OF MY FUCKING MIND

A few weeks after my father died, Marc Bolan was in Manchester recording a television series for Granada television. I spent a day with him at the studio. I had a better pair of trousers on this time, swamp-green and punk-narrow around the ankles. I remember in

Marc's dressing room I played him the Buzzcocks EP *Spiral Scratch*, where there were fast furious songs about boredom, nervous break-downs, orgasms and time sung and played as if the future of the world depended on their completion and their message. Marc thought the songs were funny and bright but a bit silly, and he called them 'bubblegum angst', like he knew what he was talking about.

He made me a cup of tea. I remember him clad in tacky silver trousers, with a skimpy little T-shirt, his grin wider than his newly skinny legs, his hair frothing around his head, carefully measuring out the tea into the teapot. My favourite pop star ever asked me how many sugars I wanted. He had the most perfect English accent. I think I liked him even more as a real man than as an idol.

I was still very shy being in the presence of someone who had been such a dream, such a central presence in my changing imagi-nation, but we were on the way to being friends. He gave me his home telephone number and asked me to call him when I was next down in London.

A month later, a couple of days before I was due in London, Marc Bolan, the idol and the real man, the fantasy and the flesh and blood, died in a car crash.

I felt I knew him so well, and yet not at all, he was so close, and yet so far away, that I just couldn't cry.

ON: FACING THE FINAL CURTAIN

I had a dream a few weeks after my dad died involving Elvis Presley. He was somehow at the same time the thin Elvis and the fat Elvis and there was something about him that suggested in the way he moved the 30s, the 40s, the 50s, the 60s and the 70s. He was in a dressing room that seemed to be at the Stockport Davenport Theatre, the venue in Stockport for pantomimes starring the likes of Ken Dodd and Shirley Eaton. It was also the place where Stockport Grammar School would hold their annual speech day. In fact, in the dream, Elvis had delivered the speech to the school, and in honour of the occasion he was wearing a black and yellow jumpsuit, with match-ing cap and cape. His speech seemed to consist of the words to 'My Way' all mixed up with the words to the Twenty-third Psalm.

I was in his dressing room with him. Sometimes as well as looking like thin Elvis and fat Elvis he would also look like my dad. He was making me a cup of tea. He took a lot of care over making the tea, he did it his way, and then without even asking me he put in just the right amount of milk and three generous teaspoonfuls of sugar. We drank the tea and had a quiet chuckle over the astonishing differences between Las Vegas and Stockport, which, he said, from where he curled his lip, were like the differences between heaven and hell. But which was which?

Then he asked me to climb on his back, and we flew high above the clouds, and out over the sea.

A few days after the dream, Elvis Presley was dead. He just sort of gave up, or gave in, or gave out. Or perhaps he woke up as someone else, as if all his life had been a dream.

I didn't cry because I had only met him in a dream.

ON: ROCK 'N' ROLL

Sometimes I feel so lonely I could die.

ON: KURT COBAIN (2) OR ERNEST HEMINGWAY (2)

I wonder if my father was aware that the bullet holes in the walls around where someone has tried to shoot themselves, and missed, are known in certain circles as 'hesitation marks'.

ON: THE LAST MINUTE

Did he choose the method he did because he considered it required the least actual will-power to succeed? Shooting yourself, jumping off a tall building, falling in front of a train. Did all this seem to require a kind of commitment that might have broken his concentration? A kind of will-power that wasn't relevant? Life would be tugging at him with all its powers of persuasion when he least wanted it to.

In the end, he sort of died in his sleep. He passed out. It wasn't at all violent. Well, it was discreetly violent. Perhaps he didn't want to leave behind a body that was mashed and mangled up beyond recognition. He was far too vain to want to destroy his body, his neck, his face.

ON: MEANWHILE

My father left his wife and three kids. I am occasionally asked how I feel at being so rejected. I have never felt any kind of rejection. Maybe I should have done. From second one, as soon as the door shut on the pale and chilled policeman and policewoman who arrested four lives with their harsh news, I have simply accepted it. I turned my back on it. This is what I have convinced myself: that I have dealt with it. That I got used to the idea immediately and my life started from there. From that scratch.

I was on my own now, this is what I decided. I wasn't rejected. I was just left. I've never thought I was important enough in his life for him to have rejected me. Perhaps that means that he had already rejected me while he was alive, but I don't feel that either. The decision he took was all about himself, and yet somehow not in a selfish way. I think he thought it was better for everyone that he killed himself. His life was so black it blotted out any feelings he had for his family, much as he tried to fight the blackness. He wasn't rejecting any of us. I have never thought of his suicide as being the selfish act many consider it to be. He was, in his stricken mind, setting us free from the same thing he was setting himself free from. Himself. I reacted, on my own, as if something had happened that was destined to happen. My father was never going to go grey. He wasn't going to accompany his wife into old age.

I was on my own. This is what I decided. Not rejected. Just left. Of course, I wasn't the only one left on their own. When the police called that still and moving morning I wasn't on my own. My mother was there. And at least one of my sisters. They both must have been there. I remember one and not the other. I think we all heard the news together. I remember it as if I alone heard the news. My mother and my sisters had slipped into their own dimensions, their own isolated part of the sea of despair.

ON: ONCE UPON A TIME

My little sister, just in and out of bed, darted in silly little circles, running straight into shock, and then she collapsed on her bed in a shambles of loss, crying out the first words I remember hearing in my new dadless life, some of the few words I remember hearing in the weeks to come: 'That means Mum's a widow.'

Yes, it did.

ON: REPETITION

I spent the rest of that tender fluid morning shocked to shreds by the sheer lucid presence of death, already changing the molecules of my being in preparation for a stage of my life where death was in front of me without my father living in the way. I cleaned the oven in our kitchen of years of accumulated grime, as if I'd done it before.

I scrubbed and scrubbed as if death might disappear along with the grime.

Everything seemed to be happening in speeded-up slow-motion warped with déjà vu. I'd cleaned this oven before. I would clean it again.

ON: LEARNING BY HEART

What I have done on the sly, without consciously trying, but with superimposed commitment, is to choose to prefer to know as little as possible about the facts of my father's suicide and beside that his life. I have practised sustained irrational indifference. I have exercised a long option on disinterest, for as long at it has taken. I have taught myself, casually forced myself, distantly convinced myself to think and feel and discover nothing much in particular about what to others is a ravishing, puzzling, quite monstrous act of grace and/ or disgrace.

When anybody finds out about my father it is the thing they find most curious and fascinating about my life. For me, because of the way I've acted since the episode with the oven, the oven I keep cleaning to this day, because I made the whole damned thing normal, in a manner of normal, it's just something that happened, something that I remember now and then. I'm superficially surprised that anybody should be so interested. A little lightly flattered that it seems to deflect my way some of the original glamour and fresh metaphysical lustre I've always insensibly sought for myself, lends me a thin floaty patina of the difference and depth I've always self-consciously tried to work up for myself out of myself. The abominable brilliance of my father's self-possessed plunge into inaccessible interior oblivion is, whatever I do with my life unless I equal or mimic the brutally mysterious style of his self-tended extinction, the most brilliant thing about me. The only thing about me that will be touched by a transcendent charge of infamy.

My father is a murderer, and, in decadent self-important addition, the self he murdered was his own. I should be so privileged. I should be so associated. So closely related.

It was nothing.

ON: SOMETHING THAT LEADS TO STILL FURTHER VAGUENESS

Am I suffering from an awkwardly classic case of American twentieth-century denial? Of course I fucking am. I carry it around with me like an industrial-sized oven.

ON: THE OPRAH WINFREY SHOW

Rejected? Me? Naah. I've never even considered it.

ON: BLACKENING A PAGE

Maybe I am jealous that my father's inconceivable exit is more interesting than anything I've done or will do in my life. Maybe I *am*, after all that pretence, just plain dumb angry that he left me, ignored me, dismissed me, wiped me out, passed me by, shat on me, suddenly went like he'd never even been, hadn't a last thought for me, and what I was going to do. But if I think those things, am I doing it because I think it's expected of me, it's the natural response. Do I think it was my fault? Should I think that it's my fault? Did I disappoint him? Did I think these things in the moment after the moment he dropped death onto himself, and by the way me, and then did I just give up thinking this way; or have I never thought about any of this before?

Did I let him down? Was I ignoring him, lost in my own developing world, making up things for myself that kept him out of my life, out of my way? Could he tell that I knew all of nothing about his life, and didn't really seem to care? Were we, are we, some kind of mortal enemies? Am I still on the Oprah Winfrey show?

When pushed to remember something about his little life and his massive death, I am distinctly uncomfortable about what I might find. Perhaps this anxiety is why I have up to a voided point suspended any animation of feeling for my father. It's been easier to numb whatever pain there might be, to numb the possibility of pain so as to never even find out the level of the pain that there is.

Am I like my father? Am I my father's son? Will I share my father's fate? If I look too hard at my father's life and death will I see similarities that will pull me towards the same feeling that life is so useless it can be got rid of in a few breaths? Will I start to appreciate that nothing is closer to life than death? Will I find that I am as prepared for death as my father?

Like father, like son. Yes, thank you, Oprah. I've never thought of it like that. I don't know if I would want to put it like that.

ON: KIERKEGAARD

The secret of the father splits the son.

ON: FOOTSTEPS

Is it in the blood?

The bloody Morley blood.

Will I be inspired by what he did? Was this his advice to me? His parental guidance? Do away with yourself as I would do with myself. Was this all he could make of himself so that I would closely follow? Will my brain genetically chase his into whatever distressed shape it ended up in? Is the past of my father the future of me?

Did he have any idea what he was doing?

Will I ever have any idea?

ON: SUICIDE AS COSMIC JOKE

Taboo or not taboo?

ON: MISHEARING

Was that the question?

ON: HELP

Could I have done anything to save him? Was there something that I should have noticed? What was he thinking? What was I thinking? Did I let him down?

ON: SYMPATHETIC APPLAUSE

Oprah is asking the final question. Have I ever had suicidal feelings?

Funnily enough, what with one thing and another, to all intents and purposes, I have.

She says, Sorry, we've run out of time.

Just like my father, I say.

(Laughter.)

ON: TREPIDATION

So far, I think, I have survived, and I have kept the thought of his routinely self-centred act, or his defensible madness, or his fantastically courageous encounter with the unknown and the

288

unknowable, in the shadows of a complacency that I have carefully and, yes, carelessly arranged for myself.

For the sake of personal security I have kept his death at a distance. I have vanished much of his vanishing. I have taken the coward's way out and so far I have only regretted that attitude, felt it as a sorry pressure, with a life all of its own, when the night is at its most immense, when the night threatens to peel back nothing, when sleep, that paraphrase of death, that decorous little implication of eternity, seems the most difficult thing in the world to achieve. Sometimes, in the midst of a night, I might think to myself how the death of my father seems a matter of months ago, if you measure it by the amount of thought I've given it. Long amounts of time pass by without me thinking with much attention about my father, and his life, and his death.

I have never allowed myself to think too hard, or too nimbly, or too face-on, about his crime against nature, his decent action, his obscene gesture; I have never thought of what he did as being anything more vivid, more troublesome, more phenomenal than just, you know, 'suicide', something that was bound to happen, something that was just an obstacle in the otherwise smooth and bumpy way life simply goes its own way. I have never concentrated on whether he was weak or strong, hero or villain, good or bad, because I have never wanted to find out too much about myself. The sense and senselessness of his suicide seemed to me, on the margins of my universe, at the edge of my thoughts, a direct route to the sense and senselessness of my self. I didn't want to know the answers to the questions that I should have been asking. And yet I did. I didn't want to remember. And yet I do.

And now that my mother and my two sisters have gathered on this empty beach, perhaps we can talk, swap stories, remember my father as a man, not a mistake, a shocking act, a ghost, an end, a forgotten life.

ON: BEING FORGOTTEN

Is naming names necessary?

289

ON: AN UNDERTAKING

I don't remember my sisters being at the funeral, or my father's mother. Or his sister. That's because they weren't there. They were miles away.

ON: A LITTLE SUDDENLY

I thought my interest, my need to know, would dwindle. Instead, it's grown. I've grown restless, annoyed with my own lack of understanding, my own diminished memories, my own lack of feeling for my father.

There's been a killing. I know who the killer is. I'm looking for a motive. I thought I had one, but I'm not so sure now. I have to know why the killer killed. What prompted him. A sudden urge, a mental aberration, a long-drawn-out sense of dread? I used to think that for my peace of mind it was better that I never knew why; I am beginning now to think the opposite. Is it time to start taking it for granted that my father killed himself, or is it time to stop taking it for granted? It's like he's turned into a story that might or might not be true. He's turned into a myth that's always about to dissolve. He almost doesn't exist beyond the fact that he doesn't exist.

ON: MEASURING UP TO DEATH

I remember that my father killed himself. I don't talk about it much, but I've never forgotten. At times all that was left of my father as far as I was concerned was the fact that he killed himself. His whole life was telescoped into the black hole of his suicide.

For all that, I don't remember the day, the month, or the year. I must have forgotten the day that it happened the day after it happened. Or even on the day that it happened.

I'm not clear in my mind if he died in 1976, or 1977, or 1978. I'm not sure if he was forty-two, or forty-three, or forty-four. I suppose it doesn't help that I can't remember if he was born in 1934, 35 or 36. As far as the day of the week he died is concerned, for all I know it was the eighth day. Farawayday. Lostday. Someday. Deadday.

Dadday. I'm obviously metaphysically prejudiced towards it being a Sunday, but it probably just felt like a Sunday, the worst of all possible Sundays, prone, mournful, deadended, one that started with a minor English farce, or the conclusion to a farce, or the setting up of a farce. I have a one in five chance of guessing what month it was – somewhere between February and June, although, now, come to think of it, July looks good. Or bad. I don't know why I think it was in the first half of the year, but not January. Something to do with Christmas, I think.

I know that he was born on 10 May. I've always known that.

I should be able to pin down the year of his death by working out when Marc Bolan and Elvis Presley died. The dead year. Even when I do, I still can't quite work out when my father died. The date doesn't seem to settle down. It doesn't seem to belong in the same year. It doesn't seem to belong on the same planet. His suicide seems something too big to have actually been a date, something to commemorate. It didn't happen one morning in the English 1970s. It happened one lifetime in a corner of space.

It happened in dreamtime in a country lost for eons at the bottom of the sea.

ON: CLEARING THE AIR

Perhaps I should ask my mother these simple questions. What was the date? What was the year? How old was he? A book would need these details. And there are other questions too. Now that the sea is calm perhaps they can be asked, and answered.

ON: JEAN-PAUL SARTRE

Sartre, in *The Wall*, describes how his principal character loses interest in everything around him as he gets closer to his execution. Indifference replaces emotions like anger or hatred. He realises that he is not even going to miss the things to which he thought he was the most attached in this life. 'Death had disenchanted everything.'

ON: JORGE LUIS BORGES

Now, like the gods, he is invulnerable.

ON: SELF-CONTROL

What were my father's last words? What were his last deadened utterances before he so truly interrupted himself? Perhaps the last words he spoke were when he paid for some petrol at a garage. 'Thank you,' he said when he received the change. 'Thank you' was the last thing he ever said. Muttered half to himself and half to a God he didn't believe in.

I have about as much idea what his last words were as I do about what his last thoughts were.

I do wonder what he was thinking as he drove to his death from Stockport to Stroud. Didn't it seem completely absurd for him to be stopping at red lights? To be following the highway code? Wasn't it hard for him to muster up the enthusiasm to drive, knowing that it was all heading nowhere, fast. Did he think, Well, that's the last time I will do that, the last time I will touch that, the last time I will smell petrol, grass, summer, me? This is the last time I will taste tea, the last time I will turn left, the last time I will go downhill, the last time I will take off my spectacles and rub the sides of my nose.

ON: WAITING

Did he escape, this last time, like he always did, as regular as fear, out into the open, run away from the tightening responsibility of his life and his family, intending to do no more than escape? Did he think, I'll return home, as I always do, and then my life, and the life of my family, will be picked up, and knocked back into shape, as it usually is? Until the next time. Or did he think, This time I will escape for good, and begin a new life? Kill the old me without killing myself. Did he spend a few days happy to be away, from Stockport, from the walls of the house, from the bills, from the trap of his mind and the trap of his circumstances? Was there no intention of suicide, or was he always sure as soon as he drove out of Stockport? Did he just enjoy a last few days of solitude, before the forgone conclusion of his suicide.

Perhaps he intended to go back. Just a few days of peace away from it all to gather his senses. And then he looked at the situation. He had run off in the company van. It didn't belong to him. He couldn't imagine going back home one more time to have to piece his life back together knowing he'd always see the cracks. More and more cracks. More cracks than whole pieces. The cracks of a cracked and cracking life.

How long, in the end, the alien end, did he give himself to live? A week, a weekend, a day, an evening?

Tonight's the night.

It was still a surprise.

ON: JORGE LUIS BORGES (2)

He walks slowly under the lindens. He looks at the balustrades and doors, but not to remember them.

ON: DOUBLE TIME

The last time I will look in a mirror. I won't need to cut my hair any more. I won't have to shave. When he shaved that morning, or the night before, looking at himself in the mirror, did he think, This is the last time I will ever run a blade over my face? The last time I will ever run a blade over the stretched skin of my neck. Did he stare at himself, stare at the other man in the mirror that had followed him through life, stare into those deep-brown eyes and connect himself, this image of himself, this haunting double, with the sorcery of what he was about to do?

This is the last time it will be midday. The last time it will rain.

The last time I will think of this and that and carpet and Shell and so on.

The last time I will ever blink.

This is my last breath.

What was he thinking? Perhaps it had all grown beyond that.

Beyond thinking. Thinking is for this world. He was already passing into another world. He wasn't thinking at all. He was in such a state thought couldn't penetrate. He had sunk so far into himself that the superstructure of language and thus the fictive netting of thought were a receding illusion, a deceasing fact of life, no use to him in death. He was slipping out of life keeping only those things that would be useful to him in death. He journeyed through the last day of his life propelled by lingering habit, driving and signalling and eating and drinking on remote control.

He had backtracked backslid backsensed to a former form of formlessness where the nips and tucks and hooks and tips of language hadn't yet come along to trace his presence, and help and hinder him in this mortal life. In quiet preparation for his ultimate isolation, his preferred destination, he was returning to a statelessness of mind where he couldn't even begin to think. Approaching death had hypnotised him: he was falling . . .

But before then, before that happened, there must have been a last time to think, there must have been some last thoughts. And who knows, I don't, he could have been thinking to himself about himself, pure himselfness, right up to the first moment the gas began to mist his mind to mist his life to mist his last thought this is the last time I will ever have a chance to change my mind this is the last time I will ever remember this seat is sticky this is the last time the nail on my middle finger is really long . . .

He might have been thinking something right to the stoned end, letting his thoughts flow freely like a river racing to the open sea, thinking something right up to the crammed primordial end, right up to the dead delights of thoughtlessness. Thinking something, however fierce, however gentle, however chaotic, from something slipping into nothing, as if it was always that way, the something of his life dissolving away away away . . .

The last time I will ever smoke a cigarette. Twenty Guards, please. Maybe those were his last words. He didn't bother saying thank you. Not this time. The time for thank yous is over.

He deserved this cigarette. The whole of his life led to this cigarette. A last smoke before the self-execution. A deep drag on the filter sucking the life out of the thing. He sighs the smoke away into the atmosphere, watching as the swirls of smoke dwindle to nothing. He blows a perfect smoke ring and manages a weak smile as he monitors its spiralling neatness. He takes a final drag and flicks the butt away. He doesn't see where it lands.

ON: JORGE LUIS BORGES (3)

He meets an acquaintance and tells him a joke. He knows that for a time this episode will furnish an anecdote.

ON: NABOKOV

'I want you to concentrate. You are about to die.'

ON: NATURE'S WAY

I wonder what the moment of death was like. A slow drizzle into unconsciousness. A staggering moment of incandescent euphoria. A guillotined slam into ferocious blackness. A psychedelic sham of disintegration and horror that induced last-minute panic as he was sucked down a plughole of nothingness and it was too late he couldn't pull back all the sense of him located in one instant stared death full in the face and then it was all over. Sheer terror.

ON: W. B. YEATS

A blaze of heaven in the brain.

ON: SAMUEL BECKETT (2)

Was there a final rattle as he passed away?

ON: MORE THAN HIS SHARE OF HAPPINESS

What was he thinking whenever it was that he gave up on thinking?
Was he thinking about me me me, about how his dejection and his
rejection would damage me, or was he thinking about his wife, the
weather, or the birds and bees? Thinking about the night. The last
night. No dawn followed.

Was he thinking about the last time he went to the cinema, to see
Jaws, was he thinking how his wife fell asleep as they were watching
it? Their last date together. She fell asleep. She didn't even see the
shark. He watched the film on his own. He stared at all that water.
His wife was asleep in the cinema and he stared at the water and he
was drowning.

Was he thinking that he was scared, or was he thinking that this is
all so inevitable, was he thinking that this was always going to be the
time, his time, or was he thinking about the colour of the van, the
van he used to destroy himself? Was he thinking, There's no time like
next week, or, Don't put off until tomorrow what you can do today?
Was he remembering to laugh at a favourite Ken Dodd joke? Was
the thought of death drowning out thought, or was the thought of
death illuminating thought? Was he thinking about everything and
nothing, the next few seconds, about following through with his
plan, about how well it was all going, about his closeness to closeness, what an absurd way to die, was he thinking help me, was he
thinking this is the last time I will ever cry, was he wondering I
wonder if anyone would ever care what he was thinking, what a
perfect way to die? Was he thinking . . . I can't take it any more?

Was he happy?

ON: ARISTOTLE

'We are only truly happy in death.'

ON: LATENESS

Was he thinking, It's too late to stop now . . . who cares . . . did he
think of his mother . . . his father . . .?

ON: EXPERIENCING TECHNICAL DIFFICULTIES

It was, from his point of view, a good job that the van didn't run out of petrol.

ON: THERE IS NOTHING LIKE A DAME

. . . did he have the radio on, was he listening to music, was he listening to some singer and some kind of song about love and loss, or was the last sound he heard just this mesmerising matter-of-fact forgettable hiss? The sound of the serpent reaching in to take him away.

I can't imagine him wanting to finish things off by listening to music. I never think of him as being interested in music. The only records I remember him owning were a Jerry Lewis EP – 'I've got her picture hanging upside down 'cos I can't stand the sight of her face' – 'Never Smile at a Crocodile', 'Sunday Driving', the soundtrack to *South Pacific* and a Victor Borge LP. Did he once have a single by Adam Faith the whitest man in the world, or do I just think he should have, because it would have fitted in to what I think of his life? Listening to Adam Faith on the Isle of Wight. Until the day he died he wore enough Brylcreem in his hair to suggest that he might once have been a weekend Teddy boy.

We once had an argument about music. Well, not so much about music, more about appearance. It was the only time I remember we ever came close to having a conversation about ideas, one of the few times my world of pop floated close to his world of intensity. It must have been the early 70s, we were in the Woodsmoor house, and I was watching *Top of the Pops* and he was in the room . . .

ON: BEING CARRIED SUDDENLY INTO THE PAST

I guess I got the feeling that everything was too much for him. That he was continually striving to keep a terrible temper under control. That if I had to describe him quickly in a few words I would say that he was irritably lethargic. There could be something frightened and frightening in his look. There would be times when we would be in the same room watching TV together silently on the edge of his nerves. I would look at him but not at him out of the corner of my eye sizing up his deft suppressedness anticipating at any second for no good reason a sudden flash burst of anger. He was never seemingly settled even as he slumped. He wasn't happy. Well, sometimes he was. Sometimes he seemed relieved in himself. Occasionally, he was even relaxed, as relaxed goes, building up to some eruption or another, some sinking of the heart, some need to run out of the door and never come back. Mostly, he just seemed latent. He could fill a room with tension quite easily. He could pack it out with silence. He could decorate it with mood. He could shift it with his brooding into another dimension.

He didn't want to be disturbed.

ON: OPINION

. . . and I mustered up the courage, like I was a rebellious teenager or something, to announce to my dad with all the knowing provocation I could drag into the room that Roy Wood the Wizzard singer was a genius. I knew that really this was an opinion guaranteed to wind my father up. Any hint that my generation was enjoying teenage years in a way his generation never could seemed to hit a raw spot.

My father was thirty-something at the time, but I suppose an evacuated war-child national service kind of thirty-something, someone who lived through a much different 60s from the one that has gone down in history. His 60s wasn't a pop 60s. It wasn't even a trad jazz 60s. His 60s was the one that wasn't really that long after the end of the Second World War. His 60s was more wartime than Warhol.

He glanced with his mother's dismal superior eyes at this glammy explosion of hair and paint singing with brassy monotony some boisterous nervy rhyme about jumping and jiving. He gave a snort and began to correct me. This person, he said, is just a silly clown. He wasn't a genius. Of course he was, I said. It seemed obvious to me at the time that Wood was. After all, appearances can be deceptive. Here was a musician who had written 'Blackberry Way' and 'Flowers in the Rain' and 'Brontosaurus'. He had formed the Electric Light Orchestra. I tried to put forward my point in as grown-up a manner as possible, but my father just snapped that I was being silly. He began to get angry that I didn't agree with him. I got angry that he didn't agree with my point of view. After all, pop was my territory – I knew what I was talking about.

He was right, though, More right than me, anyway.

He liked to think that he was always right, a little more intensely and vulnerably than most people like to think they're right. I suppose he thought he was right right up to the end. Right up to the last time that he thought he was right.

Who's to say that he wasn't?

Not me.

Not him.

ON: FRANZ KAFKA

There were few books in our household. There were no bookshelves crammed with volumes that could say something about the growth of my father's intellect, that could suggest something about his interests. We had a small cabinet the size of a medium-sized suitcase where paperback books were placed. I remember my father read the English horror of Dennis Wheatley. I remember a copy of Nevil Shute's post-apocalyptic *On the Beach*. There were some Agatha Christies, but I think they were my mother's. There was an *A–Z* of Manchester. There were a handful of torn and tattered *Reader's Digest*s.

In the midst of this comprehensive lack of literature, I have a memory, as faint as any, of my father bringing home one day to Hawthorn Grove a copy of some stories by Franz Kafka. The book included Kafka's classic fable of transformation and self-sacrifice, 'Metamorphosis'.

My father reading Kafka goes entirely against the character I have routinely assigned him in my mind. Perhaps I have conjured up this fantasy of my father reading Kafka in the last months of his life, because I need to feel that there was some kind of consciously poetic, or existential, ultimately deeply thoughtful reason for his suicide. I want to think of it as an act that burnt with ideas, that it was a determined, articulated response to a predicament that my father identified, and transcendentally negotiated. I have this strange, probably snobby need to interpret my father's suicide as an intellectual decision, rather than some sloppy descent into random madness. It was a revolt against the homely, the domestic, the provincial.

He was a glorious pessimist. He was a hard, brilliant nihilist. He was Hemingway-heroic. He was Dostoevsky-dark. He was an artist of alienation. He was a philosopher who'd lost his way and was quietly trying to find it. He wasn't a sick man, or ineffectually weak, he was an idealist too good for the real world. He needed a release for his dark feelings, and he saw that the ideal release, the greatest relief, certainly as far as he was concerned, and, for good reason, he had no other concerns, was death.

He always felt that he was being accused of something and his defence was: suicide.

He was searching for significance, for meaning, and he walked, purposefully, towards his suicide as if it was a great work of art, his one all-encompassing artistic statement. He knew very well that Albert Camus wrote that judging whether life is or is not worth living amounts to answering the fundamental question of philosophy. My father judged that, under his circumstances, unique, Stuckport circumstances, life was not worth living, it was fraught with unrealness. His death was his way of writing a wasteland poem, creating a work of art, conceptualising existence, breaking it down into desolate abstraction. Suicide was his way of achieving realness in the silence of his heart in a way he never could when he was alive.

Kakfa becomes a key in opening up this notion that my father turned death into an art form. Kafka's Gregor Samsa, the man who turned into a man-insect, who sacrificed himself so that his family could resume their lives relieved of his tedious presence, was part of my father's research into the meaning of life and the manners of death. Kafka captured the sense of unreality that my father felt about life: it never quite made sense, it never really added up. He envied the quiet of the empty and contemplative mind that Gregor obtained just before his death, perhaps the only time and place such a state of mind can be found. My father was a thinker. A deep thinker. A self-analyst. He thought himself to death. His death was a thought. A peaceful thought. A thought that took everything inside itself and disguised it as nothing.

I think.

ON: A THEORY OF THEODOR ADORNO'S

'He over whom Kafka's wheels have passed has lost for ever any peace with the world.'

ON: ANOTHER THEORY

A man's troubles are sent by the ghost of his grandmother.

ON: VIRGINIA WOOLF

My father decided not to drown himself. He was such a good swimmer.

ON: THE END OF THE CENTURY

I have a grumbling suspicion that my father was forty-three when he died. I tend to believe that he was forty-three, and to all intents and purposes still is forty-three, because I have been aware for some time now that I will be forty-three in the year 2000. I have been thinking about how old I would be in the year 2000 since about the time my father died. There's something very neat and fateful about the fact that I will be the age my father reached in his life in the year 2000, if only mathematically. There's part of me that thinks of it as quite a piece of destiny.

Because I presume that my father died at the age of forty-three, and because of the year 2000, it is an age that I have become sensitive and anxious about. I have started to wonder, as I speed towards the age of my father, what it will be like to be older than my father ever was. I think of it as being like walking off the ledge of time out into my very own unknown. To be more grown-up than my father ever was.

The age forty-three has become some kind of emotional pain barrier, a mental milestone. Once, it seems just a few pages ago, it just seems for ever ago, as I was scrubbing an oven, forty-three seemed old. The year 2000 seemed a long way off. At the time my father replaced himself with sheer nothing, he seemed older rather than younger. Now, for my own sake, I can appreciate how young he really was. He only made it halfway through a life really. In many earthly ways, he'd only just begun. His corpse was not the corpse of an old man.

The years after the age of forty-three will be a mystery to me now. The years before forty-three have been a mystery, thanks in part to my father, but the years after forty-three will be a different kind of mystery. A new kind of mystery. My father left no clues about how to manoeuvre through these years. There have been no hints about how to behave, how to adjust, what to avoid. Actually, he left one big clue. Not even a clue. Just a massive mission statement:

Don't bother.

Avoid everything.

ON: WHAT TO DO FROM MORNING TILL NIGHT

I remember that after, or during, or at the beginning of my father's third, or fourth, or fifth nervous breakdown the local GP swooped down on our house in Offerton. My father refused point-blank to budge from his bed. Why bother? What's the point? What's out there? There's nothing of any interest to me.

I remember this rummage of action and inaction in my parents' dark alien bedroom. My father presumably laid out flat slumped into an engulfing apathy, the kind of apathy that can eventually stretch out to death (death being a permanent apathy, within unreason). The doctor, no doubt profoundly dazed by his own life in Stockport, gruffly told my father, dumped far and futile into his very own enigmatic nausea, estranged from the conventions of everydayness by a well-equipped sense of self-loathing, sealed into his thickly coated indifference, to snap out of it. The classic advice to give to someone who is clearly suffering from a depression so real everything else is not real. The doctor tried to shame my father out of his thick, soaking depression. In terms of such an invisible, suspicious thing as depression, the sunken Stockport 1970s was the dead backward centre of the Dark Ages. It was still a good twenty years before such things would be talked about, freely, frankly, on day-time television, day in, day out, as if depression was something serious, something common, something dangerous.

'Snap out of it,' the doctor told my father, as if this would instantly lift my father out of the depths of despair.

'Snap out of it,' the doctor said, as if this would make all the difference to a man who was up to his neck in the sheets and blankets of hopelessness. 'Snap out of it,' the doctor said, as if my father was play-acting and malingering and wasting everybody's time. 'Snap out of it,' the doctor snapped, as if a simple click of the fingers would cause my father to leap out of bed and become a paragon, a positive virtue, a man of action, a man with a mission.

My father didn't move a muscle, but his being shrank a little more.

He thought he could hear someone talking to him . . .

He thought he was thinking about something, but he must have been mistaken.

He stared right through the doctor with the X-ray vision of a superman who has given up. Life had become so unreal he could see through the unreal walls that hemmed him in – right through to another set of walls. And through that to another set of walls. And through that to a mirror that circled the earth. He stared at himself in the mirror and thought to himself, I need to relax a little. I need to relax a lot.

I suppose a few years after the doctor ordered my father to snap out of it, I suppose my father did indeed snap out of it. Right out of it. Out of his mind. Out of this world. Snap.

He could even see through a mirror to what lies beyond the reflection.

ON: JORGE LUIS BORGES (4)

Now, like the dead, he is invulnerable.

ON: BEING A PRISONER

I remember that my father and I liked to watch the television series *The Prisoner* starring Patrick McGoohan. This was perhaps the most directly philosophical television show there has ever been, as McGoohan's character tussled from episode to episode with all manner of notions regarding identity, location, reality, sanity, meaning, freedom. Alongside the Kafka, this is another clue that my father had definite views on, say, the ineluctable banality of existence, the disconnected nature of reality, the irrelevance of society. That he perhaps believed that the world was uniformly zany and corrupt and not all that it was cracked up to be. Life was a kind of sloppy nightmare made up of mildly hallucinatory sensations dressed up as something normal for the sake of effect. Life was enigmatic, futile, unignorable, a parade of stuff and nonsense that is at best a playful waste of time. The jolly trapped terror and routine chases and silly puzzles and incongruous whimsy of *The Prisoner* must have been right up my father's street. He could easily identify with the dearly maintained aplomb, the helpless anger and frustration of McGoohan. They were of a similar build. About the same age. They both had something about their look that could wryly appraise the given situation of the apparent world around them, and dismiss it as bogus. They could fly off in a rage at the drop of a meaningless hat. They could snap a command with furious precision. They tried to prove themselves and win and find a way out of their predicament, even as they kept losing, and losing their way. They were bewildered by the moment, moment to moment, but would work hard not to let it show too much.

McGoohan, as the Prisoner in a place called The Village where society was shrunk into a small wonderland of vaguely menacing pretence, was given a number. He was number 6. In each episode, apart from whatever else he had to deal with in this place uncannily separated from the rest of the world, McGoohan determined to find out who number 1 was. Who ran The Village? Who was in charge? Who made up the rules? Who put me here? Why do I have to live where I live and do what I do? Why can't I go somewhere else, be someone else, do something else. Who is number 1?

Each episode, a different number 2 would reply quite simply, 'You are number 6.'

The puzzle remained. The Prisoner still quested after the identity of number 1.

As the series progressed, and the identity of number 1 proved increasingly elusive, you kept watching to see how extreme the fantasy, the religious imagery, the parade of intrigue would become, believing that by the end of the series, there would be some kind of answer – to the Prisoner's fate and to who number 1 really was. As we approached the finale – itself a piece of flushed nonsense that gave away nothing and just wrapped up the whole series in a gleeful 60s blast of psychedelic absurdity – my father believed that he had cracked the mystery. 'Listen to the way number 2 always answers the question who is number 1?' he said. 'Imagine that there is a comma in his answer. Who is number 1? He doesn't say, You are number 6. He actually says, You are, number 6. He's giving McGoohan the answer, it's just that McGoohan doesn't realise it.'

I was very impressed. We are all prisoners, with our own numbers given to us by the randomness of society. But we are also our own number 1s. We are our own Gods. We make the rules. We decide what happens. We decide who to be. It's all a matter of free will. Whatever the apparent circumstances of your life, whatever the immediate surroundings, whatever you're meant to believe, you are ultimately in control of yourself and your destiny.

At least, I think that's what he meant.

ON: A MID-LIFE CRISIS

Nothing ventured, nothing gained.

ON: STANDING UP IN COURT

Uncle Graham drove my mother and me to the inquest. We probably followed pretty much the same route my father followed as he drove himself to his death. The rest of the world was carrying on around us at its usual pace, but my father's wife and her husband's son, the sorry pair a few days into a life newly packaged as post-suicide, were well off the pace.

I remember the inquest like it was an old courtroom TV drama where I just happened to somehow take part. It was the first time I had ever been in any kind of court. It reminded me of school. The room, neatly, brownly parked inside a bureaucratic bubble, had been dried out by years of deathly details, and quietened by a strict need to get things done, to turn things around, to file away lives and deaths on distant shelves. There was a medium gloom of correctness and pleasantness hanging around, and a polite sense of staginess. Everyone seemed to quickly slip into a slow old routine.

My mother stayed in the corridor outside the courtroom, unable to hear the details of her husband's recent death. If she had gone inside the room, her brave face which she had brought especially for the occasion, and which looked so poignant, would have burst the bureaucratic bubble. I went inside the room, because it was my responsibility to contribute the thoughts of the untogether Morley family.

A young couple who had found the body were represented by a young boy who explained how he had seen the blue van parked in the dark. Then he had seen the tube linking the exhaust and the driver's window. Then he had put two and two together to make, as it often does, something not quite right. He and his girlfriend had called the police. Oddly enough, the young couple seemed to be played by the same people who had played the policeman and policewoman who arrived to tell us that as far as my father was concerned there was nothing further to say.

The police arrived some time later and found that in this case two plus two made death. In the front seat of the van they discovered a pink-cheeked body that appeared to be in the bloom of health.

As I listened to this evidence, I started to put another two and two together myself, and wondered if, when the young couple first discovered the van, hooked up for death, my father was in fact still alive, having just begun his last journey. The young boy had apparently not checked in the van, he had just quickly called the police as soon as he had completed his two plus twos. Perhaps in the time it took for the police to arrive there might have been time to save my father, to break the circuit of death he had created, to pull him out of the van and bring him back to real life. I felt a sudden urge to shout out this point, as if it was my duty to cross-examine, make points, investigate closely. Was my father still alive when the van was discovered? Could he have been saved? But what good would any of that achieve? Saying it now wouldn't save my father. All it would do was make two young people even more traumatised about their trip to a lonely lovers' lane than they were now. It wasn't their fault that my father died, any more than it was the fault of the person who invented the internal combustion engine.

And if they had 'rescued him', if the process had been stopped before my father had died, then he would probably have suffered from brain damage. It is the one real risk involved in such a method, which is one of the safest, cleanest and efficient methods of self-disposal. You are 'saved' before you suffocate, and the time you have received no oxygen to the brain means you are, to some extent, still alive, but mentally impaired. Not dead, still wanting to be dead, but now not capable of organising your own death. This is the worst possible result of a serious suicide attempt. To survive this time with the chance of trying again is a much better result. It is also the worst possible result of a non-serious suicide attempt – the cry for help attempt, the attempt you hope will actually lead not to death but to a new life. It is not the response you were expecting to your cry for help to wake up paralysed, or brain-damaged, or disfigured. Semi-dead. It's enough to make you want to consider a serious suicide attempt, except now, of course, you may not have the physical means to try.

Sometimes you save someone by letting them die as they had planned it in their head, the head where all their life ended up, crushed by itself.

My father was probably dead when they discovered the van. The couple whose smooching had been brutally upset could probably tell without checking because everything was so still. I wonder what the couple did as they waited for the police to turn up. Shiver? Marvel? Watch the grass grow?

Then it was my turn to speak. I suppose I was wearing the same clothes I wore at the funeral. I was not conscious of my trousers. There were about fifteen people in the room as I delivered to a gentle-looking and perfectly cast coroner my feelings about my father's feelings, my opinion about why he ended up so alone, so lost, and then, so found. I don't know if what I said was something I had recently discussed with my mother, or if it was a theory I had developed over the years as my father broke into pieces. But it was a version of events I felt sure enough about to present to a group of strangers who stared at me with practically concerned faces.

I reported how his mother had told him around 1970 that the father he thought had died during the war had in fact run off with another woman to Australia and had actually been alive all these years. But now he was dead. Definitely dead. So he had thought he hadn't had a father for over thirty years but really he had but now he hadn't.

I went on to say that this news had triggered the first nervous breakdown in my father's life, and that ever since then he had suffered a series of depressions that had got deeper and deeper until there was nowhere deeper to go.

I suppose I blamed his mother, and indeed his father, for his death.

I was just trying to say that something had caused his depression and then once he had this depression it ate away at him. Like a cancer of the soul.

The inquest came to an end and this particular bubble burst when it should have done.

The verdict was suicide.

There was a last look of concern from everyone concerned, and one or two of those present even put the verdict in their pipes and smoked it, and then we all left the room, some of us more permanently touched than others. Some of the people present went through this process every day of their lives. Outside in the corridor my mother, who went through this process once in a lifetime, was no longer wearing a brave face. I think she had flushed it down the toilet where it went through a series of pipes and streams and rivers before finally arriving in the sea.

She was now wearing no face at all.

Her husband had killed himself.

There was no doubt about it.

ON: THE SUICIDE NOTE

There was one thing that gave away what my father had done. He had left a suicide note. As far as the good and gentle coroner was concerned, this sealed the matter.

On the day of his death my father had got dressed, written a suicide note, and concluded a life in a way that verged on the English ritualistic.

The coroner showed us the note as evidence K, or something. He said that the family would receive a copy of the note, but the real thing had to be kept for the record. He mentioned the number of years the real suicide note would have to be kept. In some file. On some shelf. In some room. Ten years, I think he said. It could have been a hundred. I don't believe my mother or my sisters ever made an application to have the real suicide note returned to us. We all made do with the fake suicide note. The copy.

I seem to remember seeing the note, and holding it, although I don't know if what I held was the real note, or the fake note. It was written on a small piece of lined notepaper. It wasn't a great piece of writing. It wasn't a note written by someone who had been run over by Kafka. He didn't talk about death being a limitless pleasure, about everyone's right to kill themselves. He didn't mention that he had been working on his suicide all through his life. He didn't write that as soon as one is born, one is ready to die.

It was a note that seemed to have been copied out of some book that offered do-it-yourself advice on how to write a suicide note. It seemed hurried. There was not a great deal of final contemplation going on.

I can't go on. I've not been the same since the last breakdown. It's better this way. Sorry. Love to you and the kids.

The letters and words of his handwriting were slanted down as if they were under a great deal of pressure. The note said so little, looks like rain, that you could tell he was thinking about something else.

At the end of the letter, flatly, he wrote his name. It was like he was putting a signature at the bottom of his life. Or signing his single conclusive all-inclusive work of art.

At the end of everything he named himself. The last thing that he ever wrote was his name. It was all he had left.

And then, stunningly, he un-named himself.

ON: TEARS

I didn't cry when I heard that my father had killed himself. I didn't cry in the days that followed. I didn't cry at his funeral. I never cry when I think about his suicide. The funny thing is, the most stupidly sentimental films make me cry, a great sporting come-back makes me cry, the death of a fictional character makes me cry. These may be deferred tears for my father. I have yet to cry because of my father's death. I might cry because of something going wrong in my life, some frustration, some disappointment. Sometimes the tears come because of something good happening, because of some happy surprise. The tears can come ridiculously easy. Perhaps they come so readily because they are all stored up waiting for the moment to come when I finally do cry because of the death of my father.

I cried at the end of the film *Forrest Gump*, I cried when the Europeans won the Ryder Cup, I cried when the grasshoppers were defeated in *A Bug's Life*. I cried during the funeral of Princess Diana, but really I think I was crying because I remembered how the coffin of my father was disappearing from sight. I was remembering to cry. There is something about the matter-of-fact world, and what happens as it goes around, that reminds me of my father. The whole world, and how he once belonged to it, spinning with it, sticking to it, this wide resourceful world full of trivia and tragedy, trial and tribulation, triumph and trauma, and how, now, he doesn't belong. He's missing, and he's missing out on things he could quite easily have been aware of.

I have never cried for my father, but every time I do cry, I cry because, once, he was alive, and then, he wasn't, and he could easily be alive now. Perhaps not easily, stickily, maybe, suffering, still scared, but still alive.

Still alive but for a journey to the south-west of England that took him from one end of his life to another, but for a change of heart, but for the sake of some more obedient molecules. If the chemistry of his mind had been a little different and the pull of the atmosphere around him a little stronger he could now be still alive, and crying his own tears.

ON: VIRGINIA WOOLF (2)

'A feeling of death is upon me, as if we were old and near the end of things.'

ON: HOLDING ON

If my father could have just held on, say, another five years, then his children would have left home, he would have been back alone with the woman he had loved and married twenty-odd years before and his mother would have died. He could have moved back to a vacant, green and pleasant Kent, and walked down to the sea every morning, breathed the clean air, connected cleanly with his past, put the pieces of himself back together again. He wouldn't even have been fifty, he could have wiped out all the parts of his life that had conspired to wipe him out. He could have begun again, concentrated on the welcome cliché of a fresh start.

He could have returned home, lived a peaceful time in his own vague, certain way, without the nagging of his mother, away from the slumped skies and enclosed air of Stockport. He could have lived out his life in the sandy spread-out milds of Margate, with a wife, and visiting children, and gathering grandchildren, negotiated a routine that suited him, found a job that didn't break him, a future that didn't mind him.

Perhaps from where he was in the middle of his life in the middle of the 70s in the middle of Stockport in the middle of another life-crisis, all this middle, he found himself becoming such a muddle, he couldn't see ahead, he couldn't see next week let alone the next decade, or the next century. It never occurred to him that he was born in such a time that he was meant to live to see another century. He never thought about that. The beginning of the next year seemed an eternity away. He didn't think about changing circumstances, he didn't think how his life didn't have to be as complex, as baffling, as it seemed to be. It wasn't really such a mess, his life, he only thought it was. He could have thought about it another way, that it was just a period in his life he was passing through, the middle period, the hardest period. Once he'd made it through this hard time, this muddle of middles, if he could just stick it out, stare it out, outgrow it, outmanoeuvre it, there might be a future. A future where he could articulate his own sense of self, and cope with the growing shadow of death, deal with his own past failure, the way he was fading away.

If only he had thought that there was plenty of life left for his life to change, and sort itself out.

Perhaps he did think about a future like this. Moving back to Margate. Living for thirty more years with his wife. Having to impersonate sanity more and more, having to act every day every moment as if the world wasn't really as sinister, as secretive, as seedy as it seemed to be. Seeing his children grow into their twenties, thirties, even their forties, clearly, innocently reminding him of the difficult journey he had made through life. Seeing his grandchildren flaunt the possibility of youth and a massive future in his face as his future was shrinking and his body was shrinking and his mind was shrinking. Staring out to sea and seeing, now, not possibility, not potential, but a fluid wilderness of nothing, a waste of space, a pointless sway of motion, a dark sinister endlessness that was waiting for him, always waiting for him.

Perhaps in the middle of his life, in the middle of the 70s, he saw this future, and ones quite like it, stretching out to nowhere, to the pathetic early years of the twenty-first century, and he was even more convinced that he was going to have to turn the middle of his life into the end of his life. He knew exactly what was ahead of him if he lived. More life. He also knew exactly what was ahead of him if he died.

When he died.

No life. An empty bliss beyond words.

ON: MARGATE SANDS

As a young boy my father would sit on Margate beach and think of everything he was going to do and everything that was going to happen in the future. The future was all his. Years later, with a wife and a family of three young children, he would sit on Margate sands and begin to think of nothing. The future was everybody's but his. The last time he visited Margate, the last time he went home, he sat on Margate sands, his sands, the sands of his time, his fate, his ill-fortune, and he connected nothing with nothing. There was no such thing as a future.

He looked out at a murmuring, lashing sea, the big rhythms of a nearing tide. He felt the sea-wind blowing in from the dark horizon of his future, and heard the melancholy gulls as they hovered and howled above him.

He wondered how far down under the surface of the waves you would have to go for the sea to be silent.

He turned to leave, but before he did he took one last look at the joy that descends from the sky to the sea.

Soon the tide would reach the soft dry warm sand where he had been standing and measure, chill, wash away, dampen, flatten, eat, drink, absorb, remove, his footsteps.

ON: THOMAS HARDY

'& that I be not bury'd in consecrated ground.
'& that no sexton be asked to toll the bell.
'& that nobody is wished to see my dead body.
'& and that no murners walk behind me at my funeral.
'& and that no flours be planted on my grave.
'& and that no man remember me.
'To this I put my name . . .

ON: THE HORRIBLE AND DIRTY
ADVENTURE OF DEATH

I remember that my father killed himself. I read about it in a local Gloucester newspaper. They even quoted me. 'He was depressed because he thought his father had been dead for years but then he found he had been alive all along but now he was dead.' I don't know where that clipping is now. My mother used to have it. A neighbour in Heaton Moor had rather oddly given it to her – the neighbour had a relation in Gloucestershire who had spotted the item, and noticed the address. Did you know that a man in the street where you live has killed himself? He lived at number 14. Can't remember his name. Morley . . . I think . . .

Oh, I must give it to his wife. Yes, that's just what I'll do.

I must ask my mother if she still has the clipping, carefully cut out by a helpful neighbour.

I remember that he killed himself. Because he did, because there was no real warning, apart from the warning of his whole life, that he was about to die, we never found the time, he and I, to get close, to discover each other. If he had been suffering from cancer, so that the warning about his death was not his life but his death, then I imagine we would have found ways to break down the barriers of a lifetime and . . . talk to each other. If his death had been drawn out over a number of years or months, then I would have had time to get to know him. I could have used the time, this dreadful time, to make him vivid in my mind, to illuminate him, to record his voice, and trap his smells, and remember his touch. I could have concentrated on him, as a person, as an individual, as somebody real. I might have begun to understand him, appreciate him, and know how much I loved him.

By dying suddenly in the middle of life, in the middle of me moving out of home and away from the family, I was left with the indifference I felt at the time, the naturally evolved indifference of a teenager about to leave home. This indifference was fossilised by his suicide. Other things were suspended with it – incomprehension, ignorance, bitterness, fear. I wasn't ready. From my point of view the timing was terrible. I hadn't been paying attention to him. I'd been paying attention to me, my own life, my own need to separate from him, and become my own self. At the time he died I wasn't getting closer to him. I was moving further and further away. There's always later, I suppose I thought, to find my father, to make up for lost years, to become a friend.

My father wasn't really a friend when he died. He was just my dad. Somebody you expected to be around all the time, or at least for a bit longer. Always a bit longer. He was just my dad, sad, strange, quiet, shy, angry, lost, dressed in brown, watching TV, acting as if everything was all right. If I'd known he was dying I would have found ways to remember him more. But I didn't know. Something as sinister as suicide doesn't announce itself in advance in a way that those around the self-murderer can really prepare for. As the would-be self-murderer plans his way out, he is in no mood to really let people close, and he is in such a strained, distant, bruised mood no one really wants to get close. At the moment perhaps in all of our life together when I was thinking about him least, taking him most for granted, when I was more than ever avoiding his gaze, embarrassed about his diffidence and plainness, annoyed by his narrow mind, this is when he killed himself. Exactly at the moment when I had stopped looking at him and listening to him. When he killed himself he was, for his reasons and mine, just a shadow in my life. I was forgetting the man who lived even as he was alive. I didn't mean to completely forget him. I just needed to at that moment, as I prepared to make myself me.

And then he died and I almost forgot him as completely as he forgot himself. It was almost as if he had never existed, as if he hadn't been real, or anything to do with me, as if memories had been planted in my head that I was obliged to react to. He killed himself as a man, as a thing that did things, and he also killed himself in my mind, as the reason I existed as a man, as a thing that did things because he did. As the reason I was here.

Slowly, he has returned. Gradually, the man, my father, has made a sort of appearance, as a memory, as an important link with my past, as a reminder of who, for better or worse, I am. He has made his near presence felt in the strands of my thought as an abstraction of my future.

He used to be dead. Doubly dead. Dead, dead and gone.

Gone.

I never even went to where he was cremated and where his ashes are collected. I have never visited his place of death, to remember him, to think about him. For the first ten years he was dead I barely thought about him. Now he has come back. Where has he come from? Where has he found the strength to return?

I think he has found his way back into my life, found a way back to life in my memory, through my dreams. In dreams, even the dead dead, the gone gone, the self-sacrificed, the suicides, the utterly mindless, the ones who have given up on everything including dreaming, can find the strength to re-materialise. To begin to become as real as anything.

ON: A SONG THAT'S AS GOOD AS ANY TO CHOOSE TO BE THE FAVOURITE SONG OF A MAN IN THE MIDDLE OF THE ROAD WHO WAS EXTREME ENOUGH TO KILL HIMSELF AND WHO NEVER SEEMED TO HAVE A FAVOURITE SONG

'It's good to touch the green, green grass of home.'

I wake up from a long deep dream-filled sleep. I have had one of those dreams that seem as deadly real as waking life. One of those dreams where my father is still alive, matter-of-factly, like he never died. He's part of the family, one of us, like he always has been. I have such dreams occasionally, dreams where my father never killed himself, and he just carried on living, as naturally as if he had done. Sometimes I have dreams where my father has, apparently, killed himself, but then after years and years of him not being around, he suddenly turns up. He walks back into his ex-family's life as suddenly as he disappeared. In these dreams, he's been living another life, hiding out, as if he partially killed himself, as if he just killed off his identity. He returns to his wife and his children with very little fuss, he just joins in with us again, and in these dreams it's very disorientating and oddly pleasurable and tempting. He returns, and he's been alive throughout the 80s and the 90s, he knows all about Princess Diana, Michael Jackson, Bill Gates, Paul Gascoigne, President Clinton. His favourite film is *Forrest Gump* and he has even developed a soft spot for Simply Red and Neil Diamond. He looks pretty much like he used to look, maybe dreamier, softer, happier. He still smokes, still about a packet a day, but as they stopped making Guards cigarettes not long after he died, he now smokes Benson & Hedges. He jokes that the gold colour of the packet is the colour of the Vauxhall Viva he used to own, what, twenty-seven years ago.

I wake up in the middle of talking to my father, the one who never went away, who never killed himself. I'm jarred out of simply chatting with my father, who seemed in the time of the dream as real as the sea. Before I even know where I am or who I am I notice instantly that my father, the father of whoever I am, isn't alive, and hasn't been for over twenty years, and in fact he killed himself. I work out that I must have been dreaming that I have a father, and then I remember who I am, and where I am.

I'm on an isolated sandy beach and a few yards away my mother and two sisters are also waking up. I somehow know that they are waking up from the same dream.

We all walk towards each other and look out at the vast sea. It is a sea of dreams, a sea of pastness, a sea of nothing. It is very calm, its waves softly rippling as if with hard-earned contentment. We have remembered our dream, and remembered that our father is not with us. He's somewhere else. He's a dream of something else. He's a dream under the sea that stretches out before us.

We look out to sea and we begin, at last, to talk.

PART FOUR

ONE

Suddenly, my mother and I are talking about something we've never talked about. We find ourselves in a room that seems to have nothing in it but the chairs we're sitting on, in a room that seems surrounded by a blank darkness waiting for some light to come.

We open a bottle of wine, and we just begin taking each other through my father's life, right up to his death, and beyond. She's a little giggly, a little excitable, but then that's how she always is. She is, I think, the friendliest woman in the world, the softest, and in some ways the saddest. Put her on a train or a bus, and within a matter of minutes she will be chatting to everyone around her. She lived in a situation for so long where the person she thought was her best friend, hoped was her best friend, was turning against her, or himself, or life, or all three, that now she wants everyone to be her friend. She wants everyone to like her. She wants to like everyone. She wants everyone to be all right. There's a nervous tic she has developed over the years which means that every two minutes she will be asking anyone near her if they are all right. For so long, she couldn't ask her husband if he was all right, and he clearly wasn't, because this would have meant that he would have exploded with defensiveness, and aggression, and hurt, and tenderness. So now she liberally distributes all those saved up 'Are you all rights?' that she collected during the two decades they were married.

Then there's all the pointless, rambling, bubbling small talk that she saved up during the time he was alive. All the little bits of gossip and tiny intrigue and silly talk. Her husband wasn't one for small talk, let alone large talk or medium talk. There was no sense of anyone feeling able to just talk for the sake of it. There seemed some family need to keep everything we talked about rigid with pertinence, at least as he interpreted it. He became more and more a demanding kind of censor, and he censored her from the necessary comforts of just being general, loose, imprecise, chatty. In the end, from just relaxing by not having to be so serious about the bread and the butter, and the next day, and the price of petrol.

So since his death huge amounts of sweet, soft pent-up nonsense have seeped and flowed out of my mother. She's made up for lost time. She's become a virtuoso of small talk. My mother can talk about nothing better than anyone else in the world. She can talk for half an hour on why she painted this wall green and that wall lilac. Longer about the neighbours, and of course longer even about the weather. Sometimes her talk about Woolworth's, her car's exhaust, her sister's bad leg, feels as if it could unravel for ever. Unravel like the huge balls of wool she uses when she's knitting. Knitting things like the sweater she's been promising me for eighteen years.

She can provide a running commentary for making toast, parking the car, buying a newspaper, closing the door. A commentary punctuated with a few regular 'Are you all right?' questions, requests, demands, slender threats, tired hopes. If the world isn't all right, she feels that she's failed. So you say that you are all right, even if you're not. Perhaps she's asking it all the time because she wants everyone else to ask back, Are you all right? just so that she can check that, what with one thing and another, she is all right, or at least she can quite easily pretend that she's all right. She's all right, she's still here, she survived, demonstrating immense resilience both before he died and after.

There's a darkness about her, how could there not be? and there's a wildness about her that might well be part of her Welshness. There's a sometimes wonderful, sometimes forgivably infuriating childishness as well, something that rushed in with the storm and chaos and distorted relief of her husband's eventual death and which has never really left her. Most of all there's an ebullience that any melancholy can never totally undermine.

My mother's name is Dilys. Just Dilys. No middle name. My father called her Liz. She's much more a Dilys than a Liz, at least she is now. Eccentric, lovely, simple. I suppose she was a Liz when her husband was alive. She was also a darling. The way he called her darling was straight out of the side of him that was, I suppose, the charmer that he could be. But as time went by, as he became less and less of a charmer, she became less and less of a darling.

Her maiden name was Young. He made her a Morley. Mrs Morley. It never seemed to suit her. It doesn't suit her now. She's a grandmother, and it doesn't sound right calling her Grandma Morley. She's not the kind of woman who would ever stop anyone watching their favourite television programme.

Her husband forced her, just by drastic personality, by the sloppy force of his erratic nature, to be plainer than she really was. He was an inhibitor, of emotion, of energy, and she was inhibited. He was a kind of control freak, and she was controlled. She lived in his dark, unpredictable shadow. She fell in with his regimes, his rules, his regulations. She spent a lot of time, I think, keeping him together, watching him, waiting for things to happen, fitting her life around his so that it eventually took on some of its miserable shape.

When I was little I thought of them as having been together for ever, as if they were born together, and grew up together, and they seemed profoundly inseparable. They had rows, but they seemed normal, everyday, what happened in life. I remember my father hurling plates at her in fury, and it was electric, and scary, but in the end it was accepted as what mums and dads did. I had nothing to compare it with. For all I knew on that day everybody's dad was chucking dinner plates at his wife. It was the day for it.

I remember my mum in the morning shouting his name up the stairs louder and louder trying to get him out of bed and off to work. It was like she was shouting into a dead space. Surely there was no one there? Eventually, he would force himself out of bed, the grumpiest man in the morning you could imagine. And then somehow he would fill his mouth with dry Weetabix smeared with a quarter-inch of Stork margarine. Maybe even a knife-size slab of marmalade.

I remember that, maybe out of a slightly perverted affection, or something a little spiky and provocative, he used to say his wife looked like the comedian Benny Hill. Maybe he meant she was round, lovable and cuddly. Maybe he meant she was not as pretty as she once was. As long as I can remember, my mum has been trying to lose weight. 'I'm going on a diet,' would be her catchphrase, one that lost a little of its sincerity later in life when she would announce this while wandering around with a crust of bread the size of a Jackie Collins novel reinforced with crudely sliced chunks of Cheddar cheese. But she was never really fat. She was three children big, she wasn't as slim as when she got married, her shape naturally changed more than her husband's. I don't really remember my father making much of her weight, not openly but she has always been incredibly self-conscious about it. She could write a short book about the history of Weightwatchers, from its early days when it was organised with the olive-green discipline of the armed forces to today when it is softer and more daytime TV friendly. Over the years, from after she had her third child and reached a weight that she felt was unacceptable for her five-foot-three-inch height, she has lost perhaps seventy-nine pounds. Over the years she has put on perhaps eighty-seven. She now looks exactly the shape she should be as a grandmother in her sixties, but she still wanders around clutching some monstrous snack insisting that she is on a diet. Sometimes the snack consists of two slices of Ryvita, which is a start. Then you notice that between the two slices is a stupendous wedge of hard cheese that could inspire a feature-length Tom and Jerry special.

I think of my mum and dad as close, but maybe it was routine closeness, habit, well-rehearsed appearance. A lot of what went on between them went on in other rooms. In their bedroom, a room that always seemed dark, off limits, and vaguely mysterious. The houses we lived in were so small they couldn't be anything else but close. I remember as their marriage progressed, he became more and more helpless, and she became more and more the leader, the supporter. And then he died and after years and years of trying to keep him going she crumpled up into her own shapeless helplessness.

She has had a boyfriend for ten years now, and he is so much the opposite of her husband that it is almost funny. Her husband could look like he was modelling clothes in some 1950s American catalogue. Her boyfriend Danny looks as if he might eat the catalogue. Danny is a North Wales fisherman/handyman who looks like Oliver Reed if he was playing Desperate Dan. There's a bit of Popeye's arch-enemy Bluto in there as well. There are sailors' tattoos all over his body, his knuckles are emblazoned with 'love' and 'hate', and he has 'kiss' tattooed on the inside of his lower lip. Actually, it might be 'fuck', but I've never wanted to look too hard. They're not mum and dad, they're Dilys and Danny, a couple inhabiting a different world, a different lifetime, from where she was with her husband. I think the fact she enjoys being with Dan, pottering about doing nothing, entering quizzes down at the local pub, watching television, eating whatever they want, whenever they want, falling asleep while he fills in a crossword, is her most eloquent statement about what her husband did to her.

She still feels guilty, even after all these years. She still seems to shoulder a lot of the blame, as if she created the problems that led to his suicide, as if she contributed to his burden. Sometimes there's a faraway look in her eyes, as if she's still collecting all kinds of 'what ifs' and filing them away in some book in her mind where she imagines what things might have been like, could have been like, should have been like. I think the last forty years of her life have been made up of a first section, where she started off her adult life young and whole and innocent, and then as she lived out her time with her husband there was a gradual increase of bewilderment, anxiety and apprehension that reached its appalling zenith with his suicide. Then, in a second section, she began her new life at a pitch of bewilderment, anxiety and apprehension that eventually, jerkily, wound down, until, in her early sixties, she is in temporally blurred, edgy harmony with her young, wide-eyed, twenty-year-old self. She has, after everything, made a return to herself, or at least a stained, pummelled twenty-year-old version of her self.

The suicide is behind her. It doesn't possess her any more; her husband possessed her, and then his suicide possessed her, and now she has managed to break free. The suicide tails her, it watches her, but it hasn't got the energy it used to have. It's not the hard-hitting horror it once was, pressing down on her from all sides, pushing her to the limits of her own sanity. The suicide is facing its own death. A death by natural causes.

At last, at least, she can talk about it. The fact that she thinks she is to blame doesn't eat her up, it's delivered matter-of-factly, a mantra, a residue of the torment she felt in the years after he died. Something she thinks she should say, something she thinks people want to hear. That it is an explanation for the inexplicable. A way of making sense of the senseless. I suppose she has been trying to do the same thing that I've been trying to do – separate the suicide from the man, the death from the life, the myth from the banality.

There's a brief bit of nonsense as she puts off the inevitable with some fine small talk about my tape recorder, the wine, the absurdity of the situation. Then I ask her a question, and she starts to remember. As she remembers, it seems to get tougher and tougher. It takes a tremendous effort of will to remember things that she never really wanted to think about, first of all, because it is all over, and secondly because she's not sure how much it might still hurt. Not sure how real all this is. By the end, she is finding it harder and harder to find the words. It's as if she's running out of breath, out of emotion, out of memory. She'll be happier to get back to talking about the squeak on the garden gate.

More bottles of wine to be opened as I talk to my sister Jayne, three years younger than me, and then Carol, nine years younger than me. To my surprise, they both smoke. Because I have been so religiously an anti-smoker, I have always assumed they were as well. Or at least, I remembered that they used to smoke, coming out of teenage rebellion, but I always thought they had given up. It turns out I'm the only non-smoker in the family. Maybe I would smoke as well if they still manufactured Guards cigarettes, just to keep one tradition going.

Of the four of us, Jayne has always been the one who wanted to talk it out into the open. She's taken what happened very personally, much more than Carol and I, perhaps even more than Dilys. As she talks about her memories of her father, and of a home life she has cast in the darkest of lights, she positively seethes with bemused resentment. She remembers the houses we lived in as empty vessels echoing with the erratic rage of her father. She remembers the rooms we lived in as if they were temporary and artificial film sets which we dutifully occupied while we waded through the sedated motions of a hopeless family drama. Whereas her mother, after everything that happened, is content to wrap herself up in small talk, Jayne has turned the other way, and looks for every exchange to be fraught with meaning. She wants big talk. She wants to stay up all night talking problems into the ground or up into the sky or round the bend. If her father by killing himself, right in front of her, right in the middle of her teens, opened up a vast chasm of nothing, she has spent the years since trying to fill in the hole. Dilys, Carol and I have not put up too much of a fight against the way we have sunk into a family inarticulacy regarding the suicide. Jayne has seen it as a dreadful impotence, a thing that doesn't deal with the suicide but merely continues it. For Jayne, talking about it would not maintain the connection, as I certainly have felt, and I think Carol and my mother also, but sever the links, liberate us from the past. She also admits that she is worried that if she stops remembering, stops talking about him, it's as if he never existed. She won't let go. Of all of us, she has inherited the most sensitivity, the most anxiety.

Carol's journey from a frightened eleven-year-old saw her suffer badly, both from the loss of her father, and then within a year, from the loss of her elder brother, who moved away to London, and who she was looking to as a kind of father figure. And indeed from the loss of her mother, who took all of Carol's teenage years to begin to recover from the impact of her husband's death. Carol descended into years of drug and alcohol abuse, and tested herself and her relationship with reality to the limit. At times she seemed to indulge in a kind of teenage excess that could easily have led to her own death. She had seen what family life could do, and she seemed determined to avoid it. She ran away from the past and she ran away from the future and she smashed head-on into the present without caring if she disappeared under it. It was as if she was chasing her dad to the ends of the world.

Both Jayne and Carol talk about how they feel much younger than they are in the sense that, emotionally, psychologically, they blacked out for years after their father died. It's like they lost ten years before they could start their lives up again. It's not that they didn't live lives, and have relationships, it was just that they seemed to be operating on automatic. They didn't know where they were going, or what they were running away from. The centres of their lives, any sense of stability, had been ripped out, not by death, but by suicide, and the lead-up to suicide, and the corrosive fact that this suicide happened to be committed by the man they wanted so much to be their father, because he was their father.

Jayne still swats away at the shadows like they're flies that are annoying her. Carol has realised that it isn't actually going to kill you if you settle down. Routine need not be lethal. I think you could say that Jayne is a Morley, inheriting something unpredictable and elusive, and Carol a Young, where the demons have their daft side. I'm somewhere in the middle. I'm the one turning on the tape recorder.

And also, I'm a father now. My daughter Madeleine was born in 1992, and she started asking about my father when she was about four. Where was he? Where was her grandfather? I wasn't prepared for it. I wasn't ready to talk about death, and my father's death, so early. Whatever I had done to my father in my mind, wherever I had put him, as far as she was concerned, in her brilliant innocence, he was just a missing part of the great puzzle of her life that she was beginning to piece together. He would have been her granddad. She wants to know about him. When she started asking about him I didn't have anything to say. I didn't know his story. I didn't really know where he had come from. Perhaps having these conversations with my mother and sisters is, apart from anything else, preparing for the time when Madeleine asks other questions. Who was he? What was he like? It's always going to be difficult to answer. I can see that now that she has started to ask how he died. I tell her that he was very ill. That does for now. Eventually I am going to have to be better prepared. I'm going to have to create a grandfather based on some kind of reality, and find a way to explain what I've had so much trouble explaining to myself.

THREE

My father finally got out of Stockport, and, one by one, the family he left behind did as well. I was the first to leave. A year after he died, I moved to London to work full-time for the *New Musical Express*. Jayne moved to London a short while after. My mother moved a couple more times within Stockport, first to a flat not far from Hawthorn Grove in Heaton Moor, then to a large house on the main road from Stockport to Manchester. She ran this for a time as a bed-and-breakfast establishment. Then she moved into Manchester, to Rusholme, about half a mile from Manchester City's Maine Road ground. She had finally managed to claw her way half a mile out of Stockport. Carol bounced around with her for the years she had to, and then moved into her own flat in Moss Side. By the early 80s we had all in our own battered ways followed the light-blue Ford Escort van out of Stockport.

Over two decades later, we are all a long way from Stockport. I still live in London. Jayne lives in East Sussex with her two children, Natasha and Florence. Carol lives in east London. Our mother, after many restless moves around the country, has now settled into a house overlooking Conwy Castle, in Deganwy, North Wales.

Before the interviews that follow I had never talked with my mother or sisters about what had happened to my father. I have spent years interviewing pop stars and politicians and actors and comedians, and it occurred to me that perhaps I could find a way to confront this black hole by interviewing my family, one by one. There were things I now needed to know, and after over two decades of avoidance, after all that, all I had to do was ask some questions. They were the kind of questions I could ask now. Perhaps

I could have asked them ten years ago, but I don't think even then they would have come. Before then, I couldn't ever imagine asking them. I didn't want to know what the answers might be. I didn't even ask myself these questions. By the time I do get to ask these questions, everyone is very ready to talk. Some of us are more confused than others. Some of us more intense. We all remember and we all don't remember. It's a long time ago and it's very recent. We're all in our own ways nervous, and also, in our own ways, pleased that we are finally talking, however contrived the circumstances, about something we have been wanting to talk about. We just didn't know where to begin. And then we just decide to begin wherever we decide to begin. Somewhere near the beginning, which has a tendency, if you think about it, to lead somewhere approaching the end.

FOUR

The story starts with my mother, Dilys. Actually, the story starts with her father, George Young. The son of a master bootmaker, and a cobbler himself, he is the reason that the Morley family ended up in the North. He is where the North began for the Morleys.

My mother's mother, Sarah, was from Anglesey, North Wales. She was engaged to a Welshman. One day she was working near Manchester as a nursemaid, and found herself sitting on a bench in a park in Salford. George was cycling through the park. I imagine him as an industrious figure on a bicycle among many other industrious figures in an L. S. Lowry painting. He passed her on his bicycle, spotted her, and turned the bike round. He asked her out. They fell in love, and she gave away her engagement ring to a friend. They married in 1934.

They had five children. David, the oldest, born in 1935, followed eighteen months later by Dilys, and two years later by Jill. Their two youngest children, Sally and Elizabeth, were born after the war. They lived in Handforth, Wilmslow, Cheshire. George had a small shoe-repair shop in Wilmslow town centre.

A million miles away in Margate, Kent, a master grocer, Leslie Alexander Morley, was marrying a dressmaker, Edith Lemon. They had a daughter Eileen, and then they had a boy.

A few years later, war broke out.
The rest is history.

FIVE

DILYS: The war began. Very quickly he was evacuated from Kent to a very little village in Staffordshire. He must have been about three and a half . . . I think that was what he remembered first. Being taken away from his parents. Being brave about it. Trying to be brave. He stayed at a clergyman's house for a couple of years, away from his parents . . . He spent some time in London with his grandmother. He spent his early years away from his parents because of the war . . .

D: His father was a master grocer trained on the Edgware Road in London. His mother trained as a high-class dressmaker. She had a bit of a strange life. At thirteen she spent a year in hospital because of really bad rheumatoid arthritis, and they fixed her hip, but it was never right. I don't think she went to a normal school because of it. She lost out in her teenage years because of her bad hip. She had a sister, Cath, and a brother, Chris. There was lots of Morleys, I think your dad's father had eight brothers and three sisters. There were a lot of Morley's in Margate . . .

D: I don't really know how Leslie and Edith met. Your father never talked about it. I don't think he knew, to be honest. They got married in 1930, 31, they were both about twenty-five or twenty-six. They had Eileen just after they were married, and then five years later in 1936 Dad was born . . .

D: Up until the war his father had run a guest house in Westgate, near Margate. Then they bought a grocery shop, which she ran, and during the war he worked for the fire service. I don't think your grandfather was much use in the shop. She told me later that she always felt that because of her rheumatoid arthritis she had become anaemic, and she always felt very tired in the shop, and he was quite careless about things. He wasn't very organised. She gave me the impression that he liked to spend money, live for the moment, whereas she was much more careful, and she was always wanting to pay the bills on time. She liked to save. To be careful. So I think from very early on, because of the war, because they weren't really suited, because she was very low because of her hip, I think their marriage was in trouble. I think most of all the war broke them up. As soon as it was over he just had to get out and get on with his life . . .

D: The shop opposite was bombed. She was very stressed by this. The war was right on top of her . . .

D: What happened was, as she explained it to me many years later, she used to be in the shop all day long, and she was very tired, and they were trying to live normally while the war was progressing. They'd managed to buy a little house, 53 Laleham Road, Clifton-ville, in Margate, and she'd be working in the shop, which mustn't have been much fun during the war with the rationing and everything, and she never saw much of her husband. She seemed to be very lonely. None of the other Morleys in Margate seemed to be helping her. Then when the war was over they sold the business. One day she went to the shop to show the new people the ropes, and she went back to the house and all his stuff had been cleared out of the wardrobe. He had run off with another woman . . .

D: Your dad was ten. Just about to take his eleven-plus . . .

D: Your dad's mum never had any idea that something was going on. The woman Leslie Arnold ran off with had two children. I think he just wanted a different type of woman to Edith. Edith could be very tough, because she'd had a tough time, and I think he wanted things opened up more. I think he felt stifled. Anyway, he went to London and I think she went after him to try and persuade him to come back. But he wouldn't. It was all over. It hit her very hard. Your dad never saw his father again . . .

D: Your dad failed his eleven-plus, and his mother went to the school and explained that he had been under a lot of stress because his father had walked out. So he was allowed to go to grammar school. He was given a place at the grammar school in Canterbury, which meant he had to travel fifteen miles to school and fifteen miles back every day . . .

D: I don't know what she told your dad about what had happened. He never talked about it. As far as he was concerned, his dad just disappeared one day. Eileen used to write to her father, she was fifteen, and working, and had broken away a little from her mother. Your dad didn't seem to have any contact at all. The impression I got was that she wouldn't allow your dad to go to see him or even write to him. I think she didn't allow her husband to see your dad. He must have wanted to. He came back to Margate to see his relatives, but he never saw your dad . . .

D: I think she was a very good woman, she tried very hard to do things the right way as she saw fit, but she just wouldn't forgive. She couldn't forgive. She never forgave her husband. I think she carried it with her all her life. It made her very odd when it came to how anyone lived their life. She became very domineering. Very cold. She was very tough inside. I think she had to cover up all this insecurity and guilt. It made her very inflexible. She thought she was right about everything. She could never admit to any mistakes. There was no room for manoeuvre with her. What she said went. That was half the trouble I think between her and her husband. The impression I got was that your father was brought up in a funny atmosphere both before and after his father left . . .

D: She wouldn't divorce him. I don't think she could bear the stigma. In the 40s and 50s, it was hard to be a divorced woman. She got a ten-shilling postal order from him every week, and then when she was sixty-five she got his pension. A very little pension. But she stuck out for it. She was always struggling for money. She did bits of dressmaking, she took lodgers in during the summer months. But she would not divorce him . . .

D: I don't think she liked men after that. I think she thought they were very weak. Her tendency was always to put your dad down. There was never any praise for her own son. And she seemed to praise other people just to spite him . . .

D: He was quite bright, but he was very lazy at school. He didn't work at all. He passed his maths O level. Just that one. I don't think his mother ever had any ambition for him to go to university or anything. She was very much of the opinion that you never rose above your station in life. But he loved table tennis. He was the Isle of Thanet junior champion. He played for Kent juniors . . .

D: I think she restricted him a lot. Home life was very mundane and austere. Every day there was like a set menu. He knew from day to day, week to week exactly what he was going to eat . . .

D: There wasn't much display of emotion in that house. No one dared to cross her. No one dared to raise their voice. I don't think Eileen had an argument with her mother until she was thirty-seven . . .

D: He left school at sixteen, and he went to work in Margate Hospital as a laboratory technician. He worked for Eric Morecambe's wife's father. Because he worked in the hospital, when he did his national service he joined the Royal Army Medical Corps. I think he enjoyed his national service, maybe because it got him away from his mother. He became a sergeant, but I think that was because they promoted the most senior person in the unit. But it certainly didn't seem a traumatic time or anything . . .

D: I met him when he was nineteen. I would have been eighteen. He seemed quite happy. Very outgoing. He was funny. We actually met rather romantically. I was an army nurse and together we were taking a woman in an ambulance down to Norfolk. This poor woman had been given sandwiches the size of doorsteps. Me and your dad were roaring with laughter. When we got down to King's Lynn, we dropped this woman off at the hospital, and then it was too late to get the train back. And he said, Well, we'll just have to sleep on the beach. I was getting really worried. He was really cheeky. I was very serious back then. I thought he meant it. But we managed to get the last train back to Liverpool Street.

No we didn't sleep together on the beach. Don't you dare say that! But we did start going out together immediately. He used to love me in my Norman Hartnell blue and red nurse's uniform, and he used to laugh because I would never take me hat off . . .

D: We were both away from home . . . everything seemed very exciting . . .

D: He wanted to marry me after three days. He was chasing me like mad. He thought I looked like Doris Day . . .

He would say, When we have children, we'll have a girl like you, and a boy like me . . .

D: We got engaged and went up north to see my parents. We bought the engagement ring in Stockport, funnily enough. At Morley's Jewellers. It was called Morley's! And then we bought a bottle of whisky and went round to my parents and he asked my mother and father for permission to marry me. He did it all very properly. He was that type of person. He was very good with my mum and dad. They liked him. He liked me mum's pies. I think he really liked the atmosphere in my mum and dad's place. He felt more relaxed at my parents' house. Everything at his house had seemed so repressed. I always thought there was something funny about his house when I visited it. No one ever seemed to talk about anything. Nothing real. They just seemed to talk around things . . .

What I noticed about people in the South is that they even ate their fish and chips off plates. It was nothing like the North . . .

D: We got married in the end three months after we met. September 1956. His mother seemed all right about it. I mean, because we were under twenty-one she had to sign a form to say it was OK. But I suppose inside she didn't really like the idea. She didn't say anything but I think she thought it very peculiar that we were getting married . . .

D: And six months later you were born. March 1957 . . .

D: Are you all right?

PAUL: Did you get married because you were pregnant with me?

D: We were madly in love. We were. Of course we were. I think we would have got married even if I hadn't been pregnant. You just sped things along.

P: But you got pregnant straight away. Didn't you feel forced into things?

D: At the time we were so wrapped up in each other it just seemed that we were meant for each other. It didn't seem wrong what had happened. It seemed right. You don't think how this is going to affect the rest of your life . . .

D: Nobody in the family knew you were arriving . . .

D: We lived in a little village near Farnham in Surrey and he was very smart in his sergeant's uniform and very proud of you. He earned £9 a week and we payed three guineas a week for a flat and we were quite happy. We had a couple of bad arguments. He slapped my face once when I wouldn't go to the sergeants' mess with him, and he told me to go back to my mother's. But it just seemed like, you know, a normal relationship . . .

D: I wrote to my mother saying that you were born and she sent a telegram saying congratulations, darling. We didn't hear a thing from your dad's mother. Then suddenly a package arrived. Inside there was a shawl she had knitted. She wrote a note explaining that it hadn't been finished when you were born because she didn't think you were coming for another couple of months . . .

D: At first she didn't think that you were your dad's baby. She was very suspicious. But she came down to see us, and she took one look at you, and you were the spitting image of your dad. She knew then . . .

D: You were christened when you were six months old, but all the family thought that you were only three months old. So they were all saying, Well, he's very big for three months.

P: What did my dad want to do, what did he want to be?

D: When he left the army, he was twenty-one, and we'd already had you, he knew that he didn't want to go back and live with his mother. He didn't really know what he was going to do. And then he saw an ad in the paper for a prison officer, where you got a house with the job. This was how he got into the prison service. Junior prison officers started at Borstals, and so he went to work at Dover Borstal . . .

D: We had to go and live with his mother for three months in Cliftonville while he waited for the job to start. That was hell. She wouldn't let him sign on, although he could have done, but she was just so ashamed of it. So we had no money. Neither of us had any money.

D: He went on a lot of courses and trained really hard. And he got sent to Parkhurst Prison on the Isle of Wight. I don't think working there did him a lot of good. I think prison officers are like prisoners themselves. But he took it very seriously at first, and he went on courses to become an assistant governor. He sat exams and came second in the whole country. He went up to Wakefield Prison for three days of tests and interviews and he came back absolutely shattered. You were interviewed by everyone, including psychiatrists, to gauge how suitable you were. I think really you were treated as if you were a prisoner. It was all so rigorous and punishing. His friend got the assistant's job at Wakefield and eventually became governor at Maidstone. He was over thirty. Your dad was only twenty-five, and just didn't have the experience. If he had stayed on maybe he would have done really well. But because of his medical background he went to work in the hospital and I think he experienced some very dark things.
P: Did he talk about it at all?
D: A bit. Not much. He didn't like to bring the prison home with him. He liked to keep the two things separate. A lot of the younger officers started to leave. They couldn't keep up with the pressure. It was difficult. You would mix with a lot of hardened criminals. Murderers. Rapists. He started to do nights in the hospital. I think there were some very dangerous men in the prison. Your dad started to change a little. He became a bit more quiet about things. Not so outgoing. The trouble was, once you were in the service, it was very hard to break away. You had the house,

it was all wrapped up together, and by then I was expecting Jayne . . .

D: He passed out a couple of times, just fainted. He started to complain of a bad back. And then of course he had the Bell's palsy, which they do say could be triggered by stress. He would get really down. I think they were just signs that he couldn't cope. It was all too much for him. But he kept it inside. He never talked about it. He never just said, Oh, I'm really fed up. I suppose he never wanted to show any signs of weakness . . .

D: My mother thought that he really changed after Parkhurst. She thought working at the prison did him a lot of damage. He was a different man before he worked there. He was never the same again . . .

D: And then Jayne was born. February 1960.

JAYNE: I don't remember anything about the Isle of Wight. For years to me Dad was just a vague presence in the background. He didn't seem to be around much. I suppose he was always at work. My first memories of him seem to come when we were at Reddish. I don't remember anything about Eccles. I remember when I was young, I just seemed to spend a lot of time on my own. I played a lot of make-believe things with myself. It took quite a few years for Dad to come into focus, and by the time he did, really, as a man he was out of focus. He was somewhere else. He was already living a life that was outside the family.

D: One day we were visiting my mother's in Handforth, and while we were up there he said he might just have a look around to see if there was any work. He really wanted to get away from the prison. I didn't really take it seriously but he came back and said that he'd managed to get a job. He had found a job at British European Airways in Deansgate, Manchester. As a reservations clerk. After Parkhurst it seemed very exciting and glamorous and of course it meant moving even further away from his mother. We went back to the house on the Isle of Wight and we sold everything we could so that we could make the move. We sold an insurance policy, your rocking horse, Jayne's pram. We were very determined to get away from the Isle of Wight.

P: Why did we move to Eccles?

D: It was the only place we could quickly find near Manchester. We rented a flat for £3.50 a week, and immediately we were always struggling for money. He had been quite well paid at Parkhurst, and there was the house, and now by the end of the week we were always breaking open your money boxes for pennies and looking down the back of the settee for money. Just so that we could pay the rent. We were always scrabbling for change so that he could get the bus to work. I used to walk miles for cheap eggs and stuff like that. You went to your first school in Eccles.

P: You had to drag me through the school gates. I remember at that school I tried to climb over the toilet door in the outside toilets. I fell and I remember banging my head really hard on the wet concrete floor. Perhaps I'm still unconscious and everything else has been a dream. I remember playing the innkeeper in the school nativity play, and I only had one line: 'The inn is full.' I forgot it.

J: I remember, and this is a weird one, the kind of memory that can come out strange if you were in therapy, but I remember when I was very young my dad bathing me. And he had very soft hands. I remember his soapy hands washing me and he seemed very tender. I only remember it happening once, but I think it must have happened regularly. On a Sunday. It's the only affection from him I really remember.

There was always that ritual, the bath the night before the school week began. He did try to create these rituals, as if he felt that this is what a family did. He didn't seem to do family things out of any kind of instinct, but because it was expected. As if it was a kind of superstition.

D: Your great auntie Cath, Edith's sister, lent us £150, and we used it as a deposit on the house in Reddish. It cost £1,850. Your dad was earning £12.50 a week, and money was still incredibly tight. And your dad was going into the centre of Manchester to work at BEA, a very exciting place to work, and there were lots of high-powered go-getter office types, and your dad worked hard to keep up with them. He was always very smart. They couldn't believe he had two kids at work. I was at home with two kids, no money, sometimes by the end of the week absolutely no food in the larder. And then he had an affair.

P: I never knew that.

D: It was my fault, actually.

P: Why was it your fault?

D: Well, there was this social club at BEA where they had these dos and he was always asking me to go with him. I had about two dresses and I was always feeling so tired. I used to say, No, it's OK, you go. So he did ask me. So it was my fault.

P: Why wasn't it his fault?

D: I should have gone with him. I didn't. And then one of these parties, I went to stay at my mother's. I think it was a Christmas party. I should have gone really. And he met this woman. A divorcee. She was twenty-eight, twenty-nine. Apparently she sat on his knee at the party. I think he was a bit flustered by it all. He came over to my mother's and I ironed one of his shirts for him. I actually found lipstick on the collar. I didn't really think much of it at the time, stupid me.

P: Was it serious?

D: Not at the beginning. You were only little. Six or something. One day I went through his pockets. I was only twenty-five for God's sake. I found this diary with her name in it.

P: What was her name?

D: You know, I'm not sure. Jean something. Jean Smith. What a name, hey? And then I found payment slips that showed he'd been doing overtime and not telling me that he had more money than he said he had. And I'd been really struggling. He'd been spending it going out with her. Well, it all got a bit nasty. I would stay up all night waiting for him to come back. I would go through his pockets and his case. And then one day he left, I think it was a Saturday, he threatened to walk out. And then he decided not to. We didn't have a phone so I made him march to a phone box and ring her with me there to tell her that he wasn't coming. And then later, it still seemed to be going on, I went into Manchester, stormed into the BEA offices in Manchester, went up the stairs and demanded to see the boss. There I was in my headscarf and everything. And I said to this man, his boss, He was all right before he came here. There was nothing wrong with him. What's happened to him since he came here? Your dad got a letter from BEA asking him to explain himself. She got the sack. She was the head switchboard girl. She was from Wythenshawe. He always said that she wasn't as nice as me. He was so young, you know, he had two kids, I think he just needed to find some freedom.

P: But you were angry at the time?

D: Oh yes. He finally did run off with her one weekend. I was so angry, in my madness I cleaned out the whole house, I turned all the mattresses over, and then I found a letter from her under the mattress, like he wanted me to find it. So I thought, I'm not waiting around for him to come back, and I took you two kids and went off to his mother's.

P: Why his mother's and not your own?

D: I don't know. I suppose I thought my mother had enough on of her own. Maybe I thought his mother could control him, make him see sense. I borrowed the money off my sister Sally for the coach. Grandma Morley knew as soon as she opened the door. There I was with my bags and you two kids. It was as if she expected it . . .

D: He'd gone to Chester with her, I don't know what for, but it didn't seem to work out. Your dad came back home after a few days to find everything all boxed up, everything cleaned away, an empty house. He rang my sister Sally and he said, Do you know where Liz is? And she said, No, don't you? And my mum and dad went around to Reddish and found him on his own just sat there. They took him home with them and my mother sent me a telegram asking me to ring them at eight that night. We didn't have a phone at Reddish and Grandma Morley didn't have a phone. It was all quite complicated. I rang, and he answered, and he seemed really sorry, and I said I would go home the next day. Grandma Morley actually told me that I shouldn't go straight back. She said I was giving in too easily. She said, You should let him wait. It was odd, she seemed to want to side against him. There was never any attempt to see his side, or have any kind of sympathy for him. But I went straight back, and we met at the station, and my mum and dad looked after you, and we went back home and just sat on the settee talking. He promised me the affair was over. He was very loving. And we decided that we would have another baby.

P: How long did the affair last?
D: Only for about six months. I think he just got in over his head and didn't know how to get out. We were always so broke. There was an utter lack of money. I think the affair was like respite for him. I sometimes think he might still be alive if I'd let him go off with her. I don't know.
P: Is that you just trying to punish yourself?
D: I just wonder if it might have made him feel less hemmed in.
P: What would his mother have thought?
D: I think she thought that's what men did.

J: He was a really attractive man. Really charming, a very nice man, certainly to the outside world. He didn't slouch around or anything. He was very fit and agile . . .
   I remember, at Reddish, we used to go round to the corner shop to buy a bottle of pop. It was like a really big occasion. And one day, I bought my bottle of pop, and I dropped it. I was terrified that Dad was going to shout at me, because I had wasted money. But he didn't. I remember being really surprised that he actually didn't shout at me. And then one day he gave me nine old pence to buy some sweeties for all my dolls, and I came back with a block of Galaxy, and that did make him really angry. I could never work out when he would be cross and when he wouldn't be.

D: And then Carol was born. January 1966.

CAROL: I have this feeling that I'm going to read this book and find out that I'm not my father's daughter after all . . .

P: Is Carol Dad's?
D: Oh, for God's sake . . . what do you think?
P: I was just asking. . . she doesn't quite have the Morley look.
D: Of course she's Dad's . . . I never ever looked at anyone else . . . your dad was the first man . . . you know . . . the only person . . . sometimes it has crossed my mind that if I'd had

affairs . . . But through it all, whatever happened, whatever he did, I just felt that we were married, and we had to make it work. We were meant to be together. I really believed that.

J: I was so happy when Carol was born, because it meant I would have someone to talk to. I think I felt terribly isolated.

P: I wanted a boy to play football with.

C: I was born at home. In Reddish. I don't remember much about that home. I remember the back garden. I remember there used to be a lot of shouting. I remember being quite scared because there was all this shouting and I didn't really understand what was going on.

J: And then Carol became like his plaything, and that's when my jealousy crept in. It was like Carol was the golden child, they had her to keep their marriage together, and I felt that they were treating her better than me. I had a lot of anger about that.

P: Anger?

J: Yes. Why are you being sarcastic about that? I wanted affection, and as far as I could tell, he was showing much more affection to Carol than to me. That's how I felt.

P: I never really thought of it as being a battle for affection.

J: Well, I was the middle child. You notice these things more. I really did think that he loved Carol more than me.

D: I didn't feel the same towards him after the affair. I used to think everything he said and did was right, but not any more. Before then, I never really wanted to go to work or anything. After the affair, my attitude changed. I started to work. I began to get some independence. He was never that keen.

J: I'd love to speak to the woman he had the affair with. He must have been very different with her. Here was someone who he was intimate with. There was no intimacy in our house.

P: Isn't that slightly far-fetched? Have maybe the memories of his death blasted away the moments that must have been normal. I remember moments of closeness.

J: I want to remember nice moments. I really do. But the way I remember it was that there wasn't much affection, there wasn't

342

much structure, there wasn't any sense of future. Everything was just crowded in day to day. Maybe because you were older, you remember a time before he started to have his affair, before his breakdowns. You remember when perhaps it wasn't so fraught. And you had the football. You and Dad were able to share something and get close. I think the father and daughter relationship is very special, and I was looking for an emotional closeness that he wasn't able to give me.

For me, as I was becoming a teenager, I just remember a lot of tension. He was very cold. He was very distant. He was very self-obsessed. You know, Mum is a very bubbly and emotional person, but she couldn't afford to be with Dad around because he was so dominant and so serious. It was like from my point of view everything was always on tenterhooks. His depression was just too big, and however hard any of us tried to make it all happy families it just wasn't going to work.

P: But as part of some survival instinct, do you remember a strangeness, a coldness, because you don't want to remember anything normal? You don't want to recall good times and a friendly father because it was all so brutally taken away from you.

J: I don't know. I really don't think so. I felt that he was so wrapped up in his depression that there was never any guidance, and that I was lacking attention. I'm surprised I didn't end up the kind of person who sets fire to buildings because I felt that I was so starved of attention. There never seemed anything to hold on to. Everything always seemed to be falling apart.

I felt very insecure. There was never a sense as a family that it was like, Here we are, this is where we are going, and this is how we are going to get there.

At the time, you know, his breakdowns started when I was ten, eleven, and I didn't really know how serious his depression was. Nothing was ever explained. So I just felt a lot of guilt and bewilderment.

P: Guilt?

J: I felt guilt because I thought that maybe it was my fault he was running away. I thought that I was being really naughty and bad. I couldn't understand it. I didn't take drugs or anything. I thought everything was my fault . . .

343

P: I don't think I felt that what he did was anything to do with us.

J: It was everything to do with us!

P: Well, yes and no.

D: He couldn't argue properly. It was never like a normal argument where you'd argue and then it would be all over and forgotten. He never forgot an argument. All the arguments just seemed to keep accumulating. I don't think he'd been brought up to understand how to deal with a difference of opinion. He always took everything so personally . . .

D: He had to leave the BEA job really, because of that woman. It was a good job. You got cheap fares, even though we couldn't really even afford them. And he went abroad a lot with BEA, he went to Amsterdam, he went to Germany. You think how it might have been if he'd just been allowed to carry on there . . . but he left, didn't really find another good job for a while. Then I saw an advertisement for a job at Shell and BP in Wythenshawe. He was very dubious that he'd get it. He always seemed to lack confidence. But he got the job, and he was very well thought of. Very boring work, though. Petrol accounts. But he did well, and was pretty soon getting promoted . . .

D: You passed to the grammar school, and I borrowed £50 from my uncle to pay for your uniform. Your dad was always very upset that we had to borrow the money from relatives, but there was no other way. There was never, ever any spare money. It all went on the mortgage and food and travel. There was nothing left over. We were very chuffed, though, that you were going to that school, and during your first year there, just before Christmas, we decided to move. We didn't move house particularly to be near your school, but we happened to find one that we really liked nearby . . .

D: I think he started to feel guilt for what had happened with that other woman. I think he started to worry that he was like his father. Somewhere along the way he lost his sense of humour. He used to roar at comedy. And then somehow it changed.

J: He used to scare me when he laughed. He used to watch Morecambe and Wise and there was something frightening about the way he laughed. I didn't understand it. It seemed so uncontrollable. I remember once asking him to stop, and he said, Don't be silly. I'm just laughing.

C: I remember during Sunday dinner you and Dad would be listening to comedy on the radio and really laughing. I think it was *Round the Horne* or something. I used to laugh with you even though I was too young to understand what you were laughing at. I just wanted to be in on what you were in on.

P: I remember Dad taking me and Jayne to see Ken Dodd in pantomime at the Opera House in Manchester. It must have been about 1966. We had a box. He loved Ken Dodd. I remember Dad loving *Some Mothers Do 'Ave 'Em* with Michael Crawford. It must have been 1973. I remember him in the early 70s going to see Tommy Cooper in cabaret and telling me all about this routine Cooper performed. Cooper took twenty minutes to set up this complicated trick and then having set it up and built up everybody's expectations he asked the back of the club if they could see. Someone shouted no, so Cooper said, Well, I better not bother with the trick then. Dad loved that. And then in 1975 he didn't find *Fawlty Towers* funny.

D: After a while it was like he didn't have the energy to laugh like he used to.

P: I suppose you've got to have a lot of belief in the stability of life to be able to laugh at it . . .

P: Do you remember him ever reading to you?

C: No, I don't. I remember reading to *him* . . . I read him a Noddy book. He just listened and then he walked off. He didn't say anything . . .

D: We were meant to move that Christmas. It got delayed, because there was a border dispute with the old woman who lived next door. He seemed to lose his rag about it. He couldn't take the stress of it. He shouted at her that she was a stupid old woman. And then his mother came to visit.

D: It was 1968 turning into 1969. His mother came for Christmas. She took him upstairs. They were there for about twenty minutes.

I don't know what they talked about. Then your father came down and he said, 'My dad's dead. My father's died.'

Apparently, he'd died six weeks before and no one had told your grandmother. Eventually, she heard from Australia. She heard from her husband's brother. No one had bothered to tell her.

It was sad, your dad was going to see his father when he met me, but instead of going to see him, we went out together, and he never got another chance.

P: For some reason, I always thought my dad's father lived in Australia, which is why he never saw him. I thought he died in Australia.

D: No, it was your dad's uncle that lived in Australia. Your dad's father lived in London. And then he died. At the time I just didn't think how much impact this had on your father. I had never had anyone die on me, and we just didn't know his father. He hadn't seen him for over twenty years. But I think it just devastated your father, and combined with lots of other things to completely change him.

I remember, your dad used to go very quiet on his birthday. He never liked his birthday. When he was twenty-one he was very odd. I think he was sad that his father wasn't there. It makes you wonder if his father ran away on your dad's birthday.

P: So you still carried on with the move from Reddish to Woodsmoor?

D: Oh, yes, he didn't show any effects. That was the thing. He never talked about anything. He just got on with things, so I presumed everything was OK. I didn't think that maybe he was really hurt by the news. And eventually we managed to finish off the move to Woodsmoor. We moved on March the thirteenth, 1969.

P: A Friday?

D: It might have been. We bought the house from somebody who had a brain tumour. He was always shouting at his wife. I sometimes wonder if these things sometimes stick in the atmosphere of a house.

Aaah, I loved that house. We had to do it up and we didn't have much money, but I really thought that we had made a brand-new start. It reminded me of the one I grew up in at Wilmslow. I was

346

quite happy there. I thought it was a much better place than Reddish, a big garden, apple tree, nicer people. It wasn't so towny. It seemed more your father's type of area. He always seemed the odd one out at Reddish.

J: I remember going out with my dad and his friend from Shell, Jim. Jim is the only friend I can remember him having. He had two daughters, Leanne and Gail, and we all used to go swimming, the five of us. You never came. Not to swimming. And Dad used to be so energetic and strong, and very funny. He was a good swimmer. He made people laugh. This really sticks out in my mind, because he wasn't like that at home. I used to go with him when he played squash, and he was a different man to how he was at home.

P: I remember Jim Heaton as being the only friend he had. He lost touch with him after the first nervous breakdown. One day in Heaton Moor I saw Jim being interviewed on the TV about Manchester City signing Rodney Marsh. I excitedly told Dad that evening, but Dad just blanked me and acted like he'd never heard of Jim.

J: I shared a bedroom with Carol, and I really liked to read, and one day I picked up a book and dropped it and woke up Carol. He raced into the bedroom and hit me around the head. I told Mum about it, and she just didn't believe me, and that was really weird. Or she didn't want to believe me.

C: I remember him hitting me ... I remember him hitting Jayne because she was eating Sugar Puffs at the wrong time. This broke all the rules.

P: I don't remember him ever hitting me, but oddly enough I always remember feeling scared that he might hit me.

C: I wouldn't say it was persistent violence, but there seemed to be violence in the air. I felt this from very early on in my life. Something seemed as if it was always about to happen. I just thought of the atmosphere as being quite scary. Maybe it was because I was young. I remember a lot of shouting.

D: There were lots of arguments about money. We just never seemed to have any.

C: It's wrong to say that we were deprived compared to how things were during the war, but I know from talking to other people that we had less, materially, than other people, even those

347

that lived in council houses. We were pretty impoverished. We had the bare essentials, but sometimes there was just no food in the house. Absolutely no food.

J: They were always getting themselves into a situation where the lifestyle they were after was more than they could afford. That made things really difficult . . .

D: I think your father wanted to give you this idealised home life, and I think it stretched him further than he could really go. He was always chasing something, always under pressure. He wanted to give us things.

C: Part of me thinks that as a family we would have been happier if we'd lived in a council flat that we could afford. And then have had money left over to live a little. Everything was always so tight. But Dad, and therefore Mum, insisted on this aspirational idea of ownership. All of this Tory nonsense. Dad was a Tory! There was no reason for him to be a Tory considering his background. But he was a kind of snob. I remember he hated the fact that you were a Labour supporter.

P: He hated Wilson. He was a Heath man through and through.

C: He didn't seem to understand that the Tories were of no use to someone at his level. They were not interested in helping the likes of him. But he was always so determined to own his home, even when it was continually breaking him. He was a very old-fashioned Little Englander. Very stubborn. Thought that there were ways a family behaved and sort of forced us to behave like that. Maybe towards the end he gave up a bit on that.

It was like he acted old. I think of him as being a man of the 50s stuck in the 70s. He completely seemed to miss the 60s. And yet he was so young.

P: Would he have liked Thatcher?

C: Oh, no. She was far too flash and ostentatious. And as bossy as his mother. Like you say, he was a Heath man. He was an old-fashioned Tory. I don't think he would have liked the 80s. He would have been very adrift . . .

J: I remember when I was about eleven we would all be watching *Top of the Pops*, and Pan's People would be dancing, you know, in bikinis and short skirts, and I remember looking at you and dad to see if you had erections.

P: You need help, you do. And did we?

J: No. Never . . .

D: At Woodsmoor, as soon as we moved in, little things started to go wrong. The car would break down, our lovely little Mini. We sold that and got another one, and then that had problems. It was all little problems, but he seemed to be affected as if they were really big problems. He was starting to take everything incredibly seriously. Early on in our marriage, he never took things so seriously. I was the one who took things seriously. But gradually, that changed . . .

D: That summer, a few months after we'd moved to Woodsmoor, we went on our annual holiday to Grandma Morley's.

P: That was such a strange ritual – the annual holiday. What was that all about?

D: I always used to say, Shall we not go this year? But no, we always had to go. It wasn't so much that he wanted to see his mother, more that he was determined we would have a holiday every year.

P: They were these tense mixtures of pleasure and trauma. It was like being forced to have fun.

D: We used to give her money and after a week she would always say, Well, I've run out of your money now, and I'm using my own. We'd feel dreadful. I hated those holidays. I really never wanted to go.

J: Those holidays were such a formula. Every day we would do the same thing. We'd sit on the beach from nine to six. We'd have our beach hut, which we would call a beach chalet. At the end of the fortnight we'd go to the Dreamland Funfair. One day we would go to the park. It was the same day in day out every year.

C: His relationship with his mother was absolute torture. As far as Grandma Morley was concerned she had given her entire life up for her children, and that was it. She lived a life of absolute stoicism.

349

Grandma Morley would boil cabbage for forty minutes.

J: The atmosphere at her house was so odd. It was like walking into the 1800s. I remember once you spilt a cup of coffee and it was a drama for three days.

C: It was like she had some form of control over Dad. He was shrunken whenever he was with her.

J: I remember once he grabbed hold of a carving knife and shouted that he was going to kill her. I don't know what happened then . . .

D: We came back from the holiday, and he was very strange there, you know, the first time he had been back in that house since he found out about his father, and on the drive back we stopped off somewhere for a picnic. He went and sat by himself. He didn't want to sit with us. He just sat on his own in a world of his own. We got back home and he went back to work. He had just been promoted and he had lots more work to do. Quite hard work, pretty boring work. And then one night he didn't come home . . .

D: I really thought it was another woman. It got really late and I rang Shell. It must have been about eleven at night. A night-watchman answered and he said, There's no one here. The next day there was no sign of him. I was just about to call the police, and then at about seven o'clock in the evening he rang. He said, I feel really dreadful. He said he was near Derby or Stoke, and that his car had broken down. I have no idea what he was doing.

P: Had he gone off with a woman?

D: I don't know for sure, but I really don't think so. I said, What are you going to do? and he put the phone down. It took ages for him to come home. When he got home he really did look dreadful. This is what made me think it wasn't another woman. It looked as though something terrible had happened to him. He sat on the settee and he just sat with his head in his hands, really defeated. And you know, the thing about your father is, he never showed his feelings . . .

J: Oh, and do you remember the way Dad sat!

P: How did he sit?

J: He always had his head in his hands.

P: Mum reckons the opposite, that it was only very rarely that he sat with his head in his hands.

J: Oh my God no! . . .

D: The doctor came round, and he was all very jolly and matter-of-fact, and he said, Oh, I get a lot of men driving up and down the motorway. It's the stress, he said. You're just working too hard. He gave your dad some tablets. That's what they did then. Tablets . . .

D: The tablets absolutely zonked him out. He was at home with me for a few days recovering, and I said, Do you want to come to the launderette? And we walked, it was about a mile, and halfway there he was completely gone. He couldn't even walk with the effect of these tablets. So I sat him down on a park bench, raced off to the launderette, did my washing, knew he'd be OK because he just couldn't move, raced back, and there he was. Sat on the bench staring into space. It was awful . . .

D: And that's when I started to learn to drive . . .

C: I remember he didn't have many clothes. He had two pairs of shoes. A pair of brown laced shoes and a pair of black slip-ons. But he kept everything very nicely. He was a very stylish man.

J: Other dads wore jeans and T-shirts. But I only remember my dad in a suit. Always in a pair of pressed slacks. I thought this made him special. But I think now it was a kind of defence. A kind of fear. He didn't want anybody to know how he felt inside, so he always tried to, you know, keep up appearances. He was the kind of man who would pretend to go to work even if he had lost his job . . .

D: He went back to work at Shell. He went back to doing exactly the same work and the same amount of work he did before he ran away. And then three weeks later he did it again. He went to work the Friday morning, and in the evening he didn't come back. That second time was the worst. He didn't come home from work, and, most peculiarly, the phone was dead. I went out to a phone box to ring his friend Jim, and he was most upset. His father had apparently done the same thing. Disappeared out the blue. When they found him he didn't know who he was or where he was.

I'd got this job at a local pub, to help out with the money. Nine until three. It was a good little job, I could do it while your dad was at work and you were at school. It got me out of the house. I had to give it up when your father ran away. It was strange that the phone was dead. Jim persuaded the telephone people to come around to fix it, because it was an emergency. The man who fixed it said it looked like the line had been cut.

It was awful. We rang the police but they didn't seem to be able to do much. He was just gone.

On the Tuesday a package arrived. Inside there was your dad's wallet and £600 in cash. No letter or anything.

On the Wednesday your dad's car was found in the car park at Piccadilly Station. It had been sitting there since the Friday. I don't know why it took so long for the police to find it. Jim went to collect it. He was really worried by now. I just didn't know what to think. I think we were all in a kind of daze about it.

And then on the Wednesday someone rang from Grayling Well Mental Hospital, near Chichester in Sussex. It was a psychiatrist, forget his name, very nice man, he said, We've got your husband. We were so relieved.

P: What did you think had happened to him?

D: Well, I thought that he might have killed himself. The thought really did cross my mind. Especially when we got the wallet with all the money in.

He'd checked into a hotel under the name of John Ford. He had taken about a hundred aspirin. He realised that his ears were really hurting, so he staggered out to a phone box and called the local hospital. He was taken to the hospital and he had his stomach pumped out.

He had forgotten who he was. He couldn't remember his name or where he came from. They sent him to Grayling Well and he'd been there all week and of course he'd sent his wallet home so they didn't know who he was or where he lived. They gave him electric shock treatment to get him out of that state. Three shock treatments. They didn't have any permission, but then they didn't have anybody to ask.

352

He came onto the phone and said, I'd really like you to come down if you could. So Grandma Morley came up to look after you kids and I went down to see him.

P: What did his mother make of all this?

D: She just seemed to take it all for granted. She never talked about it. She never really seemed to react. She just seemed to block it out.

C: I remember Mum telling me that when she went down on the train to get him she met loads of stars from *Coronation Street*.

D: Everyone looked perfectly normal in the hospital. I don't know what I was expecting. And your dad seemed fine, considering that a few days before he really did have no idea who he was. He'd made a friend there and we went to the pub with him. He'd been running away for ten years.

We had an interview with the psychiatrist, and he said, Perhaps the level of work is just too much. Perhaps he needs to lighten his load.

When stress gets so much you can't bear it, you can lose your memory.

P: Was this suicide attempt more a cry for help than a serious commitment to kill himself?

D: A bit of both I think. He didn't really want to be in that type of job. It had a kind of responsibility about it that he didn't really like. And ultimately he just felt it was pointless, a pointless job.

We stayed in a hotel before we came home, and we had quite a nice time. Winston Churchill had stayed at the hotel. It was lovely. We had dinner, and it was all quite sweet. He didn't want to come home. He wanted to stay away for a few weeks. I think he just wanted a break that didn't involve his mother or the kids.

We came home. He carried on working. Shell sent people round to try and help. I think they were worried they might be blamed for what had happened. We decided to move again, to Offerton. We made a profit on the house, we were now near Carol and Jayne's school. We were trying to find another brand-new start.

We'd just moved to Offerton, and his Aunt Cath came to visit. And one morning he went to work and in the evening he never came back. He disappeared. We wouldn't hear from him for a few days.

We'd hear about a body being found on the News, on a railway line, and you couldn't help but think, Maybe it's him.

This went on for seven years . . .

J: I remember that time he was in the hospital, I'd just started school. I spoke to him on the phone, and this voice asked me how school had gone. I remember telling him that I'd made a blanc-mange and that when I brought it home it was raining and the blancmange shrank. He didn't say anything.

It's funny, but I remember him running away as bringing some excitement into life. Everything seemed so boring and weird that it at least gave the sense of something happening. It was like nothing ever happened in our family apart from what always happened, the day-to-day grind, so it was almost like here was something interesting. Here was adventure.

D: It was all a bit Walter Mitty after that first breakdown.

J: There was such secrecy about him. It was like this was how he lived his life, as one big secret even though there was all of us around him. It was as if we were part of his secret life. Perhaps this was something to do with his father, and how his father was never talked about.

D: Grandma Morley rang up one day and said, He's here. He'd run away and he just turned up there. She said, He looks very peculiar. He was just staring and very quiet. It was like he thought he was a little boy again.

C: Back in the 70s you didn't get the feeling that there was any help around for someone like Dad. It was very much 'pull your socks up'. You never heard the word 'depression' back then. Now you hear it every day on daytime television. Nowadays it's very much a confessional age. Everyone's queuing up to talk about their fears and anxieties and fucked-up families. It was nothing like that back in the 70s. He probably thought he was the only one who felt like he did. Maybe he felt ashamed.

D: I remember once after he came home, I looked through his pockets and I found some cards from strip clubs in Soho, London. It made you think that he was just running off and having some fun, and then realising that he had to come home.

C: I remember when I was at school at Offerton, I'd broken my front tooth and someone had to come and pick me up. Jayne

354

came, not Mum, which upset me. And we went back home and Mum was crying in the kitchen, and I thought it was because I had broken my tooth. But it was because Dad had gone again.

J: He had a look that could kill. Absolutely kill.

He didn't give out any energy. I think that affected us all. It sucked us in. Sucked us into this emptiness. He was like a hollow man. He didn't really seem to believe in anything.

D: They say that even doing sport can help with depression. But he'd stopped doing his sport when he was thirty, thirty-one, just before all this happened. He lost interest. Table tennis just didn't mean anything to him any more.

P: Did you get angry with him? Try and shake him out of it?

D: If you got angry with him he would just completely withdraw. I tried to talk with him but he just wouldn't listen. After a while I realised that shouting at him, or pleading with him, just made him drift further away. You couldn't reach him at all by talking about what he was doing. You had to find other ways to deal with it. You had to pretend that everything was normal because that seemed to be what he wanted, and he couldn't bear to think that it wasn't.

C: I don't think of Dad as mad or mental. I just remember it as being always very unstable, and when you're a kid all you really want is stability. It was chaos. We tried hard to make it seem stable, but really it was chaos.

J: Everything seemed so slow, so dead. There never seemed to be any rush, any get-up-and-go. The mornings always seemed so quiet. There was none of that rushing about for work and school, just this sense of, you know, defeat. It was like we were all in our own space being maudlin, taking our lead from Dad.

P: He went off a lot, but I don't remember it as being particularly disruptive. It was almost just one of those things.

C: It became predictable behaviour. We incorporated his behaviour into our lives. You can see it with the Fred West family, how the most extreme events can be normalised into daily routine. How could anyone not notice what was going on? With us, we normalised what he did to ourselves, and to the outside world.

It was normal but it wasn't normal. We made it normal. It was what we knew. This was what family life was. Our father ran away and then he came home.

J: We just accepted that Dad ran away, at least to each other. We pretended to accept it. We put up with it. It was what happened. But I never understood what was going on. I was always very confused. It was never explained to us. For me and Carol especially, we would be just kept in the dark. He would run away and there was never any hint of an explanation. It was just not mentioned.

C: I think he was very much wanting our family to be like a normal family. The more he wanted it the less it happened and this just made things even worse.

I used to lie at school and pretend that everything was all right. Maybe all families lie about their home life, make it out to be better than it is. But I so wanted everything to be normal and I never ever let on that anything out of the ordinary happened.

When you're a kid you're quite conservative. All you want is everything to be normal . . .

C: I remember he used to say, If you keep quiet for ten minutes I'll give you ten pence . . .

D: So he'd run away again. I had a Mini then because of the job I was doing. We got the phone call from him and I said to Aunt Cath, I'm going to pick him up now. He told me he was at the last service station on the M1 before London. He couldn't get home. I had to go and help him. I'd never been on a motorway before, but off I went. It was a real strain. So I left Aunt Cath looking after you kids and I chased off down the motorway, and at first I went north instead of south. I was completely out of my depth. Anyway, it turned out he had hired a car from Manchester and it had run out of petrol and he didn't know what to do. I finally managed to get to the service station, and I saw him walking towards me. He seemed quite normal. We drove back. I drove because I didn't trust him. We ran out of petrol. We had no money so I had to give my firm's name as security, and they weren't very happy, and I lost that job. The car came with the job so I lost that as well . . .

D: He ran away and he called me and he was in Chester. I had to get a taxi to go and get him. It was about forty miles. He was just sat in the bus shelter waiting to be collected. As if that was what happened – he'd run away and then he would be collected. He was very quiet. Didn't say anything, and I wasn't expected to ask anything.

I would always have to talk him back. I would have to work really hard to persuade him that it would be OK . . .

D: When he came back after he had run away he always seemed shattered. As if he had really bad flu. It took him a day or two to get back to normal and he always seemed very uneasy about you kids, worried what you were thinking about him. He never said this, but I could tell. He never really said anything about why he went away and I was always too worried that he might do it again to ask.

We called the doctor, and I was really at my wits' end. I pleaded for him to help me. I said I really must know exactly what's wrong with him.

The doctor would say, He's suffering from clinical depression, as if by telling me that I would know what it meant and what to do, as if by saying it that was the solution. It meant nothing to me. And the doctor would act as if there was nothing you could really do.

I said to the doctor, What's wrong with him? why does he keep running off? and he said, these were his exact words, 'Well, he can't be a loony, because he wouldn't have been able to hire a car if he was!' I said, Don't you dare use the word 'loony' in relation to my husband. I tried to change doctors, but they wouldn't let me.

C: I remember he came back, and I went upstairs into Mum and Dad's bedroom, and they had this massive dark-brown fitted wardrobe in there. I used to hide in it sometimes, and there were hardly any clothes in it. One dress and one suit. Dad was in bed there, and I showed him my broken tooth. He just smiled at me. He didn't say anything. He just looked at me. Then he looked away.

P: For all his running away, I don't really remember the comebacks. I don't remember big reunions or anything.

C: Well, for me it was always very important that he came

back, and I remember coming home from school, and he would
be there.

P: Exactly. He just seemed to creep back in. He would be gone.
Then he would be back.

D: I think it would have been quite a normal life if it wasn't for
the fact that he kept running away. Why didn't he just go and get
blind drunk?

P: Did you think of him as lonely?

D: Yes. I think he was lonely. He was a lonely man. Nothing
could really change that . . .

   Eventually it became obvious that he wanted to stop working
at Shell. It had all become too much for him. The work, the fact
that the firm were monitoring him, not really caring for him but
just watching their own backs. He felt stifled. So he decided to
leave Shell. He didn't really know what he was going to do next.
We started looking at various businesses in Blackpool. We toyed
with the idea of running an off-licence.

P: Is this where he started to drift a little?

D: It wasn't that he couldn't hold down a job or anything. It
was just that in a way he was too smart for the kind of jobs he
was getting and he just got really bored with them. He couldn't
get better jobs, ones that might have suited him, because he had
no qualifications, and in a way because he had no confidence in
himself. He looked like he did. He held himself very straight, he
never gave the outward signs of being depressed. It wasn't like he
mooched around unshaven in scruffy clothes. But he never felt
that he could get the different jobs, the interesting jobs. At
Offerton, after he left Shell, he did different jobs, he worked for
the Gas Board for a bit, he worked for Everest Double Glazing for
a while. Nothing lasted.

C: I think he thought a lot. He was a very thoughtful man. Trapped
in the body of a salesman. And of course he was in the wrong
place. He got himself trapped. In Stockport. He found he could
get himself out of Stockport, by running away. But he couldn't
get his family out. He kept having to come back.

   I would be scared of him. Not so much because he was always
shouting, and I remember that, maybe just because I was young,

358

but because he could be so quiet. What I remember most actually is him thinking. You'd ask him a question and he would dwell on it and dwell on it. There would just be this silence. I think we all tapped into that. I don't think this is something we've made up after he died. There was definitely an aura about him. The aura of the depressed man and all that. It was very strong, and we got caught up inside it . . .

D: With the money being tight, we decided to buy down. To give us some flexibility. We got £12,000 for the Offerton house and we bought the house in Hawthorn Grove, Heaton Moor, for about £7,000. This was at the beginning of 1976. We were just trying to take the pressure off your dad really.
P: Another new start.
D: By now we were just trying to keep things going . . .

P: Can you remember his voice?
C: It's strange. I think about that a lot. I really can't. I know that he talked posh as far as I was concerned. I had a real broad Stockport accent. He didn't like it. I tried to talk like him, but I couldn't. I taped his voice once. I know I did. I had a cheap tape recorder we got from Woollies, and I definitely taped it. But we never kept things, did we? It's got lost. It's weird. I'll never know what he sounded like. It's another one of those gaps. Trying to think who he was, I realise now that I never really knew who he was. Not because I was young, but because he seemed to slip through your fingers as a person. I can't really pin him down in my memory. He just floats past me.
P: Do you remember anything nice he did with you?
C: I remember once we drove out to Lyme Park. Just me and him. It was really nice. We drove out but when we got there it was raining so we drove straight back. I don't remember what we talked about. I remember there was a hitchhiker and I really wanted Dad to pick him up. But he wouldn't.
    I remember we played table tennis at Offerton. We had this net you could fix to the dining table. That was nice.
J: I remember he gave a birthday party in Offerton, I was about fourteen. He took me and my friends to the cinema. He was really good with all my friends. He was at ease. At times

like that you could see what a totally charming man he could be.

J: The time I really got to know him was at Heaton Moor. I have this image of him getting up every morning and sitting in this chair in the kitchen eating cornflakes. Because his clothes had just been stolen from the dry-cleaner's, he only had one pair of trousers, and I remember as he sat there in his underpants Mum would be pressing his trousers. He always seemed to be in this state. I didn't like the fact he sat there in his underpants . . .

C: My birthday presents would be really shit. Because it was the fourteenth of January and it was really close to Christmas and there was no money left. I would always be excited and optimistic. Once I was so excited that I sleepwalked and went into the front room at Heaton Moor and grabbed hold of my present. Dad was there, and Jayne, and Dad said, not angrily, What are you doing! I woke up. I opened the present and it was a half-pound box of Milk Tray chocolates. I lied at school about what I got.

J: Christmas was a strange time, because you were allowed to choose presents up to a £4 limit. There was always a limit put on our presents . . .

C: I was a very nervous girl. I was very nervous at school. I played the recorder really well but they wouldn't let me in the school recorder choir because I was too nervous . . .

P: How long were we at Heaton Moor before he died?

D: (Pause) About eighteen months. It was a very big old house, I said to him, Well if you can't get a job, let's rent out a couple of rooms to students and get money in that way. But he was having none of that. He had too much pride . . .

P: So eventually his last job was working for Singer, the sewing machine company?

D: No, actually it wasn't. He did work for Singer, but only for a few days. He didn't like it. He got a job with a collection agency. He would go round to people's houses and collect money for things they had bought out of catalogues, and he would deliver goods they had bought. They weren't really jobs he wanted, they were just all he could get . . .

J: I remember at Heaton Moor coming home one day from school and Dad was there. And I hadn't had a good day at school, I was feeling miserable, and I said, Oh, life's really shit, there's nothing to do. And he got really angry. He shouted at me, No, life's great, there's lots to do.

I suppose I wanted some help from him, but I think he needed help much more than me. I suppose I wanted him to say, Well, sometimes life gets you down, and sometimes life makes you feel up. It'll be all right. You don't expect to be yelled at, told that life is great, which as far as he was concerned was a total lie.

P: That was his way of helping. He might have felt like agreeing with you but he must have felt that you couldn't really hear him agreeing with you.

J: Probably. But it wasn't what I needed . . .

C: Do you think we can only talk about all this when there's a recording device in front of us? . . .

J: He was a classic case of someone with depression who couldn't see a way out and it filled the whole house, even one as big as the one in Heaton Moor . . .

C: I remember towards the end Grandma Morley left her house less and less. I never really saw her outside of her house. I think she was an agoraphobic. She even sent us into the garden to pick the peas. She was picked up by a car to go to church. She had her groceries delivered. I don't think she left the house throughout the 70s.

P: Was Dad like he was because of his mother?

C: I don't know. She wasn't much of a help. She might have been the start of it. She wasn't really the end . . .

J: I remember he was decorating the hallway at Heaton Moor. It was a school day, so I suppose at that time he didn't have a job. I was off school. I was feeling really down myself. I was in the sixth form and just needed some time off. And Dad asked me to wash his car. I remember feeling very close to him then. I remember putting my arms around him and telling him that I loved him.

Now, I think, Well, did I really do that, or do I just think I did, that I must have? He didn't say anything back as I remember it. I feel that it was about two weeks before he died. Perhaps I'm just hoping that it happened.

I popped in to see him at the Singer shop in Mersey Square. He looked really pleased to see me, but the shop was so empty, and I remember feeling awful. He looked so young. Why was my father selling sewing machines? It didn't make any sense. It didn't map onto the man. It wasn't my dad. He was selling sewing machines. Hanging around in this empty, dead shop. It was such an awful image.

P: Do you remember the last time you saw him?
J: Well, I've got it in my head that the last time I saw him was when I told him that I loved him. Everything seemed so normal that day. He was doing something to the house, I was helping him. It was how I wanted the family to be. Together. So I've made that memory up, or I've made the memory better than it was, or it really did happen. I don't know. Those last few weeks, even months, they're all such a blur. I suppose Dad was on some dreadful slide and we were all just following behind . . .

D: When we had sold the house in Offerton, we were in dispute with the estate agent. We said that in the end we had found the person who bought the house. We didn't think that the estate agent had anything to do with it. But they insisted that they had introduced the purchaser. Your dad got very annoyed about this, and he refused to pay the commission. It was about £250. But your dad was insistent that it wasn't fair, that really the estate agents had done nothing to help the sale. Why should he have to pay? This dispute dragged on through all the time we were at Hawthorn Grove.

Talking about all this job business, it sounds like he couldn't keep a job down. But he could. It was just after the business at Shell, he seemed to lose the heart for doing all these nothing jobs.

He gave me a watch a few weeks before he died. He seemed so apologetic because it was a bit cheap.

Two weeks before the final disappearance, he ran off again. He came back that time, but by then to be honest I was sick to death

of him running off. You kids just accepted it by now as something
he did, so I wonder if that time he just didn't feel that we weren't
that bothered to see him back or something.

C: The disappearance I remember the most is one at Hawthorn
Grove. It was the one before the last one. He came back from
wherever he had gone, and I always think that he went away for a
week, every time, one week. And he came back and I remember
he was sat in this chair in the kitchen. Mum was doing kitchen
things around him. And he was just sat there. Just sat there looking at nothing. Emptied out.

P: I don't remember that he ran away a couple of weeks before
the last one. Maybe I have the vaguest, vaguest memory. By then I
was so wrapped up in my own life, and so used to the fact that
sometimes he went off. It was just something he did, they were
little trips he made that we had almost made official.

D: He wouldn't talk about what was happening to him. He wasn't a
talker. I had no idea what was going on in his mind . . .

C: I remember in those last few months he bought his first
pair of flared trousers just as you were buying your first pair of
punk drainpipes . . .

P: I remember him working for Singer right up to his death.

J: Yes, he did . . .

D: The weekend before the Monday, which was going to be his
first day at John Blundell's, he put down the carpet in the front
room.

P: I'd repaid the loan he'd given me so that you could buy the
carpet.

D: I don't remember that. I never knew he lent you any
money.

P: Yes, so that I could have *Out There* printed. It cost about
£100, and he lent me the money.

D: I never knew that. It was only a second-hand carpet. I don't
understand that.

P: Do you think he kept a lot of things from you?

D: I don't know. I suppose he must have done. He looked after
all the finances and everything.

He fitted that carpet really well.

C: I don't remember the carpet . . .

C: How could he afford to lend you the money?

P: I don't know. I do remember now and then, very rarely, he seemed to have some spare cash. Maybe he was a secret gambler.

P: When was the last time you saw him?

C: On the Monday morning, he drove me to school. It was the day he was starting his new job.

P: At Singer.

C: I'm sure it was at Singer.

P: But hadn't he already been working there for a bit?

C: I definitely remember it was his first day at his new job. I think that he got the job because it meant he had a car. He needed a car. I remember the preparation that morning. Brushing his clothes. He had that silver clothes brush. He really took his time to make sure he looked good. And I remember he got this new car the day before.

P: The Ford Escort van.

C: No, it wasn't a van. It was small.

P: A small van.

C: Maybe, yes.

P: It was sky-blue.

C: I don't remember the colour. You probably think it was sky-blue because of Manchester City.

C: I was the last one in our family to see him. He drove me to school and he was incredibly quiet. It was towards the end of the school year, and the next year I was going to start secondary school. And I would have to travel from Heaton Moor to Offerton. And I remember asking him if he would drive me to school then. And he was very thoughtful. He didn't say anything for ages. Eventually he said . . . 'Maybe.'

C: He tried to kiss me. At that age I was a bit funny about people trying to kiss me. He went to kiss me on the cheek, but I pulled away, and he ended up brushing my ear.

He dropped me off down the road from the school. He drove off, but I remember that he went left instead of right. He didn't take the turning back to Mersey Square. I thought he was going off to buy cigarettes or something.

I remember later Mum really pushing me about which direction he had driven off . . .

P: When was the last time you saw him?

D: . . . It was that Monday morning. He was driving off to his new job. He gave me a kiss and that was that. I tell you what did happen though. There was some stuff he was delivering that morning. One of the things he had to deliver was a big hairdryer, one with a hood that you put over your head. Part of the dryer was a long tube thing. He'd left it behind. I remember saying, 'Don't forget this.'

P: How did he seem?

D: He seemed all right. No different from usual.

I went to work. I was working in the office at Victoria Wines. You were the only one at home. And then John Blundell's rang to ask where your father was. He hadn't turned up for work. You called me and I came home.

P: I don't remember that.

D: And when I was at home that afternoon a solicitor rang, asking whether my husband was still OK for court on Wednesday morning. I didn't know what he was talking about. Apparently, the estate agent had sued over the £250 commission for the Offerton house, and the case was in the county court that Wednesday. I had no idea. Your father had kept it all to himself. It was typical. I told the solicitor that my husband wasn't in at the moment. He would be back later.

And then we waited, like we always did . . .

C: I was absolutely certain that he was coming back that last time.

D: I wasn't really worried at first. I just thought, He's done it again.

J: By now we knew how to keep our life ticking over while he was away. We had learnt to expect him back.

D: On the Monday we called the police. They said there was nothing they could do for twenty-four hours. We were starting to get slightly more worried. But you, it was like you didn't want to give

365

all your attention to worrying, because it was just as likely that he would come back any moment, or he would call. So it was a strange mixture of old fears and new sort of indifference. And because we were just so convinced that he would come back, we never reported him missing on the Tuesday. We just kept waiting . . .

D: On the Tuesday night, I slept with Carol. I couldn't sleep in my bed without your dad there. At about three o'clock in the morning I remember she started to shake like mad.

C: Mum was sleeping downstairs.

P: I slept downstairs.

C: You did not.

P: I was definitely downstairs, in the front room.

C: Well, she wasn't in her room.

D: I came downstairs early because I couldn't sleep. I must have been sat in the kitchen or something early on the Wednesday morning.

P: There was a knock at the door, and I answered.

C: No, Mum answered.

P: I answered . . . I'm sure of that.

C: Look, this is my version of events which you might find quite interesting if you'd only listen . . . There was me at the top of the first set of stairs, Jayne at the top of the second set of stairs, you were at the top in the attic room, and there was a knock at the door. It was very early because I wasn't dressed for school. Mum opened the door. It was a policeman and a policewoman, and Mum just groaned. And they asked her if she was Mrs Morley, and she just went, 'No!'

D: I knew as soon as I saw the police.

P: You knew he'd killed himself.

D: Oh yes. At that moment I knew instantly that he was always going to. The times he had run away sort of put us off guard, but as soon as I saw them, I knew that he was always going to kill himself. He was a suicidal person. It just took a long time to get there. All those dreadful false starts. All those rehearsals.

P: What did you think first of all? Anger, hate, sadness?

D: I was angry that I hadn't done the washing-up. When I found out, I just remember thinking, I wish the kitchen was tidy . . .

D: It took a long time for me to feel angry at what he had done. A year. Maybe more. Angry because of what he had done to all of you, really. I was very cross. He didn't need to have done it. There could have been a way out. We could have found one. The thing is, because of the way he had been brought up, he just felt such a failure if he wasn't in control of things.

J: I didn't really understand what was going on. I felt it more than understood. I just remember us all standing around. Not really saying much.

C: I got dressed and put on my jeans because I knew I wouldn't have to go to school that morning.

P: Do you remember saying, 'That means Mum's a widow'?

C: Not at all. I don't remember saying anything really. We all just seemed to move around the house as if we didn't belong there.

D: The police came into the house. They were only in for a few minutes. They asked if there was anyone they should ring.

I rang up your Uncle Graham. I asked if I could speak to Jill. He said, She's got a sore throat. I told him what had happened. He said, We'll be straight over.

C: Mum rang the mother of Jayne's school friend, Jane Fiddler. She lived round the corner. She came round, and she gave us tasks to do.

P: I thought it was Aunt Jill who got me to clean the oven.

C: Jill and Graham were on their way, but it was going to take them an hour or so to get to us. Mrs Fiddler came round and went into hyperefficient mode. I remember her whispering to my mother that a cremation would be best. It would be cheaper.

P: So Mrs Fiddler made me clean the oven. I don't remember it being her at all.

J: It was Mrs Fiddler who got us all busy. She got us all doing things to take away the shock. She got me ironing. I found that I was ironing one of Dad's shirts, and I got really upset. I just broke down . . .

D: Jayne rang up Mrs Fiddler. It was funny, because her husband's parents had both killed themselves. They'd gassed themselves in

367

an oven. She came round straight away. She was a doctor's receptionist. She gave us all some Valium.

P: Valium? Even Carol?

D: I think so. She just felt it was the only way to get us through it. I'd never had Valium before in my life.

P: I never knew I had taken Valium. No wonder the day feels even stranger than strange to me when I remember it.

D: She was doing what she could to help us. It made me feel oddly normal. It was the most normal I'd felt for weeks. The whole day was this mixture of strange and normal.

C: I was given Valium? God, no wonder I felt so distant from everything, like it had all happened already.

D: I rang up his sister Eileen's husband Michael, and told him. I said, Will you break it gently to Eileen, and to his mother? I was really worried how the news was broken.

C: Jill and Graham arrived, and I remember that Jill was wearing a fur coat. It was the middle of summer, but I remember Jill in this fur coat. It was like a symbol of what I thought was their wealth. I always think that Mum and Dad aspired to the middle-class appearance of Jill and Graham. The bank manager and his wife. The large house in the country. That's what they were after. She can't have been wearing a fur coat, but that's how I think of her. Hair just done, full make-up, bags of confidence. Graham all sure and certain. It makes you wonder about Mum sometimes. She could have quite easily married someone from Wilmslow who went on to do really well in business. Just like Jill. Instead of marrying a man from the strange South who took her on this bumpy road towards suicide. It could have been so different.

J: I don't remember much after doing the ironing. I remember Jill and Graham took us all back to their place. I remember when we got there, there was a tapestry that Jill was in the middle of sewing. It seemed like a symbol of the real life that we had lost, that we had never had.

C: We all went round to Jill and Graham's house.

P: I didn't.

C: Where would you have been? No, you were definitely in the car. There was Jill and Graham in the front, and in the back there was Mum, you, and I was sat on Jayne's knee.

P: It worries me that I have absolutely no memory of that.

C: You were with us. We got to Jill and Graham's, and it was the first time I had met their daughter Lesley, our cousin. It's like we hadn't seen Jill and Graham for two, three years. I remember playing on the floor with Lesley, and she asked what had happened to my dad. I said, My dad's dead, like it had happened years ago, as if I was already completely used to the idea. I think we all went into some kind of catatonic state after we found out. It's like there's some kind of survivalist instinct takes over, to help you survive such a thing. You were there.

P: I also wasn't there.

C: Then I was sent to stay with my supposed best friend at school, Collette, only she wasn't really. I haven't got much of a fucking clue what happened next. What happened over the next few days, weeks, months. Except that I went back to school the following Monday. As if nothing had happened, you know . . .

D: I think it was the next day – or was it that day? – you had to go down to identify the body. Was it the same day? I can't remember. Uncle Graham drove you down.

P: Maybe it was the same day. That might be why I can't remember being at Jill and Graham's. I do remember the drive down to Stroud. And I didn't identify the body. Graham did.

J: I didn't know that. I thought you saw the body . . .

D: The inquest was five days later. Do you remember, I wouldn't come into the courtroom? By then we knew how he had killed himself, and I realised that I had handed him the means to kill himself. He had used the tube of the hairdryer, stretched it from the exhaust pipe to his window. I'd said, Oh, you've forgotten this. I handed it to him. And that's what he used.

He was due in court on the day that he killed himself. Maybe that was the final straw. Who knows? Maybe he was going to come back, like he always did, and then he thought of the court case, and he just couldn't face it. If only he'd turned back . . . it was only a stupid little thing. It could have easily been sorted out . . .

P: What do you remember of the funeral?

D: Very little. It was all so hazy. I remember after the service having a little walk to where your dad's ashes were going to be put, and the undertaker looked at me very funny.

P: In what way funny?

D: I don't know. I just remember thinking he gave me a very funny look . . .

P: You weren't at the funeral.

J: Yes, I was.

P: Why don't I remember?

J: We were all in our solitary dream-worlds. I came down with Mrs Fiddler.

P: She came down? I don't remember that. In fact, I don't remember there ever being a Mrs Fiddler. Maybe she gave me some more Valium.

C: I wasn't allowed to go the funeral. That really pisses me off.

D: That was a mistake. We should have let Carol come. But we thought it would be too much for her. My mum and dad didn't go either.

P: Why not?

D: They didn't really know what had happened. It was all such a mess. It was difficult to keep a clear head about what to do. Jill and Graham didn't come. Grandma Morley didn't come.

C: What happened at the funeral?

P: It was very perfunctory. I remember the Lord's Prayer and a general feeling that the whole thing wasn't really happening.

C: Did they play any songs?

P: What were they going to play? Something from *South Pacific*? 'There Is Nothing Like a Dame'? With new lyrics – 'there is nothing like a dad'.

C: I remember Mum bought a new navy-blue dress and matching handbag for the funeral . . .

D: Eileen gave me some money, over a hundred pounds, in the toilets at the crematorium. I used it so that we could all go out and get something to eat. Do you remember? That place opposite the station. We all got really drunk.

P: I don't remember Aunt Eileen being there at all.

D: Yes, she was there. I don't remember what she said and did, but she was there.

The woman from the bed-and-breakfast place we'd stayed at in Gloucester the night before was in the restaurant. I remember her coming up to me and squeezing my hand.

P: What happened to the suicide note?

D: I don't know. We had that copy and now I don't really know where that is.

C: I had it for a while. I found it amongst some papers of my mum's. I took it and put it inside a book. She must have taken it back because one day it wasn't there any more. She never mentioned it.

P: What do you remember it saying?

D: Nothing much: I can't go on. Sorry. Love to you and the kids.

C: I hated that he said 'the kids'. He never mentioned our names. We were just 'the kids'.

C: At least he didn't take us with him! You read about that, don't you ... depressed men killing their children and then killing themselves. That's one way of looking on the bright side ...

C: What the fuck was he doing? The bastard!

P: Is that how you feel?

C: Well, sometimes you think that's how you should feel.

P: Was it just a case that he was ill? He couldn't help it?

C: Well, that's one way of rationalising it. The fact is, he left. He did it. He could have got help.

J: You just think, If all this is just because he was ill, well how pathetic is that? He could have been helped. Surely it has to be about something more than the fact he was just chemically imbalanced.

I sometimes worry that I'm like him. That I'll want to do the same thing. I get unhappy, and I think, Is this how my dad felt? But I know that I'm not suicidal, because I love life too much. But then you think, Shit, is it hereditary? which is kind of out of your control.

P: I sometimes find myself shouting at Madeleine about something silly, or because I'm tired, and I think, Oh God, I'm just like my father. She's just going to remember me always shouting at her.

J: You're nothing like him. You don't play table tennis for a start.

C: I think it's different for us than it is for Mum. With us, you think, It could be in the blood. We have the same blood. Mum doesn't. So we have a different kind of worry: can whatever happened to him just rear up and attack us? Mum can't really know what that feels like.

P: When I feel tired and depressed, I just go to sleep. That's one thing I've learnt. Dad never seemed to be able to get enough sleep. I make sure I sleep. All day if necessary. Just to stop those feelings, which might lead to feelings which might trigger off whatever happened to Dad . . .

C: This is my childhood!

J: There's a part of me now that feels guilty that I'm alive and he's dead. Because I just do not know why he wanted to die. I feel I'm only guessing when I say, Well, he was ill. I don't know for sure. No one ever told me. Not at the time. This is just something I've learnt later. I don't know what to make of that. Nowadays we'd go as a family to a psychiatrist and we'd talk it through.

P: Would we? I don't know what Dad would have made of that. I don't know what I'd make of that. Would it really help?

J: Yes, I think it would. I think talking about things, making them open, is really important. The fact that Dad didn't talk about things, the fact he wouldn't have wanted to go to any kind of therapy, that in the end is what helped kill him. He kept everything to himself. You need to know what is going on to begin to help. He was just so secretive. Thinking about it now, it's like his whole life was a mystery.

P: But would the talking have really broken down that mystery? It's apparently a more confessional age now, there's more talking, people are more aware of depression, but the suicide rate seems to be going up.

J: It would have been good to have felt involved in what was happening to him. It would have helped the rest of the family to know what was going on if not Dad. I mean, I know Spike Milligan's daughter. She is very aware of his depression, she knew when it started, she knows what it is. She feels involved. She can talk to people about it, as weird as that is because he's famous. But it's something she has come to understand. If, God forbid, Spike Milligan killed himself, she would know what had led to that, how he felt, why he had to do it. But for us it was such a bloody shock when the police came round and told us. It was a shock, it wasn't a shock. It was a relief, it wasn't a relief. There were all these mixed emotions. And then we still didn't talk about it! . . .

J: It's the not talking about it which has always deeply frustrated me.

P: We're talking about it now.

J: Only because you're writing this bloody book. We didn't talk about it five, ten, fifteen years ago. I bet we don't talk about it again.

C: Not talking about him has sort of magnified him, magnified the idea of him as something demonic . . . not talking about him makes him seem more powerful and strange than he actually was . . . talking about him now, it normalises him. Maybe we never talked about him because we didn't want to diminish him. But in a way it's good to remember that after everything he was just a bloke, he wasn't a big mystery, he wasn't a hero, he wasn't insane, he was just a bloke struggling to live a normal life and it was all too much for him. Marrying young, having children, he created too much pressure for himself. He was just a bloke, someone who was difficult to know, someone who ended up giving up. But he wasn't a monster . . .

J: It's probably why I talk too much about things now. I can't bear this silence that goes with everything. I want to talk about everything. I want to talk and talk and talk. In that sense I'm the opposite of Dad.

P: Does all this talking do you any good?

J: Maybe! I'd rather talk than keep it bottled up . . .

P: Do you think in the end he killed himself to get out of our way?

J: Maybe.

P: He did it to let us get on with our own lives?

J: Maybe.

P: It was a selfless act as much as anything?

J: Maybe.

P: Perhaps he really wanted to go the first time he tried to kill himself, and he battled on for seven years, trying hard to stay with us despite the pressure he felt. He fought to stay alive.

J: Maybe . . .

J: You know, a few years after, I was living in London, and I was in bed, and suddenly I felt Dad was there at the bottom of the bed. It was as if he was saying, I know you've moved a lot, but I still know where you are. I'm still with you. It was quite incredible. I know you don't believe in things like that.

P: I'm quite prepared to believe that you believe.

J: Well, it was incredibly reassuring. I lost him when I was very young . . .

C: I think if he had carried on living, it wouldn't have got any better. I think this was the solution for him. There would have been more breakdowns, more downward spiralling. I think he would have become more difficult and more violent and our lives would have been even more clouded. It went on about as long as it could . . .

D: He had eight copies of your *Out There* magazine in his briefcase with him when he died. Didn't you know? Why did he have them with him?

P: What else did he have with him?

D: Oh, not much. His watch. His cigarettes . . .

C: You're eleven years old and suddenly the centre of your universe disappears. You're going to be very puzzled. And for better or worse up to that point my dad was the centre of my universe.

I remember at my school, a girl told me that her dad had died of cancer. She asked me how my father had died. I said that he had killed himself. She just laughed. The thought was just too weird.

I think if he had died of cancer or something, we might remember the day that he died. But because it was suicide, it's not something that we can remember. It's not a date you think back to. I never have. I know you haven't. I've never thought, Oh, it's the anniversary of dad's death.

J: If I had a real choice, and if I was completely clear-headed about it, I wish that Mum was living somewhere with her boyfriend, and that Dad was alive with his girlfriend, and that he would have got over that period. I wish that it was only that – a black period that he survived.
C: Was it brave to keep living a life that just wasn't working for him to try and keep the family together? Or was it foolish? At the time, maybe it seemed a brave and good thing to do. Not to run away with that woman, or another woman. Not to try and change his life. But now, I think it's foolish. I think, What a damned twit . . .

C: The fact that you've never learnt to drive. I always wonder if that's got something to do with the way Dad killed himself. You know, that he used a car. It's like it completely put you off being in control of a vehicle.

D: His mother died four years later. She never really acknowledged what had happened to him. She had a sad last few years. She mellowed out a bit. She wrote to me a few days before she died, Christmas week. She seemed fine, she sent a few money-off coupons. A funny thing – she said the horses were acting strange in the field at the bottom of her garden. She wondered what it meant . . .

D: You wonder how planned it was. You know that he killed himself a couple of weeks before my fortieth birthday? You have to be forty to be able to claim a widow's pension. They let me have one in the end. You wonder if he knew that. That he hung on until he felt that I would be eligible.

P: He killed himself two weeks before your birthday?
D: Yes. I don't think he liked birthdays.

P: How old was he when he died? I've always thought he was forty-three.
J: He was thirty-nine.
C: He was forty.
D: He was forty-one.

P: When did he die?
D: It was Wednesday, June the twenty-ninth, 1977. About three a.m.

D: I don't know why.

PART FIVE

1) It was just after midday. I rang for a mini-cab. I didn't know what time the train would be. I had decided that I would just head for the station. There surely wouldn't be more than an hour's gap between trains, and anyway, I was feeling optimistic that the train travelling where I wanted to go would be on the hour, every hour. I would make the one o'clock train, as long as the cab arrived within fifteen minutes. At this time of the day it should. No rush hours to contend with. Drive around the back streets and it shouldn't take more than half an hour to get to Paddington station. Paddington – the London station from where trains head out to the West of England, to Bath, to Gloucester, to Bristol, and beyond that to South Wales.

2) I'd been unexpectedly nervous about this trip, even a little disorientated. I hadn't got to sleep until five that morning. That's why I was catching a train in the early afternoon. This type of journey was one of those where it seems appropriate to get a good early start, but by the time I woke up it was gone eleven. I was on writer's time. Except I hadn't done any writing the night before, I'd just done a lot of thinking. Thinking is what happens before the writing. In this case, a lot of this thinking was what happened after the writing. I was thinking about what I had written in this book, about how I started not knowing where I was in relation to my father, or where he was in relation to himself. I started a long way off from my father and then in a roundabout way, in a conscious way, in a random way, I moved in closer and closer. Wary, in case he bit, in case he lashed out. Cautious, in case he disappeared even further from view, round the back of himself, up his own exit.

3) I thought about this until five in the morning. I also worried about what I was going to wear, and I fretted about the fact that I hadn't had a haircut, and the hair around the back of my neck was thick and tufty and a little scruffy. I'd washed my hair, which had made it fluffy and shapeless, which annoyed me more than it usually would, and I'd had a shave that had cut my face open. I didn't have any shaving foam, so I had used the lather from the shampoo. I just felt that it was important that I shaved. I wanted to be clean and fresh. As I shaved, I ran the blade up to a point on my cheek, the line my father had once advised me was where you went up to when you shaved. I remember as I stared into the mirror, older, I now realised,

than my father had ever been, that he liked to shave just before he went to bed. One less thing to do in the morning, the awful, degrading morning. I went to bed with blood on my face. One thing I've definitely inherited from my father is a tough beard. Gentle Young skin and virulent Morley bristles. The Youngs and the Morleys never did quite go together, and you can see the mismatch after I've shaved, in the bloody little cuts and the spiky patches of sore rash.

4) And then eventually I fell asleep, roughly, restlessly, as if the next day was a tantalising mixture of an examination, an appearance on live television, and, oddly enough, a plane journey. I didn't dream, or I didn't remember my dreams. Unless I dreamt of assured blackness, a conspiracy of blackness, a me blotted out by all the blackness in the known and unknown world, a flawless blackness that stretched around my sleep and between the sleep and over the top. A dream about two halves of ingenious blackness that fitted together perfectly with no air between, no slit of light, no marble of colours, no hint of sound, a blackness floating in its own blackness, drifting past its own shadow. That dream I remember. I have that one a lot.

5) I woke up feeling vaguely irritated with myself. I wasn't as prepared for the journey as I somehow thought I should be. After all, it had taken over twenty-two years to make. For the first time in twenty-two years I could now confidently report how long it had been since I last made this journey. I could tell you exactly. And after those twenty-two years and those exact hours and days and months, I should, by now, be ready, prepared, calm. But I wasn't. It all felt very last-minute. I suppose in a way it was, and it would have felt last-minute if I'd planned the trip down to the last meticulous detail. I could never be prepared enough to be on top of this particular situation. No amount of unbloody shaving, fresh haircut, advance-booked train would have made me feel that everything was under control. The last-minuteness of it, I convinced myself, was perhaps the only way this journey could have happened.

6) I worried about what to wear. It seemed quite a warm autumn day, but there were also heavy storm clouds in the sky. Usually on such a journey I would just wear my soft Gap trousers with the elasticated waist, an old T-shirt, my comfy jacket with the rain stains, a pair of well-worn-in shoes. This didn't seem right at all. But, adding further to my sense of annoyance with myself, I had not

been to the dry-cleaner's for ages. I had nothing ready. My good shirts were a handful of wears beyond the decent. My suits were badly hung up and creased or, worse, crumpled into dustbin bags awaiting a trip to the dry-cleaner's. But suits seemed too dramatic, too pompous a statement to make, and I felt a stupid burning shame, all to do with myself and nothing to do with what my father would have thought, that my suits were all two, three years out of date. The material was too light, or too heavy. The lapels were the wrong shape, the widths of the trousers were too small, or too wide, the buttons were in the wrong place. I was the middle-age man one, two steps out of time with the fashion of the time, the middle-age man who had never found his own style to make such thoughts redundant. This made me feel even more disappointed with myself. I wanted to show my father, in the shape of myself thinking about my father, that I was above such things, because I was in control of such things. Getting dressed on such a day brought attention to the fact that, after approaching twenty-five years of adulthood, I still hadn't sorted myself out. I was still not instinctively smart, groomed, balanced, hard as I tried.

7) I needed to find clothes to wear that wouldn't wrap themselves around my sensitivity and compound it, clothes that wouldn't scratch my pale nervousness with their itchy irrelevance, clothes that wouldn't add edge to the edge that had built itself around my edginess. I had to find clothes that fitted me, that weren't too casual, that weren't old and out of date, clothes that suited an occasion for which there seemed to be no precedent.

8) I decided to start with my favourite shirt and take it from there. A deep-blue shiny Nicole Farhi shirt that I love because it is so soft and smart and timeless, and which streams down my body like a piece of metal made out of silk. It also has a welcome tendency to sweep over my bulging belly and keep the front of me looking straight. It also reminds me of a shirt my father used to wear, a nylon sports shirt which he played squash in and which I used to wear after he died.

9) The shirt was still squashed into a suitcase that I hadn't got round to unpacking, but one of the beauties of this shirt is that it takes really well to a form of ironing that I have invented. It works surprisingly well. I put creased clothes into the dryer for a few minutes, and the drying action gets rid of all the creases. You end up

with an item of clothing you almost believe has been newly dry-cleaned. Once I had the shirt, the rest of my outfit fell into place. A pair of black narrow flat-fronted Dolce and Gabbana trousers that are a bit old but which are comfortable, and which take well to the ironing-in-the-dryer method. The combination of this shirt and these trousers meant that my hooded mac or hooded coat were out. There was only one jacket I could wear, a heavy black woollen DKNY piece that might be a little warm but which was plain enough, and neutral enough, in terms of cut and lapel size, not to upset my fragile equilibrium.

10) Then I got upset with myself for feeling that I had to dress up in such a manner. But the choice was, dressing down, or dressing up. Dressing up won by a neck, a neck with only a couple of little cuts still visible.

11) Finding socks was a tough little battle. I found two black ones that didn't quite match, and fought hard not to let this completely knock me sideways. For a moment there was a surging rush inside me that suggested that my inability to have a fresh pair of perfectly matching socks immediately available on such a day meant I was a total failure. I faced up to it, acknowledged the fact that at least there were no holes, and beat the feeling back into its horrible little home. I chose the one pair of shoes I have that are elasticated at the side. They hadn't been polished since I bought them, because unlike my father I am not a religious shoe polisher, but they didn't look too scuffed, and I had to wear them because my father was always fond of a nice pair of black shoes with elasticated sides. I was ready, in an unready sort of way. I was black and blue from head to toe, which seemed, what with one thing and another, pretty fitting.

12) In between ordering the mini-cab and it arriving, I had a sudden urge to hoover the hallway, and the stairs, and the upstairs landing. I quickly did this, and then I washed up the previous night's dishes, and cleaned some surfaces in the kitchen. When I came back home later that day, I wanted everything to be as tidy as possible, and as I made my journey into an English unknown I didn't want the fluff on the carpet or the dirty cups and the breadcrumbs on the bread board to be nagging away at my mind. A mind that somehow I was going to be sharing with the mind of my father.

13) I made myself a cup of tea. A cup of green tea. No milk, no sugar. Sort of hot water stained with possible flavour. My father

would be spinning in his grave, if he had a grave. What's the cremated equivalent? My father would be swirling in his urn? There is a packet of Weetabix in the house, but I resist the temptation to eat one covered in butter.

14) A knock at the door. It's the cab driver. I open the door and wave to him as he walks back to his car. I notice that the driver is one that I don't really need on such a day. I've had him before a few times. It's the driver that chats mercilessly, the driver that seems on the edge of his own catastrophe involving the self and destruction. The driver who has the drooping face and sunken voice of a worried man, the driver who takes time during every journey to communicate in dry detail how rotten his life his, and his marriage, and his job. I had been wondering how the day would unfold, and how I would respond to it knowing that, as well as it being an important day from a personal point of view, I was going to write about it. Would I be too self-conscious about certain details, aware of the context, of self-discovery, of potential completion, that I was going to place them in? As soon as I saw the driver, I realised that I was just going to have to let the day unfold in its own way, at its own pace. The details would form their own shape without any help from me. I was destined to have this driver, a man in his forties who had no particular place to go in life, whose marriage was a sham, whose future was grey, whose past was forgettable, and who used his passengers to confess his misery and recite his essential boredom with his life, and life in general.

15) It's a quarter past twelve. I decide to send a last-minute fax, just to get one other task out of the way. One more thing that wouldn't be preying on my mind as I made my journey. As I send the fax, I start to daydream about the cab ride I'm about to take, with this particular driver and his dead tales of sneery woe. I mustn't tell him what I'm doing. If I explain about my father, and his suicide, and the crematorium I'm about to visit for the first time since his funeral twenty-two years ago, who knows what the driver might say, and do? He might talk about his own suicide attempts, one of which involved sticking two sharpened pencils up his nostrils and then banging his head sharply down on a desk. The pencils snapped. Then there was the time he tried to decapitate himself by placing his neck on a railway line. The line was shut down for engineering works. He might even use the journey to the station to

have another go, driving at a hundred miles an hour into a bridge support.

16) He might ask if he can come along with me. It's his idea of a really enjoyable day out. Yes, don't bother getting the train, I'll drive you down. You don't want to do it on your own.

The fax won't go through. I lock up and leave the house. The last thing I do before I leave is grab an umbrella. Just in case. After all, I'm going to a cemetery. It's bound to rain. It's a last moment of preparation that makes me feel that, after all, I am ready for anything. Come rain or shine.

17) The driver is fiddling about suspiciously in the boot as I climb into the back seat of his car. He peels open his undertaker's grin and gets into the driver's seat. I'm hoping for silence all the way to Paddington, I just want to wrap myself up in myself and sink into the back seat of the car. He starts chatting immediately. He speaks in the voice of a man whose catchphrase is: 'If I should happen to die one of these days . . .' He has the pallor of a mushroom and eyes as grey as faded newsprint.

'Where to?' he asks in his forced jolly voice. I forgive him this, as he does have to know where we're going.

'Paddington,' I reply, trying to say it in such a way that communicates without hostility my need for a quiet trip. He's the kind of man who even if he picked up on the signals I'm trying to give him through voice and body-position would take it as a challenge. Nothing is going to stop him talking. It's one of the reasons he likes this job so much. In the back seat of his crumb-filled six-year-old car are captive victims who can do little but listen as he drones on about his life. 'Mustn't grumble,' he'll pretend, as he drives his Nissan Futile nought-point-nothing and drops passengers off where they say they want to go, as if they really know.

'Going anywhere nice?' he asks as he turns out of my road and heads up towards Highgate Hill. Here we go. He says it so innocuously, as if he's really interested. As if he really cares about you, and your life, and what you're doing today, tomorrow, for ever. Really, he's just looking for a way to talk about himself.

I toy with being rude, and saying nothing, or saying something curt and dismissive, but in the end I know he'll still find a way to talk. He probably talks to himself even if there is no one in the car with him. Silences inspire him. Rudeness challenges him.

'Nowhere special,' I lie. Should I say any more? I can't help myself. 'Just down the road,' I mutter, trying to be as non-committal as possible. I catch his dreadfully expectant eyes looking at me in the front mirror. Oh no, don't catch his eyes. He can read my mind. Look out of the window. My eyes must be giving it away, that I'm travelling by train to Gloucester, and I'm going to visit the crematorium to visit at last the place where my father was cremated. My eyes will give it away that I'm strangely nervous about the day. My eyes will give away the fact that it took twenty-two years to talk to my mother and my sisters about what happened. My eyes will give it away that only now, after I have talked to them, can I make this journey. My eyes will give it away that I don't really know what I'm doing, if I'm doing it for me, or for the book, or for my father. My eyes will give it away that I haven't even prepared enough to know what time the train is. Don't let him look in my eyes . . .

'What time is your train?' he asks, as if he's being humbly concerned. Damn, he saw it in my eyes. He read my mind. He knows full well that I have no idea. He lulls me into telling a lie.

'Well, they're very regular, trains to Reading.' Yes. Reading. I'm going to Reading. Nothing that will make him think I'm doing something more exciting than he is. Nothing that will incite any kind of envy.

'Yes, of course,' he says, as if he's humouring me. 'And then it only takes about half an hour, doesn't it?' He knows damn well I'm not going to Reading.

'Yeah,' I sigh, as I sense the trap of his depressed talk about to snap around me and my badly clad ankles. We turn a couple of corners, driving away from Archway Bridge, a favourite suicide spot, one I fancy he's eyed up many a time, just think, a hundred-foot plunge onto beautifully hard black tarmac, and pass the definitively Gothic Highgate Cemetery. I glance at a few gravestones overrun with tangled trees and unkempt grass. The gravestones are softened by the misty rain that has started to fizzle down from the low-hanging skies. As usual, I recall that this is where Karl Marx is buried. Even though it's only half a mile from where I live, I've never been to see his grave. I've never been to visit anybody's grave, although I once tried to find Marc Bolan's grave in Golders Green.

We head down towards Parliament Hill, and then we'll drive

along Gospel Oak towards the lower reaches of Hampstead, making for St John's Wood. There are no more cemeteries to pass.

18) The cab driver is talking about some holiday he's planning to take in Cornwall. Lovely hotel. In St Ives. Rooms need a bit of refurbishment but they can't really afford it. Food is lovely. You get a five-course dinner. Great full English breakfast. Usually they charge £45 a room, but during September and October it's only £25. Including dinner and breakfast. It's just what I need. Total relaxation. A real break away from it all.

I realise that he's implying that he will be going on his own. He's trying to create an opening in which I will ask him a question about his trip, but I stay stubbornly silent. He dribbles on. Yes, a lovely five-course meal, and then I just walk along the sea for an hour. Then I go back to my room and watch television for an hour.

He makes the holiday sound more and more depressing. There's something about the way he explains his plans that is tinged with self-pity. I imagine that any minute he will start to sob, and admit that in fact he's going there to kill himself. By the sea. In a small room nine feet by nine. Above a bed that's been slept in by more sad people than any other bed in all of south-west England. He'll hang himself. I estimate that a man of his height and weight would need a drop of nine feet. Perhaps he'll try and find an unusual way of disposing of himself. Maybe he'll sweat so much as he contemplates the void that he'll drown in his own fluid.

19) I remember a silly way of killing yourself that I read on the Internet in a list of bizarre ways to kill yourself. This one involved the American comedian Jerry Seinfeld, whose comedy has always been based on how much nothing there is in the world. Basically, you commit suicide by bashing yourself repeatedly with Seinfeld. You died with the satisfaction of knowing that you would then enter a Seinfeld routine, one of those he used to begin his television series.

'What is it about those people that are using me to kill themselves?'

I wait for the cab driver to take a sharp turn from his story about his holiday into a story about his suicide attempts. I've still got Jerry Seinfeld on my mind. I remember one of his routines.

'The thing I don't understand about the suicide person is the people who try and kill themselves, don't succeed, and then that's it. They stop trying! Why don't they keep trying? Pills don't work? Try a rope! Car in the garage won't start? Get a tune-up! I mean, there's nothing more rewarding than reaching a goal you've set yourself.'

20) The cab driver grumbles on as we drive through St John's Wood towards Maida Vale. As I thought, going this way, there's little traffic. We should make it before one o'clock. The driver is humming with self-regard, gnawing at the humiliation of life. He's talking now about a couple of accidents he's had recently. Of course, he explains, they weren't his fault. Other cars just kept driving into him. Well, of course, they would. The other drivers were probably passengers he had once driven who recognised him. They didn't know how to drive until they were driven, to distraction, by him. The first thing they did after he had driven them round the bend in his car was book some driving lessons. They passed their test as quickly as possible. And then they searched him out so that they could drive their cars into his.

The cab driver can't stop talking as he speeds towards a set of traffic lights. The lights are changing, and right ahead of us a black cab is waiting to turn right. The black-cab driver reasonably assumes that the mini-cab driver will slow up in readiness for the red light. The black cab moves forward ready to take the right turn. But the mini-cab driver doesn't stop. Instead he rather gleefully and definitely provocatively speeds up. The black cab has to brake quickly and jerks to a halt. The black-cab driver rightly looks furiously at the mini-cab driver. The mini-cab driver, having narrowly escaped his third accident in a few days, merrily speeds on. 'It's perfectly legal on amber,' he explains, grinning inanely, as if he also considers it to be perfectly legal to drive through the lights on red. Perhaps he doesn't care if we live or die.

21) He keeps talking, and in my mind the whining Jerry Seinfeld mixed up with the whining cab driver somehow becomes the eighteenth-century philosopher David Hume. It's an easy mistake to make. I can't hear the cab driver talk about his last accident, and the Americans driving the other car, from California, nice people, I might go and visit them, that'll surprise them. Instead, as we drive down by the canal in Little Venice, I hear the cab driver, dripping with drear, speak some words by David Hume from his 1783 essay on suicide:

It would be superfluous to magnify the merits of philosophy by displaying the pernicious tendency of that vice of which it cures the human mind. The superstitious man is miserable in every scene, in every incident in life, even sleep itself, which banishes all other cares of unhappy mortals, affords to him matter of new terror; while he examines his dreams, and finds in those visions of the night prognostications of future calamities. I may add that although death can put a full period to his misery, he dares not fly to this refuge, but still prolongs a miserable existence from a vain fear lest he offend his maker, by using the power with which that beneficent being has endowed him. The presents of God and nature are ravished from us by the cruel enemy, and notwithstanding that one step which would remove us from the regions of pain and sorrow, her message still chains us down to a hated being which she herself chiefly contributes to render miserable.

22) We swing around the roundabout under the Westway and approach Paddington station. The mini-cab driver finally seems to have run out of things to say. Perhaps he is just enjoying the decomposing fragrance mournfully wafting from the little green Christmas-tree air-freshener that's dangling gruesomely from the driver's mirror. Perhaps he's wishing his breath smelt as sweet.

Occasionally I sense him sneaking last-minute looks into his mirror, still trying to catch my eyes. He's still trying to read my mind. He's still angling for an invitation. He's still dying to tell me about the time he tried to kill himself by swallowing bleach. Unfortunately someone had put lemonade into the bottle. What kind of person does that? What is it with the people who put lemonade into empty bottles of bleach?

We pull up outside Paddington station. It's just coming up to one o'clock. I've got £9.60p on me. The fare is usually about £8, so I complacently assume I've got enough money. I could even tip him, if I had the desire. Unfortunately, all desire, for anything and everything, has left me after spending half an hour in the cab with this man. He turns round and with a thin, definitely quite sinister smile, the smile of someone who feels he's doing everyone a favour by not shooting them there and then, he tells me that there was ten minutes waiting time. That bloody fax. I don't believe I kept him waiting that long, but I can't be bothered arguing. I get the feeling if I do argue with him he might abruptly drive off and take me to a field on the outskirts of London where he would bury me alive. And then bury himself alive. I imagine he knows how. I expect he practises all the time.

'So that's £10,' he says. Christ, I tell him, sorry, I haven't got that much. He says, with all the shredded charisma of a hopeless man, 'Well, you seem like a nice man. Give me what you've got.' I hand over the change I'd collected thinking I was fully prepared for the first part of my journey, and I leave the mini-cab feeling let down that I end up owing this sour, defeated man a favour. Feeling somehow abused that he felt able to call me a nice man. I don't want to be his nice man. Both the words 'nice' and 'man' leave me with a stale taste in my mouth. As if I've just chewed his vomit-green air-freshener.

He drives off into a doom of his own making, and I imagine him smiling slyly to himself in his driver's mirror and muttering to himself that the life of a man is of no greater importance to the universe than that of an oyster. Oh yes, and no one ever lacks a good reason to commit suicide. He then crashes into a bus, both out of a kind of spite for the rest of humanity, and as another attempt to kill himself. As he crashes into the side of the bus, he screams, 'To think that we could have spared ourselves from living all that we have lived!' I feel mildly grateful that in the end I managed to tip him minus forty pence.

23) You used to go to Paddington and feel that you were stepping back in time. Now you are stepping into a film-set future. It's been brutally modernised, so that it now looks like a cross between the imposing dingy Victorian structure that it was and the hyper-developed overlit twenty-first-century travel centre that it is becoming. The dusty rusty past merges head-on with the shiny see-through future. Charles Dickens meets Philip K. Dick. Trains from Paddington can now deliver you in fifteen minutes of hushed cushioned efficiency to Heathrow Airport, and the station has been transformed into an airport terminal. The station isn't now only the gateway to Ealing Broadway, Reading, the West of England. It's a gateway to the whole world. The station is crawling with serious-looking people coming through and going out of the gate that can take them anywhere from Bristol to Buenos Aires.

I scan the many hi-tech screens that are now spread around the station encouraging you to feel you are slap bang in the mostly modern world. I'm looking for a mention of Gloucester. It's one minute past one. I see no sign of Gloucester. In the end, I have to find an old-fashioned printed timetable. Trains to Gloucester. Yes, there was one at one o'clock: the InterCity to Swansea, change at Swindon. Platform 4. Damn. Just missed it. As I work out what to do next, I notice that there are a lot of people milling about the entrance to platform 4. The train to Swansea has been delayed. I rush to the ticket office and buy a first-class day return to Gloucester. I get a first-class ticket as if there is a way that somehow it can possibly impress my father, who, I now know more than ever, has been dead for twenty-two years.

24) The Swansea train is ready for boarding. I race to the platform, and at six minutes past one I sink into a seat in carriage H of the one o'clock to Swansea. It's as if the train waited for me, knowing I was on a special journey. But then there are probably other people on the train who think that the train waited for them and their special journey. At quarter past one it leaves the station and slowly curves its way out of West London. Paddington station's measured, borrowed future becomes the approximate present of London. But that's out there, beyond the train. I'm in here. Inside myself inside the train. A train that smells very nearly new.

I am on my own. Facing forward. Sealed inside my very own journey. No one is seated near enough to talk to me. The mini-cab driver has not followed me onto the train. I can think again. I can talk to myself in a discreet, acceptable, silent, thinking fashion. On the train there are hundreds of people talking to themselves in the privacy of their own heads. I can't hear them and they can't hear me. It's just as it should be. As the train confidently speeds up and pushes its way out of London, the people on this train are all together and all on their own. Sharing a universe, and imagining their own. Thinking that we're all clinging to the same planet, and the same reasonably consistent reality, but thinking it in our very own way. Everyone on the train sees the same thing as everyone else, but they see it differently. They see things from their perspective, they see things as they fit into the rest of their life, as they make sense in their life, or no sense at all. Everyone has their own sense of the sense of things, and of the nonsense of things.

Everyone sitting on the train going forwards and backwards is inside their head surrounded by massive bone, and the skin that keeps up appearances. Everyone is surrounded by the late 13.00

from Paddington to Swansea. Outside, on either side, the English country, all brick, grass, glass and leaf, comes towards us and hurtles past us. Hundreds of little houses formed into homes line up in rigid patterns as if to salute us, for having such courage to move. As we finally make a clean break out of what can safely be called London, green fields start to appear. There are horses in the fields, standing perfectly still, all placidly looking at the train, silently marvelling at something that can move so fast, and contain so many people, who have so many thoughts, most of which will never be heard out loud. Two days later these horses would stand looking at a train speeding in towards London, and on this train would be people thinking thoughts about their life and their day and a simple next few minutes. A few minutes later this train would crash into a train leaving Paddington, and thirty people would lose their lives. Their thoughts would stop dead in their tracks. None of them knew that on that day sudden death was where their thoughts were aimed.

On my journey, going another way, up above the thinking train and the thinking horses, blue sky occasionally manages to peek through a mix of ugly, muddy clouds and plump white clouds, as if it cannot believe its eternal luck. It's not raining. Then it is raining. Sometimes gently, sometimes quite ferociously. The train charges on as straight as the moment as if it is plunging through the thoughts of someone who cannot make up their mind whether to be happy or sad.

25) I know now when my father killed himself, and how old he was, and it seems absurd that I didn't know and didn't want to know before. Now that I know, I still find it strange that he died in 1977, when I was twenty. He must have, because I was writing about Buzzcocks and Joy Division in the *NME* after he died. I always felt that I was younger than twenty. I thought I was a teenager.

It's as if there must have been two 1977s. The year Elvis and Bolan died in their own smashed ways. The punk rock year. The Queen's Jubilee. Anarchy in the UK. There was all that stuff and nonsense going on. And in the middle of it all my father killed himself, in another 1977, somewhere on the other side of the sun.

1977 seemed such a big year, but not a year made big because he died. Surely he died the year before? Or the year after? The senselessness of his death meant that even though I just had to ask when he died, I just didn't think there could possibly be enough sense in the world to explain that he just died on a day when other people died, other people were born. On a day that wasn't something he plucked out of nowhere and took with himself over the edge of his mind. Surely it was a day he made up for himself? Surely nothing else happened on the day he died? Surely the year was emptied out by his death? No – it was just one of a million things that happened that moment, that day, one of a billion things that happened that year. He was this side of the sun. He took part in the one and only 1977, until he opted out.

My mother had known all along exactly when he died, and she just assumed I knew. She wonders how I never noticed that every year around that time she gets a little withdrawn, a bit quiet. I suppose I thought she was still thinking about his birthday, or thinking about hers about to come.

I know now that he died in 1977. He carved out his own anarchy in the UK. He gobbed into the face of God. I thought I was being the rebellious one, but I was just playing. He wanted to destroy. Really destroy. Everything in his path, including himself.

Since we talked, out in the open, of our new closeness, my mother has sent me my father's death certificate. A piece of paper that if I'd seen it in the late 70s, or early 80s, or most of the 90s, would probably have caused me physical pain. Or perhaps failed to penetrate my continuing numbness and therefore caused no pain whatsoever and made no real sense. It's a piece of paper I have never even considered actually existed. A piece of paper that brings his death down to form-filled earth with a dull thump.

She's sent a copy of the certificate along with other certificates that become the formal confirmation of the way that a family comes into being, the way that people come together and change the shape of their lives, their futures and their needs.

I have my father's birth certificate, and I can see in lifelike black and white that he was born on 10 May, 1936, in the Northdene Nursing Home in Madeira Road, Margate. I can see his name and his sex and the fact his father was a master grocer called Leslie Alexander Morley. I learn that his mother's middle name was Mary, and she was the parent that signed the certificate, the piece of paper that announced for all the world like it mattered that he was out of the womb.

And then, press forward through a lifetime of guesses, hopes and hesitations, through leaps of faith and perplexed fervours, the piece of paper that announces that, for the sake of argument, he is in the tomb. The piece of paper that could have told me all along, whenever I wanted, the dirty-dated details.

DEATH, it says at the top of that part of the form that is to be filled in. Death, because what else is it meant to say? Death, because that is why we are all here. Entry 102. Registration district Stroud. Sub-district, Stroud. Administrative district, County of Gloucestershire. Name, sex, date and place of birth. Occupation: Financial Assistant. How did anybody know that? What does it mean? Name and address of informant: Certificate received from K. C. Brooks, Coroner for Cheltenham District, inquest held 4/7/1977.

Cause of death: carbon monoxide poisoning due to inhalation of exhaust fumes.

Suicide.

This still reads like a damned, sabotaging surprise.

Another surprise is the place of death. Bull's Cross, Painswick. I have never heard this place mentioned before. I have no idea where it is. But I'm on the 13.00 Paddington to Swansea InterCity change at Swindon to find out. I'm aiming my thoughts towards this bull's-eye. I'm going to finish this particular journey where he finished his particular journey. I'm also going to visit the crematorium where he is buried, which I find out, now that my mother and I are talking about the death like it's the most natural thing in the world, or at least like it's something that happened in our lifetime, is actually in Gloucester.

26) Not Stroud.

27) He died on a Wednesday, just another day, as ordinary as itself and the next day and the day after that, an ordinary day in the middle of summer. Not one of the days suicides statistically favour, those being Monday and Friday, but certainly a month that seems to be popular, suicidally speaking. Flaming June.

28) The train slows up to pull into Reading. There on the left-hand side is Reading Jail. The rain starts to slash noisily down the window next to me. Huge drops smash and splash against the glass, as if the water is trying to force its way into the warmth of the train. The sky seems to sink down towards us as we glide into the

station. I'm not looking for signs, and I've let Reading Jail disappear behind me without reading anything into it, but I have to say that the sky over Reading has a livid, bruised quality that verges on a colour you could call 'corpse'. You might go as far as to call it 'zombie-yuk'. We pull out of Reading, and on the other side of the station the rain has stopped, and there's sunshine, and blue sky, and white clouds that are mockingly voluptuous. As we pick up speed, the sky changes shape and colour. It gets greyer, and heavier, and huge bulbous clouds rumble with theatrical menace. Abruptly, it starts to rain again. For a few moments there's sunshine, and there's rain, and trees sway in time with what happens next, and the elements are clearly, and darkly, enjoying themselves, creating atmosphere at will.

Some cows in a field look into the train, and pick up on my thoughts. They're clearly bored that all I'm thinking about is the weather. Cows just don't have the wit to appreciate that, really, deep down, beyond the weather, my mind is full of stranger human things. And, it might interest the cows to know that there's now a place in my mind for somewhere called Bull's Cross.

29) I change trains at Swindon. It's raining hard as I get onto the 14.16 to Cheltenham, stopping at Gloucester. The train is just a couple of carriages in length, and filled with the kind of basic seats you usually see on a bus. It's about half full. The people on the train are all strangers, and they all look deeply familiar. I've seen these faces before, all around Britain. I recognise the way they sit. I've seen all these expressions before, expressions which are actually pretty much the same expression. An expression you could call expressionless, or an expression which is on the verge of being an expression. They must be thinking about the weather.

On the InterCity train, you got the feeling that you were connected in some way to the end of the twentieth century. This train seems ready to slide into the past, and take all the listless and familiar-looking strangers with it.

Looking around, there's not much evidence that these people belong to 1999 and not 1977. The train has sliding doors, in the way it wouldn't have had twenty years ago. There's no mention of British Rail anywhere, and the train is completely non-smoking. A woman in front of me speaks softly into a mobile phone. But you couldn't really tell from the clothes we're wearing, their colour and their shape, and the blank timeless look on people's faces that this isn't 1977, or any time since.

The passengers are spaced around the train in a pattern that might mean something. We've all tried hard to avoid sitting too near each other, so that there are lots of seats filled with tired preoccupied-looking people, separated by lots of empty seats that might represent something.

When the train starts to move it actually chugs. It seems to be shuffling down the track. It takes a long time to pick up speed and all the slow while everyone on the train just stares into their own space, or out of the window, or nowhere special, wherever they can avoid eye contact with the others on the train. They must be thinking about death.

It's as if we're all on this train with the same mission in mind. We're rocking gently down a green, green artery towards the actual dead centre of England and each of us is heading towards a secret location with a magical name. This is the lacklustre 14.16 suicide special from Swindon. Out in the fields, the horses and the cows turn their backs on this train.

As we head into Stroud station, a woman sitting a few seats in front of me to my right starts talking to herself. Or someone sitting in the empty seat next to her who must be invisible. She's got a lot to say. She's found a good listener. She catches my eyes as I look at her. I look away very quickly. Out of the corner of my eye I sense her gesturing with her hands. Nobody else is paying attention to her. Maybe I'm the only person on the train who can see her. Or maybe I'm the one who is invisible.

30) I now know not to get off the train at Stroud.

31) I arrive in Gloucester at three in the afternoon. The train doors slide shut behind me, and the ghost train continues on its dead way through green leaf and changing atmosphere to Cheltenham.

Gloucester station is as flat and humble as it must have been twenty years ago, tentatively brought up to date by new public phones and a café/newsagent where you can buy cappuccino and layers of magazines devoted to soaps, fashion, music, home decoration and something called 'lifestyle'.

I head towards the city centre and find a shopping mall, a shiny chip off the old Mersey Square block, where there is a WH Smith. I

395

buy a local *A–Z*. I'm not sure why, but the first thing I look for in the index is any street with the name Morley. There's a Morley Avenue, just off the Golden Valley bypass. I then look up the cemetery. Page twenty. 4D.

My father was cremated at Coney Hill Cemetery, and I decide to walk. It doesn't look too far. I walk up Eastgate Street, out of the shopping mall, where essence of 90s has been dropped into the City of Gloucester, and head towards Barton Street. This takes me through a tightly packed inner-city area full of small terraced houses and small run-down shops that could easily have been transplanted from Eccles, or Reddish, or some of the other sadder parts of Manchester. It starts to rain, although the sky stretched above me more than it would be in Stockport is as filled with blue as it is smeared with grey. But mostly Gloucester seems like a cracked reflection of Stockport, and my father, after all that, didn't escape as far as he hoped. He swapped one insignificant town trapped in time and timelessness for another. In a way, he proved that he was right all along to think that, whatever you do, there is no way out. Everything and everywhere is the same.

I cross over the railway line that took me into Gloucester, and cut through some streets where the houses are semi-detached, but still working-class, and find myself separated from the cemetery by a busy modern dual carriageway, Eastern Avenue. It takes a few minutes to cross, either by bridge or by waiting at some traffic lights.

The cemetery is surrounded by trading estates, a fire station, factories, schools, community centres, a driving-test centre. It's surrounded by life, and traffic, and movement, and there's a betting shop a couple of hundred metres away, and yet it has a simple stillness, and because a large playing field backs onto it, there seems to be a hint of country and openness. There's a monstrous concrete circle of big road that contains it, the M5, a couple of big bypasses, the Eastern Avenue, but the cemetery is very self-contained, very orderly, and, considering all the activity that crowds around it, incredibly quiet. It has created its own atmosphere, and nothing from the outside world can interfere. In the distance, the Cotswold Hills keep eternal watch, sending down into the city, cutting across the modern mystery of the M5, some of their ancient grace.

As I walk towards the cemetery I recognise it instantly. How could I ever have forgotten? I remember it as being underwater, and

I remember it as if it was miles above the surrounding area, isolated from streets and houses, almost up in the clouds, but I know immediately that I've been there before. The little pale brick chapel built with doll's-house neatness is placed exactly in the centre of a space that is split into a graveyard and a series of lawned gardens where plaques and flowers and trees mark out those who have been cremated. It looks exactly as it did twenty-two years ago, if a little dryer, and more in focus.

As I walk towards the gate, it seems so recently that I was there, I half-expect to see myself treading water outside the chapel waiting for the other mourners to arrive. It is 1977 here. It's also 1973, 1985, 1993. This is a place where the past never escapes itself, and the present is constantly dissolving into the past, and the future is unheard of.

I stop at the gates and look in. Gardeners are mowing grass and tidying pathways. If the place wasn't so full of death you might think how pretty it all looked. You might think how well death can be decorated, and disguised, and how discreetly the meaning of it can be so delicately deflected into a patchwork of leafy, grassy denial. You might think that remembering can be lovely.

It's raining harder now and I'm grateful for the umbrella. Apart from that, I've not prepared myself very well for this visit, and I have no idea where my father, who I've seen no sign of for twenty-two years, would be placed, if that's the word. I'm never sure how to refer to the cremated. It's easy with the buried. They're dead and buried. A big stone marks the spot. There they are. Underground. With the cremated, it's less obvious. They're not quite anywhere, really. Where will my father be positioned, marked, plaqued, hidden, available, numbered, filed . . . scattered?

As I look up the path towards the little chapel, I notice something that slightly spoils the cute proportions of the clean, boxy building. A wide brick chimney rises up a little higher than you would really like. It tries very hard, as hard as a chimney can, not to draw attention to itself. It wants to appear dignified. The trouble is, this is a chimney that is used, very regularly. And you know what it's used for. Any smoke that comes out of this chimney is the smoke of human kindness. After I saw my father slide down the slimy conveyor belt and disappear behind cheap brown curtains, he would have been burnt, and most of him would have gone up in smoke, up this chimney, into the open air, which becomes thin air, which becomes nowhere.

I look at the chimney and I wonder if that's what I should be paying my respects to.

32) There's a large notice board by the entrance gate. I look at it as if it might give me a clue where my father is. It's actually a price list. Death is always a business. Remains remain a part of the cost of living. I count the cost of burial versus cremation, big gravestones versus little gravestones. Every letter on a tombstone has its price. I notice that a plaque marking the presence – or non-presence – of a loved one is removed after twenty years. You pay a fee for a twenty-year period, an estimate of the length of a generation I suppose, and then the plaque is removed. I'm not sure what they do with any ashes that might also have to be removed. It seems that if you don't renew the spot where the plaque is, you lose it. It dawns on me that I might not be able to find where my father is, to a point, positioned. It has been over twenty years since his funeral, and the Morley family have lost the plot. None of us knew that you had to pay for more time. We just supposed that death lasts for ever. We thought that even though we never made the trip to this end place, he was still here, somehow, named, and permanent. By the time any of us could even think of talking about him, and our grief, his name had been wiped away.

I won't find his name here after all. He's in some dreadful equivalent of an unmarked grave. We haven't looked after his memory. I haven't looked after his memory, and I feel that everyone buried and cremated in this cemetery, and the birds flying overhead, and any fantastic fish that might still be around from the day of his funeral, can sense how terrible I feel.

33) I walk around the gardens. Perhaps I've read the notice wrongly, or perhaps whoever paid for the plaque in the first place made sure that it would be around for forty, sixty, eighty years. Perhaps they do a special rate for being permanently fixed in your permanence. There are flower beds with plaques stuck into the ground. Plaques are lined up at the edges of the path. There are hundreds and hundreds, some more looked-after than others. I look for half an hour. I can't find his name anywhere. There doesn't seem to be a suicide corner.

I wonder how his plaque must have looked, placed at the side of a path amidst other plaques with other names on, the name on his plaque never looked at by anybody he knew. Screwed in place for twenty years, and then unscrewed, as if it had never been there in the first place.

34) There's an office at the side of the chapel. I go in, and ask a lady behind a counter, a counter where you can order your plaques and your headstones and your inscriptions, if she can tell me what happened to my father. Her name is Mrs Evans, and she's in her fifties. Plump grey and familiar looking. She checks some records. Eventually, she finds out that his plaque was removed last year. His ashes were scattered over lawn seven. She tells me this firmly, as if she's ready for me to break down, or argue with her, or shout wildly, or moan at the bureaucratic nonsense of it all. She has a manner that suggests she is used to dealing with the distraught, the bewildered, the numb.

I ask her what I should do. She carefully explains, as if I'm a touch stupid but she quite understands, that they might still have the plaque in storage. If they do, it will cost £75.60 to place it in the gardens for another twenty years. If they can't find it, it will cost £150.75 to make a new one and put it in place. Or, if I wanted, I could have his name written into a memorial book. A few lines could be written to remember him. I ponder this for a few seconds, wondering what the point of that might be, and she continues to look at me as if I'm much more vulnerable than I really appreciate. The memorial book sounds like a hotel register to me, or a visitors' book.

I tell her that I would really like to put a plaque into the gardens, to have things back how they were. In the limbo of the cemetery, surrounded by hundreds of people who still have their names in place somewhere on the planet, and not just in a book, I can't bear the thought that he's nameless. After everything that happened to get him into this place, even if it's a place he never knew, even if it's a place he ended in by chance. After everything he did to find some place where he could rest. After all the time he's been here without anyone paying attention. Even though he knows nothing about it, about where he is, about where he isn't, about the removal, about the neglect.

I have to put his name back, as if he does know, as if he's felt desperately lonely. He has to be somewhere, even if he's not. He has to be here, because this is where he's been, even if I didn't know it.

He has to be here, named, fixed, planted, because now I do know that he was here. All the time I wasn't thinking about him, this is where he was. An eight-inch by five-inch brass plaque that a whole life had shrunk into. I want it put back.

Mrs Evans registers no emotion whatsoever regarding my decision. She's just very keen to ensure I understand the pricing system, as if I might protest to her that I think it's pathetic that I have to pay for this. He's dead, for God's sake. He's been dead for twenty-two years. Nor does she offer a hint of disapproval that I march off the streets after twenty-two years, his only son, and want everything back to how it was. Where've I been all these years? Mrs Evans deals with death as if it is an excursion that needs to be organised with brisk matter-of-fact unfussiness.

She tells me that she will call me the next day to report whether they have found my father's plaque. I leave her office, walk past the gardens where my father is and isn't, where he is in a limbo inside a limbo, and leave Coney Hill Cemetery.

I walk back down towards Gloucester city centre. It stops raining.

35) The next day, Mrs Evans rings me at home. If I didn't know better, I'd swear she sounded just a tiny bit excited. They've found the plaque. I ask her what it says on it, because I don't think I ever knew. She says, 'At Peace.' It seems so obvious, but then I suppose death is the place for this kind of obviousness. Death is the greatest cliché in life, and we surround it with padded clichés, little cushions of triteness for us to rest our weary imaginations on. I wonder for a moment what else it could say.

'Suicide is painless.'

'How tickled I am.'

'It's grim up north.'

'God does not exist. I am God. I do not exist. I commit suicide.'

'Never smile at a crocodile.'

I imagine telling Mrs Evans that I want it to say, 'I am alone, I am bereft, and the night falls upon me.' She would simply tell me how much it was going to cost.

'At peace' is fine, I say. It is bad form to play around with the firm, banal etiquette.

Is it definitely his plaque? I ask.

400

'Oh yes,' she says. 'Lionel Roland Morley.'

That's not his name, I say.

'Well, the plaque is a bit dirty,' she says, as unflustered as always, 'I can't quite make out his first two names. But it's definitely Morley, and it's definitely the right one. When we've renovated, the name will be much clearer. If you write to us formally asking us to clean and replace the plaque then we can send you an invoice for the amount.'

36) I walked back to Gloucester station to find a taxi to take me to Bull's Cross, Painswick. My new *A–Z* of Cheltenham and Gloucester had shown me that Painswick was a small village midway between Gloucester and Stroud. Even though it was out of the range of the *A–Z* squares that covered Gloucester, Cheltenham and Stroud, it was special enough to have its own inset. Tucked away into the corner of page 31 were eight squares that revealed to me the existence of Painswick. Bisected by the A46, made up of Stroud Road which becomes Cheltenham Road, which in turn is fed by Gloucester Road which in turn becomes Gloucester Street, the names of places in this little inset suggested that Painswick was a classic, quaint Cotswold village. I wondered how my father had found it.

There was nothing in the index that helped me find Bull's Cross, but I hoped that a taxi driver might have heard of the place. There are two lonely-looking cabs at the rank by the station. I slip into the first one, cab number fifty, a smart new toffee-coloured Rover. The interior is the colour of Weetabix when it has been turned into a mush by some milk. The driver is about fifty, well dressed, in gentlemanly beiges and fawns, skin the colour of rich tea biscuits, and he appears to exude easy English pleasantness. His manner makes me feel comfortable, and the car itself is very comfortable. Plenty of legroom, very soft seats. I ask if he could take me on a round trip to Painswick and back. How far away is it?

'About nine miles. Anywhere in particular you want to go?'

Nowhere special. Well, I'm not sure. I just want to have a look around. Perhaps we can just drive through. Even at this stage, I'm not completely sure I want to go to Bull's Cross. What will I find there? A plaque recording the suicide? Some sign of something or other that explains everything? I can't imagine what I'm looking for, really. Truth? Reality? The ending of a book? A happy sort of an ending? The beginning of a book? A sad beginning? A rusting sky-blue Ford Escort?

I don't get the feeling that the driver is being intrusive, or that he's going to be unnecessarily talkative. He doesn't fight to catch my eye in the rear-view mirror, but I don't feel ready to explain why I am making this trip. I haven't got a clue what I will find in Painswick, and perhaps in the end I will just drive through and vaguely wonder how on earth my father ended up there. Perhaps he just took a fancy to the first four letters of the name of the village. It's a journey I decide to make in contemplative silence. I decide to just let things happen.

The taxi turns out of the station car park. I decide that this soft beige man is the perfect neutral driver for me to have on such an occasion, whatever the occasion is. There's something about his manner that calms me down. I decide it's OK that I ask him if he has ever heard of Bull's Cross. He thinks about it for a polite second. He thinks he might have.

As we wait for the lights to change so that we can pull out of the station car park onto Bruton Way, a hearse containing a coffin passes in front of us. Of course, this means nothing at all. It's just one of those things.

37) We turn left out of the station, onto Bruton Way, and make our way out of the city centre up Metz Way. We then turn right along Eastern Avenue, which takes us past the trading estate and factories that are in front of Coney Hill. I can see the chapel chimney sticking into the sky in the distance. The sky behind the chimney looks tormented and turbulent. It starts to pour down, the rain hammering down so hard that after one swipe of the windscreen wiper the screen instantly fills up with racing water. We make another left turn, onto the Painswick Road, the B4073. As we head towards Painswick, it suddenly stops raining. The sun decides to follow us out of Gloucester, but it can only follow us so far.

I sense that the driver is perhaps mildly puzzled by my determination to make this round trip to Painswick. He tells me that he remembers Bull's Cross because there's a squash club there. Remembering how my father used to play squash, remembering his battered squash racquet, I react a little overexcitedly to this news. A squash club? Isn't it a rather strange place for a squash club?

'It is. It's also a blues club.'

A blues club? In the middle of the Cotswolds?

'It's very popular, so I believe, although in thirteen years I have only had one passenger ask me to take him to the squash club. I've forgotten where it is, to be honest. Bull's Cross is somewhere down the lanes out of Painswick, but I'll have to ask when we get to Painswick exactly where it is.'

I can't make my mind up whether to explain to the taxi driver what I'm doing. The atmosphere in the car ever so slightly starts to change. He's picking up on my edginess, I'm picking up on his gentle curiosity, or none of this is happening and I'm just imagining it. I decide that I won't tell him why I want to go to Painswick. I don't want him to feel that I'm burdening him. When I tell strangers that my father killed himself, I always giggle, or smirk. I can't help it. I don't want to sour things, so I sort of shrug, and laugh, as if to say, My father killed himself, but it's not important or anything. Don't let it spoil your day.

We drive past an attractive-looking country pub, The King's Head. The pub sign outside is of a painting of Henry VIII. I imagine my father going in there for a last drink. A last pint. A drowning of his sorrows. I don't think of him as much of a drinking man. Carol reckoned he once said to his wife that he never wanted to start drinking because he was worried that he might end up an alcoholic. My mother admitted she sometimes wondered if it might not have been better if sometimes he'd gone off and gone on a drinking binge, just to get things out of his system.

We pass the Hatton Court Hotel. A place to stay on the night before you die, perhaps. The roads are getting tighter and tighter, the corners more numerous. Houses are further apart, occasional road signs feature more obscure and slightly symbolic-sounding places. Massive, old, graceful trees create twinkling canopies above us. We glide through an England that has barely changed in a hundred years and slip smoothly into the village of Painswick. It's a little darling of a place, the quintessential English country village preserved in aspic. The English past in a well-kept nutshell, a clear million miles away from shopping malls and McDonalds, occupying a different twentieth century from the one we're used to. There's not a leaf, or a brick, or a roof-tile out of place. It seems a shame that cars are allowed to drag in the noise, dirt and scandal of the twentieth century.

At its centre there is the most immaculate-looking church, the Parish Church of Saint Mary, with a garden ornamentally caressed into heady perfection. Everything is proportioned as if the church and its surroundings were built in exquisite miniature and then blown up in size. We drive past it onto the Stroud road, and then my taxi driver pulls up at the side of the road to ask directions. The first people he asks are American tourists. This is no surprise. If an American wants to see England in a way that is all at once intensely real and intensely unreal, as solid as the established past and as transparent as a dream, then Painswick is the perfect place. It is a painting of the perfect place, and to visit the village is to enter this picture, and be tempted to stay, for ever. I'm not sure what is more ghostly – the outside world, of cities and towns and factories and movement, or the inside world of Painswick, of nothing and still-ness, which is a tiny model of an English paradise.

The taxi driver faithfully perseveres on my behalf, and I stay in the car as he finds someone else to ask. He returns, and tells me that a local lady has given him directions. We turn round, pass the church that looks too good to be true, and then plummet down steep windy lanes that seem to be taking us towards the very centre of the earth. Deeper and deeper we seem to fall, down roads that are just wide enough to take one car, surrounded by trees and hedges and fields, hemmed in by unnatural nature. We twist and turn in such a manner you can't believe that you could find your way out again. The twists and turns become so severe it's like we have entered some ancient maze. We veer to the left, shoot downhill, then suddenly we're head-ing uphill, and to the right, and then again to the left. I can only imagine that my father found himself in such a dark, dense, unsignposted part of the country because he was lost. Then again, it seems as if you have to know your way into these mysterious lanes. You have to possess the secret, know the local codes. You can't really stumble into this tangled nowhere by being lost. You have at least to know where to begin. Or you have to be very committed. You have to keep going, turning this way and that, uphill and down, round and round, in and out, over and under, through and through. You mustn't panic that you will never know your way out. That mustn't be a concern. You just keep driving until it seems as though you have driven right through into another time.

You drive until you have passed through a barrier into another dimension. You drive until you are immersed in leafy, empty, untimed otherness. You feel you could drive round and round in circles for ever and never get out and it doesn't matter nothing matters but driving deeper and deeper into a part of England that is deep under its own past, present and future. And then you peak and abruptly burst over the top of a sharp hill and find yourself at a crossroads, surrounded by fields and trees, surrounded by nothing but epic, unyielding English countryside, surrounded by nothing but views of sun and cloud and forest and space and time. You have arrived.

A signpost tells you that you are at Bull's Cross. Bull's Cross is simply a crossroads in the middle of somewhere or nowhere that offers you four different directions. You can go this way or that way. You can go back the way you came. Or you can go your own way.

My taxi driver has brought me to this isolated spot with uncomplaining persistence as if he was born to do it. I ask him to pull into a lay-by. I tell him that I am going to get out and walk around. He simply accepts this. I'm glad I haven't got the mini-cab driver I had on the morning of my journey, trying hard to read my thoughts, to climb into my journey. My Gloucester driver sits very still as I get out of the car. He's very good at keeping himself to himself.

Just off the lay-by there's a little rutted jut of muddy tracks hooded by trees, next to the entrance to a farm, Trillgate Farm. This jut is about twenty yards long. I walk down it. Ahead of me is a sharply sloping field bordered by a dense line of dark-green trees. As far as the eye can see there is nothing but the hedged green, yellow and brown of the country and the steady blue, grey and white of the sky. There is no sign of a modern world. No roads, no wires, no cars, no factories. No buildings whatsoever. At the far end of the field there's a black horse quietly revelling in all the isolation and staring at nothing in particular.

I stand at the edge of the sloping field and look out over this expanse of countryside. You could easily pull a car, or a van, into this leafy tunnel, and point it out towards the dreamy distant horizon. You could easily lose track of time. You stare out into a part of space decently covered up by growth and undergrowth and you let your mind wander.

I decide that this is where my father lethally connected his van, the hair-dryer and himself. In the dark of a lovers' lane he chanced upon. It was as good a place to die as any, if you can make the choice. You could call it a beauty spot. He did his best to die beautifully, considering he was poisoning himself. He arrived in the bright daylight of a hot June day, picked his spot for its rolling peace and dead-end splendour, and waited until it became night. It was dark and he closed his eyes and made it darker still. Darker and darker. He imagined himself seeping into the countryside around him. He didn't know where he was, but it was very dark, and very quiet, and very still. There was something deeply comforting about the place. He started to think the same thoughts as all the surrounding trees with all their unbelievable leaves. He became smaller than the smallest thing in the world and bigger than the biggest thing. He disappeared. The whole surrounding area disappeared with him.

He took Bull's Cross with him, or Bull's Cross took him. It's the kind of place you can imagine only materialises once every few years. It flickers in and out of existence. Sometimes you can find it. Other times you can't. It moves in mysterious ways.

I walk back to the taxi. My driver doesn't seem to have moved a muscle since I left him. I get into the car and we drive down more steep hills and find the squash club, a converted farm. The area is a curling maze of lanes that wind steeply around farmland, and you spot other potential death-traps, dirt tracks that go nowhere, cul-de-sacs of mud and grass, lots of places where you can lose yourself and just fade away. I bet my father couldn't believe his luck when he found this part of the country. He could even treat himself to a last game of squash before he found some enclosed nook and hooked up the tube his wife had reminded him about, and turned on the ignition.

There are other places he might have stopped to consider his fate, including one likely-looking lane right next to the incongruous squash club, a building so out of the way I have the feeling strange cultish things happen inside. I'm still convinced that he killed himself at the place I first found. I ask the driver to take me back. Nothing about his expression questions this decision, and up a hill, and round the bend, and down again, and up again we drive until we burst upon the bull's-eye of Bull's Cross. We stop in the lay-by again. I take a last look at the bit of muddy track overlooking the sloping field next to Trillgate Farm. It looks like some kind of primitive launching pad.

This is where he did it. I don't feel any awful pull. I don't feel as if I am standing at the edge of a tall building. I don't get the urge to slip a strong rope over one of the branches hanging nine feet and two inches above me. I see no reason to follow the route my father took from this idyllic spot to the chimney in Gloucester nine miles away. I just know this is where he did it. He killed himself, right here, at the dead centre of the country, and twenty-two years later his son arrived, took a look, and then left, a little in shock, feeling intimately connected to his twenty-year-old self the day he heard his dad had died.

I stand there looking around for a few seconds, and then I think, That's it. I've seen enough. This is where his life ended, but it's got very little to do with my father. As I feared, it explains nothing. But of course nothing is in its own way everything.

38) The taxi driver and I drive back towards Gloucester. I must be filling the interior of the car with my thoughts and my quietness. The driver retains the same polite, professional expression. I assume he must be extremely curious about what I've just done, but as we pull out of the excess prettiness of Painswick, I still can't bring myself to tell him my story. What's he going to say, to do? Will he turn out to have had his own suicidal associations? Did his son perhaps kill himself? Or will he have strong views on suicide that he suddenly starts to discuss.

'Do you think it's an insult to our culture?'

'How confusing do you think it is?'

'Is it an absurd thing to do, or a valid response to absurdity?'

'You know, they say it is less likely to happen the older you get.'

'I tried to kill myself once. I tried to take a hundred and fifty pills. Couldn't get them all down. Dry mouth. Then I started to get this buzzing in my ears . . .'

We drive back towards the bricked-in possibility of modern civilisation, speeding sweetly down the B4073 towards Upton St Leonards. I keep nagging to myself about whether or not I should tell the driver what I'm doing. I'm thinking about this more than the fact I've just found the place where my father committed suicide. I realise that I absolutely need to tell him. More for me than for him. I don't know about him, but I can't bear the fact he doesn't know, and that he's being so dead centrally English and reserved and not wanting to intrude.

I decide I'm going to tell him. I prepare to tell him in what I hope is an appropriately mature and articulate fashion. I want to tell this incomplete stranger why I'm here and I want to do it in a way that doesn't make me out to be a bit odd. Is it possible? All of a sudden, as a surprise to me, I start to explain to the inscrutable driver the point of my trip. The words I speak are also a surprise to me. I begin by saying, You know, well, I don't want to be morbid, but the reason I wanted to go to Bull's Cross was that it was where my father died. I hold back the key bit of information, which means the taxi driver, motivated by professional politeness, must ask the question, 'Oh, was it an accident?'

I'm now in the dilemma I was hoping to avoid all along. Can I manage to say, 'My father killed himself,' without smirking nervously, without sounding almost autistic? Can I just say it clearly and cleanly and matter-of-factly, because I've got used to it, because I've recovered from the shock?

I rehearse what I'm going to say in my mind. When I finally manage to reply, after a very long ten seconds, it sounds like somebody else speaking. 'Well, I don't mean to be morbid . . .' I smirk nervously, just as I always do, like a little boy who's done something wrong, like it's all some ridiculous farce. 'Actually, my father killed himself.'

The taxi eases past The King's Head. The driver doesn't flinch, but I detect slight discomfort. 'Oh, I'm sorry,' he murmurs. I get the feeling he really didn't want to know anything after all.

We close in on Gloucester and it starts to rain. Both of us are trying to find something to say next. I make the first attempt. 'I think it's so interesting that he drove all the way from Manchester and somehow found this beautiful out-of-the-way place.'

The taxi driver doesn't say anything. I think he wants to, just because he's a polite man, but he can't think of anything. I think he wants to go home for his tea. He doesn't say. 'Yes, it is interesting.' He doesn't say, 'Mmmm.' He doesn't say, in the words of David Hume,

> That suicide may often be consistent with interest and with our duty to ourselves no one can question, who allows that age, sickness or misfortune, may render life a burden, and make it worse even than annihilation. I believe that no man ever

threw away life while it was worth keeping. For such is our natural horror of death that small motives will never be able to reconcile us to it: and although perhaps the situation of a man's health or fortune did not seem to require the remedy, we may at least be assured that any of us who, without apparent reason, has recourse to it, was cursed with such an incurable depravity or gloominess of temper as must poison all enjoyment, and render him equally miserable as if he had been loaded with the most grievous misfortunes. If suicide be supposed a crime tis only cowardice can impel us to it. If it be no crime, both prudence and courage should engage us to rid ourselves at once of existence, when it becomes a burden. Tis the only way we can be useful to society, by setting an example, which if imitated, would present to everyone his chance for happiness in life, and would officially free him from all danger of misery.

The driver stays quiet as we glide back into Gloucester, and so do I. I've brought old departed death into his clean and tidy vehicle, his place of work, his ordered life. I imagine he's not looking forward to the next time somebody asks him to drive to Bull's Cross, which, in the end, is just a place you get to on the way to somewhere else. You wouldn't really want to stop there.

39) Monday, 27 June, 1977. After he had dropped his daughter Carol at school in Offerton, Stockport, my father would have driven off towards Marple, crossed the A6 onto the A523 and driven towards Macclesfield. He would have turned onto the A537, which leads all the way to Knutsford, and then turned left onto the A535 to Holmes Chapel. He would have used motorway junction number 18 to join the M6, heading south. The M6 would have taken him out of Cheshire, into Staffordshire, and down towards the Midlands.

He had already made the decision, or he made it on the road, to leave the M6 and take the M5. This would take him towards the west of England. Maybe Monday night he stopped somewhere, say Worcester, where he caught his breath and gathered his thoughts and didn't ring home. He had a lot on his mind. Such as, the feeling that he would like to die. Such as, the feeling that he would like to live, somewhere else, as somebody else. Such as, an appearance in court on Wednesday morning. Such as, he had run away with a van that didn't belong to him, and by now he would be missed, and perhaps the police were already looking for him.

Perhaps he travelled by night, feeling hunted. He was being chased, by others, by himself, by versions of himself as stranger and madman that had accumulated over the years. Chased by his life, his wife, his children, his past, his exhaustion. His exhaustion was mighty and strong and could easily outrun him.

He kept on going down the M5, and at some time on Tuesday the twenty-eighth, he found himself twenty miles or so outside Bristol. There was something about the thought of Bristol that made him leave the M5 and head away from the River Severn into the country. He left the M5 at exit number 13, and took the A419 into Stonehouse.

Perhaps this was the last joke of a man who used to laugh a lot and then slowly stopped. He had seen the name Stonehouse, and was reminded of the Labour MP John Stonehouse, who had faked his own suicide. Stonehouse the MP had left his shoes and clothes on an isolated beach and left clues to suggest he had swum out to sea and drowned. My father drove into Stonehouse the village and thought he had found a good way out. He would fake his own death, but live on.

This is me holding onto the vain idea that my father had deranged surrealistic tendencies, and was the kind of man who would have enjoyed disappearing in mysterious circumstances in a place called Stonehouse having left the M5 at exit 13. Another way of looking at it is that he left the M5 because he had decided he wanted to go back home. He decided to face the music. He drove into Stroud, and turned onto the A46 heading north. He thought he could drive up towards Cheltenham, stay the night there, and rejoin the M5 at exit 11 in the morning. Maybe he thought he would drive all night under cover of darkness in case the police were looking for him. Or maybe he thought he would drive into Gloucester, where he would make a late-night call to his wife, and ask her to come and pick him up. She would understand.

Driving up the A46 at Pitchcombe, the road forked two ways. Right towards Cheltenham, left towards Gloucester. A couple of miles up the road towards Gloucester, there was a place called Edge. He thought this was tempting fate. He took the road towards Cheltenham, which would take him via Painswick.

In the dense tangle of small lanes around Painswick he got lost. The roads were so narrow and intertwined that he simply lost his bearings. Perhaps it was dark by now and this made navigating his way through this sticky web of roads even more difficult. He found himself driving in ever-decreasing circles. He lost himself in a swirling whirlpool of wood and road. He had got trapped in a labyrinth and he didn't have the energy necessary to haul himself out. He found Bull's Cross, and took the road in the opposite direction. Five minutes later, he was at Bull's Cross again. He took a way out he hadn't taken before. Five minutes later he was back again. The place had some magnetic force he couldn't escape.

He stopped the van in a lay-by. Just off the lay-by he noticed a small gap in the trees. He pulled the van into it. Perhaps he would just sleep here the night and find a way out in the morning. He shut his eyes. His mind might have raced and skidded and collided into itself as if it was going to burst into flames. It might have slowed down until there was no sign of it. He thought about his father who never was. He thought about having to return to Stockport, the place he had had to leave a couple of days before, the place he always had to leave. He thought about losing this job and getting into trouble with the police because he had stolen the van. He thought about his wife and children losing patience with his running away. He thought about the court case in the morning. He was never going to make it back in time. He would lose. He would have to pay £250 to those bastards. He thought . . . fuck it. He thought . . . fuck me.

He thought . . . fuck everything.

He thought . . . fuck.

I didn't hear him say it, but I felt it.

40)
a. At the end of a book about dysfunction, a book about defection, a book about destruction, a book about damage, a book about degeneration, a book about deformity, a book about distress, at the end of a book about something a little defunct, at the end of a book called *D for Death*, I wrote that there couldn't possibly be a climax to the story that had been told, and that I hoped the reader would understand. Perhaps the nature of the anti-climax would in itself be a powerful climax, perhaps the fact that there would be no clear

answer to any of the questions proposed and implied in the book would actually be the answer.

b. Another book required a different ending. The ending to a book about a man who killed himself leaving behind a family in a state of shock. They eventually realised, looking back on their life, and his life, that when he was alive they were also in a state of shock. They were in shock before he died, and then they were in shock, the same but different, after he died. Both forms of shock were the result of a relentlessness that only reality could contrive. They suffered from a kind of concussion, and it's difficult to say which was the stronger – the concussion they felt while he was alive, or the concussion there was after his death. The concussion didn't necessarily get in the way of living a moderately normal life, it just meant that sometimes it felt as if you were suffering from a kind of drained, draining intoxication. Sometimes you felt this more than other times. Sometimes it felt as if you were part of his dream, a dream he was having in the seconds before he died, in the seconds before he was born, a dream of a life you had together, but apart, and then a death you had together, but apart. You felt that your feelings were at his mercy, the mercy of the madman, or the sad man, or the bad man. So the ending to a book that was effectively about shock simply suggested that this family had spent a long time reeling from the effects of a shocking man. By the time he killed himself they were so shocked by his behaviour as a living man that his suicide merely topped up the shock, and ensured that it would endure, almost as a replacement for his memory. The shock would always be there.

c. The ending to a book about death decided that, for the living, death is no conclusion.

d. There was a happy sad ending to one book, a book called *Death in the Family*. The plaque marking his death was restored and replaced, at a cost of £150.75, and Dilys, Paul, Jayne and Carol all made the trip to Coney Hill Cemetery, Gloucester. They held hands and huddled around the gleaming plaque and finally put their father and their husband to rest. They cried together. They felt better. They put back together the family that he had pulled apart. Each year they would return and hold hands and keep the family together. There was a but, but it was a but that would have turned the happy sad ending into purely a sad ending, and there are enough sad endings in the world.

e. There was an ending to one book that was almost exactly like the ending to the above book. Except in this book the family went to the cemetery, joined hands, finally said their goodbyes together, and then never returned to Gloucester again. I suppose that was the but that never made it into the above ending. Just because there are enough sad endings in the world doesn't mean there won't be more.

f. A book about itself ended at peace with itself. That was quite a happy ending.

g. It doesn't matter where someone is buried, or scattered, as long as they are still alive in your imagination.

h. He looked at the sky, and he cried, If I die, it is because everything must die!

i. On: Rousseau, or, the memoirs of a dead man. Night was coming on. I saw the sky, some stars, and a few leaves. The first sensation was a moment of delight. I was conscious of nothing else. In this instant I was being born again, and it seems as if all I perceived was filled with my frail existence. Entirely taken up by the present, I could remember nothing. I had no distinct notion of myself as a person, nor had I the least idea of what happened to me ... I felt throughout my whole being such a wonderful calm, that whenever I recall this feeling I can find nothing to compare with it in all the pleasures that stir our lives.

j. At the ending to a book about death, called, for the sake of argument *Putrefaction*, I described how when I died I would like to be cremated. My dream would be for the ashes to be sent into space, but I suppose being placed into the earth somewhere pleasant somewhere on the planet is a form of being in space. I would like it to say on the plaque that marks my final position: 'Kiss my ash.'

k. At the end to a book on suicide called *The Fiasco Itself*, I summed up how a suicide is a different death. It is less than a death, it is more than a death. It's death and a half. It's minus death. It's death turned inside out. It's death that's not quite finished off. How can a human being choose to die, and not be chosen to die by God, or fate, or time? There's a dead body, but it's hard to find something or someone to mourn. The suicide places a big black endless glow in the way of the body, the life, the death.

l. At the end of a book about my father called *Slaughter of the Self*, I decided that he was a cheat. He cheated life, he cheated those he left behind, he cheated himself, he cheated his depression out of a few more years' nasty work.

m. A book called *Ifs & Buts* that was full of ifs and buts ended with three last buts and one massive if. But who could blame him? He had killed himself, but really he had been forced to kill himself, by an illness, by a disease of the mind that fought him from within, and bent his will, and bashed his brain in. It was as if he had been hit by a car, or suffered a heart attack. He may have arranged his death, he may have turned the key, or pressed the button, or flicked the switch. But it was something else, an outside force, a depression the size of a burnt-out sun, that compelled him to go through with it. If only . . .

n. Stockport got away with it. It had an airtight alibi. It was somewhere else at the time of the death.

o. I am now older than my father ever was. I still think of him as being older than me. He had me when he was twenty-one. I had my daughter when I was thirty-five. She's seven now. In a way, you could say that I am the equivalent of what he was at twenty-eight, when he had a seven-year-old child. He had a twenty-year-old child when he was forty-one. I'll be fifty-five when my child is twenty. Maybe then I'll think of myself as being somehow as old as my father was when he died. Perhaps my father will always seem older than me. When I'm seventy I'll still think of my dad as someone who was older than I could ever be. I'll only catch up with him, be as old as he was, as old as you can get, when I die.

p. The ending of a book is like a death. The book finishes, its life is over. Suddenly all the words and emotions that have piled up stop dead in their tracks. The end finishes off the shape of a book, of a life, of a mind. And most endings to books are voluntary. A decision is taken to end it all. It is over. And after the end, some kind of mysterious afterlife, some kind of ghostly presence in other minds. Some answers, some questions, some interest, some indifference.

q. At the end of a book called *Finished Off*, I wrote that I had a dream about my father at about the time I finished off a book about his life and death. He appeared in the dream to confirm that he was indeed dead, and in that sense the book I had written was quite accurate. 'And guess what?' he says, in a voice I can almost hear. 'I know Elvis.'

r. 'But you got it wrong,' he then said, in a voice so toneless, so colourless and so extraordinary it summed up the sensational secrecy of the man. 'My favourite comedian wasn't Ken Dodd. It was Victor Borge. Dodd was all right, but it was Borge that made me realise how ludicrous consciousness is, and how faithless the mind is. You could learn a lot about the twists of fate from the way Victor Borge fell off a piano stool. I know him too.'

s. 'And Kafka. Actually Franz and Victor are very good friends, as funny as each other.' Then he grinned, a little strangely, the smile of a man killed by pain and time. It was as if he didn't know what he was saying, as if he couldn't possibly be saying anything, because he was dead, because he was nowhere to be seen, or heard. 'But I don't know my father.'

t. He continued, as if he was answering a question I hadn't even asked. 'I just wanted to turn off the sun. Imagine my surprise when I found out that I could.' There was a somber confidence about him, and he looked much better for not being so bothered by life, and light, and assorted mental effort. 'Death is so simple,' he sighed, as if he hadn't got a care in the universe.

I suppose you could say that he suited disappearance. He was a very vague man, and as he stood there in my dreams in front of me, but behind me, I could see that he had merely turned his vagueness into death. Death is a fine refuge for the vague. You can be vague to your stopped heart's content. So vague you end up quite specific. 'I always felt kind of temporary about myself,' he said, as if he was acting out someone else's lines. 'I feel much more permanent now.' He paused.

Forever.

u. I rang up my mother from Gloucester station just before I caught the train back to London. 'Mum,' I said, 'I'm in Gloucester . . . I've been to the cemetery to see Dad . . .' There was a pause. 'Oh,' she said, 'you're not going to do anything silly, are you?' No, I'm not going to do anything silly. I tell her that I've also been to the place where he killed himself. I tell her it's a beautiful location, because somehow that might make the thought more palatable. She is pleased, as pleased as you can be under the circumstances, to hear that he chose somewhere lovely to die. Then she asks me, 'Are you all right?'

v. I ring up my mother as I finish a book in which she has featured. In fact, I ring her at exactly this part of the book, just after the moment I have written the words 'Are you all right?' It's Paul, I say. She says, 'Are you all right?' I tell her that I have just written those exact words. I've made it your catchphrase 'Oh, don't! It's not only me who asks it all the time. They say it a lot in Liverpool, and in Wales. Perhaps I started a fashion . . .' I tell her that I am just finishing the book. Is there anything else she might have remembered? Something nice? 'Oh he was a lovely man, really, before he had the electric shocks we had some wonderful times. I sometimes wondered if the shocks made him forget the good times we had, made him forget himself, really, how funny and warm he could be. He was very romantic . . . he used to buy me lovely Valentine cards.' Up until when? 'Well, until he started to get ill. He used to look after you as a baby, he loved taking you for walks to local beauty spots. He was quite artistic, as well. He used to choose all the colours for the houses. I just think he wanted more money. I mean, everybody does, but it really used to get him down, that there was never anything to spare. Did I tell you when we were at Reddish he started gambling? Him and a mate started betting on the horses. They did well for a time, and they started winning. He kept saying, everything's going to be all right now. But then they lost it all. I sometimes wonder if I had been prim and proper, a different kind of woman, whether it might have suited him better. I don't know . . . I was talking to my friend Betty the other day, and she's had a really bad time, she buried her husband and son-in-law within three and a half weeks three years ago. And we were having a drink and talking about our lives, and she said, Well, after everything, do you think your life's been worth nothing? And I said, Do you know what, it's been all right really.'

w. A few minutes after I have spoken to my mother I notice that there is a message on the answer machine. I must have been in another room, because I didn't hear the phone ring. It's my mother. She tells me that she loves me. This slightly panics me, as it isn't something she regularly does. In fact, I don't remember her ever doing it. Not that I really notice: I suppose she says it in other ways. I worry that perhaps all this talk about her husband is starting to get her down. I call her back. 'Are you all right?' I ask her. She laughs. 'Of course. It just occurred to me that I never say it. I suppose I feel a bit funny about saying it. I just wanted to say it.' We finish the call, and simultaneously we both say 'Are you all right?'

x. There was a book about the suicide of my father, called for the sake of argument *The A to Z of Nothing*, and it ended with some facts, or at least some speculation about facts. The place my father chose to kill himself had something of a history. Bulls Cross, the exact location his end began, wasn't just anywhere, or nowhere. It was somewhere. Definitely somewhere. In the early pages of Laurie Lee's autobiography set in the small and remote Cotswold village of his childhood and youth, Lee mentions, in the most dramatic fashion, Bulls Cross.

He writes of Bulls Cross as being once a crossing of stage roads and cattle tracks which 'joined Berkeley to Birdsip and Bisley to Gloucester Market'. Every night at midnight, legend had it, a terrible ghostly scene would be replayed, the nasty chaotic crashing of a coach and horses. Each night, the terrified shrieks of the passengers, the wild desperation of the horses, the violent crack of snapping harnesses, the ghastly crunching of wood and wheel, the sheer panic of the coach driver. The coach smashed to a dreadful halt, the horses flailed around kicking out each other's brains, the passengers slowly, painfully, died in the dark cold open air. 'The image of that small but local disaster still possessed qualities to appal which the more grandiose carnage of recent times has never quite overshadowed.'

Lee calls Bulls Cross a ragged wildness of wind-bent turves, a saddle of heathland set high at the end of a valley, a place of hollows and silences. He would never go there at midnight. It reeked of being a place where travellers would meet in suspicion, or commit violence on each other, or rob or rape or murder. Just below Bulls Cross was a 'dank yellow wood' known as Deadcombe Bottom. Lee and his brothers discovered a derelict cottage there, and learned that the cottage had been the home of the local hangman. Bulls Cross had been chosen as the ideal location for a gallows. They found out that the hangman, a busy and brutally efficient man, had one bleak night, without caring to look at those pathetic, petty criminals he was dispatching so quickly, hung his own son. When he realised what he had done, he didn't say anything to the men standing nearby. He simply walked back to his cottage and hanged himself. 'Since when no one had lived in Hangman's House, which crumbled in Deadcombe Bottom . . .'

y. Did my father know of this history? Was this the greatest of all his secrets? Did he choose this place, the high, haunted Bulls Cross, or perhaps even the steeply diabolical Deadcombe Bottom, on purpose? Or would he have been surprised to have learnt that the beauty spot he randomly chose wasn't so beautiful, and innocent, and unstained as he supposed? The stain he left there was just one of many imprinted upon the leaves and trees and air over hundreds of patient, poisoned years.

Or was he drawn there by forces beyond his control? Forces that sensed his despair, his weakness, his fearlessness, his desire to retreat from reality. I wonder if the last thing he saw on this earth as a living man was the monstrous and unreal sight of the coach and horses thundering to a dead certain end. And he followed them fantastically to ghostly wherever . . .

I call my mother ask her if she remembers him ever reading *Cider with Rosie*. The question leads to a long story concerning joining a book club on the Isle of Wight, ordering *Cider with Rosie*, reading it, and then the book being sent back by her sister, my Auntie Jill, because she considered it a bit too bawdy. My mother can't remember if my father read it, and if he had, back in the early 60s, could he possibly have remembered this place, this Bulls Cross, and held onto the image all these years as a place to choose when the moment came to find a place to kill himself? Did he, through the thick and thin of his unravelling life, always have this place at the back of his mind as some kind of death target? Was it a dim, darkly tempting image that got sharper and sharper the nearer he strove to his inevitable doom?

My mother seems to remember that Jayne studied the book for O level. So *Cider with Rosie* suddenly appears in our house in the months before he died. Could he have read her copy as it lay around the untidy kitchen, the bare front room? Jayne tells me she didn't study it for O level, although she has read the book. Perhaps it was Carol who studied it for O level?

I ask her. She tells me she did, but that would be years after our dad died. It turns out I am the only member of the family who has never read *Cider with Rosie*, supposing that my father did, and perhaps he did, and when he wanted to die, he went to a place he vaguely remembered was where death was never far away.

I imagine my youngest sister, Carol, at 15, a few crappy years into her now dadless life, reading *Cider with Rosie*, as if there was some point. I imagine her reading Lee describing this place Bulls Cross as 'an island of nothing' set high above the crowded valleys all around, and not realising that she was reading about an island her lost father visited at exactly the moment his life ended. Which was some point. She read about this island of nothing, because she had to, and there was no reason to put two and two together. There didn't even seem to be a two plus two to find. It all seemed so distant, so foreign. I wonder if she still shivered a little as she read about this doomed place in the hills, as if she had felt a ghost try and kiss her.

z. 'Why do you want to know?' she asks. I tell her about Bulls Cross, and Deadcombe Bottom. I say that I think this is where he, you know, did it. I have found a location, a floating image of a fixed point where self-discovery and destiny combined once and for all with self-destruction. A dead beautiful place where grass grows, and clouds rush by, and shadows shimmer, and ghosts materialise, and mysteries create themselves out of the air that is sometimes still, and sometimes stormy. 'Oh,' she says . . . 'And will that be the end of the book?'

'Nearly,' I say.

41) I can imagine the commotion my father must have caused in Bull's Cross, Painswick, in the early hours of the morning on 29 June, 1977. The police would have been called, and an ambulance, and they would have had to take his body away. I expect those who helped carry his body can remember it to this day.

And as I think about this, I realise that I can now almost see his body. I can see it being carefully taken out of the Ford Escort van and laid onto a stretcher. Carried into an ambulance and driven away. Taken to a morgue and laid out for inspection. There would have been a post-mortem. His body would have had some last use on this earth. Then it would have been cleaned and repaired and prepared for the funeral. He would have been put into a coffin. I can imagine him lying in his coffin, a hint of a tragic, privileged smile traced onto his dead handsome face.

All the thoughts, feelings and words in this book have started to take on the shape of his body. They have formed themselves through me into an image of him that I can see when I shut my eyes. I can see him. I can see him alive. I can see him playing with me, watching television with me, walking to the shops with me. I can see him getting angry. I can see him trying to control his anger. I can see in his eyes that he's keeping all these secrets, these secrets about himself, and his mind, and his future.

I can see us playing pitch-and-putt together at Dovedale Park, near Denton, Manchester, and we're both taking less than thirty shots to cover the nine holes and we're thrilled. I'm ten years old, and he's an energetic, smiling thirty-one-year-old who will surely live for ever. He is the only man I can ever imagine being my father. He will always be my father. Nothing will change that.

I shut my eyes, and I can see the shape of his dead body. He has come to life, even if I know that this life leads, again and again, whichever way you look at it, to his death. And as much as I can see him alive, I can see him dead. I can see him dead, wrapped in pure bright white. I can see his ruddy still face, and his deep-black hair, tinted ginger around the sideboards, slicked back from his proud shiny forehead. I can see the worry lines that were always etched deep into his forehead and even as I look they seem to be smoothing themselves out. The tension has left his body.

I can imagine his dead body as if I had seen it once, in the folds of the past, in the delays of time, through the holes in the universe.

Memory is a part of the imagination. Memories form in your mind the same way that the imagination does. There is no real difference. At times you cannot tell the difference between your memory and your imagination. It's all in your head. You need the imagination to create the memory. Without imagination, there is no memory. Without memory, there is no imagination. They are both made up of images you conjure up yourself out of your own experience and versions of your experience. Where do you draw the line between what is made up and what is real? How much of reality do we in the end make up, to ensure some kind of survival? How much of reality is just a compromise we've learnt over generations of time between what happened, what might have happened, what happens, and what we want to happen.

I can quite easily believe that I didn't see the body of Ian Curtis, the lead singer of Joy Division. I only imagined that I did. I imagined it because at the time I wanted to imagine it. I dreamt it up with all my heart and it had the quality of a memory. Memories are difficult things to trust, because they happen in your head, they pass through, they repeat themselves, they change in density, they become something else, they're as ethereal as a fantasy. I didn't see the dead body of Ian Curtis, the young man who killed himself as if he'd predicted it in his songs. I imagined that I had, as if his songs persuaded me to. It is not a memory, it is an act of imagination that reminds me of a memory.

But I have seen one dead body in my life. My imagination is beginning to tell me that I have seen the dead body of my father, and it's as vivid, or as tricky, or as vague an impression in my mind as a memory. It could be a memory. It is a memory. I remember seeing the dead body of my father, showing me, right up close to my face, that he had been alive, and now he was dead, and I looked at him, lying just where he wanted to, just the way he wanted to, lifelessly, absurdly, and I realised that he was gone, he was out of my life. He wouldn't be coming back. He hadn't faked his death and reinvented himself in some hot faraway land, or Scarborough. He was dead. The evidence was as plain to see as the back of my hand, which, I could now see as I lifted up his limp hand hanging out of the white sheet covering him, was almost exactly the same as the back of his hand. The hand that used to belong to him, and that now belonged nowhere.

I looked at the body, and I realised that I loved him, and hated him, I knew him, I never knew him, he was my father, he was someone else. I want him around now. I don't want him around now. I looked at him, at his face that was slipping away from being a face, and I felt something inside me, the part of me that is him living in me, growing in me, because I came from him, came from inside him, I felt something twist and turn. I felt something shudder. All of him that he wanted dead was gone. But the part of him that he had wanted to live, the part of him that was in me, came to the surface of my consciousness, sighed a little, and then sank back into the dark depths. I looked at his body, built out of memory and dreams and imagination and out of the reality that memory, dreams and imagination conspire to create. I looked at his breathless, unapologetic body built out of the memory, dreams and imagination that mean there is conceivably something rather than nothing, and I understood that, for good reasons and bad reasons, for the sake of everything he thought and felt, he deserved to be named.

Here lies the body of Leslie Ronald Morley, who decided, because he had no choice, to make his own mind up about when to say 'The end'.

THANK YOU TO:

Elizabeth Levy for helping me to know where to start, and when to stop, and for the space, and the spaces, and the thoughts, and the love.

Madeleine for asking good questions, some of which I might have answered.

Dilys, Jayne and Carol for being in the story whether they liked it or not, and for being, funnily enough, family.

Julian Loose for pushing and pulling, for minding and reminding.

Walter Donohue for waiting for . . .

Jocelyn Targett, James Brown, Mary Anne Hobbs, Chris Bohn, Christine Crowther, B. S. Johnson, Alexie Sayle, Tim Hulse, Sally Mitchell and Kevin Hewitt: for various things at various stages in various ways.

And my father, for helping me – what with one thing and another – to write a book.

SOUNDTRACK

Music listened to whilst writing *Nothing* and music you might listen
to while reading it includes:

'A Louse Is Not a Home' by Peter Hammill
'Electric Warrior' by T. Rex
'Out There' by Eric Dolphy
'Unknown Pleasures' by Joy Division
'Horses' by Patti Smith
'Rock Bottom' by Robert Wyatt
'Five Leaves Left' by Nick Drake
'No Pussyfooting' by Fripp and Eno
'Berlin' by Lou Reed
'Solo Concerts' by Keith Jarrett
'Spiral Scratch' by Buzzcocks
'Tonight's the Night' by Neil Young
'Death Disco' by Public Image Ltd
'Brighten the Corners' by Pavement
'Heartbreak Hotel' by Elvis Presley
'Preemptive Strike' by DJ Shadow
'Music for 18 Musicians' by Steve Reich
'I Like to Score' by Moby
'The Art of the Trio Volume 3' by Brad Meldhau
'Live at the Village Vanguard' by John Coltrane
'Todd' by Todd Rundgren
'Genius of Modern Music' by Thelonius Monk
'Die Kunst der Fuge/J. S. Bach' by The Keller Quartett
'Heaven Knows I'm Miserable Now' by The Smiths
'Free Fall' by Jimmy Giuffre
'The Velvet Rope' by Janet Jackson
'Angel Song' by Kenny Wheeler
'Zero Tolerance for Silence' by Pat Metheny
'Golden Greats' by Ian Brown
'Now He Sings, Now He Sobs' by Chick Corea
'Unplugged' by Nirvana
'Kanon Pokajanen' by Arvo Part
'The Affectionate Punch' by The Associates

'1984' by Hugh Hopper
'Conversations with Myself' by Bill Evans
'Another Green World' by Brian Eno
'Hard Normal Daddy' by Squarepusher
'This Charming Man' by The Smiths
'Getting Away with It' by Electronic
'The Man Who Sold the World' by David Bowie
'Eternity and a Day' by Eleni Karaindrou
'Outside the Dream Syndicate' by Tony Conrad and Faust
'Boys Don't Cry' by The Cure
'Death and the Flower' by Keith Jarrett
'Real Life' by Magazine
'Happy Sad' by Tim Buckley
'Never Smile at a Crocodile' by Jerry Lewis
'In Darkness Let Me Dwell' by John Dowland